Women and Property
Early Modern Englan

Women and Property in Early Modern England

Amy Louise Erickson

London and New York

First published in 1993
by Routledge
11 New Fetter Lane, London EC4P 4EE

Simultaneously published in the USA and Canada
by Routledge
29 West 35th Street, New York, NY 10001

First published in paperback in 1995

Reprinted 1997

© 1993, 1995 Amy Louise Erickson

Typeset in 10 on 12 point Times by
Ponting–Green Publishing Services, Chesham, Bucks

Printed in Great Britain by
T.J. International Ltd, Padstow, Cornwall

British Library Cataloguing in Publication Data
A catalogue record for this book is available from the British
Library

Library of Congress Cataloguing in Publication Data
A catalogue record for this book is available from the Library
of Congress

ISBN 0–415–13340–8

Contents

vi *Contents*

Figures

A note on the jacket illustration

This is a woodcut showing a court of women. It is one of very few early modern representations of women with written documents, but it survives in several copies. The one reprinted here comes from *The Parliament of Women* (1656), which satirizes gender roles in the civil war. The same woodcut appears on a later seventeenth-century ballad in defence of female hairstyles entitled *The Women and Maidens Vindication of Top-Knots* (H. Weinstein (ed.) *A Catalogue of the Pepys Ballad Collection* (1992), vol. 4, p. 367). This picture is a copy of a version in an earlier style that appeared on the play *Swetnam, the Woman-Hater, Arraigned by Women*, published in 1620.

Tables

Abbreviations

AgHR	*Agricultural History Review*
AHEW	Joan Thirsk (ed.) *Agrarian History of England and Wales*
AJLH	*American Journal of Legal History*
als	*alias*
BL	British Library
BIHR	Borthwick Institute for Historical Research, York
C&C	*Continuity and Change*
CRO	Cambridgeshire Record Office
CUL	Cambridge University Library
DRO	Dorset Record Office
EcHR	*Economic History Review*, 2nd series
HRO	Hampshire Record Office
JFH	*Journal of Family History*
LAO	Lincolnshire Archives Office
LPS	*Local Population Studies*
MCC	Magdalen College, Cambridge
n,N	number (proportion), Number (total), in tables only
NRO	Northamptonshire Record Office
P&P	*Past and Present*
p.a.	per annum
PRO	Public Record Office
SRO	Somerset Record Office
TRHS	*Transactions of the Royal Historical Society*
WMQ	*William and Mary Quarterly*
WSRO	West Sussex Record Office

Preface

CONVENTIONS

In the transcription of early modern manuscripts and published works, spelling has been modernized only in so far as the inversion, for twentieth-century eyes, of u/v and i/j, and the substitution of 'th' for 'y' where necessary. Capitalization is standardized and abbreviations are spelt out. In manuscript transcription, first names are standardized where possible and an occasional comma has been added for clarity. Dates are modern – that is, the year is taken to begin on 1 January, instead of 25 March, as it did until 1752. All numerals, whether Roman or Arabic in the original, are rendered in Arabic notation. Archaic monetary values (marks, nobles) and all variations of monetary expression are rendered as pre-decimal pounds, shillings, and pence: 12 pence (d.) to the shilling (s.), and 20 shillings to the pound (£). Common early modern expressions such as 'twelvepence' and '40s.' become 1s. and £2 in this text, for consistency.

References to documents in manuscript take the following form.

Probate accounts, inventories and wills: Name, social status, initial estate value/net estate value (date) Parish, Record office: reference number(s), except

Yorkshire wills: Record office: Name (date) Parish, Deanery.

Chancery Court records: Plaintiff *v.* Defendant, County of origin (date) Public Record Office: reference number.

All information necessary to locate the document follows the record office designation. Other information, such as names or dates, which is given in the text may be omitted in the reference. Estate values are rounded to the nearest pound. The net estate value is that listed by the early modern probate clerk, and not the actual total which may be derived with the aid of a modern calculator.

References to printed records take the following form:

Statutes: Regnal year Monarch chapter (date). Thus 22 & 23 Car.II c.10 (1671).

Legal case reports: Plaintiff *v.* Defendant (date), *Report*, page. Thus Waterhouse *v.* Wytham (1595) *Croke Eliz.*, p. 466.

The report titles are abbreviated in standard form. They do not appear in the bibliography, as case reports are most conveniently found not in the original editions but in the more widely available collection, the *English Reports* series. They may be located there by the plaintiff's name in the index volumes, or by the title of the report or name of the reporter.

ACKNOWLEDGEMENTS

The research for the PhD thesis which formed the basis of this book was completed with generous financial support, in the form of the Winston Churchill Memorial Fellowship of The English-Speaking Union of San Francisco (1985–7), Una's Fellowship in History at the University of California, Berkeley (1984–5), the Ellen McArthur Studentship in Economic History at Cambridge University (1987–8) and a Research Studentship at Corpus Christi College, Cambridge (1987–8).

For early encouragement and inspiration in the research which ultimately generated this book, I am indebted to Robert Brentano and W. G. Sheils. Helpful comments were offered on various aspects of the original thesis presented to conferences of the International Economic History Society (Bern, 1986), the Centre for Seventeenth-Century Studies (Durham, 1987), the Economic History Society (Norwich, 1988) and the Western Association of Women Historians (Asilomar, California, 1989), and to the Women's History Seminar at the Institute for Historical Research in London (1988), both the Legal History Seminar and the Social and Economic History Seminar at Cambridge (1988), the Manchester Women's History Group (1989) and the informal workshops of Margaret Spufford's research students. I am especially grateful to Margaret Spufford for her patience, criticism, support, and the suggestion to explore this new document, the probate account. Advice on particular points from Steve Hindle, Mark Overton, Tim Stretton, Joan Thirsk and Helen Weinstein has also been very helpful. Many other colleagues made specific offers of their discoveries relating to women's property, and these are acknowledged individually. For help with archival research, my thanks to Molly Erickson, whose fits of giggles over probate inventories in the hushed record office ('It's how I always wanted to spell!') revived my occasionally flagging interest in document transcription. Alasdair Palmer has contributed greatly to the book's stylistic refinement. The staffs of all the archives I have used were most helpful, and the staff of Girton College Library cheerfully assisted with my obscure reference queries.

Permission to reprint material previously published has been given by the British Record Society, for 'An introduction to probate accounts', in Geoffrey Martin and Peter Spufford (eds) *The Records of the Nation* (1990), and by *The*

Economic History Review, for 'Common law *versus* common practice: the use of marriage settlements in early modern England' (1990). The Lincoln-shire Archives Office has granted permission to reproduce the documents in Figures 1 and 3.

Map of places cited in the text.

Part I

Background

1 Introduction

English legal writers from the seventeenth to the nineteenth centuries never tired of claiming that women were 'a favourite of the law' and even, in the hybrid professional language called law French, 'lour darling'. The position of a married woman in England, although admitted to be '*de jure* but the best of servants . . . *de facto* is the best in the world'.[1] This despite the fact that the legal restrictions placed on English women at this time were exceptionally severe even by the standards of other early modern European countries.

In the twentieth century all overt legal restrictions have been removed, and yet women as a group remain at a profound economic, social and political disadvantage. Women today predominate among those receiving income support or welfare from the state – at the identical rate that they predominated in the seventeenth century among those in receipt of parish poor relief. And an equivalent proportion of the poor then and now are single mothers, although the causes of their singleness have shifted. Women today earn only about two thirds of what men earn. But women have earned approximately two thirds of men's wages for the last seven centuries. How is it that such severe economic disparity between women and men persists when the laws have changed so dramatically? What is the relationship between law and practice?

Historically, the most important component of wealth was not wages, but inheritance, whether that inheritance consisted of a landed estate, or of a single cottage and garden, or even of a cow, a kettle, a brass pan and a bed.[2] How did early modern women survive when not only were their wages significantly lower than men's, but the common law only allowed them to inherit land if they had no brothers, under a system of primogeniture? When they lost all their personal property and control of their real property to their husbands at marriage, under the doctrine of coverture? Coverture eclipsed the legal identity of a married woman, leaving her unable to sign a contract or sue or obtain credit in her own name. As a widow, a woman might be entitled to only one third of her husband's real property, or might even be left entirely at the mercy of his will.

This book reconstructs the lives of ordinary women between approximately 1580 and 1720, by comparing the laws of property transmission with women's everyday experience of inheritance, marriage and widowhood. The traditional tripartite division of women's lives into before, during and after marriage – into maids, wives and widows – was not only socially but also legally defining. (A 'maid' was simply a girl or unmarried woman in early modern England. A young female employee was usually a 'maidservant', and 'maid' alone did not connote servanthood exclusively until the nineteenth century.) The rich historical sources of the long seventeenth century afford evidence of how a daughter was brought up relative to her brothers, how her inheritance compared with theirs, and what happened to her inheritance upon marriage; what property a wife actually enjoyed or considered her own, in spite of the law of coverture; and what benefits a widow received from her husband's estate, what she did with that property in her widowhood, and to whom she left it when she died.

The sources in which it is possible to trace actual property ownership, as opposed to property law, are those resulting from death and marriage: probate documents and records of lawsuits over marriage settlements. Virtually every death and every marriage involved a transfer of property, and the ways in which property was distributed shaped the structure of society. The relationship between property ownership and class structure in early modern England has received considerable attention in legal history, social history and family history, but the role of gender has been conspicuously absent from these discussions. This book outlines the patterns of property ownership and property transfer among ordinary women and men in early modern England.

Understanding these basic economic patterns of property movement is essential for three reasons. First, it is vital to know about women's economic position in order to say anything at all about social relations in a society in which more than half the population was female. Second, many sweeping generalizations about early modern family relations have been made in the last twenty years. But when these have been grounded in evidence of actual families – and they haven't always – the evidence used is the marriage settlements and inheritance of very wealthy families. Thus most of the population has been left out. By looking at the patterns of property distribution in ordinary families, this study grounds generalizations about emotional climates in the lived experience of the vast majority of the population. Third, while much has been written about women's 'status' in the early modern period, the great majority of this work is based on literary sources in which it is difficult to disentangle theory from practice. Property offers an excellent means of comparing the theoretical ideal, in the form of the law, with actual practice, in terms of ordinary women's ownership. While gender has been expertly analysed in legal philosophy, tracing the exclusion of women from concepts of 'the individual' since the later seventeenth century,[3] no connection has been made between the theoretical individual and real individuals making property decisions in their daily lives. Even in social history, the prescriptive evidence of the law is still taken largely as reflective of practice, especially where women are concerned.

PROPERTY LAW

The best known aspects of the law respecting women and property are the common law doctrines of coverture in marriage and primogeniture in inheritance. Historians, lawyers, social scientists and literary critics all emphasize these doctrines. It is widely assumed that only landed families cared about property at all. They traced wealth from father to eldest son, while daughters were married off for familial interest. Marriage settlements were negotiated between the bride's father and the groom or his father, women not participating in the arrangements.

This patriarchal scenario founders first on the rock of demography. Early and frequent death in early modern society made the completion of the cycle unlikely. Only 60 per cent of marriages produced a son, and even if a son were born he was unlikely to be of age at his father's death, so his inheritance 'wandered' to his mother.[4] It is certainly true that land pulled inexorably towards males, but it spent a good deal of time in female hands along the way. Another 20 per cent of marriages produced only daughters, who inherited land together jointly. And since a wife regained her legal identity on her husband's death, in practice a mother was almost as likely as a father to negotiate her children's marriage.

The second problem with the common law focus is that it ignores the other four bodies of law which regulated property ownership in the early modern period – and in fact from the middle ages until the nineteenth century. The common law is the best known because it is the shorthand description for the system which, through colonization, came to dominate nearly one third of the globe. But in fifteenth-century England the system called 'equity' originated in order to modify what was perceived as the harshness of the common law, and throughout its history a considerable part of the business of equity courts consisted of cases involving the property of married women, which the common law did not recognize. Ecclesiastical law regulated the division of personal property, and in so doing it followed Roman civil law, which was considerably more egalitarian than the common law in so far as it advocated a form of community property within marriage and the equal division of parental wealth among all children. Manorial or borough law varied locally, affecting the inheritance of land within the manor or borough. In many places this land was partible among all sons rather than impartible to the eldest son. Finally, parliamentary statutes, made by common lawyers sitting in parliament, also played a crucial role in regulating property transmission, principally by intervening in ecclesiastical law.

The common law, equity, manorial law and ecclesiastical law operated jointly to produce a workable legal system in early modern England. The common law was never meant to be exclusive – it would have been wholly untenable on its own. The specific provisions of each jurisdiction as they relate to women and property transfer are outlined in Chapter 2.

The balance of power between these multiple legal systems shifted over time, but very gradually. Throughout the late medieval and early modern period, the ecclesiastical or civil law idea of community property in marriage and partibility in inheritance came into conflict with the common law idea of coverture in marriage and primogeniture in inheritance. The religious controversies which racked England in the sixteenth and seventeenth centuries gave rise to an increasingly secular state in which common law and statutes came to dominate. As increasing centralization strengthened national over local law, the medieval manorial and borough courts also declined. Equity was ultimately incorporated with the common law in the nineteenth century. The long-term winners and losers in the jurisdictional struggle can be identified by twentieth-century terminology: manorial and borough law, and even ecclesiastical law, are today usually referred to as 'custom', which is of lesser authority than 'law'.

The resolution of conflicting legal principles, usually in favour of the common law, is euphemistically called the 'rationalization' of the law. Over a period of five hundred years, between about 1300 and about 1800, this 'rationalization' had deleterious effects for the economic security of daughters, wives and widows. The deterioration of women's legal and economic position in the early modern period does not imply that the middle ages were a 'golden age' for women. What it shows is that a restrictive system tightened even further, possibly in a series of 'backlashes' against women's perceived liberties. The two statutory changes which restricted women's already limited entitlements to property occurred in the later seventeenth century, in an atmosphere of general conservatism and retrenchment following the restoration of the monarchy. Their ostensible purpose was to secure the exclusive control of the male head of household over his – that is, the family's – property. The details of these statutes are discussed in Chapter 2, and their ramifications for ordinary women in Chapters 4 and 10.

The progressive dominance of the common law doctrines of marriage and inheritance make it impossible to subscribe to the traditional 'celebratory' type of legal history which hypothesizes a progressive evolution towards sexual equality throughout history.[5]

FAMILY RELATIONS

The most prominent school of family history also takes a 'celebratory' view of its subject, positing a progressive evolution in familial emotion. According to this theory, marital, parental and filial affection have emerged gradually in the family over the last few centuries, in much the same way that technology or sanitation has evolved. The first glimmerings of 'affect' have been dated anywhere from the late sixteenth to the mid-eighteenth century, but the turning point is widely considered to be around 1700. Prior to that time, marriage is supposed to have taken place for reasons of financial interest, rather than personal attachment, and the significance of children for their parents is presumed to have been limited to the production of a male heir. By contrast, from the eighteenth century marital and parental relations gradually ceased to be dominated by mercenary economic considerations, and the modern family form (with which we are all undoubtedly familiar) emerged, in which '[p]atriarchal attitudes within the home markedly declined, and greater autonomy was granted not only to children but also to wives'.[6]

But one man's 'companionate marriage' is another woman's 'gentle tyranny'.[7] The idea of emotional modernization is widely discredited among social historians, aware of the preponderance of evidence in support of the idea of an essential continuity in human emotion, whose expression varies in different historical contexts. The seventeenth-century Buckinghamshire physician who thought marital strife 'the most lacerating of all grief' and the Essex clergyman who, on the death of his 8-year-old daughter, mourned 'a precious child, a bundle of myrrhe, a bundle of sweetness; shee was a child of ten thousand'[8] are not so foreign to the twentieth century.

Certainly the early modern family was largely defined in political and economic terms, masking the emotions which may now seem invisible. But this is partly due to the type of records that survive. There are simply far more court cases extant than there are intimate letters, there being no administrative body with a remit to register and preserve private correspondence. Those letters which do survive come largely from the upper echelons of society, which do not necessarily represent the majority of the population. In the twentieth century the family has been through a process of privatization. It is now defined in emotional terms, which conversely mask any economic and political motivations in marital and parent–child relations. But while the growth of literacy ensures that there will be more personal letters surviving from our own day, it is inevitable that most of the documents available to the historian in two hundred years will also be primarily economic and legal.

Most proponents of essential continuity in familial attachments have maintained an academic diffidence, and emotional progress remains the most popular theory with historians and non-historians alike. This, I think, is for political rather than historical reasons.[9] It is profoundly reassuring to believe that our own century represents the apex of romantic affection and parental love. It helps to salve the current moral and political anxiety about the disintegration of the family – in particular, worry over rising divorce rates and unmarried mothers.

The romantic ideal of companionate marriage still so heavily propounded today was articulated in the eighteenth century, and is the basis of the claim for emotional progress at that time. However, feminist historians observe that these romantic ideals were simply a new means of maintaining male dominance at a time when overt demands of submission were no longer acceptable.[10] In the words of the more outspoken advocates of historical continuity in familial relations, the idea of emotional modernization amounts to little more than a 'male generosity theory' of increasing status for women and children, 'a great self-serving myth of the modern world'.[11]

The distribution of property within the family has been largely omitted in the discussion of familial relations, although economic patterns clearly reflect emotional ones. Modernizing historians who assume the exclusively economic basis of families prior to 1700, if they mention property, refer to the common law doctrines of coverture and primogeniture as evidence of mercenary attitudes in marriage and inheritance. It is not surprising that women are largely omitted from this history. But neither do women feature prominently in the works of more careful historians who produce detailed studies of particular parishes or families. In an England in which the household was 'a little sparke resembling' government – a miniature model of the kingdom, ruled by the husband as a lilliputian monarch[12] – historians of that household, with few exceptions, have proved insufficient to the challenge of writing about both women and men.

THEORY AND PRACTICE

The same cannot be said of literary historians, who have spent considerable energy in analysing gender in both published and private literature. This focus is largely due to women's predominance in the academic field of English literature. By comparison, women are relatively scarce among social and economic historians.

Peaks of high status for women in early modern England have been variously attributed: to the Elizabethan period on the basis of Shakespeare's heroines, the humanist interest in women's education, and the queen herself; to the interregnum on the basis of women's pamphlet-writing, and petitions, and ladies' accounts of defending besieged country seats; to the Restoration on the basis of the prominence of female playwrights and Queen Henrietta Maria; and to the eighteenth century, for its novelists, letter-writers and blue-stockings, and, in the last decade, its radicals.[13] But for ordinary women there are more radical continuities through the early modern period than there are peaks and troughs in their 'status'.

The second wave of women's history in the later twentieth century has concentrated on the representation of women and ideology. (The first wave, at the beginning of this century, focused on women's political, legal and economic position.) The most frequently discussed component of women's 'status' now is therefore ideology – that is, how people (mostly men and some women) thought women ought to behave. The sixteenth- and seventeenth-century explosion of the printed word spawned a huge volume of didactic literature churned out to instruct women: sermons, conduct books and moralizing tracts abound. While didactic literature certainly illustrates what women were told, and possibly what they heard, it does not say a lot about what women as a whole actually thought or how they went about their daily lives. The relationship between theory and practice is highly complex, and while it is little explored, it must be continually borne in mind.

To take one simple example, it is one thing to observe that early modern male writers invariably described women's place in the social hierarchy, the 'great chain of being', entirely in terms of marriage. It is quite another to remember that they did so in a society in which most adult women in the population at any given time were not married – they were either widowed or they had never married. By contrast, we today live in a society in which the majority of adult women at any given time are married.[14]

To take another example, early modern conduct books notoriously exhorted women to silence, obedience and chastity. Richard Allestree, for example, devoted whole chapters of *The Ladies' Calling* (1673) to modesty, meekness and affability. But it has been convincingly argued that upper class girls were enjoined to be quiet and obedient *ad nauseam* precisely because these were not obvious and natural patterns of behaviour but had to be forcefully inculcated in the female sex.[15]

Ladies and gentlewomen, clerics' and merchants' wives read conduct books. The vast majority of women did not. Certainly ordinary people were familiar with exhortations to female subservience from the pulpit, and many women, like men, would no doubt have subscribed to this idea, as they would have to other aspects of a hierarchical society. But the evidence of both public and private literature provides many salutary reminders of women's opposition to their subjugation in the seventeenth century. The puritan William Gouge complained that of all those groups in subjection wives 'are most backward in yielding', and when he preached in London's Blackfriars that a wife ought not to dispose of the common goods of the family without her husband's consent, 'much exception was taken' in his congregation. The view that a man might 'discipline' his wife with physical force was at least hotly contested in the later seventeenth century in manuscripts privately circulated in London and Oxford. Even in far away Lancashire it could prove socially unacceptable to propound a view of female inferiority. The mercer's apprentice Roger Lowe wrote in his diary that he 'was in some greefe' when it was reported locally 'that I said such things concerneinge women's naturall infirmities, which I never did, and troubled me extreamly'.[16]

One of the main thrusts of didactic literature on women's behaviour of the early modern (and of the medieval) period was that women ought to keep themselves indoors and men ought to busy themselves with matters outdoors. This is, of course, the same dichotomy which would be characterized from the late eighteenth century as the split between 'public' and 'private'. Richard Brathwait's 'English gentlewoman' (1631) 'made a covenant with her eyes never to wander' and to be 'no common frequenter of publike feasts'.[17] Hannah Wolley, the first woman in England to make her living by her pen, in 1670 advised good girls not to 'shew themselves in the streets but when they have just occasion to go forth'.[18] A collection of proverbs published in the same year included 'A maid oft seen, a gown oft worn / Are disesteem'd and held in scorn'.[19] The philanthropist Thomas Firmin in 1678 advocated regular spinning employment for poor women so that they 'are not only kept within doors . . . but made much more happy and cheerful'.[20]

Many more examples could be adduced of the necessity for women to remain within the household, but there are as many examples of women doing nothing of the kind. Both the theory and the practice are evident in the writing of the gentlewoman Celia Fiennes, in about 1700. Fiennes comments about the people of West Yorkshire that 'they live much at home and scarce ever go 2 or 10 mile from thence especially the women, so may be termed good housekeepers'. However, she herself was writing about her journeys around England, and she recommended travel to other ladies and gentlewomen – at the very least, travel within their own county – as well as the

> studdy of those things which tends to improve the mind and makes our lives pleasant and comfortable as well as proffitable in all the stages and stations of our lives, and render suffering and age supportable and death less formidable and a future state more happy.[21]

More ordinary women than Celia Fiennes commonly ventured out of doors, to make a future state more happy in the more immediate economic sense of working in the fields or commons and going to market. In household manuals like Fitzherbert's mid-sixteenth-century *The Boke of Husbandry*, one of the housewife's duties is to attend market, both to buy and to sell. In popular literature, the seventeenth-century chapbook heroine Cisley arranged to meet her beau in a tavern in the Lancashire market town whither Cisley had come to sell a stone (14 lb) of hemp. Private account books also record women's commercial activity: the Berkshire yeoman Robert Loder lists marketing among his maids' activities in his account book of the early seventeenth century; the Fell family in Lancashire, whose accounts were kept by daughter Sarah, had a woman servant in charge of marketing and dairy produce; Giles Moore paid both maidservants and his neighbours' daughters for fetching and carrying goods in the neighbourhood of Horsted Keynes, Sussex, where he was rector. At opposite ends of the country the Sussex rector and the Lancashire gentlewoman both bought small items from itinerant chapwomen, peddling laces and ribbons, pins and needles, buttons and cloth.[22] Prohibitions upon girls and women appearing in public places like markets and fairs are entirely absent from early modern ballads and broadsides, a significant omission since this form of popular literature *did* inculcate other forms of female behaviour, such as responsibility for domestic labour and the desirability of silence, often by means of satire.[23]

Women also travelled for pleasure and education. In the second half of the seventeenth century Agnes Beaumont in Bedfordshire and the female friends of Roger Lowe in Lancashire thought nothing of walking or riding between parishes alone to visit friends or to hear sermons.[24] Brathwait's 'English gentlewoman' notwithstanding, it could not have been too uncommon to frequent public feasts, like the wedding at which the fictional Lancashire lass, Cisley, first met her Simon. And women travelled of necessity. Jane Martindale, daughter of a yeoman farmer, had gone to work in London against her family's wishes, but when in 1633 she heard that her mother lay sick in Lancashire she 'posts downe with all speed, having bought an excellent swift mare to that purpose, which performed the journey in a short time'.[25]

These may seem obvious examples of obvious activities, but they are worth restating because such common acts potentially violated acceptable female behaviour. The distinction between the bad (outdoors/public) woman and the good (indoors/private) woman is biblical. But even within a single book of the Bible the description of the harlot – 'her feet abide not in her house: now is she without, now in the streets, and lieth in wait at every corner' – is flatly contradicted by the good wife who 'bringeth her food from afar', who 'considereth a field, and buyeth it' and who 'maketh fine linen and selleth it; and delivereth girdles unto the merchant'.[26] The simultaneous injunction to stay indoors and to provide for the household by going outside of it is simply a trap, hanging the threat of misdeed over the head of any woman outside her front door.

SOURCES

Fortunately, the historian of early modern England does not have to rely on didactic literature. A considerable amount of literature of all kinds was published by women, notably in the colourful, vicious *querelle des femmes* – the debate on the nature of women which raged in print throughout Europe in the sixteenth, seventeenth and eighteenth centuries.[27] Women made heated contributions to the pamphlet war in the early seventeenth century, with titles like Jane Anger's 'Protection for women', Esther Sowernam's 'Ester hath hang'd Haman' and Constantia Munda's 'Worming of a mad dogge'.[28] In the second half of the century defences of women grew longer and more philosophical, giving specific details of legal restrictions and men's evasion of moral responsibility, while the attacks remained largely at the level of cheap satire.

Male hacks wrote on both sides of the woman question for financial gain. Men not infrequently published under female pseudonyms, ranging from the decorous 'One of the fair sex' – intended to boost credibility and sales – to the farcical 'Mary Tattle-Well and Joan Hit-him-Home'.[29] Men's writing about women has been aptly described as a litany of 'alternate eulogy and vituperation'.[30] The words of the Duchess of Newcastle in 1668, describing court gallants, also extend to a larger group of men who 'raile of all women generally, but praise every one in particular'.[31]

The sheer number of women writing on every conceivable topic in the early modern period has received considerable attention in the last twenty years.[32] Women were probably always more likely than men to publish anonymously. But in early modern England they were not obliged, as were the Bronte sisters and George Eliot two centuries later, to assume male names in the hope of publication. What kind of misogynous society was it in which so many women could get into print on a commercial basis? The 'insignificant' woman writer may be more important for the fact that she was able to publish than for what she published.

Aristocratic ladies and gentlewomen wrote private literature too, in the form of diaries and letters, and some of it has subsequently been published. The diary was used particularly for religious reflection by the austere Lady Margaret Hoby in Yorkshire in the years 1599–1605, and by Grace, Lady Mildmay in Northamptonshire, who recollected fifty years of married life, spanning Queen Elizabeth's reign, during which her principal solace was in doing good works.[33] Letters show a more public but also a less self-conscious face. In the letters of Lady Brilliana Harley (1600–43) she defends her castle against royalist attack one day and sends pies and dried apples to her son at Oxford the next. Dorothy Osborne's letters in the early 1650s show a woman chatty, catty, earnest, and very much in love. The intrepid Lady Mary Wortley Montagu in the early eighteenth century, after a passionate but lucid courtship and a peripatetic married life during which she reported to friends in England on her travels, established herself in Italy, maintaining from there an amicable correspondence with her husband in London until his death twenty-two years later.[34] Celia Fiennes, mentioned above, recorded her travels around England at the end of the seventeenth century in a journal in which she meant others to read about her discovery of 'curious' things, like a history of Pope Joan in the library of Hereford Cathedral, the latest waterworks in great house gardens and a skeleton in the Barber Surgeons Hall in New-castle.[35] The letters of Dame Joan Thynne from Longleat House in Wiltshire to her husband at the Elizabethan court were for private eyes only, although she addressed him always as 'Good Mr Thynne' while he wrote back to 'Good Pug'. Memoirs are the most stylized form of life story: the adventurous royalist Anne, Lady Fanshawe (1625–80), retained her breathless adolescent tone even when writing her memoirs at the age of 50, for the only surviving son of her fourteen children; Margaret Cavendish, Duchess of Newcastle (1623–73), published a slim autobiography in addition to copious philosophy and fiction, much of it of an autobiographical nature.

All of these women were very well-to-do and not overburdened with domestic cares or children at the time they wrote. The personal thoughts of someone like Mary Green – who married her barrister husband at 15 and died in childbed with her eleventh infant at the age of 33 – are one of the great unknowns of history. It was her husband who kept the diary.[36]

Apart from the attraction of reading these women's personal opinions, their diaries and letters also tell us something about their property. It is clear that these ladies and gentlewomen were personally involved in the financial management of the combined marital property. The Duchess of Newcastle, for example, while publishing enormous quantities, also manipulated the finances of her husband's vast estate, using skills acquired as a girl on her mother's sheep-farming estate in Essex.[37] Dame Joan Thynne managed the family property, as well as a house she had inherited, while her husband was away – which was most of the time. Bathsua Makin, former tutor to the daughter of Charles I, put the case succinctly in her *Essay to Revive the Antient Education of Gentlewomen* (1673): 'We cannot be so stupid as to imagine, that God gives ladies great estates, meerly that they may eat, drink, sleep, and rise up to play.'[38]

One diary and one autobiography deal especially overtly with property matters. The tenacious Lady Anne Clifford fought the most publicized property battle of the century on two fronts: to recover her inheritance in Westmorland from her male cousin, and at the same time to defend that inheritance against her husband in Kent. She kept an almost daily diary of her trials and triumphs, some of which has been published. Much of the autobiography of the widowed Mistress Alice Thornton in mid-seventeenth-century Yorkshire testifies to miraculous deliverances from illness and death. But she also dwells on the financial tribulations of her widowed mother, and defends her own honour against allegations from her brother and her in-laws of irregularities with her own and her dead husband's property. Because the ladies and gentlewomen are and always will be more visible, they – and particularly Anne Clifford and Alice Thornton – appear occasionally in the following chapters, to illuminate the silent actions of more ordinary women.

Both of these women had a very clear sense of what they were entitled to and of the importance of women owning property in general, at least at their social level. They were by no means alone in these views. The artist Mary More in the 1670s, the high church tory Mary Astell in the 1690s and the anonymous 'Sophia' in her *Woman Not Inferior to Man* (1739) held that economic dependence on husbands was one of the principal reasons – if not *the* principal reason – for women's subjugation, and that the constraints of marriage and motherhood could reasonably be compared with slavery.[39] The most acid and thorough exponent of this view was, perhaps of necessity, fictional: Daniel Defoe's Roxana, in the novel of the same name.[40]

In general, early modern feminism was more immediately concerned with education than with property and law. The idea that women's subordination was due to a lack of education, rather than any 'natural' inferiority, was widespread. By the early eighteenth century, when overt advocacy of female inferiority was less acceptable, even Richard Steele's *Ladies' Library* took this view, but it was more forcefully put in the second half of the seventeenth century by Margaret Cavendish, Bathsua Makin, 'Sophia' and Daniel Defoe. Like Mary Astell's famous *Serious Proposal to the Ladies* (1694), Defoe also proposed academies for women – one in every county and ten for London – but, unlike Astell, Defoe's ultimate aim in educating women was to make them fit companions for men, and his proposed curriculum was rather less rigorous than hers.[41] Similar arguments about the need for education were voiced a century later by Mary Wollstonecraft, Catharine Macaulay, Mary Hays and even Hannah More. Some of these women, in both the seventeenth and the eighteenth centuries, adopted the language of female virtue, asserting their own chastity and denying any aspiration to social

equality with men. This can be seen as a means of protection and legit-
imization, whether conscious or not – the early modern equivalent of today's
disclaimer, 'I'm not a feminist, but . . .'. Such a preface represents the
publicly acceptable face of female activism, allowing the speaker to voice
criticism of male dominance and mechanisms of control to a relatively more
sympathetic audience.

Most early modern women were not concerned about equality with men,
but redress for the specific wrongs they perceived had been done to them was
of considerable importance to many. Petitions to parliament during the
interregnum were presented *en masse* by crowds of women, like 'The humble
petition of many hundreds of distressed women, trades-men's wives, and
widdowes' (1642). The practice of imprisonment for debt, 'whereby wives
and children are exposed to unexpressible misery', gave rise to 'The women's
petition' (1651). Individual gentry women published their own petitions –
'The humble petition of Alice Rolph, wife to Major Edmond Rolph, close
prisoner at the Gate-house Westminster' (1648) or 'The case of Mistress
Mary Walker, the wife of Clement Walker, Esq. truly stated' (1650) – asking
for a husband's release from prison or protesting the sequestration of his
lands, especially when those lands included his wife's jointure.[42]

In the following chapters it is the ordinary women, the unexceptional
women, who are most important – the women who never filed a petition, and
who for the most part never sued in any court over property issues. 'Ordinary'
people here encompasses everyone who was neither very rich nor very poor
– everyone who was not aristocratic or gentry on the one hand, nor in chronic
poverty on the other. Thus 'ordinary' describes perhaps 70–80 per cent of the
population. The word was not common in the early modern period, but it has
the advantage of being compact, non-negative, and universally under-
standable today. There was no appropriate contemporary term. Most early
modern descriptions of the social hierarchy, being written by gentlemen or
aristocrats, carefully list the aristocracy in descending order but stop after the
gentry, resorting thereafter to broad general terms like the 'middling sort' and
the 'poorer sort'. The 'middling sort' includes the yeomen, the clerics and
perhaps the husbandmen, but for my purposes it is not accurate because it
excludes the labourers, some of the craftsmen, and the widows of many men.

Sir Thomas Smith in 1583 descended as far as yeomen, but all men below
that were members of the 'rascabilitie'.[43] While 'proletarian' was a seventeenth-century adjective, it has since acquired industrial and political over-
tones which distort its application to rural early modern England. Both
'ordinary' and 'common' were derogatory in early modern parlance; one
could be presented in court as an 'ordinary railer' or a 'common hedge-
breaker'.[44] The ordinary man – the common man – was not yet exalted as he
would be in the later eighteenth century; the common woman, of course, has
yet to be eulogized. One contemporary, Richard Baxter, referred to men who
had incomes of £40–£50 p.a. as 'very ordinary'; those with £200–£500 were
the 'better sort'.[45] The great majority of the people examined here are very

ordinary by Baxter's definition. A few are of the better sort.

Most ordinary women worked for wages or sold their own produce in addition to their work in the household. But wages amounted to, at most, a shilling a week, or a little over £2 a year if work were steady. And most of the work for which women were paid – agricultural labour, needlework, spinning, lacemaking, cleaning, washing, helping out in the manor house occasionally, hauling, carting, tending the sick, cleaning and wrapping the dead – was seasonal or sporadic and informal.[46] Although work and property inheritance are obviously the two essential aspects of any woman's economic life, it is not possible to integrate the two in the early modern period, since the historical documents which deal with property do not deal with work, and those documents which deal with work, while they may refer to wages, do not mention any other aspect of wealth. Only an in-depth parish reconstruction could match individual women in each type of record.

Ordinary housewives, married to yeomen, husbandmen, labourers and small craftsmen, left no personal memoranda of their household expenses, or their income from the sale of butter, cheese, eggs, ale, honey and pies, or their wages, let alone their thoughts and experience. The principal source in which to locate the property transfers between ordinary men and women where one party was not contesting the situation – that is, aside from litigation records, which represent only contested cases and are likely to be out of the ordinary – are probate documents. Wills, inventories and probate accounts had to be publicly registered, and although the courts were not required to preserve them indefinitely, enough survive – 2 million wills, 1 million inventories and 30,000 accounts[47] – to outline the actual practice of property distribution over a period of nearly two centuries.

Probate documents are records of the ecclesiastical courts. Wills were made principally by dying men; inventories and accounts were filed mostly for the estates of dead men. But approximately three quarters of all those who presented wills and inventories in court and filed accounts in court a year later were women. These women were clearly not unusual because they had to travel often some distance to appear in public court, where they made up the majority of those doing so. The ideological debate on the nature of women does not appear in such mundane transactions. In the sources used here there is not even oblique mention of individual women's piety, modesty, confinement to the house, or silence.

These documents were rarely written by the people whose estates they deal with. In the case of probate accounts, if the information brought into court was originally scribbled on a piece of paper by the woman filing the account or a friend, it was written again in a 'fair copy' in court by the clerk. It is almost always the fair copy, and not the original notes, which survives. The most information that can be amassed on one family is three probate documents (a will, an inventory and an account), and sometimes their birthdates in the parish register. In most cases only one or two documents survive, of between one and five pages in length, much of which is taken up with legal formalities. (Even these three documents are catalogued and stored separately, and in order to be certain they are about the same person – at a time when four or five Mary Smiths might have lived in a single parish – it is necessary to match dates, sums, children and so on.)

The individual acts of property transmission in probate documents are isolated and random in themselves, but cumulatively they add up to a pattern of action, of general practice, of early modern habit. Inventories and wills have been used extensively by historians in the last twenty years, but probate accounts are the most important document for the study of women's property. This is the first study to make systematic use of probate accounts, and for that reason the nature of these documents is discussed fully in Chapter 2.

Both the chronological and the geographical spread of this study are determined by the survival patterns of probate accounts. Of all probate documents, accounts are the rarest, and they survive in numbers only between 1580 and 1720. The procedural changes giving rise to the creation and preservation of probate documents resulted from governmental anxiety about the enforcement of probate, including the recovery of any property due to the crown, and from jurisdictional conflicts. Wills are the longest running of the three documents. But even they survive in smaller numbers before the mid-sixteenth century (when the devising of land was restricted and ordinary people simply owned less moveable property) and after the mid-eighteenth century (when other means of property transfer increased and the value of individual household goods fell, relative to the value of liquid assets and land). Neither the legal procedure of administering estates nor the prominence of women in the business were unique to the early modern period. The same basic structure prevailed in the middle ages and in the eighteenth and nineteenth centuries.[48] But the documents which detail the whole process survive only between the late sixteenth and the early eighteenth centuries.

Geographically, probate accounts are limited to England. They exist only in small numbers in Wales, and not at all in Ireland. Scotland had (and has) a different legal system, derived from the European continent. While the laws of marital property were not too dissimilar,[49] Scotland, not unified with England until 1707, escaped the Tudor passion for administration that produced quantities of documents. The probate accounts discussed here come principally from four counties: Lincolnshire; Cambridgeshire; the southern half of Northamptonshire; and West Sussex, hereafter called simply Sussex. Smaller numbers of accounts come from Somerset, Dorset and Hampshire. These probate accounts all originate in the ecclesiastical southern province, the province of Canterbury, incorporating all of England up to the southern borders of Cheshire, Nottinghamshire and Yorkshire (see map on page xiv).

The probate accounts which survive in the northern province, the province of York, are neither numerous nor readily accessible, being uncatalogued and mixed in storage with other documents. Nevertheless, because ecclesiastical law differed between the north and the south, it is important to learn whether corresponding differences arose in practice. These variations should be apparent in wills, as they did not affect those dying intestate, and so I have included a sample of wills from the rural north and east ridings of Yorkshire and from the market town of Selby, at the southern end of the Vale of York, which had a population of about 1000 in the seventeenth century.[50] All told, approximately 2000 probate documents are represented in this study – mostly probate accounts (1500) with corresponding inventories and wills where available. These come from more than 500 different parishes. Most are villages, some are market towns, and a few are in the quiet cathedral cities of Chichester and Lincoln, the university town of Cambridge and the county town of Northampton.[51]

The geographical spread is wide for two reasons. First, the survival of probate documents is erratic. Second, it was desirable to look at different regions in order to generalize as much as possible about English women's property ownership. Focusing on a particular county, manor or parish may have yielded greater detail about individual women and why they made certain economic decisions, but would have limited conclusions. Almost all previous studies of wills and inventories have been local, and I will refer to these often, collating them wherever possible in tables so that they can be easily compared. Only by putting these local studies together is it possible to spot the anomalous parishes. Generalization is important because the subject of women's legal history has had so little attention that a broad outline of women's property ownership in law and in practice is needed before the specific areas which require further research can be identified. To move beyond a history in which women can be relegated to an index entry because there are so few references, to a history whose analysis of the past is based upon an understanding of the gendered structure of society requires studies like this one to map the terrain.

ORDINARY WOMEN AND PROPERTY

The emphasis on the common law in legal history, on hierarchy in family relations and on didactic sources in women's history is an emphasis on the upper classes. The assumption is that ordinary people have nothing to say about property. Those without land are regularly described by historians as 'propertyless'. This is a macroeconomic perspective based on the assumption that 'wealth' refers to the wealth of the nation, which was owned by relatively few people. Two thirds of all cultivated land and all forested land in early modern England were owned by the church, the crown, the aristocracy and landowners of 300 to 10,000 acres.[52] Ordinary people were not members of this elite; they were the 'small owners' with pieces of the remaining third of cultivated land or a house in the forest. But while they owned a minority of the total acreage, ordinary people comprised the vast majority of the population.

The approach here is microeconomic, to investigate normal conditions of property transmission among the small owners and those who did not own land at all. Most people owned property of some sort, even if it were only household goods and a cow, or the lease of a single cottage. Regardless of its dynastic repercussions or its implications for national wealth, this property had significant value for its owner. Despite the truism that land was the basis of wealth in an agricultural society, replaced by cash and financial assets in a commercial, industrial society, the relative value of land and moveables on an ordinary household scale was actually much closer than it is today (see Chapter 4). In the seventeenth century our modern phrases 'domestic economy' or 'household economy' would have been redundant. Retaining the spelling of the Greek word for household, 'oeconomie' on its own still referred to the small scale, defined as 'the knowledge of well ordering matters belonging to the houshold'.[53]

Other historians have commented on the limited application of primogeniture among ordinary people, or on the actual independence of women compared with their theoretical legal subjection.[54] But new models have not taken the place of impressionistic evidence because no comprehensive analysis has been undertaken of the actual patterns of inheritance and marriage. This study specifies the particular ways in which early modern women were disadvantaged by the law of property, what means were employed by both women and men to circumvent restrictions and what financial decisions they made about property.

It has been objected that one ought not to write a 'separate' women's history.[55] Whether one ought to or not, one cannot. Even concentrating 'exclusively' on women, they are seen through the lens of a law made by men, whose procedures were followed in documents written by men, which were exhibited in courts staffed by men, and still most women are obscured to the historian by their husbands until the shadow is removed by his death. The historical records themselves are obstructive. Mary Prior has aptly described tracing women as cutting across the grain of the historical record.[56] Mothers' names are not always recorded in parish baptismal registers; the most common social phenomena, such as women exchanging their family name upon marriage – *every* marriage – create enormous obstacles for the historian. Even for historians not specifically tracing women, kin by marriage are difficult to identify, which has implications for the study of debt and credit networks, as well as kinship ties.

The dependence of the historian on male channels to write about women is wholly non-reciprocal. There is no such concept as men's property rights or men's legal position. Hence my title, 'Women and property', whereas a book entitled 'Property and political theory'[57] need make no excuse for its total failure to mention that there are two sexes in the world and that this had any effect whatsoever on ideas about property. The relativity imposed on the study of women is made clear by an observation of anthropologists: whereas research on women may be based entirely on conversations with men, the reverse – talking only *to* female informants *about* men – would be impossible 'without professional comment and some self-doubt'.[58] This study aims to make it an occasion for professional comment and self-doubt for any historian to summarize English women's legal and economic position in the early modern period without asking the women themselves.

While the components of women's 'status' in any particular society are variable and disputed, their economic position – including inheritance, financial security and wages – is at all times crucial to 'status'. The research presented here clearly indicates that in early modern England daughters inherited from their parents on a remarkably equitable basis with their brothers. The costs of raising girls and boys were identical. When it came to distributing the patrimony, fathers normally gave their daughters shares comparable in value with those of their brothers, although girls usually inherited personal property and boys more often real property.

No amount of equal inheritance could counteract the law of coverture and its legal 'fiction' that a husband and wife were one person – the husband – and therefore their property was his. However, in practice wives maintained during marriage substantial property interests of their own. While marital property settlements are assumed to have been made only by the wealthy, ordinary women in fact made them too but the records are extremely difficult to uncover.

Widows commonly enjoyed much more property from the marital estate than the law entitled them to. But while ecclesiastical courts and dying husbands entrusted their wives with far more property and financial responsibility than the law required, at the same time a man very rarely went so far as to allow his widow complete discretion upon his death. The intent was to give her an ample maintenance, not to make her independently wealthy, and certainly did not extend to any principle of gender equality. The wealthier a man was, the smaller the proportion of his estate left to his widow, and also to his daughters.

Widows and women who never married had different ideas about property from men. These women gave preference to their female relatives in dividing their property, they enabled their daughters or nieces or female cousins to live independently in cottages and smallholdings, and they gave bequests to the poor, tacitly recognizing women's susceptibility to poverty. If widows remarried, they took greater care to protect their property than they had on their first 'venture', on behalf of both their children and themselves. Although 'venture' was used of either spouse throughout the seventeenth century, it was particularly appropriate in reference to a husband as 'an undertaking without assurance of success', since women's economic security from the day of marriage depended so heavily upon their husbands' good will.[59]

Despite the fact that women exercised considerably more power over property than has previously been allowed, both the legal system and individual men still kept women firmly subordinate. Women's dependence on their men's good will increased over the period, as the limited ecclesiastical protections of their property were eliminated by statute. The reality of women's receiving large amounts of property and exerting power over it in a distinctive way does not change the fact of oppression, but it does highlight the disjuncture between theory and practice. It also exhibits the ingenuity of many ordinary women in working within a massively restrictive system. Individually, they registered their collective disagreement with the principles of inheritance and marital property laws.

2   Law, society and documents

Four early modern treatises dealt specifically with the law relating to women. The earliest was *The Lawes Resolutions of Women's Rights: Or, the Lawes Provision for Woemen*, published in 1632. This spelling of 'women' had been used previously to imply that women were the woe of men, but the sardonic comments on the common law's attitude to women made here by the anonymous male author implies rather that the law could be the woe of women. In addition to its witty asides, the *Lawes Resolutions* was intended to provide a practical manual for lawyers, but also for women readers, as opposed to 'the deeplearned'.[1]

In 1700 there appeared *Baron and Feme: a Treatise of the Common Law Concerning Husbands and Wives*, followed in 1732 by an extended version, *A Treatise of Feme Coverts: Or, the Lady's Law, Containing All the Laws and Statutes Relating to Women. Baron and Feme* itself was reprinted in an enlarged edition in 1738. These were dry, straightforward manuals designed for reference principally by lawyers and possibly by gentlemen and women.

The only volume written by a woman appeared in 1735 with the impressive title of *The Hardships of the English Laws. In Relation to Wives. With an Explanation of the Original Curse of Subjection Passed Upon the Woman. In an Humble Address to the Legislature*. Not intended as a practical legal guide, *The Hardships of the English Laws* is an impassioned and cogent argument for changes in women's property law, employing both biblical and philosophical arguments. It is simultaneously an appeal to parliament and a warning to as-yet-unmarried women. Like the other three, this author is anonymous, although it was rumoured at the time that she was the wife of a Gloucestershire clergyman. Perhaps to defend her against accusations of personal bitterness, it was also observed that she had 'a very good husband' and 'only writ for the good of her sex in general'.[2]

Gentlewomen and those who were relatively well-off appear to have been reasonably familiar with legal texts, and particularly with the laws relating to marriage which affected them most directly. The Cambridgeshire gentlewoman Anne Docwra, who later published several Quaker tracts, was only 15 years old when her father pointed to the great Statuet book that lay upon the parlour window and bid her read that; saying it was as proper for a woman as for a man, to understand the laws, because women must live under them and obey them as well as men.[3]

Books of more general interest than collections of statutes made frequent reference to technical legal terms. *The Ladies' Dictionary* (1694) was compiled almost entirely by men, but men who expected their readers to take an interest in – and to have a working knowledge of – property law. Its 600 pages include entries for Coverture, Alimony, Dowry, Dower, Feme Covert and Jointure, scattered in between entries like 'Body, the beautifying thereof' and 'Table behaviour'.

Playwrights of the late sixteenth and early seventeenth centuries regularly punned on sexual and property meanings, which shows that, at the very least, audiences readily recognized the legal terms. These puns, familiar in Shakespeare, also provided a rich well of humour for his less famous contemporaries. John Fletcher's riposte to *The Taming of the Shrew*, for example, *The Woman's Prize or the Tamer Tamed* (1611), is replete with entails, demurrers and rejoinders. Petrucchio, on at long last bedding Maria, declares 'What may be done without *impeach* or *waste*, I can and will doe . . . here's a coyle with a mayden-head / Tis not *intayl'd*, is it?'[4] In the anonymous *Thomas of Woodcock*, written about 1591 but set in the fifteenth century, men 'meddle with . . . women in the blanks', blanks being medieval pre-written charter forms. The distasteful multiple puns in this work layer legal meanings on top of archery terms, on top of sheer scatology.[5] Although the puns fell out of favour over the course of the seventeenth century, the technical terms remained and marital property arrangements were still central to the plots of Restoration playwrights like John Dryden, Aphra Behn, William Congreve and Susannah Centlivre.

Legal 'evidences' – deeds, bonds, charters, contracts, wills and so forth – were enormously important at all levels of early modern society. Thomas Phayer, in his preface to the *Newe Boke of Presidents*, attributed wondrous consequences to the use of written securities:

> for by such evidence . . . are matters in the lawe continuallye decysed, truthe is made open and falshed detected, ryght advaunced and wronge suppressed, matters of doubt are put out of questyon . . . is justyce and equitie to everyman yelded, sute and contention avoyded, unitie and concorde induced, vertuous and polityke ordre observed, fynallye love and amitie encreaseth, wyth all kynde of goodnesse in quyet, which is the chefe parte of felicitie or happynesse in this life.

Phayer was one of the earliest authors of conveyancing manuals, or books of legal forms or 'precedents' for the purpose of drawing up property deeds or 'conveyances', contracts or wills. Along with all other forms of publishing, technical legal writing burgeoned from the later sixteenth century. The *Newe*

Boke of Presidents first appeared in 1543 and was reprinted five times by the early seventeenth century. It was followed in 1594 by William West's *Symbolaeography*, which remained the principal conveyancer until the civil war.[6] The manual best known today is the *Conveyances* of Sir Orlando Bridgman, who dealt with 'the most considerable estates in England', including those of the Percy family; Bridgman advised on the marriage settlement of Dorothy Osborne and William Temple, among many others.[7]

· Even ordinary people in rural areas who owned no conveyancing manuals secured their transactions with evidences. In a Lancashire market town Roger Lowe used the writing skills required for his work as a mercer's apprentice to draw up documents for neighbours and friends. In 1664, for example, after the successful conclusion of negotiations between a father and son 'att suite' over money, Lowe noted in his diary 'we all went to alehouse togather, and I made bond for to pay such a summe of moneys att such a time, and so parted'. Even villages by the late sixteenth century probably contained several people who could write.[8] Debts, sales, marriages, gifts of property both pre- and post-mortem, were all transactions to be secured in writing. For those unable to purchase a legal treatise, there was *The Country-Man's Counsellor: or, Everyman Made his Own Lawyer*, printed anonymously in the seventeenth century. Sold by peddlars for a mere tuppence, this chapbook included instructions on writing wills, drawing up bonds, and even how to go about suing in the Court of Chancery. For those who contracted debts on a regular basis, pre-printed bonds and bills could be had for less than tuppence apiece in the later seventeenth century, at least in London, where the Sussex rector Giles Moore bought them by the dozen.[9]

The litigious nature of early modern English society has often been remarked upon, but usually in the context of physical and verbal violence in the community. That private civil issues were as readily taken to court is vividly illustrated by a recent study of the Norfolk port of King's Lynn, where in the 1680s the courts dealt with approximately 2000 cases of debt alone every year. Almost every household in King's Lynn was involved in debt litigation within a period of a few years.[10]

Popular awareness of legal issues is all the more striking because of the confusing coexistence of four separate but overlapping legal systems. Common law and equity were applicable to all of England; ecclesiastical law differed slightly between the northern province and the southern province; manorial customs in the countryside and borough customs in the towns varied locally.

These four jurisdictions governed two principal types of property – real and personal. Personal property, called chattels by the common law, is more aptly described by the ecclesiastical court's phrase 'moveable goods', including money, debts, clothing, household furniture, food and so forth. Land was divisible into three categories – freehold, copyhold and leasehold – but only freehold was real property, unlike today when real property means any land or house. Copyhold land was held of the manor, either 'at will' of the lord or lady or according to the established custom of the manor.[11] Land was leased for a term of years (usually twenty-one or forty), or for lives (generally three – that is, lasting the length of the lives of three named individuals).[12] Leases of land were classified as 'chattels real', halfway between real and personal property.

The legal rules governing property can be divided into those relating to marriage and those relating to inheritance. I will sketch the multiple jurisdictions which apply and their terminology, first for marriage and then for inheritance. These next two sections are technical. The reader may skim them if she likes, but because I know of no other overview of the interplay between the different legal systems in all the published work on 'standard' legal history or on women's legal position, it seems important to venture it here. For reference, the laws and terminology of inheritance are summarized in Table 2.1, and all technical terms appear in the glossary.

Table 2.1 Legal jurisdictions and terminology relevant to the transmission of property at death

	Law			
	Common	*Ecclesiastical*	*Manorial*	*Equity*
Property jurisdiction	Freehold	Moveables Leasehold	Copyhold	Any
Husband may dispose of by will	2/3 military tenure to 1645, then all; all non-military tenure	1/3 in north, Wales, London; all in south; all everywhere after 1724	Varied by manor, none to 2/3	–
Widow's right in husband's property	Dower	Thirds	Freebench or jointure	Jointure
Division in husband's intestacy	Primogeniture; coparcenary if sonless	Thirds	Manorial custom	–

MARRIAGE

Under common law a woman's legal identity during marriage was eclipsed – literally covered – by her husband. As a 'feme covert', she could not contract, neither could she sue nor be sued independently of her husband. The *Lawes Resolutions* in 1632 referred to coverture drily as 'the conglutination of persons in baron and feme'.[13] The property a woman brought to marriage – her dowry or portion – all came under the immediate control of her husband. The moveables she lost permanently; the leases she might recover if she survived her husband and he had not disposed of them during his lifetime; the freehold or copyhold he held 'in the right of his wife' and received the profits thereof, although he could not permanently dispose of the land without her consent.

If she survived her husband a woman was entitled at common law to dower for her lifetime. By the fourteenth century dower consisted of one third of the real property her husband had held at any time during their marriage.[14] The widower's equivalent of a widow's dower was his 'curtesy', by which he was entitled for life to *all* of his deceased wife's real property, not just one third, as long as a child had been born. Whereas a married man could dispose in advance of his wife's dower after her death, according to common law a married woman was unable to make a will, so she could not dispose in advance of her husband's curtesy upon his death. It descended automatically to her children.

Manorial law made provision for widows comparable with common law dower: a widow's right in her husband's copyhold land was called her freebench, sometimes widow's bench, or simply bench. The proportion to which she was entitled varied between one third and all of her husband's copyhold estate, but usually consisted of half or more. The duration of her interest might be for life or for her widowhood.[15] Like freehold, a wife also recovered at her husband's death any copyhold which was hers by inheritance or purchase prior to her marriage.

The formulation of dower, and sometimes freebench, as a proportion of the land her husband had held *at any time* during the marriage presented difficulties for apportioning and enforcement, both from the point of view of wives and in the interests of an efficient land market. If a husband sold land without having his wife sign a deed of release of her dower in it, the new owner might be subject years later to a suit from the wife, now a widow and claiming her dower. Conversely, if a woman had to go tracking down a series of subsequent owners of several different pieces of land which used to belong to her husband, she was not receiving adequate security in her widowhood.

The alternative to dower was a jointure. The medieval jointure was a joint tenancy of land by husband and wife, in which the survivor of the two enjoyed the income from the land so held. Either copyhold or freehold land could be held in joint tenancy, enforceable in manorial or common law courts.[16] The word 'jointure' did not appear until 1451, although by the early sixteenth century jointure had in practice largely superseded dower.[17] But by this time jointure generally took the form of an annuity arising from a rent charge on specified lands. The cash portion a woman brought into marriage was generally used to buy land to provide an annual income, first to support the new couple and subsequently to support the wife should she survive to become a widow. Among wealthy families the jointure had the advantage of allowing the patrimony, or the main estate, to remain intact for the heir. At the same time, jointure was also more suitable for protecting the wife's interest in families which had primarily leasehold land, or land settled in a trust, in neither of which a widow enjoyed common law dower or manorial freebench.[18]

The terms of the jointure were usually set in a pre-marital settlement, involving a trust to protect the annuity which would otherwise be lost under coverture. The trust and/or the marriage settlement was defensible not in manorial or in common law, but in equity.[19] The system of equity originated in the fifteenth century specifically in order to mitigate the harshness of the common law. The business of equity was largely with trusts (or prior to the mid-sixteenth century with their precursor, uses), which the common law did not recognize. In addition, it was possible to sue in equity even if the litigant did not have possession of the bond, deed, contract or other evidence to prove title to property, where a suit in these circumstances was not possible at common law.

A marriage settlement might also protect three other categories of married women's personal property, in an attempt to circumvent the most uncongenial effects of coverture. First, a 'separate estate' could be established, consisting of specified property held in trust for a wife's use during coverture, which was to be at her disposing. Second, 'pin-money' was an annual allowance with which a woman was to outfit her household and 'deck her person suitably to her husband's rank'. The payment of pin-money was virtually unenforceable during marriage, but a widow might claim it up to one year in arrears at her husband's death. According to one parsimonious Victorian equity text, the purpose of pin-money was

> to save the trouble of a constant recurrence by the wife to the husband, upon every occasion of a milliner's bill, upon every occasion of a jeweler's account coming in; not the jeweler's account for the jewels, because that is a very different question − but for the repair and the wear and tear of trinkets, and for pocket-money, and things of that sort.[20]

The seventeenth-century *Lawes Resolutions* took a more romantic view of pin-money: a woman, herself her husband's ornament, 'glittereth but in the riches of her husband, as the moone hath no light, but it is the sunnes'.[21] Finally, 'paraphernalia' consisted of a wife's clothes, jewels, bed linens and plate. Paraphernalia, originally under ecclesiastical jurisdiction, was recoverable in equity by the early modern period. While these goods could be disposed of by her husband at any time, any remaining at his death reverted to the wife.

INHERITANCE

For the purpose of inheritance, the common law regulated only real property. In the absence of a will specifying the distribution of land, a dead man's freehold was divided according to the canons of descent, fixed by the mid-thirteenth century and unchanged until 1925. In the first instance, this meant by primogeniture, or to the eldest son. In the absence of any sons then the land went to all daughters, who inherited jointly. Following common usage I refer to the whole system, in short, simply as primogeniture, but it is important to bear in mind that unlike many continental European systems of land distribution, which sought a more distant male relative in the absence of sons, in England the law preferred a daughter to a collateral male.

Manorial customs of inheritance determined whether copyhold land could be disposed of by will (mostly it could), and whether it was partible or non-partible in cases of intestacy. Non-partible manors followed either primo-geniture or ultimogeniture, in which the youngest son inherited. Partible customs usually divided land among all sons, but very occasionally included daughters.[22] Much early modern copyhold descended by partible inheritance, particularly in pastoral regions, including the north, Kent and the East Anglian fenland, although the practice of primogeniture was spreading. While the system of partible inheritance was more egalitarian, in the presence of any population growth it produced what has been called the 'extreme pulverization' of land.[23] Not only was land divided into smaller pieces, but partibility encouraged earlier marriage which led to a higher birthrate, which produced more and even smaller pieces.[24] A partible system might be maintained in the long term only where it was accepted that one son would buy out the interests of the others in the land.

In any event, both freehold and copyhold could be disposed of during the owner's lifetime or by will,[25] so common law or manorial customs of inheritance only operated in cases where no previous arrangement had been made. As for leased land, a lease for lives, upon the death of one lessee, simply transferred to the next; the remainder of a lease for years could be willed, or it was treated as other moveables in the absence of a will.

Wills themselves, as well as the division of moveable goods in cases of intestacy, and the entire administrative procedure of probate, came under ecclesiastical jurisdiction. From their origins in the twelfth century until 1857 the ecclesiastical courts decided not only church matters (clergy discipline, church repairs, tithes and so on); they also held jurisdiction over the probate of wills and the administration of intestates' estates, on the grounds that the ostensible motive for bequests was the soul's health after death. In the early modern period the ecclesiastical courts also licensed schoolteachers and midwives, and dealt with drunkenness, scolding, marriage, adultery, forni-cation and defamation.

The first standard guide to ecclesiastical probate procedure was Henry Swinburne's *A Treatise of Testaments and Last Wills*, which appeared first in 1590 and was reprinted six times over the next two centuries.[26] (For convenience, 'probate' is used throughout to refer to cases of intestate administration, as well as to will registration.) In 1668 George Meriton, deciding that Swinburne was nearly out of print – the most recent edition had appeared in 1640 – and too dear for the 'honest countrey-man', published his *Touchstone of Wills, Testaments, and Administrations*.[27] The third edition of Meriton's *Touchstone* in 1674, at only 1s. 6d., was reasonably accessible to country men – at least to country lawyers, country clerics, and perhaps the occasional yeoman. Its price was substantially less than that of a leather-bound Bible, and the equivalent of nine newspapers, but it cost a full day and a half's wages for a labouring man.[28] Another edition of Swinburne's *Testaments* followed in 1677.

The ecclesiastical rules of inheritance in intestacy followed Roman civil law in so far as all children, regardless of sex, were entitled to equal portions of their parents' moveable goods. Similarly, the goods of unmarried people dying intestate were equally divided among all their siblings. An intestate man's widow was entitled to one third of his moveables, and the other two thirds were divided equally among his children. The ecclesiastical law of the province of York, Wales, the City of London, and 'other great cities',[29] further protected the family of a man who did make a will: his widow was entitled to one third of his moveables and his children one third, so that the head of household could only bequeath one third, sometimes called the 'dead part'. A married but childless man might bequeath only half of his moveables; the other half was his widow's. The widow's and children's entitlements were called 'reasonable parts' or 'thirds'. In the middle ages reasonable parts had been recoverable at common law, but by the fourteenth century the common law had abjured the idea, leaving it to the ecclesiastical courts. Even the ecclesiastical law of reasonable parts had disappeared by 1500 in the province of Canterbury, where a man had complete freedom to disinherit his children and leave his wife penniless.[30]

Swinburne explained both the northern rule of reasonable parts and the southern rule of no reasonable parts in terms of moral desert. 'For what if the sonne be an unthrifte, or naughtie person, what if the wife be not onelie a sharpe shrowe, but perhaps of worse conditions?' In this case, the head of household's complete testamentary freedom 'might be a meanes whereby they might become more obedient, live more vertuouslie, and contend with good desert, to winne the good will and favour of the testator'. On the other hand, 'what if the childe be no unthrifte, but frugall and vertuous? what if the wife be an honest and modest woman? which thing is the rather to be presumed?' Then the testamentary power of the husband, who was after all 'perhaps also greatly inriched by his wife', was justly restrained.[31] Unluckily, however, 'disobedient wives and unthrifty children' were not exclusive to the southern province, with freedom of testation, nor were 'lewd husbands and unkinde fathers' geographically restricted to those areas where widows enjoyed the right to reasonable parts.

Between 1692 and 1725 the ecclesiastical right of widows and children to reasonable parts in the province of York, Wales and the City of London was abolished by statute.[32]

THE BALANCE OF LEGAL POWER

It is clear from this summary of the laws governing property in marriage and inheritance that the different legal jurisdictions were at odds with each other on several points. The balance of power between the different jurisdictions shifted as the laws themselves changed over time. The overlapping jurisdictions of local manorial or borough courts, regional ecclesiastical courts, and regional and national equity courts were, increasingly over the early modern period, dominated by the common law.

The first major shift in the balance of power between the common law and ecclesiastical law was the English reformation. From the middle of the sixteenth century ecclesiastical law, based on the continental system of civil law, could be regarded by English common lawyers as alien. The centralization of governmental administration under the Tudor monarchs and the constitutional disputes of the early seventeenth century accelerated the 'hardening' of the common law. From the 1630s it was politically necessary to assert that the common law was immemorial and immutable, in order to back up parliament's claim to authority over the monarchy. For that reason the mid-seventeenth-century movement for legal reform, which proposed to unify and rationalize the legal system, got nowhere.[33] The victory of the parliamentarians in the civil war and the subsequent restoration of the monarch on constitutional grounds further consolidated the position of the common law. In the two centuries after 1660 the common law steadily encroached upon the jurisdictions of both ecclesiastical and manorial law. This was done ostensibly in the name of 'rationalizing' the legal system and clarifying rights of private property, but in practice it consolidated the narrow common law view of marriage and inheritance, and established absolute rights to private ownership of property for men only.

The legal trend towards national standardization has been observed in the gradual enclosure of land over the sixteenth, seventeenth and eighteenth centuries, which led to the elimination of local customs and common rights to land. Alongside this abolition of local custom and common rights should be included the almost wholly ignored series of late seventeenth- and early eighteenth-century statutes cutting down women's ecclesiastical rights to reasonable parts from their husbands' and fathers' moveable goods, as well as the innocuously named Act for the Better Settling of Intestates' Estates of 1670 (22 & 23 Car.II c.10), which cut in half the right of a childless widow to her husband's goods. These statutes probably did not greatly impinge on daughters (see Chapter 4), but they were potentially extremely damaging to widows (see Chapters 9 and 10).

Most legal histories are written about one or another of the systems of law, most frequently the common law. This is unfortunate, since despite its egalitarian name the common law was the creation of the medieval landed classes to preserve dynastic hegemony through practices like primogeniture and coverture. The pre-eminent English legal historian F. W. Maitland thought that 'the habits of the great folk are more important than the habits of the small'.[34] In light of the common law's increasing influence, his thesis may have some validity in the long term. But it seriously misrepresents the actual experience of most of the population in early modern England.

In the early sixteenth century Christopher St German had been more circumspect in his comments on the common law's treatment of women.

Considering the relation between law and morality, he conceded that the disparity between the wife's dower and the husband's curtesy, the bride's loss of all her moveables, the principle of primogeniture, and the ability of a husband to cut his wife off with a shilling by will 'cannot be proved onelye by reason . . . although they be reasonable'.[35] Perhaps St German was recalling late medieval disagreements over the law of women's property; perhaps he was responding to the humanism of his own day in its relatively benign attitude towards women as human beings. But the 'reasonableness' of the common law was still throughout the early modern period facilitated by the ameliorating effects of the other legal jurisdictions.

The early modern treatises on the law relating to women deal primarily with the common law, and secondarily with equity. Nevertheless, it is clear that ordinary people did not attach the same overriding importance to the common law that later centuries have done. Throughout the early modern period, relatively equal access was available at a regional level to at least manorial, ecclesiastical and common law courts, although equity was more limited.

The common law was administered in quarter sessions and assizes. Quarter sessions were held four times a year, in the county towns and also on perambulation. Here Justices of the Peace (JPs) dealt with criminal charges and recognizances to keep the peace, but also with non-violent matters: local rates and national taxes, the poor law and vagrants, the maintenance and apprenticeship of bastards, roads, markets and trade, religious matters, and licences to keep alehouses and to build cottages, for example. The assizes usually dealt with criminal cases; they were held in county towns and followed a rather more limited perambulation than quarter sessions. Outside of sessions or assizes, JPs also heard cases individually or in twos or threes, by the late seventeenth century called petty sessions.[36]

Manorial courts, the medieval court leets, were probably the most easily accessible courts in those areas of the countryside where they were still operating in the seventeenth century. Manorial authority was gradually undermined over the early modern period by the loss of manorial rolls through neglect, and in some cases deliberate destruction, particularly during the civil war.[37] But from the sixteenth century manorial customs could also be enforced in common law and equity courts.[38] Borough courts sat in some cities and towns as often as three times a week, dealing with matters of debt and disputes relating to bye-laws and local customs of land inheritance.[39] Manorial and borough courts consisted of the male tenants of the manor, or freemen of the borough, but substantial numbers of the litigants coming before the courts were women. Many boroughs – London and others as yet unidentified – from the middle ages allowed married women the anomalous status of 'feme sole trader' if they were engaged in business on their own account separate from their husband.[40] Exactly how this worked has never been investigated, but it did allow the possibility of married women appearing in these courts – which they could not do on their own in common law courts – in addition to single women and widows.

The most important courts from the point of view of women's property were the equity courts and the ecclesiastical courts, and it remains to examine their records and procedures and the people who appeared before them.

THE COURT OF CHANCERY AND ITS LITIGANTS

The primary court of equity throughout the early modern period was the Court of Chancery in Westminster. Other courts had equity jurisdiction: the Courts of Exchequer and of Requests, both also in Westminster, and the Councils in the North and in Wales. But Requests and the Councils were abandoned at the civil war. The three independent palatinate counties of Chester, Durham and Lancaster also had their own equity courts, but the volume of business in these declined rapidly over the seventeenth century.[41]

From the Court of Chancery the decisions (but not the proceedings) in a small number of cases were published by 'reporters' beginning in the late sixteenth century, and were used as guides to precedent. These cases in printed *Reports* generally involved titled people and large amounts of money. Original Chancery Court proceedings have rarely been explored, but the documents available include the original pleadings, depositions and court orders, and, unlike cases in the *Reports*, they represent a wide social range of plaintiffs and defendants, particularly in the sixteenth and early seventeenth centuries.

The majority of all plaintiffs in Chancery appear to have been below the social standing of the gentry. Aristocratic and gentry plaintiffs may be identified either by an honorific title (down to Mr or Mrs) or by the subject of suit being the lordship of a manor.[42] The now ubiquitous 'Mr' and 'Mrs' were in the early modern period pronounced master and mistress and designated the gentry, without reference to female marital status. Up to one quarter of all litigants in Chancery were women (see Chapter 7). The proportions of untitled people in the common law Courts of Common Pleas and King's Bench were comparable: between three quarters and two thirds of litigants in the later sixteenth and early seventeenth centuries.[43] But the social level of Chancery litigants rose markedly over the seventeenth century, reflecting the rapid contraction of its clientele with rising costs and lengthening delays.

Nearly two hundred years before the infamous Chancery case of Jarndyce *v. Jarndyce* in Dickens's *Bleak House*, Celia Fiennes commented in about 1700, 'This formerly was the best court to relieve the subject but now is as corrupt as any and as dilatory'.[44] The volume of cases in Chancery had increased tenfold between the early sixteenth and the early seventeenth century,[45] and after the influx of business following the closure of the Court of Requests in 1642 and the Court of Wards in 1645 Chancery clogged hopelessly, for the remaining 250 years of its existence.

THE ECCLESIASTICAL PROBATE COURTS: PROCEDURE

Ecclesiastical courts were divided at the highest level into prerogative courts, one in the northern and one in the southern province. The next largest jurisdiction was the consistory court, then the archdeaconry court, and finally the deanery and peculiar jurisdictions, which might cover only one or two parishes. Rural deans even made house calls for probate business, for an extra fee.[46]

The ecclesiastical courts had two sides: one dealing with religious and moral matters in which the church prosecuted offenders or individuals prosecuted each other; and one dealing with the strictly administrative business of probate. Women appeared regularly before the litigation side of the ecclesiastical courts in cases regarding disputed inheritance, tithes, religious behaviour, drunkenness, scolding and defamation, adultery and fornication, broken marriage contracts, and practising midwifery or teaching school without a licence. The litigation side of the church courts reveals a great deal about how women were supposed to behave, as well as about how they did behave, and the records of this side of the church courts have received considerable attention in recent years.

But whereas relatively few women in the population were involved in this type of litigation, vast numbers of ordinary women appeared before the administrative probate side of the court. Of all those people appearing in court to prove wills, exhibit inventories and file accounts, nearly three quarters were women. Probate documents are more representative of normal practice than litigation over property in ecclesiastical, equity, manorial or common law courts, because litigation by its nature is extraordinary.

Wills are the best known type of probate document. However, despite a will's utility in 'preventinge of suche troubles unkyndnes and controversies as doe moste comonlie growe where noe suche order is taken', as one Lincolnshire yeoman put it,[47] most people did not make a will. Most people still do not: in Britain today less than one third of adults die having made a will.[48] Estimates of the number who made a will in early modern England vary from less than 5 per cent up to 45 per cent of the adult population in different places.[49] But all calculations of early modern rates of testation err on the side of underestimation.[50] So relatively more people may have made a will in the seventeenth century than do so today. This is surprising in the light of the disparities in literacy, education and communication between the seventeenth and the twentieth centuries, but less surprising when one considers the consequences of not making a will under a system of coverture and primogeniture. Early modern wills were primarily concerned with provisions for widows and younger children, whereas both common law and local custom were preoccupied with the rights of the heir.

The use of wills as a historical source is not straightforward. The size and nature of bequests in wills may have been shaped by many factors – 'convention, affection, guilt, need, duty'[51] – which are not recoverable in individual cases. Gifts made during the testator's life are often unaccounted for. Nevertheless wills do reveal personal intentions, as opposed to the impersonal operation of law, at least suggesting what people wanted their daughters to inherit relative to their sons, what portion of the estate a man meant his widow to have, and who was to have responsibility in the positions of executor, guardian of minor children and overseer.

Inventories, like wills, survive in large quantities, but unlike wills most are formulaic and short on description. While they are the most impersonal probate document, inventories do represent a broader spectrum of the population than wills, since the moveable goods of testates and intestates alike were appraised. Technically the appraisers had to be at least two local men, who were given breakfast or supper for their services, and an inventory was only required if the estate was worth more than £5. But smaller estates were appraised, like the £3 11s. worth of the single woman Elizabeth Hodgeson who died in the Lincolnshire wolds in 1641, appraised by five men who would have enjoyed a meal at the expense of her estate.[52] The entertainment, though, cannot always have been the reason for scrupulous appraisal. Agnes Procter, another 'poore mayd' of Lincolnshire with only £1 14s. 7d. to her name, consumed her meagre estate in expenses during her last sickness in 1616. Yet her inventory was taken by four men, without the possibility of a party. Hospitality to the appraisers might be reduced to merely 'drinke' in the case of an impoverished estate.[53]

Being documents of the ecclesiastical court, inventories included no land, although leases do sometimes appear. Those moveables which were classified by arcane legal reasoning as adjuncts to a freehold – and therefore belonging to the heir – were also excluded from inventories: grass or trees on the ground; glass windows, window shutters, wainscots (panelling), coppers, leads, ovens or anything (including tables and chairs) affixed to a freehold; any object designated in a will as an 'heirloom' which 'customarily' goes with the freehold; vats in the brewhouse; anvils, millstones and mangers; keys and a box or chest with the owner's 'evidences'; hawks, hounds, doves in the dove-house and fish in the pond. Whether or not root vegetables ought to be included in an inventory was the subject of some controversy among learned legal minds.[54]

Not even all legally eligible moveables were necessarily included in an inventory. Items bequeathed by will may not appear, having been removed from the house before the inventory was taken.[55] Other goods were worth too little to be itemized, and would have been included in the customary catch-all category at the bottom of the inventory, usually 'other trash', 'etc.', 'hushlement', or a variation thereon. (The OED derives 'hushlement' from the French word for utensils, but Lincolnshire and Yorkshire appraisers clearly thought it was an elision of 'householdments'.)

Whereas pewter and the occasional piece of silver were separately itemized, wooden candlesticks and trenchers, small pieces of iron like rushlight holders, cups and spoons made of horn and earthenware plates and bowls were not. In the second half of the seventeenth century Giles Moore paid 1s. 7d. a piece for pewter trenchers, but less than a penny a piece for 'beechen' trenchers. Not only do these cheap but essential and ubiquitous items not appear in inventories, they rarely survive to be seen in museums either: wood has deteriorated, metal has been used for other purposes, horn and earthenware have long since cracked and broken. Other common items too inexpensive to merit separate listing in an inventory would have included a rolling pin or a spade or a pair of scissors, at tuppence; a basting ladle, at thruppence; a latten (brass) funnell or a saucepan or a little pocket looking glass, at 4d.; a chopping knife or a new hammer or even a 'Venice wine glass', at 6d. Even the garden rake or the goose worth a whole shilling might be lumped in with the 'etc.'.[56] Cows, pigs and sheep were itemized; chickens, ducks and geese were usually not. So inventories omit land, adjuncts to a freehold, and a great many cheap, everyday household items, but they are still the only surviving record of individual wealth at the time of death.

Probate accounts, the third and least known type of probate document, offer a snapshot of that same estate a year later, after all debts had been settled.[57] The executor of someone who had made a will, or the administrator of someone who had died intestate, was required by ecclesiastical law to file an account of their handling of the estate, usually one year after the death. (More than two thirds of all accounts were filed for intestates.[58]) This account listed, first, the inventory value of the estate, with which the executor or administrator (hereafter the 'accountant') was charged; second, all disbursements out of that estate which were owed in the deceased's lifetime, plus the accountant's costs, including primarily debts, rents, taxes and tithes, administration and funeral costs; and third, the expenses of raising and apprenticing children, if any. For all of these deductions the accountant 'prayeth', 'craveth' or 'demaundeth' allowance from the probate ordinary, or official presiding in the probate court. Finally, the balance was calculated and any residual goods were distributed in accordance either with the will or with ecclesiastical rules of intestate distribution. The account was the final stage in the process of administering an estate, serving to acquit the accountant of further responsibility for debts.

Between 85 per cent and 90 per cent of all probate accounts were filed for the estates of men, and only 10–15 per cent for the estates of women. But a man's executor or administrator was usually his widow, if he left one, and women's estates were also commonly administered by other women. In the diocese of Canterbury's 13,000 accounts, the largest collection in the country, at least 70 per cent of all people filing accounts in court were women, most of them widows, but also daughters, sisters and mothers.[59] Probate accounts are thus the single most valuable document illustrating ordinary women's economic responsibilities and financial management. Whereas in wills widows appear as relatively passive repositories of their husbands' trust, in accounts they actively take care of the business.

The two standard deductions of an accountant were administration and the funeral. Administrative costs varied between £2 and £3. The court's own 'ordinary charges' for either probate of a will or administration of an intestate amounted to about £1 15s., and additional travelling expenses varied with the distance the accountant lived from the probate court.[60] The court's fees rose very little over the early modern period, but in the case of particularly impoverished accountants the court could abate part of its own fees; this happened most often in Cambridgeshire and Lincolnshire, where more accountants were left in debt than elsewhere.[61]

As for deductions over and above the basic administration and funeral, Henry Swinburne directed that 'sumptuous and delicate expences are not to be allowed, but honest and moderate, according to the condition of the persons'. At the passing of an account the payment of any debt of more than £2 had to be supported by an aquittance or a cancelled bond. Payments of smaller amounts were attested by the accountant's oath. She paid debts out of the deceased's estate in specific order: first to the crown; then legal judgements and condemnations; statutes merchant and recognizances; obligations; and simple bills and merchant books.[62] Debts not in writing (without specialty) the accountant was not legally bound to pay at all, although she often did, especially those which had been confessed by the deceased in his lifetime or on his deathbed.

The efficacy of early modern ecclesiastical courts has been persistently doubted by historians who take contemporary anti-clerical criticisms – particularly those from the 1640s and 1650s – at face value.[63] The supposed inefficiency of the ecclesiastical courts is meant to explain their decline over the early modern period. In the later seventeenth century Henry Consett prefaced his *Practice of Spiritual or Ecclesiastical Courts* defensively with the acknowledgement 'that our ecclesiastical laws professed in this land, have lain, and at this instant, do lye under most unjust and severe imputations, I am very sensible'.[64] However, the whole question of efficacy refers to only one aspect of the ecclesiastical courts – its jurisdiction over morals, or what was called the 'bawdy court', dealing with drunkenness, bastardy, fornication, defamation and so forth. Even the bawdy court has been vindicated in recent years, by research which shows that its procedures, officials and punishments were no more inefficient than those of any other court in the seventeenth century.[65] The decline of ecclesiastical courts over the early modern period owes more to jurisdictional conflict with the common law than to ineptitude on the part of ecclesiastical procedure.

The probate side of the ecclesiastical courts, dealing entirely with administration, as opposed to litigation, was never attacked even by seventeenth-century critics. When the ecclesiastical courts were interrupted by the civil war and probate administration was transferred entirely to a single secular court in London during the commonwealth, the result was chaos.[66] At the restoration of the monarchy in 1660, probate administration was promptly returned to the ecclesiastical courts.

Probate administration was enforced by apparitors, who reported to ecclesiastical officials their neighbours' swearing, drunkenness and sexual trangressions, as well as less titillating lapses such as failing to prove a will or take out an administration. Apparitors were paid by fines collected from the offending parties, so it behooved them to seek out offences. The creditors and legatees of the deceased were called to appear in court at the account's passing by a notice posted in the parish church and by a proclamation from the local apparitor.[67]

The efficacy of ecclesiastical probate jurisdiction is attested to by the tenacity of the court in its pursuit of accountants. The court had to be persistent in the face of a high turnover of estates. In Sussex, Charity Figg *als* Vincent *als* Chandler proved the will of her first husband Chandler, a victualler, in October 1605, and that of her second husband Vincent, who died of plague, within the next two years. But in John Vincent's inventory had been accidentally included £11 worth of goods belonging to his deceased son, also John. When that son's wife died, *her* administrator in October 1607 complained that the £11 belonging to John Vincent the younger, of which his wife in turn had been rightful administrator, was still in the hands of Charity Vincent *als* Chandler. So five months later, now married a third time to Figg, Charity was called to account yet again for that £11 belonging to her dead husband's dead son's dead wife's administrator.[68]

The accounts themselves were closely inspected by the court. Expenses deemed inappropriate were crossed out and the addition of sums was corrected. In Margaret Parkinson's 1604 account of her husband's estate before the probate ordinary at Ely, marginal notes indicate that some of the accountant's claims were allowed by the court but others were not. The final balance was crossed out and refigured five times.[69] Accountants also reported to the court assets which the appraisers had overlooked at the time of taking the inventory, or extra money made by the subsequent sale of the deceased's goods. One among many was the Sussex widow Alice Hill, whose husband's inventory came to £46 in 1635. In her account she reported an additional £8 bond and £5 worth of goods which had been overlooked, plus £4 worth of books sold before the inventory was even taken.[70] In some cases these additional sums almost doubled the value of the inventory, and would have made a significant windfall for the accountant had she covered them up.

But she declared them so often that it is difficult to think that large numbers of accountants either tried or succeeded in falsification. In 1618 it was alleged against Agnes Crow, of the Isle of Ely, that at least part of the deductions she claimed in her account of her husband's estate had in fact already been paid by her husband in his lifetime.[71] Such false expenses would have allowed the accountant to reap a larger residue than appeared in the account balance. But this scam had little likelihood of success without extensive cooperation by payees, considering the proofs of debt – in the form of bills, bonds, shopbooks and acquittances – which the probate court required. In 1500 accounts, Agnes Crow is one of only two accountants accused of unethical procedures. The other was Martha Onn of the Lincolnshire fenland, widow of husbandman

Bartholomew, who was sued by Bartholomew's new administrator, another husbandman, 'for her rashe administringe of his goods'. This man then charged the litigation costs to Bartholomew's pitifully small £9 estate.[72] These two cases appear in the administrative records of the probate side of the courts, but more disputes will appear in the litigation side, upon further investigation. Testamentary disputes comprised a small proportion of all ecclesiastical litigation, but they have been ignored relative to more salacious types of cases; there are only two brief treatments of probate disputes, and only in the sixteenth and early seventeenth centuries.[73]

Although the truthfulness of accounts in and of themselves is not suspect, their use as a historical source is complicated by two questions: first, why the ones that survive survive; and second, under what circumstances they were originally required by the probate ordinary. Probate accounts survive in small numbers relative to wills and inventories. It would appear that many courts only kept them for a short time before discarding them, but the fact that the accounts which do survive in different record offices often date only from certain years, or relate only to people whose surname began with certain letters of the alphabet, suggests that their survival is entirely accidental, and that random boxes of the filing system just happened to escape discard.

Probate courts were first authorized to require an *executor* to account to the ordinary in the thirteenth century. The next legislative mention does not occur until the Statute of Uses in 1540 (31 Hen. VIII c.5), which states that an *administrator* may be called to account, although he cannot be forced to distribute the residual estate. The latter restriction was clearly an anti-ecclesiastical jab, which the ecclesiastical courts in their turn side-stepped by granting the administration of an estate only to that person who would give a bond promising to distribute the residual estate according to the ecclesiastical rules of division.[74] Swinburne in 1590 said that the purpose of an account was to avoid 'the utter undoing and spoyling of many fatherlesse, and friendlesse children', and further warns that 'no man can with safe conscience, speake against the rendering of an account',[75] which suggests some men were doing exactly that. Nevertheless, the largest number of probate accounts survive from the period beginning when Swinburne was writing.

The next legislative mention of accounts is the 1670 Act for the Better Settling of Intestates' Estates, mentioned above in connection with the distribution of residual property. This Act laid down that the ecclesiastical ordinary 'shall and may' call an administrator to account, and so allowed for enforcement, but without specifying under what conditions enforcement was to occur.

Because the 1670 Act empowered ecclesiastical courts to compel estate distribution, it has been seen as a strengthening of ecclesiastical juris-diction.[76] However, the ecclesiastical method of enforcement seems to have been working reasonably well already. If it had been ineffectual, then a significant increase in the number of surviving administrators' accounts after

1670 would be expected in the light of the newly extended powers granted to ecclesiastical courts by parliament. No such increase occurs in the surviving documents. Furthermore, ecclesiastical enforcement of estate administration was *restricted* by parliament fifteen years later in the Statute of Distributions (1 Jac. II c.17).

The Statute of Distributions confirmed in large part the provisions of the 1670 Act, but henceforth accounting would only be required in cases where there was a specific request on behalf of a minor, from the next of kin, or from a creditor of the deceased. After that 1685 Act, the number of surviving accounts drops markedly. They continue to occur through the eighteenth century, but only where requested, and so are more likely to represent disputed cases.[77] Hence the pattern of document survival argues that parliament was eroding, not strengthening, ecclesiastical jurisdiction with the Act of 1670. (The Acts of 1670 and 1685 have previously been equated to such an extent that the earlier one is often referred to as the Statute of Distributions.)

On the basis of the only fragment of parliamentary debate on the 1670 bill which survives, it appears that the intent was to extend the jurisdiction – and income – of the common law courts by reviving the medieval common law writ which would have allowed the widows and children of men who died intestate to sue for their thirds (the principal issue in the 1670 Act) in common law courts, rather than in ecclesiastical courts.[78] By 1685, those who spoke against the rendering of accounts had gained ascendancy.

Apart from the vicissitudes of the relations between common lawyers and ecclesiastical lawyers, it would seem that accounts were never made for the same number of estates for which inventories were made, so they must have been created only in certain circumstances. Two reasons in particular which might have caused the ordinary to require an account would suggest a bias in the surviving documents. The first possible reason is circumstances of actual or potential conflict over the estate. But aside from a few spectacular instances – like the Cambridgeshire widow Frances Richardson, in possession of her husband's £566, who in 1674 defended four actions at common law and a suit in Chancery in London[79] – litigation is rare in probate accounts. Among Cambridgeshire accounts, which date from the first half of the seventeenth century, 12 per cent mentioned a law suit (11 of 95); Northamptonshire accounts date from the second half of the seventeenth century, and only 6 per cent referred to litigation (8 of 140). Whether the discrepancy in litigation levels here is a difference of region or of period might be tested by a study of the frequency of probate suits in ecclesiastical courts, and a direct comparison of accounts with litigation where possible. The majority of these suits concerned not disputes over the estate itself, but the recovery of individual debts due to or from the deceased. So potential conflict over the estate was not a prominent reason for requiring that an account be filed.

The second reason why the probate ordinary might have required an account is the estate's liability to debt. However, only about one quarter of all accounts ended in debt (see Table 2.2), and so the court would have been

Table 2.2 Proportion of all probate accounts ending in debt

	%	n	N
Sussex	21	40	194
Lincolnshire	25	91	371
Northamptonshire	25	36	145
Cambridgeshire	35	85	242
Total	26	252	952

Sources: WSRO, LAO, NRO and CUL accounts.

Notes: All medians, if split, take the higher number, here and on all subsequent occasions.

Accounts with a balance of zero have been included as in debt. In accounts, a negative balance is somewhat confusingly referred to as a 'surplussage'.

The totals are slightly lower than the overall total number of accounts from each county as shown in Table 2.4 because not all accounts gave a final valuation.

remarkably inaccurate in its target group if it was calling principally potential debtors to account.

While the selectivity of probate accounts' survival is not clear, there is no pattern to suggest its being anything other than random. Obvious biases like suspect management or likelihood of debt can be ruled out.

THE ECCLESIASTICAL PROBATE COURTS: PEOPLE

The vast majority of probate documents relate to ordinary, untitled people, but discussion of social status must be carried out entirely with reference to men. A woman's social status derived from that of her husband or father, and for an untitled woman her principal identification was her marital status. In the rare cases where a man was identified by his marital status, it was usually 'bachelor'. Only one, a Sussex yeoman, referred to himself as 'Thomas Hardom the maried man'.[80] For men marital status was the second line of identification, in the case of there being two adult Thomas Hardoms who were not father and son.

An untitled man's social status was defined either by his trade or by his land ownership. A woman was almost never identified by her occupation, regardless of the work she undertook. In this study they were very few – Sarah Pepper, a victualler of Pinchbeck, in the Lincolnshire fenland, in the 1670s; Mistress Rite, an apothecary of Twerton, Somerset, in the 1690s.[81] The absence of occupational descriptions does not mean that women did not practice trades in addition to housewifery, but that these trades were only occasionally specified, as when Robert Beilby of Selby, in his will of 1703, desired that his wife Alice and youngest daughter Rebecca 'live together in love and charity and be assistant one to the other in managing the trade of pipe-making, for an honest livelihood'.[82]

Most men were described by their agrarian standing, rather than by a trade. Yeomen, at the top of the untitled agrarian social ladder, were traditionally defined as those with freehold land worth at least £2 p.a., but that standard was outdated by the mid-sixteenth century, when Sir Thomas Smith estimated it was equivalent to £6 p.a. of 'our currant money'.[83] The traditional stratification by type of landholding, according to which yeomen held freehold, husbandmen copyhold and leasehold, and labourers no land at all but only worked on others' land,[84] is based largely on the theoretical legal superiority of freehold. Most people held land in copyhold or, increasingly, leasehold.[85] By at least the late sixteenth century, the amount of land held was more significant than the type.

Yeomen in regions of arable agriculture, requiring large holdings, farmed 50 or 100 acres or more; husbandmen might farm up to 50 acres. Arable areas in this study include southern Cambridgeshire, most of Northamptonshire, the east riding of Yorkshire, the central vale and wolds of Lincolnshire, and in Sussex the coastal plain and downs. By contrast, holdings of less than 15 acres, and even as small as 3–4 acres, were common in pastoral areas like the fenlands of northern Cambridgeshire (the Isle of Ely) and southern Lincolnshire, the Isle of Axholme and the marshland in Lincolnshire, the Sussex weald and the north Yorkshire moors (see map on page xiv).[86] Smaller holdings could be maintained in woodland and pastoral areas where access to supplemental resources was available. Common land, forest, marsh or fen allowed cottagers to graze animals, hunt or fish and to gather herbs and fruits, fuel and building materials, and provided income from industries like woodworking, rushweaving or knitting. Labourers generally had only a cottage and garden with less than 1 acre of land; few had the statutory 4 acres required for the building of a cottage.[87]

Celia Fiennes quoted a proverb old in 1700: 'a yeoman of Kent with one year's rent could buy out the gentleman of Wales and knight of Scales and a lord of the north country'.[88] The same range of regional variation occurred lower down the social scale. A yeoman of Kent might not have recognized his namesake in the far north, where 'yeoman' was used loosely of poor and prosperous men alike.[89] Regional nomenclature must also have influenced the fact that in Lincolnshire 'labourers' comprised nearly one quarter of all men whose status was identified in probate documents, but in Sussex 'labourers' were completely absent, while 'husbandmen' were a larger and comparably poorer group.[90]

But the local economy was an important determinant of social standing. Labourers in arable areas were relatively poorer than labourers in pastoral fenland and woodland areas, who rented small pieces of land and even paid other people to do agricultural work for them. Some labourers, especially in the late sixteenth and early seventeenth centuries, had copyhold and even freehold houses. Miles Constable of Selby, for example, whose inventory amounted to £30 worth of moveables, disposed of a lease of land and a freehold house with garth and backside (yard and garden) in his will of 1638.[91]

The local agriculture and economy might also be expected to influence women's property, in so far as it determined land inheritance practices and the type of provision for widows. An arable economy which depended on preserving large landholdings intact in order to grow quantities of corn (grain) might have less land to spare for daughters and require that widows live with their sons rather than independently. Equally, in areas of dairying and other specifically female industries – the Vale of Pickering, the Cambridgeshire fenland or the Sussex weald and downland – women might acquire more distinct ideas about their own property than in areas where they had little opportunity to earn a cash income.[92] These propositions are examined in more detail in later chapters.

From their inventories it is possible to calculate the personal wealth of those men whose social status was identified. Despite regional variation, there is a broad correspondence of wealth in agrarian social levels. Table 2.3 compares the median moveable wealth (before debts) of different social strata across the country. Very broadly, labourers had up to £30 (£13–£28); husbandmen up to £80 (£22–£83); and yeomen up to £200 or more (£104–£229). Gentlemen, at the bottom of the titled hierarchy, had £114–£329, although this group is also represented by the smallest sample. The few gentry families included here were of the lesser sort – county, or even parish gentry, whose influence extended over only a parish or two. The median moveable wealth of Lincolnshire gentlemen, at £221 for example, certainly places them on the lowest rung of the gentry.[93] Tradesmen and craftsmen are not included in Table 2.3 because their numbers in inventories are small and their wealth too disparate, depending on the trade or craft.

In surviving wills wealthier men are generally overrepresented. (The apparent exception to this rule is the fenland, where poor men were far more likely to make wills. See Chapter 12.) In most rural areas yeomen were the largest identified group among willmakers, although husbandmen and labourers were the largest group in the population. Labourers alone probably comprised one third of all adult men in the seventeenth century.[94] Most people for whom inventories were filed had less than £50 worth of moveable goods, even into the eighteenth century, putting them in the range of husbandmen, smaller tradesmen and labourers, but even inventories overrepresent the wealthy.[95] In accounts too, yeomen were the largest self-defined group, but this has something to do with the greater tendency of those self-consciously at the top of the non-gentry hierarchy to identify themselves. If the wealth of the majority of men who did not identify their social status is considered, it appears that most men or whom accounts were filed were in fact husbandman. Table 2.4 lists the median economic status of all probated men in this study, by county.

If we estimate very roughly from individual parish studies that up to one third of any local population was in receipt of poor relief, one third neither received relief nor paid tax, and one third or somewhat more paid poor tax, then this study deals primarily with the middle and upper thirds, and occasionally with the lower third.[96] At the top of the group, many people died owing back poor rates; at the bottom, orphaned children were turned over to the Overseers of the Poor.[97]

Table 2.3 Median wealth, before debts, of agrarian social strata

		Gentleman		Yeoman		Husbandman		Labourer	
		£	n	£	n	£	n	£	n
1	Berkshire, Lincolnshire, Sussex 1556–1650	–	–	160	2172	–	–	–	–
2	Lincolnshire 1582–1698	221	11	110	81	83	68	27	48
3	Sussex 1594–1685	–	–	149	29	68	16	–	–
4	Norfolk, Suffolk 1587–1711	165–408	–	100–97	–	41–70	–	–	–
5	Selby, Yorks 1637–1709	114	14	117	34	80	13	24	8
6	Cambridgeshire 1660s	–	–	180	58	30	24	15	18
7	Powick, Worcs 1676–1775	188	21	120	48	22	13	–	–
8	14 counties 17th century	329	298	195	1071	80	470	28	103
9	Essex 17th century	–	–	229	–	45	–	–	–
10	England 1675–1725	–	–	104	952	30	332	13	28

Sources: Line 1, Mildred Campbell, *The English Yeoman under Elizabeth and the Early Stuarts* (1942) p. 238 (average, not median); lines 2–3, from Table 2.2; line 4, Mark Overton, 'English probate inventories and the measurement of agricultural change', in A. van der Woude and A. Schuurman (eds) *Probate Inventories* (1980) p. 209, or 'Agricultural change in Norfolk and Suffolk, 1580–1740' (Cambridge Ph.D. thesis, 1980) p. 24; line 5, *Selby Wills*, my calculation; line 6, Spufford, *Contrasting Communities*, pp. 37–8; line 7, Johnston, 'Probate inventories', pp. 22–3 (I have rounded his figures to whole numbers); line 8, David Cressy, *Coming Over: Migration and Communication Between England and New England in the Seventeenth Century* (1987) p. 121, Table 4 (averages, not medians); line 9, Cressy, 'Social order', p. 40; line 10, Lorna Weatherill, *Consumer Behaviour and Material Culture in Britain 1600–1760* (1988) Appendix 2, Table A2.2.

Note: Throughout, I use medians rather than averages (means) because means distort series of numbers which are mostly similar but include a few very large examples, in this case a few much wealthier men than the rest. In my own samples in this table, for example, means overestimate medians by 15 per cent for labourers, up to 53 per cent for husbandmen and 68 per cent for yeomen.

But are we looking at the same levels of society over a period of nearly 150 years? It has been observed that the individual wealth of probate records rises over the early modern period.[98] The mid-seventeenth-century gap in probate records, when ecclesiastical probate administration was interrupted, is a convenient means to compare earlier with later patterns. Table 2.5, assessing the median value of some 680 probate accounts and inventories in Lincolnshire and Sussex, half dating from before and half from after 1650, suggests that the median wealth of probated estates approximately doubled over the century, from £35 to £74 in Lincolnshire, and from £60 to £115 in Sussex. The rate of price inflation between the later sixteenth and the beginning of the

Table 2.4 Median wealth of men before and after debts 1579–1715

	Initial value (£)	N	Final value (£)	N
Cambridgeshire 1602–1709	43	223	8	219
Lincolnshire 1594–1691	62	303	15	244
Sussex 1572–1711	81	1024	38	93
Northamptonshire 1669–1685	132	147	45	147

Sources: CUL, LAO, WSRO and NRO accounts and inventories.

Note: In Northamptonshire, Sussex and Cambridgeshire (Ely Diocesan Records, not including Cambridge University accounts), the initial number represents the total number of surviving accounts; in Lincolnshire it represents a sample of the 6000 or so surviving. The very high number of initial valuations from Sussex derives from an index of probate accounts in the WSRO made by T. J. McCann which lists initial but not final value. The table is restricted to men's accounts so as to compare it with the wealth–status correlations in the previous two tables, which are entirely male.

The median wealth of women's probate documents ranges from one half to four fifths the value of men's, because men's inventories in most cases assess nuclear family wealth and women's inventories in most cases do not, being made generally at a later point in their lives. Lorna Weatherill, in her study of 3000 inventories, distinguished between 'economically active' women (identified by a trade or inventory contents), whose median estate was worth exactly the same as the overall men's median estate, and all other women, whose median estate was slightly less than two thirds that amount. 'A possession of one's own: women and consumer behaviour in England 1660–1740', *Journal of British Studies* 25:2 (1986) p. 152. I have not made the same distinction because of doubts that an inventory's reflection of a widow's economic activity will depend on the length of time elapsing between her husband's death and her own; the shorter the gap, the less likely the widow's inventory necessarily reflects her own economic activity, although it may indicate her own personal wealth in other ways, if goods appear in her inventory which did not appear in her husband's (see Chapters 8 and 11).

The regional variation in wealth does not correspond to the expected wealth hierarchy of the counties because of the agrarian regions within each county from which probate documents come. Cambridgeshire appears inordinately poor because most of its probate accounts come from the fenland, rather than from the richer south; Margaret Spufford (*Contrasting Communities*, p. 156) estimated that the median yeoman was worth only £48 in the fen, but £299 on the chalk. Inversely, most Sussex accounts come from the wealthier coast and downs, not from the poorer weald.

Table 2.5 Median wealth over time in probate documents

| | 1582–1650 | | 1650–1686 | |
	Initial value (£)	N	Initial value (£)	N
Lincolnshire	35	212	74	240
Sussex	60	125	115	103

Sources: LAO and WSRO accounts and inventories.

Note: Cambridgeshire accounts date almost entirely from before 1635, and Northamptonshire accounts entirely from after 1669, so neither county can illustrate long-term changes in wealth.

eighteenth century varies depending on the good whose price is charted, but it can be approximated at slightly over 200 per cent.[99] Since the doubling of probate wealth in this sample is roughly in line with the general rate of inflation, we must assume that approximately the same level of society is represented in probate documents throughout the early modern period.

This does not mean that the proportion of the population in each economic bracket remained the same. Labourers, for example, were increasing in number over the early modern period but declining in number among probate documents, and early eighteenth-century labourers' inventories are more impoverished than late sixteenth-century ones.[100] But strictly on the basis of personal wealth, those people whose estates were probated under Queen Elizabeth approximate to those probated under Queen Anne.

Most of these people lived in houses with two main rooms, chambered over to create at least a partial second story. The main rooms were usually called the hall and a 'house' or 'parlour' or 'kitchen'; the chambers over them were used for storage or for sleeping. The third room might be just a lean-to or outhouse, called a buttery, a pantry or a larder. In poorer houses this 'room' might be nothing more than a large storage cupboard. But in wealthier houses it was these outhouses which multiplied – adding a dairy, buttery, milkhouse, brewhouse, cheesehouse, wash house or bakehouse, plus additional chambers designated for servants. Wealthy yeomen and clerks might have nine or ten rooms all told; most people had five rooms or less, including chambers, garrets and adjunct rooms. Many had a barn, or at least a lean-to for animals. Most households had a cow, but few had more than one. Older houses were built of brick and timber, newer ones in the second half of the seventeenth century of stone. The interiors were furnished with beds, chests, tables, a chair or two, benches and stools. The interior walls of husbandmen's and labourers' houses may have been painted directly on the plaster, or pasted with penny ballads. In yeomen's houses the walls were decorated with painted canvas or panelling, although neither of these appear regularly in inventories.[101] The value of moveable goods in the inventory was not necessarily related to the size of the house. William and Helen Lowick in the Lincolnshire fenland had only £28 in their inventories in 1606, but their house had at least seven rooms, three of them with glass windows.[102]

Despite changes in social structure, and shifts in the balance of power between different legal systems, by and large the history of women and property is one of continuity. In the middle ages, research revolves around the feudal incidents affecting women's property, the details of which no longer affect early modern women.[103] In the nineteenth century, the study of women's property is inextricably bound up with questions of suffrage and political campaigns, both of which were inconceivable in the seventeenth century.[104] Nevertheless, women in all three periods, at all social levels, were faced with much the same legal structure of inheritance and marriage.

Fortunately, the survival of probate and court documents provides a glimpse of how early modern women dealt with legal restrictions. The coexistence of four codes of law was a vital fact of early modern life. In describing the land law, A. W. B. Simpson noted gently that complexity was 'an outstanding feature of the old law'.[105] That complexity is precisely what early modern women at all social levels had to deal with, at each legally significant phase of their lives, as maids, wives and widows.

Part II

Maids

Men in the characters of fathers . . . are generally infinitely more amiable, and do more justice to the [female] sex, than in any other character whatever.

> Mary Hays, *Appeal to the Men of Great Britain on Behalf of Women*
> (1798:260)

In legal documents a maid was generally a 'virgin' in the sixteenth century. By the seventeenth century she was a 'spinster'. An unmarried female of any age was a 'wench' in the popular tongue of the later middle ages and even into the seventeenth century, but that word would cause problems were I to use it in the following pages, since 'wench', like 'spinster', took on negative connotations in the eighteenth century.

The material well-being of maids in the early modern period can be assessed at several different points. The first is the financial investment in girls' upbringing relative to boys'. The second is the relative value of the portions inherited by daughters and sons from their parents. Both up-bringing and inheritance can be fairly well documented. The third stage, only occasionally visible to posterity, is the care and investment of their portions by parents and young women themselves, and the significance of the portion in negotiating of marriage. For, as the anonymous author of *The Lawes Resolutions of Women's Rights* (1632) put it, all women 'are understood either married or to bee married and their desires [are] subject unto their husbands, I know no remedy though some women can shift it well enough'.[1]

The least visible women are those who never married. A woman remained a maid until her marriage or her death. 'Spinster', originally a woman who spun, had come to designate an unmarried woman in the sixteenth century, and it had only that legal connotation, a meaning it retains today. Both the sneering epithet 'old maid' and the derogatory use of 'spinster' appeared only in the late seventeenth century. In 1688 Jane Barker's 'A Virgin Life' already flouted the opprobrium implied by the terms:

In this happy life let me remain
Fearless of twenty-five and all its train

Of slights or scorns, or being call'd Old Maid,
Those goblins which so many have betray'd.[2]

Mary Astell, in her *A Serious Proposal to the Ladies* (1697), also thought no wise woman should be ashamed of 'the dreadful name of old maid'.[3] But as late as 1707 the pejorative use of both 'spinster' and 'old maid' must have been still unfamiliar to Delarivier Manley – otherwise mistress of the up-to-the-minute put-down – since she had to resort to describing someone as 'an ugly unmarried maid of 30'.[4]

Unlike other new eighteenth-century slang – 'wench' for whore, for example – 'old maid' and 'spinster' did not replace pre-existing words. While the proverb, recorded from the sixteenth century, threatened that 'a woman who died a maid' would lead apes in hell, there was no English word to describe this person until the end of the seventeenth century. The invention of sneering names for the bitter, twisted, *unwomanly* unmarried woman co-incided with a slow but steady decline in the actual number of unmarried women in the population. In the seventeenth century the proportion of the population never marrying fluctuated between 10 per cent and over 20 per cent, substantially higher than at any time since.[5] By comparison, in the 1970s and 1980s only 5–7 per cent of British and American women had not married by their mid-forties.[6]

The reasons for not marrying in early modern England are touched on briefly in Chapter 5. The economic circumstances of women who never married can be glimpsed in probate documents, and here single women are grouped with widows in Chapters 11 and 12, since their living situations and their wills were similar.

3 Upbringing

A preference for sons rather than daughters is associated with Mediterranean and oriental cultures to the present day. Recent articles in the press are vividly illustrated by the distorted demographic statistics in China, parts of Asia, and North Africa, where females die in abnormally large numbers as a result of neglect, malnutrition and lack of health care, if not outright infanticide and sex-selective abortion.[1] It has been suggested that in Western Europe too, from late antiquity to the late middle ages, girls were more likely than boys to be abandoned by their parents – for reasons of poverty, personal defects or illegitimacy.[2]

However, no demographic imbalance is evident at the point when populations become measurable in early modern England. Seventeenth-century prosecutions for infanticide yield no difference in the rate of girls and boys killed at birth, perhaps because the reason for killing an infant was usually illegitimacy.[3] An overt preference for boy children in early modern England is relatively rare. Mrs Alice Thornton, for example, very much wanted a surviving son although she had daughters, and believed she was healthier when pregnant with boys. A late seventeenth-century sermon by the nonconformist Philip Henry expressed the same reason for son-preference elucidated by Chinese, North African and Indian parents today: 'The more children there are – the more of them males, the more likely the family is to be built up by them . . . whence tis so, they are God's gift.'[4] But in general, early modern English letters and journals are silent on the subject, in a way that is surprising, given that parents in some parts of the world today freely express their dislike of daughters to foreign journalists.

Nevertheless son-preference is certainly evident in England on a less than life-threatening level, most notably in the practice of primogeniture and lineal descent through males (the latter shared with all other European cultures, except in unusual circumstances). Historians of both the 'nasty, brutish, and short' and the 'essential continuity' schools of family history suggest that daughters were shortchanged on education and apprenticeship relative to sons, and, more seriously, that they were malnourished.[5] By the nineteenth and twentieth centuries there is evidence that adult women in Europe were malnourished. The early social reformers like Maud Pember Reeves and

Margery Spring Rice amply documented the dietary deficiency of the housewife, although the best known writer in this group, Seebohm Rowntree, was less aware of the gender dimension of poverty than his female contemporaries.[6]

In seventeenth-century England, the men who published tracts on the management of the poor certainly *thought* that adult women ate less than adult men. So did the Justices of the Peace who set maximum wage levels for agricultural labourers. Women labourers received between one half and three fifths the food allowance of men, even when they were doing heavy work like reaping alongside the men.[7] According to modern estimates, women need between 70 per cent and 93 per cent of the calories that men need to maintain health, and until the age of puberty girls and boys need exactly the same amount of calories.[8] But if early modern English women were themselves underfed, it would not be surprising if they habitually underfed their daughters as well, as a matter of either training or expectation.

Probate accounts make it possible for the first time to compare the exact sums expended by early modern parents and guardians on the upbringing of daughters and sons. Quantification is complicated by the fact that most accountants were erratic in their listing of expenses on children's behalf. A mass of miscellaneous payments are recorded, including milk and wetnursing for infants, lengths of cloth, sewing of shifts and breeches, new pairs of shoes, resoling shoes, mending clothes, refooting stockings, various medicines and treatments in sickness, and even pocket money given to the children of yeomen and clerics.[9]

However, it is possible to quantify the most systematic accounts (a minority of the total) which claimed a single lump sum, to cover either the child's annual maintenance or the cost of its apprenticeship. An annual cost for maintenance covered food, lodging, clothing, washing and sometimes schooling. The largest component of maintenance would have been food, the usual expression for which is 'meat and drink', where meat has its early modern meaning of food, not its modern one of flesh. (Kitchen accounts for 'meate' even in the later seventeenth century could include 'cowcumbers, carets, pudings, viniger, samon, cabech, fich, peper'.[10])

Among the families represented in probate accounts, which included wage labourers as well as more prosperous farmers, the median levels of annual maintenance for girls and for boys were identical, at £5 p.a. Quantifiable examples of annual maintenance appear for seventy-nine girls (in forty-seven accounts) and sixty-one boys (in forty-three accounts). Annual expenditure for girls ranged between £1 and £12, and for boys between £1 and £10, with a single extraordinary example of £26. The annual keep of 'children' was listed for a further eighty-five children (in twenty-nine accounts), and the median again was a solid £5. In listing 'children', neither the accountant nor the court clerk saw any reason to differentiate between girls and boys.

The annual maintenance deduction of £5 is only a rough guide to expenditure, and these costs varied according to circumstances. For example, when the person bringing up orphan children was a relative, costs were sometimes less because the guardian made up the difference on his own account. The three Lowick children in the Lincolnshire fenland were kept for the year 1605 at a very low rate, and no future costs were claimed although they were all still 'very younge', but they were maintained by their paternal grandfather.[11] Costs also varied regionally. In remote Westmorland in the late seventeenth century, the autobiographer Wiliam Stout and five or six other schoolboys boarded with a woman for only £4 p.a. apiece 'and plentifully provided for'.[12]

But there is no clear increase in a child's annual maintenance expenses commensurate with greater parental wealth. At the lower end of the social scale, even those children maintained by the Overseers of the Poor were boarded out, often with widows, at an annual rate not very much lower than that found among more middling families in probate accounts. At the end of the seventeenth century, most children on the poor rates in the parish of Terling, Essex, were maintained at about 1s. 6d. per week, or nearly £4 p.a., without distinction between girls and boys. Clothing costs of at least 5s. p.a. were paid by the Overseers in addition, so poor children were maintained at a rate only about 10 per cent less than the median annual maintenance cost of children in probate accounts.[13]

There are two possible explanations for the similarity between the median child's and the impoverished child's levels of maintenance. One is procedural and the other structural. The annual maintenance deductions in probate accounts may be misleading if ecclesiastical courts, or at least some of them, employed a standard level of deduction, perhaps especially in cases where an accountant could not show specific receipts for the individual expenses laid out on a child's upbringing. If, on the other hand, there was no standard level of deduction and the figures in probate accounts accurately reflect the amount spent on children, then they lend support to the idea that the average income was simply very close to subsistence level in the early modern period. This hypothesis has been put forward to explain why the rate of welfare provision in England was higher in proportion to average household income in the seventeenth century than it has been at any time since.[14] While the level of children's maintenance in probate accounts rose over time in line with rising costs, the level of poor relief remained fixed throughout the century.

Another means to compare girls' and boys' upbringing is in the premiums paid with a child at apprenticeship by the parent or guardian. Probate accounts refer more often to general service – either domestic service or service in husbandry – than to trade apprenticeship, but the terms 'apprenticing', 'putting out', 'putting forth' and 'placing' appear to have been used interchangeably. Children were not ordinarily sent to service or apprenticed to a trade until their early teens. A child could begin to help in the home or even earn wages by spreading muck or catching moles earlier, at about the age of 7, but they would not fully earn their own keep until age 13 or 14, at which time they could be apprenticed for a premium.[15] Only pauper or orphan children were put forth at a younger age, of necessity.

Premiums to apprentice or put out children in probate accounts differed not according to the child's sex, but according to its age: the younger the child, the greater the premium required to place it. The accountants of the widow Anne Chalke, who died in the Sussex weald in 1633 leaving £96 and five young children, first clothed the children and then placed them each with a different family – for £2, £3, £8, £10 and £15 respectively, in descending order of age. The cost for the only son happened to be £3; the three highest sums were paid for his younger sisters, and the lowest for his elder sister. An accountant in the Sussex downs in the same year placed ten-year-old Ann Wooles for £9, while one of her elder sisters was placed for £2, and the eldest for only the cost of writing the indentures. Ann's master was paid not only to take her apprentice, but also 'to bring her up', in specific consideration of her youth.[16] It has been suggested that early modern children were apprenticed or put to service at the earliest possible age, by wealthy parents eager to advance their children's social prospects or poor ones anxious to minimize their own household costs.[17] The higher premium required to apprentice a younger child belies any motive to minimize costs by farming children out.

The median premium paid with a child upon apprenticeship or putting forth was slightly more than one year's median maintenance. And as was the case with annual maintenance rates, the median amount expended to place a girl (forty-five examples in twenty-seven accounts) and a boy (forty-four examples in thirty-five accounts) was exactly equal, at £6. Unlike annual maintenance, there was a great disparity between the ordinary child put forth because both parents were dead and a child of the gentry apprenticed to a trade. The premiums for girls ranged from £1 to £21, and for boys from £1 to £20, plus one gentleman's younger son, whose mother Mrs Ursula Healey of the Isle of Axholme paid a staggering £50 premium for his apprenticeship to an unspecified trade, more than eight times the median rate.[18]

The disparity in premium levels between different trades is illustrated in the life of William Stout. Stout himself was apprenticed to a Lancaster ironmonger in 1680 for £20; ten years later he took his own apprentice with £20, and another one some twenty-five years after that with £35. But when in 1706 a parish apprentice was put upon him (Overseers of the Poor were entitled to place pauper children in households which could afford to keep them) Stout in turn bound the boy out to a worsted weaver for only £4. Nor was Stout stinting on this pauper child, since he also paid for the boy to learn Greek for four years.[19]

When compared over time, girls' and boys' placement in probate accounts also incurred identical median expenses: £4 before the mid-seventeenth century, and £10 in the later period, for both sexes. This chronological increase is not inconsistent with inflation, but more research is needed to enlarge the sample of children's placing. Trades were only occasionally specified for boys, put forth to tailors, cobblers, blacksmiths and the like. No trade was specified for any girl, but three girls were sent up to London, which may have involved apprenticeship to a trade. It may be significant that before the mid-seventeenth century 26 per cent of girls (7 of 28) were 'apprenticed' – as opposed to being 'put forth', 'put out' or 'put to keeping' – while after the mid-seventeenth century only 12 per cent of girls (2 of 17) were specifically 'apprenticed'. Boys were consistently 'apprenticed' over the period. On the other hand, these terms were used fairly loosely. All placement of children required much the same paperwork, in the form of indentures or bonds, so there was no particular advantage in using one form of words rather than another.

Various studies of apprenticeship indentures in London and elsewhere have found that female apprentices to trades formed a very small proportion, usually less than 10 per cent, of the total.[20] A few girls were apprenticed to what are recognizable as trades today, which are for the most part masculine, but most girls were apprenticed in housewifery. Today housewifery is comparatively devalued – a Salisbury girl's apprenticeship in 1612 to the 'mistery and sciencs of huswyfrye and flexdressing'[21] appears almost farcical to modern eyes – but formal apprenticeship is only one indication that it was regarded as a skill in medieval and early modern centuries, albeit a quintessentially female skill.

The only sample form for an apprenticeship indenture included in George Meriton's *A Guide for Constables, Churchwardens, Overseers of the Poor* uses the example of a girl placed with a widow to learn housewifery.[22] (The title of housewife expressed a relation to the house, rather than a necessary marital status, just as 'husband' – from 'housebondman' – expressed a man's relation to agriculture, as much as to his wife. By the sixteenth century 'husband' was used only of a married man, but 'housewife' could still describe an unmarried woman: in 1606 John Chamberlain referred to his friend Sir Rowland Lytton's young daughters as his 'huswives'; and in the 1670s Agnes Beaumont's widowed yeoman father, for whom she kept house, addressed her as 'hussif'.[23]) Housewifery was as important for the ordinary woman as husbandry was for the ordinary man. All that most boys in the countryside ever received in the way of apprenticeship was in husbandry. The two skills were equally admired by contemporaries, and shared the same cardinal virtue – thrift. One of the earliest dictionaries, John Bullokar's *English Expositor* (1616), defined parsimony as 'thriftines' or 'good husbandrie'. Richard Gough, an old man at the time he wrote the history of Myddle, his Shropshire parish, in 1700, exemplifies the seventeenth-century ideals of housewifery and husbandry: a bad husband was one who wasted his estates, and a housewife's highest praise was to be 'prudent, provident and discreet'.[24] The principal difference between housewifery and husbandry was that all female characteristics ultimately reflected sexual reputation. For Gough, as for many other writers, modesty implied good housewifery and, inversely, a spendthrift housewife might be assumed to be wanton.

Her excellence in housewifery was a measure by which to judge every woman from the cottager's wife to the great lady – in a way that good husbandry was increasingly inapplicable to men of rank. Even ladies and gentlewomen, whose estates may be supposed to have depended less heavily on prudence, providence and parsimony, wrote paeans to their mother's economy. According to her daughter, Alice Wandesford was not 'awanting to make a fare greatter improvement of my father's estate through her wise and prudentiall government of his family, and by her caire was a meanes to give opportunity of increasing his patrimony'. Lady Mildmay's only daughter distinguished her mother from her father in the epitaph she erected in their memory: 'She was most careful and wise in managing worldly estate, so as her life was a blessing to hers [that is, her family]'.[25]

Early modern housewives were certainly mistresses of a great variety of skills which are no longer essential in the modern practice of the art. In a volume of what must be the most execrable extant example of Elizabethan verse, but also the most frequently reprinted, Thomas Tusser's platitudes acknowledge the extent of a housewife's responsibility:

> Though husbandrie seemeth, to bring in the gaines,
> Yet huswiferie labours, seeme equall in paines.
> Some respit to husbands, the weather may send,
> But huswives affaires, have never an end.[26]

Gervase Markham's *The English Housewife* (1618) maintained, throughout more than twenty reissues, its catalogue of the knowledge necessary to the 'compleat' woman:

> As her skill in physick, chirurgery, cookery, extraction of oyls, banqueting stuff . . . ordering of wool, hemp, flax; making cloath and dying; the knowledge of dayries: office of malting; of oats, their excellent uses in families: of brewing, baking, and all other things belonging to an household.[27]

Markham's successor in the household manual market in the 1680s and 1690s was Thomas Tryon. In Tryon's many popular works – *The Good House-Wife Made a Doctor*, *The Way to Health, Long Life and Happiness*, *The New Art of Brewing Beer* and *Monthly Observations for the Preserving of Health* – the good woman was expected to run her dairy, to brew her beer (in a manner both profitable for the poor and wholesome for the rich), to practise moderation and temperance in her clothing, house and bed, to gather her vegetables astrologically, to destroy vermin, to cultivate her orchard and to treat tumours and other illnesses in both people and animals.

Even the anonymous *The Compleat Servant-Maid: Or, the Young Maiden's Tutor*, first printed in 1677 and into its sixth edition by 1700, had lengthy sections on 'physick and chirurgery'. In probate accounts, sometimes considerable sums were expended to treat sick children whose mothers, had they been alive, might otherwise have administered treatment. In the Lincolnshire fenland Isabell Blaby's eyes were cured of a 'pearle' in 1682 for £4, and

Sarah Mabbut, a yeoman's daughter, had assorted afflictions in 1684 which required worm powder, cold pills and gowns made loose, and on one occasion having her 'scald head' dressed.[28] (A recipe for treating scald head in the contemporary *Gentlewomans Companion* incorporated hot candle wax, cow dung and the 'furring' of chamber pots.[29])

Girls' apprenticeship even to housewifery, however, declined from the later seventeenth century.[30] In mid-eighteenth-century Newbury, Massachusetts, the phrase 'Art, Trade, or Mystery' on the printed apprenticeship indentures was crossed out for the girls, all of whom were apprenticed to housewifery.[31] Housewifery was no longer a 'mistery and sciencs', as it had been in Salisbury 150 years previously. The disappearance of women from apprenticeship in England and its colonies was part of a larger European pattern, in which women were gradually excluded from artisan guilds and companies over the fifteenth, sixteenth, seventeenth and eighteenth centuries.[32]

Some young women were still apprenticed, but one Chancery case of 1694 suggests why they might have appeared at least in the indentures of guilds and companies less often than they had formerly. One Barsheba Dynes, spinster of St Martin in the Fields, a seamstress who had a shop in the new exchange in the Strand, was sued by an esquire of Chichester who had apprenticed his daughter, Christiana Bickley, to Barsheba for a term of five years, with a premium of £40, plus £5 in case Christiana should get the small pox. Her father alleged that Christiana had neither been taught anything nor been made free of the city, but instead had been used as a common errand girl, and in bad weather, whereupon she did indeed contract small pox, as well as diverse other diseases, and fits too. Now at home with her father, he demanded the return of Christiana's premium.

Barsheba's side of the story is, unsurprisingly, rather different. Christiana had, by her own account, always been subject to fits; Barsheba had provided the girl with a nurse in the six weeks of her small pox, and had taken every possible care of her health, but she was never well enough to learn the trade. Most significantly, Barsheba confesses that she is no free woman of the city of London 'as many others of this defendant's trade of a sempstresse who have shopps in the said New Exchange are not and yett take apprentices in the same circumstances as this defendant did the complainant Christiana'. Furthermore, if the term of apprenticeship had been seven instead of five years, she would have taken care to bind Christiana in the Leatherseller's Hall, where Barsheba herself was bound, so that she should after seven years have been free of the city.

Her lack of citzenship, or freedom of the city, was by no means the main thrust of the complaint against her, although it may have been the implication of the charge that she had failed to teach Christiana, but Barsheba was clearly sensitive on the issue of her somehow unofficial status.[33] There may have been more 'not quite right' apprentices like Christiana in the later seventeenth century. If the women to whom they were apprenticed were themselves by that time unable to achieve status within the professional male companies and citizenry, they may have increasingly resorted to extra-legal or extra-professional means of acquiring apprentices. And unofficial apprentices do not generally find their way into official records, except when something goes wrong, as it did in the case of Christiana Bickley.

At upper levels of society apprenticeship was less important as a measure of economic activity, but young women still had to acquire expertise in housewifery. The essential skills were comparable with those required of more ordinary women, but at least by the second half of the seventeenth century the upper end of housewifery instruction included both writing and keeping accounts. The *Compleat Servant-Maid*, which was directed to the servants of ladies and gentlewomen, included 'directions for writing the most usual and legible hands for women' (starting with making a pen), as well as for arithmetic and keeping accounts – located in between a recipe for syrup of coltsfoot and directions for carving fowl. The likewise anonymous *Advice to the Women and Maidens of London* (1678) also encouraged women to learn arithmetic and accounting. The gentlewoman Sarah Fell, who looked after her mother's Lancashire estate in the 1670s, purchased for 1s. 6d. 'a booke called the younge clarkes tutor' to help her keep the accounts. Certainly for the young women who attended school in London – at Bathsua Makin's school for gentlewomen in Tottenham or Hannah Wolley's school for training servants to ladies, to name only the two best known – the curriculum included writing, arithmetic and accounting.[34]

The students at Hannah Wolley's school included the daughters of the Essex clergyman Ralph Josselin. Susan Moore, wife of the Sussex clergyman Giles, may have attended a similar school. She certainly read, since her husband is unlikely to have bought for his own use *The Compleat Midwyves Practise* for 2s. 6d. in 1657, or *The Ladies Calling* for 2s. in 1674. She could probably write too, since he pays her in his accounts for items she has purchased and for work she has done, which suggests she also kept accounts which have not survived.[35]

For the less prosperous, even such a provincial city as Lincoln had four charity schools which took girls. Throughout England in the 1690s there were more than 2000 girls in charity schools (one ninth the number of boys), and perhaps three quarters of those were outside London.[36] Rural parish registers occasionally licensed women as well as men to teach school in their own homes in the early modern period, although much of women's teaching in village 'petty' or 'dame' schools may have been unlicensed. When the guardian of four young daughters of a Lincolnshire yeoman paid 1s. 4d. to 'Mabbols wife for teaching them', it cannot have been for a long period of time, and probably was not in an established school.[37]

The curriculum even in established charity schools is not always apparent. In two schools where it is known – Christ's Hospital in London (founded 1552), which took both boys and girls, and the Red Maids School in Bristol (founded 1634), the first exclusively female foundation – the girls were taught to read and to sew, but not to write.[38] For the graduates of these schools reading was necessary for religious purposes and needlework provided a means of earning a meagre living. Reading and needlework probably comprised the standard education for the majority of girls, from the daughters of yeomen on down the social scale. In Lancashire, for example, Ellen Stout, the elder sister of the autobiographer William, was 'early confined to waite on her brother', but she had previously learned to read, knit, spin and sew.[39] For the daughters of prosperous yeomen or clerks, fancy needlework was acquired as an ornament rather than a trade. Martha Wheatley, the orphan daughter of a Sussex yeoman, in 1678 was sent five miles away to a widow in Chichester to board at school, and part of her education consisted in learning to make lace (her guardian paid 10s. for the necessary patterns), but it is unlikely Martha would ever need to fall back on her skills to earn a living, since at her majority she inherited 6 acres of land with her father's house, sufficient household goods to furnish it, and £120 cash.[40] It is not clear whether Martha ever learned to write.

While the ownership of books cannot prove the ability to read, Lorna Weatherill's study of nearly 3000 inventories in the later seventeenth and early eighteenth centuries, showing that a slightly higher proportion of women than of men owned books, is suggestive.[41] Many books, though, and certainly cheap popular print like ballads, chapbooks and news sheets, cost so little that they would not have been itemized in an inventory but simply included in the 'other trash' entry. The impressionistic evidence of wills supports the idea that some girls below the level of the yeomanry learned at least to read, if not to write, although it is impossible to quantify the difference in the cost of girls' and boys' education at this level since the length of time spent at school is never clear. One east Yorkshire labourer in 1642 gave £1 10s. to a wheelwright of the same village, 'for the keepeing of Margaret Stapleton my daughter att schoole to reade English and for keepeing her in her minoritye'. No official school was established in this village at this time.[42] In the vale of Lincoln Isabel Pell, widow of a husbandman, made her will in 1606 in which she did 'desyer' her stepfather to raise her two daughters 'at the boke and needle'. By 1700 Lincolnshire had twenty established elementary schools, usually for boys and girls together, but the Pell girls, like Margaret Stapleton in Yorkshire, would have been taught in the home of a local woman.[43]

Contemporary comment, educational tracts and clerics diaries' confirm that it was not uncommon to teach girls to read along with their brothers, at age 4 or 5. Writing was secondary and taught generally to boys of yeoman and clerical families at the age of 6 or 7, by which age all girls were more useful in the household and the majority of boys more useful in the fields or the shop.[44] Writing was also useful to less well-off boys, who could earn a few pence later on by writing out wills, deeds, letters and so forth for friends and neighbours. That is probably why one midlands labourer, whose total inventory came to only £9, owned books, pen and ink.[45] Learning to write may not have involved greater investment than learning to sew. Giles Moore's niece, Martha Mayhew, was boarded at school with a Mr John Breukes to learn to write (ten weeks at 1s. 6d. a week), and then learned to sew a sampler from Goodwife Potter while apparently living at home (seven weeks for just over 4d. a week).[46] The difference in cost could be entirely attributed to boarding.

Needlework alone – without reading – was available to very poor girls. Widows on poor relief in Ipswich at the end of the sixteenth century had daughters of between 7 and 11 who were at 'skoole to knyt' or who 'goeth to knitting schole'. An accomplished knitter could make 2s. a week, whereas these girls' mothers picked oakum for 4d., or made bone lace for 9d. a week.[47] Lincoln too had a succession of knitting and spinning schools for the poor in the late sixteenth and early seventeenth centuries.[48]

Needlework for girls was in one sense the functional equivalent of writing for boys: each skill was useful to the adult in their own household, and could supplement their livelihood with piecework as necessary. An Essex husband-man left £5 'to bring up and instruct my daughter in learning, both of the Book [Bible] and also in sewing and some other profitable exercise whereby she may be able in time to earn her own living'.[49] The idea that women supported themselves rather than being 'kept' by their husbands is rarely elucidated in seventeenth-century texts – probably because it would have been blindingly obvious at the time, so there was little need to expound on the subject. It is the most self-evident aspects of daily life that receive the least attention in writing. Ordinary girls did not have to be told to earn their own living – by their needle or by any other means available – when they grew up observing their female relatives doing just that.

At the same time that needlework was a valuable skill, teaching many girls to read but few to write was an effective means of reinforcing the maxim that 'silence is a woman's glory'. If silence did not characterize women at the time, the widespread inability to write contributed to their relative silence in the historical record. Contemporary justification for not teaching girls to write or boys to sew, in so far as the discrepancy ever had to be explained, was framed in terms of utility and appropriateness to sex. But the utility of keeping one sex substantially less able to write than the other in the keeping of that one sex subordinate is made clear by analogy with class. When in the sixteenth century the clergymen of Canterbury Cathedral objected to the sons of husbandmen attending the grammar school, it was on the grounds that they were more fit for the plough. In the late eighteenth-century Sunday School movement to educate the labouring poor, reading was standard but the teaching of writing was highly controversial, considered by middle-class philanthropists to be inappropriate to the students' station in life. In York it was the schools run by wage-earners themselves which taught writing.[50]

In early modern England the inability of most women to write meant that they kept diaries or journals or account books in far smaller numbers than men. It may also have hindered the ability of marketwomen or shopkeepers to keep track of customers' debt and credit, and of women in general to transact exchanges which involved written instruments, whether this was the sale of land or the putting out of a child's portion at interest (see Chapter 5).

It is clear, if surprising, that no distinction was made in the upbringing costs of girls and boys, at either middling or impoverished levels. Many more details of children's upbringing can be gleaned from probate accounts with further research, but even the rough comparison of girls' and boys' annual maintenance and apprenticeship costs presented here compels a revision of conventional and generalized ideas about girls' relative deprivation of sustenance and education in early modern England. The exact nature of girls' apprenticeship to trades and how it changed or declined over the early modern period is another question and requires more investigation in different sources.

Although it was assumed then and is accepted today that adult women require less sustenance than men, the gender-equal maintenance of children in early modern England actually appears to have been carried through into adulthood, to judge by evidence in the private account books kept by yeomen and gentlemen. These account books, like probate accounts, refer to maintenance in general, rather than differentiating between food, washing and so forth. The yeoman Robert Loder, in early seventeenth-century Berkshire, estimated that every member of his family and his servants cost him between £9 and £12 annually, without distinction by sex. Since Loder regularly made notes on how to economize on servants – like hiring them by the day instead of having them live in with him – it seems unlikely he would have missed the opportunity to observe how much cheaper it was to maintain a woman servant than a man. The gentleman Gregory King, in late seventeenth-century London, spent the same amount – £27 – on his own and his wife's annual maintenance, including diet, grocery, fire and candles, soap and starch, and apparel.[51] There is no hint in account books at this level of society that women in any way consumed less. Yet at the same time, the gentlemen who set maximum wage levels in their office as Justices of the Peace, and those who published tracts on the management of the poor, assumed that labouring and poor women ate less than men.

Apparently what was appropriate for women in the abstract and what was sufficient for the women of their own family were two very different things. Perhaps this divergence between theory and practice in the matter of women's sustenance is the victualling equivalent of men's habit to 'raile of all women generally, but praise every one in particular', in the words of the Duchess of Newcastle.[52] Given an evident preference for males in early modern England in terms of both inheritance and marriage customs, why are girls not undermaintained? Mary Hays, writing at the end of the eighteenth century, thought that 'Men in the characters of fathers . . . are generally infinitely more amiable, and do more justice to the [female] sex, than in any other character whatever'.[53] We might extend her observation to men in families generally, that it is easier for a man to theorize about female inferiority and sub-ordination as a general principle when an individual woman – particularly his daughter, but also his mother or his wife – is not standing in front of him, physically or metaphorically.

The same phenomenon is observable in more obviously son-preferring cultures than England. In rural Greece, for example, it seems that while boys are ardently wished for and preferred to girls when they are born, girls are equally cherished once their parents have got used to the idea.[54] Although in almost every known human culture males have been valued more highly than females, the material forms which that preference takes vary enormously. Whereas in certain parts of Asia and Africa today girls are undermaintained to the point of death, that is not merely the result of son-preference combined with inadequate resources. True, there is less need to discuss who is more valuable when there are enough resources for everyone. But in early modern England, as in many underprivileged countries of the world today, son-preference did not result in the obvious stinting of daughters, even when resources were minimal, as among the poor. The following chapter illustrates that this principle was largely carried over from children's maintenance to their inheritance.

4 Inheritance

The rules of descent of freehold and copyhold land in cases of intestacy naturally give rise to the assumption that in wills too boys were preferred in the distribution of the family land. The division of property among children raises three sets of questions. First, exactly how often was land given to sons and household goods to daughters in wills? Strictly demographically, how often were both daughters and sons present in any family to enable this division, and what happened when there were no sons? Second, was this division, where it occurred, inherently unequal? What was the relative value of land and moveables? Was land invariably the principal piece of property in a will? Third, how did men divide their property overall – as a whole – among their children? And since the majority of men did not make wills, but died intestate, how did the ecclesiastical courts distribute their moveable goods?

THE DISTRIBUTION OF LAND

Previous studies of wills, in parishes in Cambridgeshire, Essex, Hertfordshire and Westmorland, found that daughters were given land by their fathers only in the absence of sons.[1] In my own study, men in Lincolnshire and Sussex rarely gave land to daughters if they had sons, doing so in 5 per cent of cases (2 of 41). But in Yorkshire daughters did receive bequests of land even when they had brothers. In rural Yorkshire 26 per cent of men (10 of 39) who devised land and who had children (or if no children, then siblings or siblings' children) of both sexes gave it to one or more females, in addition to males.

It is not unusual to find identical bequests, such as those made by James Raynes of the north Yorkshire moors. Each of his unmarried children, daughter Ursley and son Peter, received £20 and three oxgangs of arable land (between 30 and 54 acres).[2] James Raynes must have been a very substantial yeoman to give his children three oxgangs apiece. However, gifts to females were usually in smaller parcels – say, only a close or field when their brother had a house. All but two of the ten men who gave land to a daughter when they also had sons came from the area of the vale of Pickering, where partible inheritance was customary, and where it was possible to subsist on smaller pieces of land because of the nature of the pastoral agriculture and the availability of common land and cottage industries.

However, whether daughters got land was not simply a question of partibility and the amount of land necessary for subsistence, since in other areas where small holdings were viable – in the Lincolnshire or Cambridgeshire fenland, for example – land was not given to daughters. Furthermore, in the town of Selby, at the southern end of the vale of York where partibility was not common, an even higher proportion of land was given to daughters. There 37 per cent of men (23 of 63) who devised land and who also had children (or siblings or grandchildren) of both sexes gave parcels of land to daughters as well as to sons. Even this considerable proportion should be taken as a minimum, since in some of the total sixty-three cases the daughters were already married and so would have been previously endowed and therefore not in competition for their fathers' land. Nor was it the case that men were nominally acknowledging customs of partible inheritance but expecting one child – a son – to buy back the portions of the others.[3] The greater proportion of land given to female legatees in Yorkshire carries over all the way to women's own wills: Yorkshire women devised far more land in their own wills than women in the counties farther south (see Chapter 12).

If the different patterns in Yorkshire and more southern counties cannot be explained by the local economy and manorial customs of inheritance, they may result from a more widespread regional tradition. Land may have been more commonly given to daughters throughout England in the middle ages. At least one early modern writer, the author of *The Lawes Resolutions of Women's Rights* (1632), believed this to be the case. Subsequent historical research seems to confirm it, but records are scarce, and the practice had died out by about 1300 in those areas which have so far been studied – all in southern England.[4] However, it remained a Scandinavian custom to give land to daughters, to the value of half their brothers' inheritance, long after 1300.[5] It is possible that the Norse influence in northern England may have entrenched more strongly the idea of daughters inheriting land, so that they did so with greater frequency in Yorkshire as late as 1700. It is clear that individual parishes or even counties cannot be used to generalize about whether daughters inherited land throughout England.

If girls with brothers were not normally given land in their fathers' wills, it is important to bear in mind that girls did inherit land, but through more circuitous routes than boys. One such example is the case of the two sisters Elizabeth and Mary Musgrave in the Isle of Axholme in the 1680s. Their uncle, the widowed husbandman Gregory Musgrave, died in 1669 leaving two young children, Dorothy and Robert. Gregory's will gave to his brother James one messuage (dwelling house with outbuildings and land) plus 4½ acres and three roods (quarter acres) of arable land, on condition that James pay his niece Dorothy a cash bequest of £100 at her majority. James made his own will twelve years later, at which point he had moveables worth £106. But instead of giving his brother's land back to Dorothy, who was still a minor, in lieu of her £100 bequest, he left his wife to pay Dorothy's legacy upon her majority and gave that land to his own two minor daughters, Elizabeth and Mary. His son got only 2s. in James's will, a token in recognition of the fact that he would inherit his father's own land.[6]

The Musgrave case illustrates the exercise of personal preference in allocating land and cash, while still operating a system of primogeniture for the main estate, since both Gregory and James Musgrave left one surviving son. But in many cases demographic reality seriously interfered with the dynastic ideal of primogeniture. In stationary demographic conditions, only 60 per cent of couples will have at least one son. Approximately 20 per cent will have no children at all surviving, and another 20 per cent will have only daughters at the father's death.[7] In my own collection of 666 nuclear families in probate documents, more than half of those couples with sons had only one.[8] That heir's survival to adulthood was yet another uncertainty.

Because the English system of descent preferred lineal to collateral heirs, in the 20 per cent of families who produced only daughters, those daughters stood to inherit freehold or copyhold land as heiresses. Eileen Spring has recently suggested that all the principal developments in English real property law between the later middle ages and the nineteenth century were developed by dynastically minded large landowners specifically to limit the claims of the heiress. Needless to say, her interpretation is controversial, but it is certainly plausible, since a demonstrably smaller proportion of heiresses among the upper class actually inherited during the early modern period than they had at an earlier period, and than they should have, demographically speaking.[9]

More ordinary men who made wills, however, tended to follow the canons of descent in preferring lineal females to collateral males. When a man had daughters but no sons he generally gave his land to his daughters, rather than to his brothers, nephews or even grandsons. (A bequest to a married daughter with a son 'to her and her heirs forever' was ultimately a gift to the grandson, although his mother might still dispose of it.) The rule of lineal female over collateral male extended even further: the female child or children of a dead eldest son would inherit before a living younger son. This line of descent was followed voluntarily in the will of one 'clothworker' of the Sussex weald. In 1632 John King's eldest son was already dead, leaving behind an only daughter, Anne. John's younger son, who had five children of his own, received his father's apparel and the use of his money and stock for life, but it was granddaughter Anne who was 'heire to my house and land, the waynscott [panelling] and bench in the hall, all the glasse all about the house, and the safe in the sellar'. In addition, her grandfather gave her £1 to repair the 'broom house' on her new property.[10]

The rapidity with which property changed hands as a result of high mortality, and the unexpected channels of its diffusion, cannot be over-emphasized. A good example is the estate of John Perlebine, a widowed yeoman of the Lincolnshire fenland who made his will in 1592. He named his only daughter Agnes, still a baby, his executrix, and gave her the bulk of his 'howsell' (household), worth £103, and land, appointing his brother Thomas as her guardian. In addition to a number of other bequests, John's two manservants were each to have a 'stong' (quarter acre) of wheat and a 'stong' of land until Agnes reached the age of 18. If she died before then, it was theirs for the remainder of the lease. In addition, if Agnes died before the age of 21 or marriage, then the poor of the parish guild hall were to have £10 from her goods. As it happened, Agnes died only the following year, and the parish poor, John Perlebine's two servants, and Agnes's uncle Thomas, as her only kin, were the richer. In fact, the amount that the yeoman Thomas got from the infant Agnes was equal to nearly half of his moveable wealth at his own death, childless, nineteen years later.[11]

THE RELATIVE VALUE OF LAND AND MOVEABLES

Aside from the uncertainties of early modern demography, the customary, if by no means universal, division of property into land for boys and moveables for girls raises the question of the relative value of land and moveables. It is commonly assumed that girls with moveables were necessarily disadvantaged relative to their brothers with land.[12] This assumption may be partly attributable to the historical overemphasis on the common law, which tends to equate 'wealth' and 'property' with land only, and the historical importance to the aristocracy of landed patrimony. But equally influential is the fact that in our own century the value of land far outweighs that of moveables.

The relative value of early modern land and moveable goods is difficult to judge in specific cases, but in comparison with our own century land values were low relative to other goods. Cash values for land are rarely specified in wills, and land does not appear at all in inventories. But house building prices may serve as some kind of guide. A husbandman's or labourer's two-storey, four-room cottage in later seventeenth-century Yorkshire or Lincolnshire cost only £12–£15 to build. Farther south and farther up the market, prices rose: up to £40 in 1600 for an Essex yeoman, and perhaps doubling by about 1700. A manor house in the later seventeenth century might have cost upwards of £100 to build. (Inflation did not affect Lincolnshire and Yorkshire so much, since houses there remained the same size, while houses in the south grew larger.)[13] These examples are of building rather than purchase prices, but the discrepancy was probably not too great. In 1641 Mrs Joyce Jeffries bought Goulding Hall in Widemarsh Street, Hereford, for £25 10s.[14] The house of a Northamptonshire yeoman in about 1670 was worth £60 all told – a fact known to posterity only because the house was included in the man's inventory until his widow pointed out a year later that it was 'noe chattle but a reall estate'.[15]

Most people had leasehold or copyhold, and the purchase price of a leased house may be roughly estimated from its annual rent. Cottages in southern England rented for about £1 p.a. in the first half of the seventeenth century;

a house in the city of Hereford could be had for £2 p.a. Their purchase price would have been between £10 and £20.[16] In mid-century east Yorkshire the farmer Henry Best thought a cottage rent of 10s. p.a. extortionate.[17] Its purchase price was perhaps £10. Copyhold rents were even lower; the lord made his profit from a large fine paid upon change of owner. A copyhold cottage in the Yorkshire wolds could be had for only 6d. p.a.[18]

For people who owned little land, moveable goods were proportionally more important. This is evident in the care with which willmakers – especially poor willmakers – detailed their bequests, down to the names of cows, the location of a particular table or who slept in a certain bed, and the colour of breeches and petticoats. The bulk of most people's moveable wealth lay in animals and corn (grain). Of household items, the most valuable piece of furniture was the bed.

Compare the house prices above with the valuations of common moveables in inventories: a 'furnished' bed – that is, a frame, a flock or straw mattress, rugs or blankets, and pillows (but no linens) – was valued usually at about £2, but up to £10 if the frame was posted and canopied and the mattress was feathers or down; a milk cow also cost £2 or more.[19] Thus a cottage could be bought for the equivalent purchase price of five to ten beds or five to ten cows. Although today the relative importance of cows has changed drastically, the bed remains the single most expensive item of household furniture, when its linens are taken into account. But a simple four-room terraced house at £50,000 in 1990 is equivalent to more than eighty extremely luxurious (£600) beds!

Oblique indications of the relative value of land and moveables arise occasionally in individual probate documents. One yeoman of the Sussex downs, in his will of 1616, gave his wife Agnes Mockford the best featherbed in the 'great chamber' with all its 'appurtenances', or furnishings, but only on condition that she deliver to his son a signed, sealed 'dede of release in the lawe of all hir dower', excepting £3 p.a. This was Agnes's only specific bequest from her husband, apart from the residual goods she received as executrix, and on first reading it appears to cheat her out of valuable land in exchange for a bed which might be of only sentimental value. However, the will went on to specify that if she refused to give up her dower lands she would then forfeit her right to the featherbed.[20] Hardly a ferocious sanction, but it immediately suggests that the land and the bed were of comparable value.

Some seventy years later, in north Yorkshire, the widow Anne Levet had five daughters, aged between 19 and 36. In her will she desired 'that which soever of my daughters shall after my decease become tenant to the house I dwell in' should pay each of the others £1.[21] Anne went into painstaking detail (down to individual napkins) to divide up all of her household goods evenly between the girls, which suggests that the house tenancy arrangement was also, as Anne saw it, equitable.

It was of course true then as it is true now that land appreciates and moveables depreciate. But in early modern England this divergence in value took place over a much longer term than it does today. The effects were unlikely to be significant in a single lifetime. Land appreciated only over centuries. Moveables depreciated much more slowly because they lasted much longer, being made of more durable materials. The mundane household items listed in an inventory – usually a single, frail sheet of paper – possessed a physical presence which is hardly conceivable from the vantage point of a modern terraced or semi-detached house with convenience kitchen.

At the death in 1631 of Barbara Barber, a poor Dorset widow, her estate had to be sold off to maintain her youngest children. Among her goods were a 'brasse pott' weighing more than 17 lb, and a 'brasse pane' weighing nearly 12 lb. Only Barbara's featherbed – that is, the mattress alone – bears some relation to modern mattresses, at 74 lb.[22] Estate sales occurred particularly where orphan children had to be put forth. They were advertised for a certain day by a notice in the parish church and by a cryer, and run by a drummer with someone to keep accounts. The sale accounts occasionally survive, clipped – or rather, tied – to a probate account.[23] These sales attest to the durability of moveable goods. When cooking utensils weighed as much as they did, they were passed on from generation to generation, although not necessarily in the same family. Marrying couples could purchase goods to set up a new home at such sales, with cash portions inherited from their parents or with saved wages.

The relatively close values of land and goods in the early modern period began to diverge by the middle of the eighteenth century, by which time household furniture and utensils were made of cheaper, but also more breakable, materials: woods were softer, textiles were thinner, and dishes were crockery or china, rather than wooden or pewter.

If the cash values of land and moveables were relatively close in the early modern period, there remains the question of the symbolic value of family land passed from generation to generation in the male line. This symbolism clearly resonated for individual willmakers, since they did tend to prefer sons over daughters in distributing their land. At the same time, men who had sufficient land divided it up among all their sons, or they allotted cash to buy extra parcels for younger sons, which defies the dynastic principle.[24] At an ordinary level the 'family' land was not handed from father to a single son in perpetuity. This is made vividly clear by the example of Terling, Essex, where not one of twenty-one separate freeholds remained in the male line over the course of the seventeenth century.[25] It was therefore ultimately the cash value of land that was important since, contrary to assumptions about an agrarian peasant society, land was regularly bought and sold. If fathers associated land with sons, nevertheless in a thriving market a daughter's cash portion of £20 might buy a modest house, and even £10 might purchase a cottage.

It is important to put the discussion of the inheritance of land and houses into perspective. Over three counties, only about half of all men's wills mentioned land or a house at all: in Sussex, 40 per cent (26 of 65); in

Lincolnshire, 50 per cent (15 of 30); and in Yorkshire, 51 per cent (115 of 226) in Selby and 67 per cent (67 of 100) in the rural areas. (There is no north–south differentiation: the comparable proportion in Terling, Essex, is 39 per cent, in Powick, Worcestershire, 54 per cent, and in Norfolk and Suffolk, 70 per cent.[26]) Even where land was devised it may not have been the principal holding; often it was smaller pieces acquired for younger sons or daughters; especially in the north it may have been leased; and sometimes part or all of the holding was simply given to the widow to be sold to pay off debts. Land was rarely described by its acreage, and almost never by the manner in which it was held (except by lease).

It has been suggested that local customs of land inheritance in cases of intestacy, and whether these were acceptable, may have determined the frequency with which people made wills in any particular area.[27] It would be interesting for future research to compare the rate of testation in an area known to have partible inheritance with that in an area of impartible inheritance, but the proportion of wills devising land might be a more accurate measure of local satisfaction with intestacy rules – particularly in view of the evidence that up to 60 per cent of men did not use their wills to devise land.

Studies of individual manors in Sussex and Leicestershire have concluded that land was more commonly transferred by deed or by court roll in the owner's lifetime ('intervivos' transfers) than it was by will.[28] Gifts of land to children during a parent's lifetime were not regularly recorded in either wills or accounts, and they can only be examined where a good run of both manorial and probate records survives. Wills only hint at previous transfers. In the vale of Lincoln in 1679 the prosperous John Wilson left his son John and his daughter Ellen cash bequests at their respective ages of 21, but mentioned no land. The children's mother Alice died three years later, and her will likewise devised no land specifically, but gave to Ellen a further cash sum 'besides her lands'. The principal part of the Wilson lands – what Alice called 'the estate' – went to young John as executor, but more than one parcel was carved off for Ellen. The account of Alice's estate shows that she paid at least £60 p.a. in rent, which means that the leased acreage alone must have been sizeable – perhaps more than 100 acres, worth more than £1000 on the market (see below).[29] By all appearances, both Ellen and her brother had ample lands, but it was all secured without resort to a will.

Two methods of property transfer might also be used in conjunction, even simultaneously, as in the case of the yeoman Richard Sergeant, of the Lincolnshire coast. On 8 March 1594 he composed two documents: one a highly detailed will of moveable goods, bequeathed mostly to three sets of grandchildren; and the other a deed of estate, in which he transferred all of his lands to one of his two surviving daughters and her husband.[30] The survival of deeds, which were not registered, is even more haphazard than that of wills, which were registered, and the only evidence of this deed's existence is its mention in the will.

THE OVERALL DIVISION OF PROPERTY

The allocation of property in wills may not be complete, but it is at least quantifiable. The overall distribution of property, both real and personal, among children may be estimated since a large proportion of all bequests were in cash, and approximate cash values may be assigned to many household goods. Animals were not often bequeathed. Cash or household goods were preferred, although animals were somewhat more commonly found in Lincolnshire and Yorkshire wills.[31] Where animals were bequeathed, there was no noticeable difference in the proportion given to sons and to daughters, except that those very few men who owned riding horses gave them to sons.

The distribution in wills ranged from those which divided property equally among all daughters and sons, to those which appeared to follow the principle of primogeniture even where it was not legally imposed. (Wills which appear to follow primogeniture are of two opposite types: those which give most to the eldest son; and those which give least to the eldest son, usually only a token, suggesting that he would inherit, or had already inherited, land.) Of sixty wills in the southern province made by men with children of both sexes, approximately equal bequests among all children were made by only 25 per cent; 30 per cent gave a token to the eldest son and 18 per cent gave him a larger share, for a total of 48 per cent adhering on some level to primogeniture. But in the remaining 27 per cent of wills the division among siblings was indeterminate.

It might be expected that primogeniture would have less influence in the north because partible inheritance was more common there. And indeed in fifty-eight wills of rural Yorkshire men who had children of both sexes, 48 per cent made approximately equal bequests to all their children, nearly double the southern rate; 21 per cent gave only token bequests to their eldest sons, and 31 per cent favoured their eldest son with bequests substantially larger than those given to their other children, so slightly more than half followed primogeniture to some degree. The large number of uncertain divisions in the southern province makes the suggestion of a difference between north and south only tentative. It should be remembered that those men who gave a larger portion to their eldest son may have been following primogeniture with moveables or leases in the absence of heritable land. If there was more land which descended by primogeniture in the south, this would explain why the proportion of men who gave a larger share to their eldest son was 31 per cent in Yorkshire but only 18 per cent in the southern province.

It is impossible to be absolutely certain every time land passed silently to the heir without being remarked in a will. Such is transparently the case with the Musgraves, mentioned above. Dorothy Musgrave received £100 and a furnished bed from her father, while her brother got £3. Their cousins Elizabeth and Mary Musgrave were to have a few acres of land each from their father, while their brother had only 2s.[32] But the discrepancy in bequests is usually less obvious.

It is also not verifiable when there was nothing to inherit, which would have been the case for many labouring eldest sons. But it seems probable, for example, that the Selby labourer who gave to his eldest son one heifer, two ewes, and 'the bedd with the beddinge which I ly in & one chist', and to the child in his wife's womb a heifer, two ewes, and a 'cubbert', did not have land with which to prefer his heir.[33] Conversely, there is no way of knowing when land in a will was being diverted away from the common law or copyhold heir, as men and unmarried women were at liberty to do.

What is clear is that primogeniture did influence land inheritance at an ordinary level, but that a preference for the eldest son in land did not necessarily carry over into the division of moveable goods. Clearly it was not unusual for a man to divide his entire estate equally, even at a prosperous level. The brother of the Sussex rector Giles Moore, for example, made his 18-year-old daughter his executrix in 1670 and gave her an equal share in all his lands and goods with her 16-year-old brother, an estate which comprised a copyhold farm of 100 acres plain land and 60 acres coppice which had been bought for £1600.[34]

In most cases, in order to divide property approximately equally it was necessary to balance land with moveables. There were several ways that an ordinary willmaker might do this. One was the method common among the aristocracy and gentry, to provide that a daughter's (or younger son's) cash portion was to be paid at her majority out of the profits of her brother's land. This type of provision had the advantage of preserving a landed estate intact, while at the same time providing for all children. (It is also the arrangement George Eliot alludes to in describing Mr Tulliver's sister as having 'come into the world in that superfluous way characteristic of sisters, creating a necessity for mortgages'.[35])

This same type of arrangement occurs regularly in ordinary men's wills, but unlike at upper social levels it was frequently enforced by making the bequest of land contingent upon payment of the cash bequest. If the daughter's legacy was not paid, she was to enter legally into possession of her brother's land until such time as he paid it. The severity of this enforcement mechanism and the way in which these bequests were phrased suggest that the value of the cash and the land were at least comparable. For example, a Selby cordwainer in his will of 1699 ordained that his son Joshua 'shall pay my daughter Ruth the sum of £30, when she shall accomplish the age of 26 years, in consideration of his having the messuage, and for nonpayment thereof my daughter Ruth to enter in and upon the said messuage and the same possess'.[36]

The use of this enforcement mechanism severely inhibited the power exercised by the eldest son and heir over his siblings. The kind of deference and dependence that an upper-class heir like Sir Ralph Verney exacted from his six sisters and three younger brothers[37] would have been inconceivable at the level of Joshua and Ruth Robinson. And in the absence of any clause in his father's will to encourage him otherwise, Sir Ralph did abuse his control of the estate, failing to pay his siblings' legacies and annuities. (Annuities, themselves a form of inheritance designed to create dependence, were never used for children at ordinary levels except in the very occasional case of a lunatic or – once – a crippled child.) Although we cannot be certain that Ruth Robinson received her £30 at the age of 26, she at least enjoyed the possibility of a very specific legal remedy against her brother if she did not.

Another means of balancing overall inheritance at an ordinary social level was to deny all moveables to the heir to land and use them instead to compensate his siblings for their lack of land. There were two means of doing this, one of which was available in the northern province and one of which could be used anywhere. The ecclesiastical law of the northern province, until 1670, required that one third of a man's moveables be divided equally among his children even if he made a will. This requirement was used occasionally to limit married daughters who had already received a portion, but primarily to balance sons' advantage in land inheritance. By restricting an heir's share of moveables with the statement that the bequest was 'in full satisfaction of his filial portion', while leaving that qualification off his other children's bequests, the willmaker could preserve a larger share of his moveables to be divided among his other children, and so allocate more equitable portions among all his offspring.

Two Yorkshire wills from the 1640s illustrate how the portions requirement was implemented. In the vale of Pickering Margery Walls received £10 unconditionally; her brother John received £12 but 'for his porcion'. She could claim her filial portion in addition to her bequest; he could not.[38] In the wolds the daughter of a joiner, Mary Dry, received £10; her elder brother Thomas only £2, 'in consideration of his feliall chyld parte and portion'. Mary, along with her three sisters and other brother, claimed a further portion, but Thomas could not.[39]

The children's right to a filial portion or 'reasonable part' from their father's goods was abolished in the northern province in 1692 (4 Wm. & Mary c.2). When reasonable parts were abolished in London some thirty years later it is thought that the practice had actually long been abandoned or ignored anyway.[40] This was certainly not the case in the northern province, where reasonable parts were regularly referred to in wills right up to the year they were abolished. In fact, the habitual phrase still occurred in Selby even in the later 1690s, when it no longer had legal significance.[41]

In the southern province, and in the northern province after 1670, contingency clauses – the rerouting of a bequest in the case of the legatee's death – were routinely used to exclude the heir to land from a share in his siblings' moveable goods, in much the same way that the portions requirement was employed in the northern province. A contingency clause allowed the bequests of each of two daughters to go to the other in the event of death of one of them, pre-empting the legal division of an equal share to all siblings, which would include their brother. Thus in his will of 1680 John Campleman of the vale of Pickering gave to his elder daughter Elizabeth £9 10s. and to his younger daughter Anne £9, and if either should die 'without children or som issue of their owne bodys to enjoy', then her legacy went to her sister. This clause precluded an equal division with Elizabeth and Anne's two brothers, the younger of whom was to have all remaining goods except those household items formerly given to his sisters, and the elder of whom received a bequest of only 1s. 6d. 'becaus of a former portion I gave him'.[42] The eldest son had responsibility for paying his sisters' portions. In all, discussion of his two daughters' inheritance took up most of John Campleman's will – a not unusual occurrence, since daughters were most in need of provision and legal protection.[43]

In addition to bequests, the relative position of daughters and sons may be compared in the choice of executors. A widowed man usually appointed his executor from among his children if he had any, and in the northern province a married man sometimes appointed his wife executrix jointly with one or more of his children. Joint executors were rare in the southern province, where willmakers desirous of checks and balances in the control of their estate appointed overseers or supervisors instead. Conversely, overseers were virtually unknown in the north (see Chapter 9). In appointing executors from among their children, both married men and widowers were more than twice as likely to choose daughters or younger sons, or a combination thereof, in preference to the heir. In both rural Yorkshire and the town of Selby, 29 per cent of married men with children appointed a joint executor with their widows.[44] In these the joint executors were very rarely the eldest son, but rather daughters, younger sons, or a combination thereof, or all children together. Clearly the intent was to minimize the eldest son's control of the estate in order to offset his preferential treatment by the common law of inheritance.

That primogeniture did not dominate the distribution of property as a whole at an ordinary social level should not be surprising. Throughout Europe in the sixteenth and seventeenth centuries there was an ongoing debate over systems of inheritance. Much of continental Europe had partible inheritance, and both visitors to England and some Englishmen expressed concern that primogeniture was applied more harshly in England than elsewhere. Calls for its modification, even its abolition by the most radical reformers, reached a peak during the mid-seventeenth century, when primogeniture was called 'the most unreasonable descent' by one pamphleteer. The objections to primogeniture focused, of course, on its unfairness to younger sons, rather than to daughters.[45] Younger sons were in a much better position to make their objections known, in print and in parliament. The nonconformist minister and younger son Adam Martindale was one who objected, writing in his diary, 'Many out of a desire that their houses may flourish after them ar too kind to their heires, and thereby much wrong their younger children, especially when they have means in sight to make good provision for them also'.[46]

Adam Martindale saw primogeniture as a characteristic of the upwardly mobile landowner, looking to establish a dynasty. This point of view is supported by evidence that medieval peasants and townsmen alike favoured partibility, and partibility at least among all sons was still the manorial custom in many pastoral regions in the seventeenth century. But primogeniture had probably begun to dominate manorial customs in the sixteenth century, being imposed on Wales, Kent and other smaller areas by statute.[47] The evidence in wills suggests that still in the seventeenth century poorer men were more likely to distribute what they had equally among all children, perhaps allowing for a certain threshold level of subsistence. In the wills of Powick, Worcestershire, for example, only wealthy yeomen split off pieces of land to establish younger sons,[48] probably because in this area of arable agriculture only quite large holdings were economically viable. But in many other areas of the country a more equitable division was possible. Although girls received land infrequently and circuitously, in general they were compensated by fathers who made wills for their relative deprivation of land with an extra helping of moveables.

What about the majority of fathers, who died intestate? In these cases the ecclesiastical courts were responsible for dividing up the moveable goods. The ecclesiastical law of intestacy allotted to a married man's children two thirds of his residual goods, divided equally among them; all of a widow's goods were divided equally among her children; and a child's or unmarried person's goods were equally divided among all siblings. Probate accounts which specify the division of residual goods show that in fact these rules were scrupulously applied by the ecclesiastical courts to ensure fair treatment of siblings. But the division of goods was only occasionally equal on the face of it. More often than not, modifying circumstances were considered which altered a child's portion.

According to ecclesiastical rules, if a child had been 'advanced' during the parent's lifetime – that is, given a sufficient portion of goods or money with which to start adult life – that child had no claim to a filial portion at the parent's death unless the advancement was returned to the 'hotchpot', or that part of moveables to be divided among all eligible children. The principle of advancement extended not only to a married daughter's prior receipt of a marriage portion, or the apprenticeship costs of a particular child, but also to previous legacies from a grandparent or other relative and, most especially, to the inheritance of land.

Tracing these qualifying conditions – particularly legacies from grandparents and lines of land inheritance – involved considerable research on the part of an ecclesiastical court, especially given the complexity of lineal descent at a time when perhaps 30 per cent of all marriages were remarriages, and perhaps 40 per cent of all couples in a community included at least one partner who had been married previously.[49] For example, when Alice Coolinge *als* Paternoster died in the Lincolnshire fens in 1611, her daughter by a first husband, pre-dating both Coolinge and Paternoster, was awarded only £1 of her mother's goods by the probate ordinary because she had inherited copyhold and free land worth £10 p.a. from her father. Alice's remaining Coolinge children, three daughters and two sons, were assigned £13 6s. 8d. each.[50]

Three other Lincolnshire examples illustrate typical adjustments made in cases of intestacy to balance children's portions. On the edge of the Lincolnshire wolds, Elizabeth Lincoln was left a widow in 1607 with six children. Her two eldest sons were assigned only £1 from their father's residual goods over and above the cost of their apprenticeships (unusually low in this case), since one would inherit land from his father worth £8 p.a. and the other would have land from his grandfather. But her three daughters and youngest son received £5 each, and an extra £5 portion was set aside for Elizabeth 'in case shee bee, as shee thinketh shee is with childe'.[51] (The assignment of a single amount to an unborn child of indeterminate sex has also been noted in wills, and supports the evidence for equal treatment of siblings.[52] No ordinary man ever said in his will 'to the child in my wife's womb, so much if it be a boy, but only so much if it be a girl'.)

In 1669 in the Isle of Axholme the labourer Matthew Burtoft's two young daughters were assigned 13s. 4d. each from their father's residual goods, while their brother only got 1s. because his apprenticeship had cost £3. The remaining £4 9s. was given to the accountant to raise the girls, which brought each girl's share to just under £3.[53] In 1680 Elizabeth Stow, the eldest daughter of a yeoman in the vale of Lincoln, received only one third the cash portion which her two sisters had from their father's goods, 'shee being advanced by the deceased in his life tyme by settleing an estate of coppyhold land upon her'.[54]

The same type of adjustments were made with the goods of an unmarried person. In Northamptonshire in 1680 the account of Elizabeth Douglis's estate was filed jointly by her mother, her two sisters and her three brothers. But the court divided Elizabeth's £70 residual estate only among her sisters and one of her brothers.[55] Although the court did not elaborate on its distribution, it is to be presumed that the other two brothers had received land from the parental estate.

Compensatory calculations made by the ecclesiastical courts – like those made by individual willmakers – were not merely gestures of condolence to non-inheriting children, but were meant to achieve as equal a distribution of all property as was possible, given the expectation that land belonged to the eldest son. In a 1671 Northamptonshire example, 15-year-old Susannah Sanderson was amply compensated for her younger brother's inheritance of land worth £10 p.a. (which would have sold for £200 at most), with a cash allocation from the court of £300.[56] The conscious attempt to balance is made explicit by the Northamptonshire accountant Anne Gibbs, settling her husband's estate in 1680. On her own initiative, Anne settled a leasehold parcel worth £100 on each of her two sons and at the same time gave her daughter, who had already been married with an £80 portion, an additional £20. Anne's distribution was duly approved by the court.[57]

Faced with a small residual estate and numerous children, the ecclesiastical court had no choice but to divide up the moveables. Unlike a
willmaker, the court could not require an heir to pay out cash portions to his
siblings from the profits of his land. It could only deny the heir any
moveables at all, as in the case of Giles Barker, an old Cambridgeshire
bachelor who died intestate in 1619, leaving one living brother and nephews
and nieces by two other now dead brothers. The heir to Giles's house and land
was his dead eldest brother's eldest son. This nephew's two sisters had to
share £6 between them, but the boy got no moveables because his inheritance,
apparently to the disgruntlement of the accountant, was 'more worth then all
the goods to be divided amongst all the rest'.[58] In another Cambridgeshire
case, 4-year-old Alice Cooper was awarded £3 by the court from her intestate
father's moveables in 1617, while her infant brother got 'not anie thinge for
that the sayed John Cooper shall have a free howse of his owne when he
cometh of age'.[59]

In all, the accounts of 202 intestate men and women specified the
disposition of the residual estate and named more than one child or sibling of
the deceased, so enabling a comparison of the survivors' portions. The
disposition of the residual estates of women are included in these calculations, first, because the accounts of their husbands' estates do not exist, if
they were ever filed at all, and second, because as far as the court was
concerned the estate to be divided was parental, not paternal. That means that
land which would appear in the account of the husband's estate also shows up
in the account of the wife's estate.

Of the total 202 intestate estates, the court divided the residual goods
absolutely equally between all children or siblings of the deceased in just
under half (99) of all cases. Slightly more than half (103) divided them
unequally. Most of the unequal ones (55) allotted substantially less to the
eldest son and heir. Five of this group reduced the eldest son's share to make
allowance for the costs of his apprenticeship. Twenty-six specifically reduced
the heir's share to compensate for inheritance of land (two of these were
female heirs, who had stepbrothers by the same mother but who inherited
from their own father). Inheritance of land can be presumed in the remaining
twenty-four cases where the court gave the eldest son only a token portion of
moveables but did not explain its actions. (This presumption is strengthened
by the fact that those moveable estates from which the eldest male received
only a token were substantially larger than those which were divided equally,
and thus perhaps more likely to have been accompanied by heritable land.
The median initial value of estates in which the residue was divided equally
was £56; that of estates whose residue was divided unequally, £80.)

In another thirty-eight cases of unequal distribution the basis of the
variation in inheritance is unclear, but was probably a combination of certain
children's already having been advanced, whether at the time of their
marriage or not, differing apprenticeship costs, and parental perceptions of
individual children's desert. In only 10 cases of unequal distribution (5 per

cent of the total 202) did the division of residual goods favour the eldest son. In these cases the ecclesiastical courts may have been influenced by an expectation that the eldest son ought to have land. These estates may have had no land to be inherited, but that is not apparent in the sources, nor can it be guessed from the moveable wealth of the estates concerned. There is also no way of knowing whether land was additional to the heir's portion in those estates where the moveables were divided equally.

There was some variation in the division of residual moveables among siblings in different counties, as Table 4.1 illustrates. The proportion allotting a smaller share of moveables to the eldest son was relatively high in Northamptonshire and Sussex, which may reflect a higher proportion of land descending by primogeniture in those counties than in Lincolnshire or Cambridgeshire. The highest proportion of estates divided equally occurred in Lincolnshire (57 per cent), which may reflect the influence of partible inheritance, or perhaps some other peculiarity of local land inheritance customs. To explain the regional variations in the distribution of moveable estates will require a great deal of painstaking research into local land-holding structures.

Table 4.1 Distribution of intestates' estates by county

	Equal division		Less to eldest male		Other division		
	%	n	%	n	%	n	N
Cambridgeshire	32	13	27	11	41	17	41
Lincolnshire	57	56	23	23	20	20	99
Northamptonshire	48	10	38	8	14	3	21
Sussex	48	16	33	11	18	6	33
Overall	49	95	27	53	24	46	194

Sources: CUL, LAO, NRO and WSRO accounts.

Change over time in the distribution of residual estates is more important than regional variation, because from the 1670 Act for the Better Settling of Intestates' Estates (22 & 23 Car.II c.10) the reduction of the portion of moveables given to the heir to land was actually illegal. A few years after the Act the legal writer George Meriton contended that in the northern province, in London and in 'some other places' an heir to *freehold* could be barred from receiving a portion of moveable goods, but nowhere did leasehold or copyhold land, or the payment of apprenticeship premiums, legally bar a child's portion of moveables.[60] Remarkably, in spite of the statute, the church courts did not change the way they distributed intestates' estates. Table 4.2 shows that there was no significant variation in the proportion of estates divided equally and unequally over time.

The circumstances are difficult to verify because fewer examples of specified distribution survive after 1670. Probate clerks tended to write

Table 4.2 Distribution of intestates' estates over time

	1593–1650		1650–1726	
	%	n	%	n
Equal division	65	64	63	35
Less to eldest male	35	34	38	21
Total	100	98	100	56

Sources: CUL, LAO, NRO and WSRO accounts.

simply 'Distributed according to the Act' at the bottom of accounts. Table 4.2 excludes those accounts which stated that the residue was divided 'equally' but did not specify cash amounts, since both before and after the Act the word 'equally' seems to have meant not 'evenly' but 'fairly'. For example, the clerk dealing with the estate of Anne Ockenden *als* Aylwyn in Sussex in 1608 formally stated that the residual £65 was to be equally divided between her children Alice, Margaret and John Aylwyn. But a postscript indicates that in fact Alice got £32, Margaret £33 and John nothing.[61] Even after 1670, when the £20 estate of Isaac Mobbs of Bugbrooke, Northamptonshire, was divided among his eight children 'According to the Act', a postscript records how Isaac's widow Jane told the court that her eldest son, age 30, had had much more than his portion during his father's lifetime and ought to be barred from seeking more.[62] The court's response in this case is unknown. From the few post-Act accounts which did specify residual distribution, it seems that adjustments in children's portions continued to be made along the same lines as they had been prior to the Act. The ecclesiastical courts interpreted the statute as elastically as they had the ecclesiastical law, although they usually took the precaution of formally stating their compliance with the Act.

Whether parents left a will or not, the ultimate balance of inheritance was only achieved over time, by the successive distribution of parental (and grandparental) goods. But the likelihood of a series of documents from one nuclear family surviving is slim, and so whole-family inheritance is difficult to recover. One example which is traceable largely because it took place over a relatively short period of time is the three-tiered division of the Irelande family moveables. Richard Irelande, a husbandman or yeoman of the Sussex coast, left bequests in his will of September 1634 to his elder son Richard, £2, to his younger son Henry, £12, and to his daughter Jane, £12. Their mother Joan Irelande made her will in January 1635, giving Richard £1, Henry £3 and Jane all the best linen, amounting to £3 6s. 8d. The residual goods she left to a cousin in trust for the children, generally. But when the account of Joan's estate was filed in November 1635, the ecclesiastical court divided her residual goods among the three children unequally: Richard and Henry got only 10s. 5d. each, and Jane had the bulk of the goods with £15. Overall, then, Richard had £3 10s. 5d., Henry £15 10s. 5d. and Jane £30 6s. 8d.[63]

Future research into testamentary litigation should investigate whether land-inheriting sons contested their token portion of moveable goods. Some disagreements over portions surface in probate accounts, but these were resolved by local arbitration before they reached the stage of litigation.[64] Elizabeth Perkin was married but had not yet received her portion when her widowed mother died in the vale of Lincoln in 1611. Elizabeth could not agree with her brother over the division of the residual £28, so together they paid 12s. to four arbitrators 'and other companie when they toke paines . . . touchinge the goods of the said deceased which were in controversie between them'.[65] Although the sisters Helen and Sara Knightly were both minors, they appeared personally in the probate court at Ely to testify 'that their brother Thomas . . . and they two, together with the helpe, advise and counsell of three honest, sufficient, and indifferent men, had made an equall devision of all the goods and chattels of their said father', which amounted to £24.[66]

Apparently not trusting to honest, sufficient and indifferent arbitrators, 27-year-old Hannah Fullshot resorted to self-help when her brother William died in 1624 in the vale of Lincoln. There had probably been some dispute over the division of their parents' goods since, according to the man who administered William's estate, Hannah absconded with £12 worth of William's goods before they came into the accountant's possession. She refused to give them up, and no further legal action was taken. The court absolved the accountant of responsibility for the £12 and gave him William's two sons to raise, with portions of only £6 each, leaving Hannah to go about her business.[67]

If litigation over a portion did arise, the court of first resort was one of the ecclesiastical courts, or the regional equity court if within the jurisdictions at Durham, Chester or Lancaster. Those young women who went all the way to the Court of Chancery in London were mostly heiresses who stood to get more than £100.[68]

To sum up, the consensus among ordinary people seems to have been that eldest sons ought to be privileged – but not too much. Younger sons and daughters usually had exactly equal provision. Land was symbolically associated with sons, but it was expected that both daughters and younger sons might have the equivalent value in moveables that the heir had in land. This balance was feasible because the disparity between the value of land and moveables was much smaller in the early modern period than it later became. If there was enough land to go around, it would be spread among the sons; in Yorkshire it might be spread among daughters too.

The partible approach to property as a whole, both real and personal, was taken not only by individual willmakers but also by the ecclesiastical courts. The courts went to considerable lengths to account for future contingencies, like anticipated inheritance, as well as past payments, like apprenticeship costs, in order to balance sibling shares. Even in the face of statute law to the contrary after 1670, the courts continued to bar land-inheriting children from an equal share of moveables in order to try to balance the portions of all children.

Probate accounts actually specify the heir's inheritance of land more often than wills do, and it can now be stated with certainty that while the custom of primogeniture was influential it is a wholly inadequate description of the 'grid of inheritance' among ordinary people. First, the legal application of primogeniture was restricted to freehold and some as-yet-undefined amount of copyhold land, and then only in the absence of other transfers in the lifetime of the owner or by will, which other transfers were far more common than not. Second, in practice the preference for one or more sons in the transmission of land was compensated for with moveables and, especially in northern regions, with other pieces of land to daughters and younger sons. The allocation of parental wealth among offspring among the majority of the population was made upon a basis of remarkable equality.

Because of the egalitarian approach of most willmakers, it seems likely that one of the reasons to make a will at all was to modify the effects of primogeniture, which would have been imposed in case of intestacy. This possibility is supported by the fact that a relatively high proportion of the population made wills in England. By comparison, in France, where the common custom was an equal division among all children, wills were rarely made.[69]

It is instructive to compare the situation in England with that in colonial America. There, eldest sons were rarely required by willmakers to pay their sisters' portions in cash out of the profits of the land they had inherited; daughters did not regularly receive a larger share of moveable goods than sons; and in the northern colonies the heir to land was also entitled to a double share of moveables in the case of intestacy.[70] It seems likely that the harshness of the application of the rule of primogeniture in colonial America contributed to its abolition shortly after the revolution. Conversely, the flexibility of the English application, made possible by the existence of different and to some extent competing legal systems, facilitated the survival of primogeniture until the twentieth century.

5   Portions and marriage

FINANCIAL MANAGEMENT OF PORTIONS

Once a child had received a portion, whether as a bequest from her parents or as an allocation from the court, how was the money or goods kept safe until her majority? At upper social levels the wardship of orphan heirs and heiresses was fought over by adults interested in the use of their fortunes until their majority. Among ordinary people, although the amounts of money involved were much smaller, high mortality rates among both children and their guardians could cause problems in keeping track of minors' portions. In one Cambridgeshire example, the inventory of Robert Wrinche had mistakenly included £1 9s. 3d. worth of goods which 'are constantly affirmed to be the goods of Katherine Terrington and delivered by Grace . . . her mother unto Margaret Wrinche [Robert's wife] . . . to be kept for her [Katherine's] use'. The property was eventually extricated and returned to the minor Katherine after Margaret's death in 1617, by her son and accountant.[1]

In addition to the death of parents and guardians, their potential indebtedness threatened the child's portion. Elizabeth Burnell *als* Webber, a married woman, administered her widowed mother's £69 estate in Somerset in 1703. While still a child Elizabeth had been given legacies by both her father and her grandmother amounting to £100, and these had passed into her mother's hands during Elizabeth's minority. But after paying her mother's rents and a debt due on bond, Elizabeth was left with less than £30 out of her two legacies.[2] In Sussex in 1670, William Violett's £96 estate was cut to £10 after debts, which had to be divided between his four children. Their grandmother had left the children legacies some seven years earlier of about £5 each, and had made their father executor of her will, but these bequests appear to have been lost in his indebtedness.[3]

The courts took procedural steps to protect children's portions in the traditional bureaucratic manner – by duplicating documents. When the minor Ann Friend's £40 estate was administered in Hampshire in 1672 by her married sister, Elinor Richards, three copies of the entire account were made, each accompanied by court orders directing Elinor's husband to pay portions from Ann's and from another dead sister's estate to their four brothers and two surviving sisters.[4] It is not clear how these orders were to be distributed, but the court must have kept one copy until satisfied that the portions had been paid.

The very fact that probate accounts were filed for the estates of minors suggests adherence to ecclesiastical court procedures, and that the sums were acknowledged by adults to belong to the child. When the orphan Mary Whittle died in the vale of Lincoln in 1611, for example, her £14 portion from her parents, together with her £1 worth of apparel, was duly accounted for in court by her brother even though the entire £12 remaining was due directly to him as her only sibling.[5] The wealthy Lincolnshire fenland widow Rose Westland cannot have been pleased to be called to account for the estate of her 9-year-old daughter Susannah in 1672. Susannah's only asset was a rental charge of £20 p.a. – probably a bequest from her father's will a year and a half earlier – which amount did not meet the expenses Rose claimed for her daughter's funeral and maintenance. Rose must have been accustomed to financial administration and the necessities of accounting, however; more than half her own £618 moveable estate, after fifteen years of widowhood, consisted in money owing upon bonds.[6]

When a widow with children remarried it became more important for her to file a probate account for a dead child's estate, in order to protect (from her subsequent husband) her living children's portions out of their sibling's goods. In one example from the vale of Lincoln, Susan Spaldinge and her three sisters received £20 portions from their father in 1599. When Susan died three years later, still a minor, her mother Margaret 'beinge not well able to traveile' sent her new husband twice on the 12-mile journey to Lincoln in order to take care of Susan's estate, despite the fact that there were no expenses to deduct from it except the administration and travel costs of accounting.[7]

In the fenland, the account of Alice Seagrave's £24 estate was filed in 1619 by her mother's new husband,[8] probably at her mother's instigation, in order to ensure that Alice's five sisters received their shares of Alice's portion from their own father. It was to the advantage of surviving siblings to have the proceedings recorded in writing and kept by the court rather than taken care of in private, particularly in the case of minor beneficiaries like the Seagrave sisters, whose protecting mother was only mortal.

Because of the laws of marital coverture, children were only assigned portions when their father or their widowed mother died, not when their mother died leaving a husband behind her. So the whole complex administrative procedure of keeping track of children's portions was only required of widows, not of widowers. The precautions taken by remarrying widows were not necessary for a remarrying widower since he did not surrender all his goods upon marriage.

In order to secure children's cash portions they were commonly invested. In contemporary terms, they were 'put out at interest' or 'put forth', or, particularly in Yorkshire, they were to 'go forward'. The individual investments themselves could be tiny. A labourer's widow in the Lincolnshire fen, Isabel Wharton, had very little cash to dispense in her will of 1610, but she gave 10s. to one of her young sons 'to be letten owt to his best commodytye'.[9] The portion invested might not even take the form of cash: in 1656 the Sussex rector Giles Moore recorded in his journal, 'I had a swarme of bees giv'n mee by Goodwife Pelling upon condition of the increase thereof I should afterwards vouchsafe her daughter upon marriage another swarme in satisfaction thereof'.[10]

From what has been said about the division of moveable goods, it is clear that the assets of young women more often consisted principally in bonds or ready cash than their brothers' did. Of 113 willmakers in Yorkshire, Lincolnshire and Sussex who made cash bequests to immediate kin of both sexes, two thirds favoured daughters over sons (or sisters over brothers, or granddaughters over grandsons) with gifts in cash.[11] Single people generally, and single women in particular, were a significant source of cash in the local lending market. As a group, single women were by far the most likely to hold their wealth in credits, although the amounts that they loaned out were relatively small.[12] Interest of 10 per cent could be earned on these cash sums from the late sixteenth century, falling to 5 per cent by the early eighteenth century (the interest rates specified in probate accounts always correspond with statutory maximum rates).[13] These rates of return compare favourably, especially in the late sixteenth and first half of the seventeenth centuries, with the income from land.

A municipal portion fund such as the *monte delle doti*, or bank of dowries, in fifteenth-century Florence was never implemented in England,[14] but many corporations were open for investment by small savers. The Courts of Orphans in London, Bristol and other cities and towns had a claim on the custody of freemen's orphans and their portions. These portions the city loaned out to merchants – either at a higher rate of interest than the city paid to the orphan on maturity, or in some cases eschewing profit.[15]

But probate accounts show that even cities in economic decline and without a Court of Orphans managed small investments. In 1621 Thomas Gaunt requested that two of his children's £30 portions be paid 'unto the Corporation of the Citie of Lincoln, to be put or lent forth', for a three-year period.[16] Lincoln at this time had dwindled to less than 3000 inhabitants (compare Florence in the early fifteenth century, with 40,000). Money could also be borrowed from the 'town stock' of communities ranging from the prosperous merchant town of Hull, to the 'towne' of Burton (really a village), just north of Lincoln, to the even smaller subdivision of St Andrew's parish, Whittlesey, in Cambridgeshire.[17] The intent behind the portion bank in Florence had been to stimulate the rate of marriage, after decimation of the population by plague, and to raise money for the city. Early modern England was less mercantile, in so far as its municipal investment – outside of Courts of Orphans – appears to have been run principally as a civic service, and not as a profit-making venture. The rates of interest paid to investors and charged to borrowers by the corporation seem to have been identical, but this could be better pursued in corporation records than in probate accounts.

Even more common than public investment was private investment of portions, and again of all sizes. In 1624 a small-time tailor in the Lincolnshire fens 'put forth' to a local squire a portion of £5 16s. for his daughter Anne Greene, who was less than 10 years old at the time.[18] Wills often requested that a child's cash bequest be invested or, as one Lincolnshire labourer put it, 'put forrard for his euse and bringing up', without specifying how or to whom, leaving those decisions to the executrix.[19] At the upper end of the rural social scale, in 1676 the rector of Pilham, in the vale of Lincoln, bequeathed £200 to his 12-year-old daughter Ellinor Hornby, to be put forth by her mother Mary as she saw fit and paid with the increase at Ellinor's majority. When Mary died eight years later, Ellinor duly received her portion plus £84 interest.[20]

Since Ellinor Hornby was 20 when she was left an orphan she probably took her £284 into her own hands. Alternatively, a young woman could choose a 'tutor', whose responsibility it was to look after her portion until her majority. The orphan Elizabeth Chamberline of the Lincolnshire fens received a gift of £1, and she chose for herself the man – a labourer – whom she wanted to hold her money in trust until she reached her majority. No record of this transaction would have survived had not her trustee died in 1632, leaving his wife Jane Bauger to administer his £17 estate, at which point young Elizabeth named another man trustee of her £1, whom Jane duly paid.[21]

The sense of proprietorship of their own portions is evident in the wills which young women made, distributing their modest goods. Eighteen-year-old Margaret Greave died in Cambridgeshire in 1603, carefully disposing of the £22 portion she had received from her father: £3 for her own burial and other charges; £10 to her stepsister Agnes, 'imployed to her use' until she was 16; and the remaining £9 to her eldest brother and her stepfather as supervisors, to be paid 'withe the increase' to her other two brothers and two sisters at their majority.[22] In Sussex, Elizabeth Marner was one of four orphan children whose mother died in 1640, and she found herself near death two years later. She had £41, including a legacy from her father, a tradesman of some sort, and a portion from her mother, the better part of which money she gave away. Her two sisters were the chief beneficiaries, receiving cash, clothing and 'my best childbed linen' – as the eldest daughter, Elizabeth had probably inherited her mother's special sheet to be laid over a woman after having given birth. But she did not forget the High Church (cathedral) of Chichester, nor her six cousins on her mother's side. The remainder of Elizabeth's goods went to her only brother as executor, supervised by a tailor and a husbandman, but even his share returned to her sisters when his will was proved three years later.[23] Frequent death meant that portions shifted constantly between siblings.

MARRIAGE EXPECTATIONS

The ultimate intended destination of any child's inherited portion was its use as a marriage portion. Most women, like most men, undoubtedly wanted to, or at least expected to, marry. But this expectation must be set against the extraordinarily high proportion of people remaining single, even after the possibility of monastic celibacy was removed by the reformation. The fact that up to 20 per cent of the population of early modern England never married is generally attributed by historians to economic hardship – the inability to amass sufficient capital to set up housekeeping – or to other disabilities, notably physical unattractiveness or deformity in women. But the influence of a positive decision not to marry was clearly an important factor for some women, albeit the impact of personal choice on the rate of marriage probably remained constant over time.

The writers Jane Barker and Mary Astell, for example, quoted on spinsterhood above, were not bitter and twisted because they were unable to marry. They chose not to. The autobiographer Alice Thornton elaborated on her preference when, at the age of 23 in the 1650s, she was encouraged by her widowed mother to marry:

> As to myselfe, I was exceedingly sattisfied in that happie and free condittion, wherein I enjoyed my time with delight abundantly in the service of my god [and the companionship of my mother] . . . Nor could I, without much reluctance, draw my thoughts to the change of my single life, knowing to[o] much of the caires of this world sufficiently without the addition of such incident to the married state.

Alice's resistance to marriage may be enhanced by the fact that she is recollecting in her widowhood, seeing her youth through the scrim of her disappointing marriage to Mr Thornton, who although a 'deare heart', had only a poor estate and managed both of their finances badly. In Alice's phrase he 'did not love the trouble of mannaging of his owne'. But equally, it would not have been at all unreasonable – considering that Alice had lived with her adored mother for many years and that she had, at the impressionable age of 18, lost her dear and only elder sister in the delivery of her sixteenth child – if Alice really did not want to marry.[24]

Familial pressure not to marry was also a factor in women's decisions. Ellen Stout, in Lancashire in the 1680s, 'had the offers of marriage with sevrall country yeomen, men of good repute and substance'. But she, according to her brother, 'being always subject to the advice of her mother, was advised, considering her infermetys and ill state of health, to remain single, knowing the care and exercises that always attended a marryed life, and the hazard of hapiness in it.'[25] Ellen's mother may have been genuinely concerned about the hazard of happiness in marriage, but at the same time she and three of Ellen's brothers benefited directly from Ellen remaining single, since despite being considered infirm Ellen took care of each of their households in succession until her death at the age of 63.

Forty years ago Doris Mary Stenton described the unmarried woman at all levels of society as 'a burden on her family, a failure, since she had not caught a man to keep her', and this view is still regularly voiced today.[26] Ladies and gentlewomen, without the option to earn their own living, might become an economic burden on their brothers' estates. At the same time that more people in the population at large were marrying, from the later seventeenth century, the number of women among the upper classes who never married was increasing.[27] The massive inflation in the amount of bridal dowry required at aristocratic and gentry levels over the early modern period (see Chapter 7) probably limited the number of wealthy women whose families could afford to marry them.

In a later century George Eliot described the Reverend Irwine as having 'two hopelessly maïden sisters' and 'no more than seven hundred a year, and seeing no way of keeping his splendid mother and his sickly sister, not to reckon a second sister, who was usually spoken of without any adjective, in such lady-like ease as became their birth and habits . . . he remained, you see, at the age of eight-and-forty, a bachelor'.[28] If the Irwine sisters were a burden on their brother (though he would never say so), it is important not to forget the early modern heiresses who were the issue of perhaps 20 per cent of all marriages. Gentlewomen like Mrs Joyce Jeffries or Mrs Elizabeth Parkin never married, but neither did they burden their male kin. Instead, they made a professional enterprise of investing substantial sums of money: Jeffries in Hereford, turning over hundreds of pounds annually in the first half of the seventeenth century; Parkin in mid-eighteenth-century Sheffield, dealing in thousands of pounds.[29] They are only known to posterity through their account books. Any other ladies or gentlewomen, as yet undiscovered, who undertook similar commercial enterprise probably also remained unmarried.

The lives of women who remained single, whether by force of circumstance or by choice, and their construction as 'old maids', deserves to be further explored. The idea that an unmarried woman would be a burden on her family – that is, her father or her brothers – owes more to mid-twentieth-century assumptions that a wife was kept by her husband than to the domestic reality of early modern England. Neither ordinary women nor gentlewomen were 'kept' by their husbands, male complaints about the frivolity of female occupations notwithstanding. Not only did married women work in the household, but they also contributed considerable portions at the time of marriage. The term 'dowry' is more common than 'portion' today, and it was also known in the seventeenth century, when it was not infrequently used interchangeably with 'dower'. In a particularly well-known instance, King Lear disinherits Cordelia by saying, 'Let thy truth be thy dower' – or rather, dowry.[30] Since 'portion' was the more usual term in early modern England, it is used henceforth to avoid confusion.

It is often assumed that portions only mattered in wealthy marriages. On the contrary, probably the only people to whom property was unimportant in marriage were the vagrant poor. The significance of marriage portions among the vast majority of people can be examined from three angles. First, how did young women amass their portions? Second, exactly how much in money or goods changed hands in ordinary marriages compared with wealthier matches? And finally, what was the social role of the portion in marriage: who negotiated the financial arrangements, who benefited from them, and what did they mean to early modern society as a whole?

AMASSING THE PORTION

Most young women put together a marriage portion from a combination of inheritance from their parents, gifts and inheritance from other family members, and what they could save of the wages they earned from their mid-teens. Whether they worked as servants in husbandry doing agricultural labour, or as maidservants in the household, women earned one half to two thirds of the salaries of their male counterparts. Between £1 and £2 p.a. with room and board was normal.[31] For a very poor girl, without hope of any goods at all by inheritance, her earnings might be her only source of a portion.

Very occasionally the inventories of young single women are identified as those of maidservants. Six Lincolnshire maidservants had between £2 and £14 worth of moveables. What might have been their marriage portion consisted of clothing and a few household goods, plus the principal item – either a cash sum, or one or more animals. In the fenland in 1588 Beatrice Daye had £6, of which £5 was ready cash; in the marsh in 1623, Elizabeth Atkinson had £10, of which £8 consisted of a bill of debt.[32] Both the cash and the animals could be lent at interest or rented out. The omnipresent bequests of ewes and lambs remarked in every study of sixteenth- and early seventeenth-century wills were not merely a token of the giver's affection. The recipient godchildren, nieces, nephews and grandchildren benefited by their wool, their flesh and their rent. The only sample form for a lease in an early conveyancing manual of the mid-sixteenth century is a lease of sheep for five years.[33]

By the middle of the seventeenth century bequests to godchildren, grandchildren, nieces and nephews were usually in cash, rather than as ewes and lambs. In the late sixteenth and first half of the seventeenth centuries godchildren were given bequests in 21 per cent of wills in Yorkshire, Lincolnshire and Sussex (34 of 163). By the later seventeenth and early eighteenth centuries that proportion had fallen to 7 per cent (10 of 136), but they were still more common in these counties than in the parishes which have been the subject of previous will studies. In King's Langley, for example, godchildren had virtually disappeared from wills by 1600.[34]

A maidservant might receive a gift upon marriage or a bequest from a mistress or master, as well as from her own kin. Bequests to servants were made by 12 per cent of willmakers in Lincolnshire and Sussex, and more often by mistresses than by masters. Mrs Joyce Jeffries of Hereford gave all her numerous servants substantial marriage gifts in the mid-seventeenth century. At a more modest level, one unnamed Cambridgeshire maidservant appeared unexpectedly in court at the passing of her deceased master's account in 1677, to claim that in a nuncupative will he had given her a legacy of 10s. and a coat.[35]

Like those to godchildren, bequests to servants declined in the later seventeenth and eighteenth centuries, at the same time that servants less frequently lived in their employers' households.[36] Bequests to sisters, brothers, nieces, nephews and grandchildren, however, remained constant. Approximately 20 per cent of willmakers gave bequests to each of these relations, and these small gifts provided a steady flow of contributions to young women's portions.[37]

MONETARY VALUE

Marriage portions at the aristocratic level in the first half of the seventeenth century were in the range of several thousand pounds: Lady Anne Clifford, one of the wealthiest heiresses in England, received a portion of £17,000 upon her marriage to the Earl of Dorset in 1609; the first Earl of Strafford's two daughters were to receive portions of £10,000 each; Frances Coke had £10,000 which her father, recently dismissed as Lord Chief Justice and trying to work his way back into favour, could ill afford; Mary Boyle, the future Countess of Warwick, in 1641 was promised £7000 by her father, the Earl of Cork; and Anne, Lady Fanshawe, in 1644 was promised £10,000, although like many portions hers was never fully paid because of losses in the civil war. Later in the century aristocratic portions doubled, and the inflation of portions at this level is discussed further in Chapter 7. Literary portions were even larger than life: Susannah Centlivre's 'Mistress Nancy Lovely', in her play *A Bold Stroke for a Wife* (1718), brought a portion of £30,000.[38]

Upper gentry portions ranged from £1000 to £5000. In 1612 Alice Osborne and Margaret Denton married with £2000 and £2300, respectively. In the mid-seventeenth century Alice Thornton's sisters-in-law had £1500 each, Margaret Lucas (the future Duchess of Newcastle, but from a gentry family) had £2000, Sir Robert Filmer left his daughter £2500, and Dorothy Osborne's portion came to £4000. Margaret Denton's six daughters, the sisters of Sir Ralph Verney, had only £1000 each.[39]

County gentry gave their daughters anywhere between £100 and £1000. It is to this level of society that Antonia Fraser refers in thinking £1000 a 'respectable' mid-seventeenth-century portion for an untitled woman, by which she must mean possessing at least the 'Mistress' of the gentlewoman.[40] But many 'mere' gentlewomen had less. In north Yorkshire John Legard, esquire – in 'the hazardous service' of the king in 1646, but formerly a lawyer – contracted to assure his stepdaughters portions of £500 apiece. One Callisthenes Brooke, esquire and lord of the manor of Gaitforth near Selby, in 1658 bequeathed to his three daughters and his younger son £300 each.[41]

Clerks, wealthy yeomen and tradesmen, and merchants gave their daughters usually between £100 and £500. The daughters of the Essex clergyman Ralph Josselin had up to £500 each. Martha Mayhew was married in 1673 with £300 from her uncle, the Sussex rector Giles Moore. Another Sussex clergyman, a few years earlier, gave his daughter Mercy Hinde an extraordinary £800 marriage portion. The landlord of the largest inn in Sevenoaks, Kent, married his four daughters with £175 each. There is an extensive overlap in the size of portions among the lower gentry and among prosperous men who did not necessarily append 'Mr' to their names. In two east Yorkshire examples, a 'gentleman' of the city of Beverley in 1644 left to his daughter Grace Robinson a bond of £100 which he had previously taken out in her name, and 'all such linnings and househould goods as were my owne before my marriage' with his second wife, while in 1686 Jane Lamb, daughter of a prosperous butcher on the other side of the wolds, had exactly the same portion.[42]

The litigants in the Court of Chancery fall into these categories of gentry and wealthy yeomen and tradesmen. The median portion in those marriage settlement suits which specified a portion over the seventeenth century was £300. These fell into three ranges: £40–£300, by far the largest group, including wealthy yeomen and clerks, a few gentlemen and esquires, the odd husbandman, a butcher, a maltman and a tallow chandler; £500–£700, consisting of gentlemen, esquires, a physician and a merchant; and £1000–£5000, the realm of knights and baronets, the lowest order in the titular aristocracy.

The one plaintiff who does not fit in this scheme is an ordinary tailor from Surrey, who alleged that he had been promised £30 plus extensive household goods with Elizabeth Baldwin in marriage. Even this portion hardly warranted the expense of litigation, and his wife's family countered that £10 was perfectly sufficient for a tailor.[43] Sadly, in this as in all Chancery cases, the outcome is unknown because it is not practical to trace the decision.

The size of marriage portions at social levels like that of the Surrey tailor are rarely specified, even in probate documents. Few willmakers listed the components of an already married daughter's portion, but simply stated, like yeoman Thomas Craven of the vale of Pickering, 'I have allredy given unto [my daughter Mary Cropsan] a considirable portion for her preferment in marige'.[44] In only twenty-one wills in this study was a marriage portion specified as such. Nearly all of these date from the later seventeenth century, and they range from £6 to £800, which is unenlightening except to illustrate the social variety represented in probate sources. But bequests to unmarried daughters can at least suggest the size of portions, although these figures represent minimum marriage portions since they rarely take into account bequests from grandparents or aunts or uncles, they only sometimes mention previous gifts in the parent's lifetime, and there is no reason for them to consider the young woman's earnings.

Of twenty-five bequests to unmarried daughters in rural Yorkshire, half amounted to £15 or less. They were made by husbandmen, yeomen, a joiner and a blacksmith. Two thirds amounted to £20 or less. These figures correspond to Alan Macfarlane's calculation from the bequests in one Westmorland parish that husbandmen's daughters married with £10–£50, but usually less than £20, and labourers' daughters married with a mere £1–£5.[45] Portions in the Yorkshire market town of Selby were comparable. In eighty Selby wills most unmarried daughters' bequests were for £20, from yeomen and the better-off of the town's leather craftsmen, or £10, from husbandmen, labourers, and poorer craftsmen and yeomen. In both the town and the countryside four fifths of all portions came to less than £50.

At the poorer end of the scale, several young women had only household goods. Mary Johnson of Selby, for example, had a 2-year-old heifer, a brass pot and two pewter dishes from her father, a linen weaver with a personal estate of only £9 after debts in 1671; her sister Alice had one colt, a brass pot, two pewter dishes and two swarms of bees.[46] At the upper end of the scale, the daughters of six Yorkshire men (two gentlemen, two esquires, a yeoman and a butcher, out of a total of 105) had portions exceeding £100.

The same or somewhat higher levels probably pertained farther south. In Bristol the orphaned students of the Red Maids School – ostensibly the daughters of decayed freemen, but in practice often of lower status – might be given £10 or £20 upon their marriage.[47] In Sussex wills, bequests to unmarried daughters ranged from £10 for the daughter of a husbandman in 1609 to £100 for each of two daughters of a well-to-do butcher in 1681, but like those in Yorkshire the majority of bequests amounted to less than £50.[48]

Macfarlane has estimated that at upper social levels one daughter's marriage portion constituted approximately three years' income from the parental estate, while husbandmen's daughters' portions equalled up to two years' family income.[49] It is impossible to verify this hypothesis from probate documents, which list moveable wealth at death, not annual income, and there was no necessary relation between the two. There is no correlation whatever between a man's inventory value and the size of his children's portions, for two reasons: first, the number of children affected the size of their portions; second, a son could be required to pay his sisters' portions out of the profits of land he inherited, whose value was not included in his father's inventory. The Selby cordwainer mentioned in Chapter 4, who gave his daughter Ruth £30, to be paid by her brother Joshua 'in consideration of his having the messuage', had a personal estate of only £19 after debts, which had to support his widow as well as his children.[50]

Very roughly, the portions of brides break down in the social pyramid as follows: the aristocracy, upwards of £5000; the gentry, £1000–£5000; the county gentry, £500–£1000; clerks, merchants, wealthy yeomen and tradesmen, £100–£500; prosperous yeomen, tradesmen and craftsmen, £50–£100; the great bulk of yeomen, husbandmen, tradesmen, craftsmen and labourers, up to £50 but generally under £30.

The difference between the titled woman's portion and the ordinary portion was the difference between making a daughter 'marriageable', in a recognized marriage market, and simply giving her what was available. The discrepancy between upper and lower marriage portions has already been measured for the continental cities of Genoa, Florence and Paris in earlier periods. In the twelfth century Genoese artisan portions were worth approximately 11 per cent of the value of aristocratic portions. Fifteenth-century peasant sharecroppers' daughters in the countryside around Florence had portions worth up to 8 per cent of Florentine patriciate daughters' portions.[51] But this same exercise performed on the English evidence produces the result that a £30 ordinary portion constituted only 3 per cent of a moderate gentry portion of £1000, let alone an aristocratic portion. Even if the ordinary portion is moved up to £50, it still represents only 5 per cent of the gentry portion.

The early modern English disparity between ordinary and wealthy brides is thus at least twice the disparity that prevailed in medieval Italy. Early modern Paris also displays less disparate marital wealth than England: a portion of £500, common for a city councillor's daughter in the later sixteenth century, would have taken a manual labourer three years to earn.[52] But in England the councillor's daughter's portion would have cost her *own* father three years' income. Continental European societies are generally considered to have been more highly stratified than in England, but this assumption is not borne out by the social disparity reflected in upper and lower marriage portions. It is unclear to what extent the differences are geographical, between England and Europe, and to what extent they are chronological, between the middle ages and the early modern period. But the subject certainly deserves further investigation, perhaps starting with quantitative work on medieval English marriage portions, to test the idea of chronological change.

SOCIAL ROLE OF PORTIONS

Despite the relative smallness of the ordinary English marriage portion, it was as important to the idea of marriage at middling social levels as it was among wealthy families. Three Lancashire diarists provide examples. The nonconformist minister Adam Martindale, son of a yeoman farmer, recorded in his autobiography that his eldest brother's marriage in 1633 was a 'great disappointment', since this brother had shunned a respectable £140 portion for a bride with only £40. Adam was only 10 at the time, but the financial implications of his brother's marriage made a big impression upon him.[53] The mercer's apprentice Roger Lowe, who frequently negotiated in the marriages of his friends, was himself courting a maidservant in 1663, but she dropped out of his diary when he was offered a bride with a sizeable £120 portion.[54] At the end of the century the Quaker merchant William Stout, who himself never married, often recorded in his diary the portion that a certain man got with his wife, although he usually omitted her name. One of his 'particular acquaintances' who married a £5000 portion promptly retired from business.[55]

The Shropshire yeoman Richard Gough, writing about 1700, had much the same obsession with wives' financial value. The brides he mentions, the daughters of small country gentlemen, had portions of £50 or £60; £100 portions belonged to wealthy young women. Gough's own cousin had an 'almost incredible' fortune of 'litle lesse than £3000'.[56] There were exceptions to the rule – men who married without the possibility of a portion. Gough mentions a fairly well-to-do young man who married a widow with many small children. She probably brought him very little, but in addition, because his father disapproved, she cost him at least part of his own inheritance.[57] But such examples were few.

Male diarists' interest in brides' portions is comprehensible when one considers that marriage was far and away the best (simplest, most efficient) means for a man to improve his financial condition. On the other hand, the array of possible arrangements for the bride's financial benefit – jointure, dower, pin-money or paraphernalia – is noticeable by its absence in this source. But if the security of the bride's property was not a concern of personal accounts, it was of central importance in legal treatises and conveyancing manuals, which suggests a public eager for such information.

The anonymous author of *The Lawes Resolutions of Women's Rights*, while not providing sample marriage settlements, advised young women, 'A husband *per se* is a desirable thing, but donements [gifts] or feoffments [land transfers], etc., better the stomacke, though it selfe it be good and eager.'[58] He further commented on the state of marriage negotiations in his own time, that women were

> so sweet, faire and pleasing . . . or so very good and prudent . . . that though some men get lands by them, most men are faine to assure part or all of such lands as they have (in joynture or otherwise) to them, ere they can win their love.[59]

If the bride herself did not withhold her love prior to such an assurance, her parents might, at least among the prosperous readership of the *Lawes Resolutions*:

> the greatest part of honest, wise and sober men, are of themselves carefull to purchase somewhat for their wives, if they be not, yet they stand sometimes bound by the woman's parents to make their wives some joynture.[60]

Engaged couples of more modest means are occasionally glimpsed in probate accounts, and their stories reveal the importance of even small 'donements' in respect of marriage. When a young person died while pledged to be married the exchange of promises was a matter for careful attention by the family and the court. One Katharine Browne in Somerset, still in her teens, had lived with her married sister for eleven years. As a child Katharine had been injured in a fall, and she was never completely well again, but her infirmity was apparently not enough to impair her housewifely attractiveness, for she became engaged to marry. But Katharine fell ill again and, confined to her bed for a month, she knew this was her last sickness. She chose the text for her own funeral sermon, and made her only bequest orally: £1 1s. 6d. to her betrothed that he might buy himself a ring, which bequest was honoured by the court.[61]

In a case from Grantham in Lincolnshire, Lewis Hill did 'entend to marry' one Faith Archer before his death in 1604. On his death bed, and in the presence of his two sisters, he said that Faith should have £10, which amounted to about one third of all his worldly goods. In the following year both of Lewis's sisters died of the plague, but 'in their sicknes they did acknowledge' his bequest to Faith before yet more witnesses. The court duly awarded her the amount of £6 13s. 4d., reduced from the original gift probably in view of the fact that she had since married another man.[62]

Lewis Hill's gift to Faith Archer raises the question of property transfer from the groom to the bride, rather than the other way around. Anthropologists distinguish between cultures which pay dowry (from the bride's family to the groom) and cultures which pay brideprice (from the groom to the bride's family). Early modern England may be described as a dowry culture in so far as men *thought* of marital finance principally in terms of the bride's portion, and therefore would have described their marital property practices, if asked, in terms of a dowry system. But in actual practice new marriages depended upon property from both the bride and the groom. Dowry and brideprice operated simultaneously, except that the brideprice went not to the bride's family but to the new marital household.[63] The property that the groom brought to marriage was just as much a marriage portion, but it was almost never described by that term because of the nature of the marital exchange. A bride's portion was the one at issue because under the system of coverture a wife's portion became her husband's wealth.

Had women been the courters instead of the courted, had *they* enjoyed significant financial gain from marriage, and had wives enjoyed legal control of their husbands' fortunes, we would hear more about grooms' portions. Even under the restrictions of coverture, marriage was still women's best hope of financial security. And women's writing, unlike men's, suggests the significance of the groom's financial contribution to marriage. The reason Dorothy Osborne's father and brother forbade her to marry William Temple for many years was precisely because he lacked a fortune comparable to her own. Dorothy was offered numerous alternative wealthier suitors, but remarked wisely and wearily, 'Tis much easier sure to get a good fortune than a good husband'.[64] Alice Thornton referred to her sister Lady Danby as 'married to a good estate'. Alice resented the fact that her own husband had an income of less than £400 p.a., and that amount was encumbered by his mother's jointure and his sisters' portions, while she had previously been offered two other matches of £1500 p.a. clear of encumbrances.[65] Mary Pierrepont, courting Edward Wortley in 1709, wrote to him of 'the marriage of an old maid . . . without a portion, to a man of £7000 p.a., and they say £40,000 in ready money', inverting the form in which the *Gentleman's Magazine* some years later announced marriages: 'Mr P. Bowen to Miss Nicholls of Queenhithe, with £10,000'.[66]

Whether discussed or not, it was always the case that the groom's fortune had to be of comparable value to the bride's. In the marriages of the gentry Isham family in late sixteenth- and early seventeenth-century Northampton-shire, for example, a son considered brides with the same portions as his sisters had; and cash portions were distributed equally among sons and daughters, although the heir had land in addition.[67] Similarly, men's wills at ordinary social levels – from wealthy Shropshire farmers to poor Yorkshire labourers – normally gave at least younger sons the same bequests as unmarried daughters, giving them all the same marital chances.[68] The property contribution of the groom to the marriage is occasionally hinted at in these wills. In 1627 the wealthy Sussex downs yeoman John Sowton bequeathed to his son John only £20, the smallest bequest to any of his four adult children, but in addition he asked that 'all those particulars which at the time of concluding the match betwixt my sonne John and Joan Rickman were promised by me shall accordingly be delivered . . . unto them by my executrix'. John Sowton the younger died nine years after his father with £524, half of which may be presumed to have been the 'particulars' promised by his father.[69] The equality of inheritance between daughters and younger sons was probably less and less true among the professional classes, where daughters got more because younger sons were expected to acquire a professional training and their education became part of their investment in the marriage. John Green, for example, barrister and the Recorder of London at his death in 1659, gave £1000 to each of his daughters but only £700 to each of his younger sons.[70] As the professional and trading classes increased in size over the eighteenth century the bride's portion grew proportionately more important in providing cash to fund the family 'enterprise'.[71]

Education or training was probably also one of the principal reasons that the bride's portion or dowry ultimately died out in most English-speaking countries after the First World War, albeit at different rates among different classes of people. A vestige of its former self survived until the middle of the twentieth century in the practice of the upper-class trousseau and the working-class 'hope chest' or 'bottom drawer', both consisting of household linens and fine clothing. In modern Greece dowry has only recently declined, again perhaps as a woman's contribution to marriage has shifted from her capital to her (paid) labour and her education.[72] Dowry for brides still exists to some extent in Ireland, Italy and other Mediterranean countries, many Middle Eastern countries, and India.

Historians have viewed English marital property arrangements in much the same way that early modern men did – as an issue for the bride, not the groom.[73] A daughter's marriage portion has been described as 'the price a father paid to persuade some other male to relieve him of the obligation to support his daughter for the remaining term of her natural life'. Or, from the perspective of the suitor who relieved the father, 'portions might be inimical to the establishment of dynasties, but they also helped a number of young craftsmen and merchants to establish themselves'. Peter Earle does acknowledge that 'equality of fortune' between bride and groom was expected, but concludes from this that 'nearly everyone could expect to double his original capital by marriage, a fact which might make even the most ardent misogynist a supporter of the institution'.[74]

This one-sided approach not only ignores the groom's financial contribution to marriage; it also denies both daughters and mothers any decision-making power. And it entirely overlooks demographic reality. Throughout the early modern period one child in three lost at least one parent before the age of 21. (The modern rate is only 3 per cent.) Probably at least half of all young women had lost their fathers by the time they married.[75] Among the aristocracy, where one would most expect to see a patriarch negotiating his children's marriage, we are told that more than three quarters of young men – and, one presumes, young women – were fatherless at the time of their marriage.[76]

Who then arranged marriage? In wealthier matches widowed mothers commonly negotiated for their daughters, as did Alice Wandesford for young Alice to Mr Thornton, and as her own remarried mother had done for her nearly forty years earlier.[77] The settlements in these marriages were complex, often including the maintenance of the young couple for a period of years or even for the husband's lifetime, provided usually by the parents of the groom, as in the case of Lady Mildmay and Dame Joan Thynne, but also sometimes by the widowed mother of the bride, as in the case of Alice Thornton.[78]

Where both a bride's parents were still living it might be assumed that her father made the arrangements, but even here he did not necessarily fulfil this function, as we learn from a chance mention in the diary of the 18-year-old John Green, studying at Lincoln's Inn. His sister Margaret's marriage in 1635 to the son of a barrister was negotiated by their mother, despite the fact that Margaret's father, also a barrister, was alive and well at the time. Young John noted simply, 'my mother and sister Peg came to towne' and 'Marriage concluded by Mother', in between accounts of a venison feast and a game of bowls.[79] Upper-class letters also show that marriage negotiations – which required correspondence to ascertain both the character of the proposed spouse and the security of the promised portion – were largely carried on by women, whether their husbands were alive or not.[80] These negotiations naturally included lengthy discussion of the portions of grooms and brides equally.

Unlike upper-class men, ordinary men in their wills very rarely placed restrictions upon their children's inheritance by requiring them to marry with their mothers' or guardians' consent. Even when they did a restriction was as easily placed on a boy as on a girl. In one particularly specific example, a Yorkshire yeoman in 1640 gave his nephew a messuage with the meadows and pasture belonging to it, but 'if he marrie Hugh Rotherfurth daughtter', then he had to share half the messuage with his brother.[81] Generally, restrictions went no further than urging children of both sexes to be advised by their mothers. John Legard, the Yorkshire esquire in the hazardous service of the king (pages 86–7), urged his wife Ann to be careful that the children 'may be married to persons of good fame honest life and unstayned reputacion', a sentiment which other men might have echoed had they not been paying someone else by the line to write their wills, as a former lawyer like Legard would not have to.[82]

At more ordinary levels of society daughters themselves commonly conducted their own marriage negotiations. Since most young women went out to work while still in their teens, it may be assumed that they acquired sufficient freedom and self-assurance with which to arrange a marriage. Vivien Brodsky has illustrated the differences in this respect between young women who lived under parental control in early seventeenth-century London and those who emigrated to London for work and married there without reference to their parents. The London-born women married at an earlier age, to men who were substantially older than themselves; the immigrants married later, to men of nearly their own age.[83]

Because girls did not usually inherit land and because their portion was likely to be in cash, young women were much more mobile than young men, and could – or had to – go where work was available.[84] Those who did not migrate to London also had plenty of opportunity for frequent courting. The Lancashire apprentice Roger Lowe, for example, courts and is courted at markets, fairs, races, or whilst just drinking in the alehouse before and after church. Richard Gough spoke of a teenage pair who, 'going to schoole togeather fell in love with one another, and soe married'.[85] Two fictional country maids who handled their own marriage arrangements – and expected financial contributions of their grooms – are the penny chapbook heroines, Kate and Cisley. 'Loving Kate' and her 'honest John' undertook the 'contrivance of their marriage and way how to live' in a tavern, he with £10 from his father and wages owing from his master, and she with £10 from her father in her uncle's hands and £5 saved from her wages. They conclude their plans for marital prosperity by deciding to open an alehouse. In Cisley's case, one Simon formally asked her father for her hand in marriage, but received the reply that he had better go ask Cisley herself. She proposed they two should meet on market day and 'conclude the bargain at a tavern'.[86]

The stories of real-life women of just slightly greater wealth than Kate and Cisley survive only in those cases where the negotiations broke down and litigation ensued. In one case from Durham in 1570, Katherine Marshall had a house and land worth £4 p.a., plus £10 worth of moveables. She asked the father of her intended, a tanner, to settle £13 6s. 8d. on the prospective marriage. When he offered only £5, she initially agreed, but then changed her mind and ended the relationship, whereupon her jilted groom sued in the ecclesiastical court for breach of contract.[87] Most breach of contract cases were initiated by a jilted and pregnant bride, but suits like that against Katherine Marshall specifically over marital finance occur through the seventeenth century in ecclesiastical courts.

Apart from the practical, material issues of who negotiated marriage and whether the groom's property was as important as the bride's in those negotiations, there remains the question of the cultural significance of the peculiarly female dowry. At some level, a bride's portion was not merely a nest egg for the new household – it was a token of her character, and thus of her sexual honour. Adam Martindale's memory of his elder brother's courtship, mentioned above, is particularly interesting for its elision of the moral and economic attributes of the women involved. The potential bride with £140 was 'of very suitable yeares, and otherwise likely to make an excellent wife'; the one with only £40 was 'a young wild airy girle, betweene 15 and 16 yeares of age; an huge lover and frequenter of wakes, greenes, and merrie-nights, where musick and dancing abounded'. The description of the two women's characters may have been accurate, but would Martindale have described them thus had their portions been reversed? Elsewhere, he speaks of another brother who married 'an holy young woman of pious parentage, with whom he lived comfortably at a new brick house . . . thriving fast in goodnesse and his outward estate'. The connection between moral and material worth is hard to miss.[88] Nor was this a particularly puritan or nonconformist tendency. Richard Gough, the Shropshire yeoman and ortho-dox Anglican, mentions a man who married his servant maid, 'a wanton, gadding dame, who had neither goods nor good name'.[89]

Forms of charity also attest to the symbolic significance of a bride's material possessions. Both bequests in wills and the foundation of trusts to supply dowries for poor young women to enable them to marry were popular in the middle ages and not uncommon through the seventeenth century. This 'old-fashioned and sentimental' form of charity, as W. K. Jordan called it, comprised a small proportion of all charitable donations, but he found that interest in it was more consistent than in any other form of 'social rehabilitation'.[90] Jordan did not distinguish benefactors by sex in his research, but it would be interesting to know specifically who supported dowry charities. Women in their wills were by and large more generous than men to other women and to the poor (see Chapter 12), but the symbolic significance of dowries might have had more appeal to male donors.

The unspoken assumption behind these charities is that without dowries poor women would be unable to marry and therefore forced into prostitution. Even in catholic cultures where monasteries offered the prospect of a socially acceptable celibate life, dowries were usually still required to enter a religious institution. To be sure the money helped to finance the institution, but only nuns, not monks, had to bring dowries, suggesting that sexual reputation is once again at issue. One of the most universally venerated saints in Christendom was Bishop Nicholas of Myra. In England alone there are 400 churches dedicated to him. St Nicholas's symbol is three gold balls, representing three bags of gold. These he is said to have dropped in through the window of a poor man's house to provide dowries for his three daughters, thereby saving the man from shame and the young women from prostitution. (St Nicholas later metamorphosed into Santa Claus, and it is also his gold balls which are traditionally represented on the pawnbroker's shop sign.)[91]

If there was less stress in England than in Mediterannean societies on the threat to a woman's chastity posed by her lack of a marriage portion, the size of the portion was still symbolically important for the honour of both brides and their families. It has been observed that by the sixteenth century in England the word 'credit' had a double meaning, referring both to a man's solvency and to his reputation in the community, or his honesty. The importance of a bride's portion indicates that credit also had a double economic and moral meaning for women, since a woman's reputation or 'honesty' rested upon her chastity. The cultural meaning of the dowry has been most discussed in relation to what is usually thought of as a peculiarly hot-climate culture of 'honour and shame'.[92] But its importance in England deserves a great deal more attention.

The portion inherited by a daughter received careful attention as to its financial investment and protection, by adults and by the young woman herself. This was true of portions in the tens of pounds, just as much as for those prosperous young women who sued in the Court of Chancery for their portions in the hundreds of pounds, as for the aristocrats with thousands of pounds in portion.[93] While an inherited portion was expected to become a marriage portion, it should always be borne in mind that there were proportionally more unmarried adult women in early modern England than there have been at any time since, and we know very little about their lives.

Marriage negotiations, on the other hand, are the sort of life-cycle event likely to be recorded. It is clear from the brief survey of evidence presented here that the conventional image of the bride's father treating with the groom's father or the groom himself must be jettisoned, for both demographic and social reasons. In wealthy families mothers were actively involved in negotiating their daughters' marriage; in ordinary families the daughters were likely to do it themselves.

A lively interest in the negotiation of their own marriage is to be expected from young women who enjoyed most of the same resources in their childhood that their brothers did, and who inherited with them a comparable portion from the total parental estate. The misogyny of a culture which propounded female inferiority and primogeniture did not, in the case of England, extend to scrimping on the material well-being of daughters.

Since in strictly economic terms grooms required marriage portions of comparable value to their brides, it cannot therefore be true, as Alan Macfarlane has suggested, that daughters had a slightly lower value than sons because they required a dowry, which represented a burden on the family estate.[94] Certainly daughters had a lower ideological value, and while the fortunes of both partners in a marriage were ideally equivalent, the marriage portions of brides had a cultural significance which those of grooms did not. But these values cannot be correlated to any practical economic phenomenon. Attempts by historians to provide an economic basis for cultural misogyny simply do not fit the English case, if they fit any case.

Part III

Wives

[Husband and wife] are but one person, and by this a married woman perhaps may . . . doubt whether shee bee either none or no more than halfe a person. But let her bee of good cheare, though for the neere conjunction which is between man and wife, and to tye them to a perfect love, agreement and adherence, they bee by intent and wise fiction of law one person. . . . Women have no voyse in parliament, they make no lawes, they consent to none, they abrogate none. All of them are understood either married or to bee married and their desires [are] subject to their husband, I know no remedy though some women can shift it well enough.

The Lawes Resolutions of Women's Rights (1632: 4, 6)

The title of 'Mrs' for a married woman, now universally recognized in English, only came to designate a marital rather than a social status gradually, about the middle of the eighteenth century. Edward Gibbon, writing in his autobiography (1789) about the 1740s, calls his maiden aunts 'Mrs'. But Lady Mary Wortley Montagu, whose letters cover a period of more than fifty years, distinguished a married 'Mrs' from the new maiden 'Miss' by the 1740s. The distinction is also made in Charlotte Charke's *Narrative* of her own life in 1755, and in Fanny Burney's novel *Evelina* (1778). Even this marital distinction was still only made at the gentry level, at least in England, before the egalitarian spirit of the nineteenth century slowly applied 'Mrs', 'Miss' and 'Mr' to everyone.

Below the level of the gentry the only title for a married woman in the early modern period was 'goodwife' or 'goody', but the use of these terms too seems to have been both socially and locally specific. 'Goodwife' was used to refer to married women of a certain status, perhaps yeomen's wives, by the rector of Horsted Keynes, Sussex, and by Sarah Fell in Lancashire. In New England the term was common for both wives and widows, and 'goodman' may also have been used for yeomen. But in Abingdon, Berkshire, 'goody' was used synonymously with widow, rather than wife. In the English chapbook 'Loving Kate' expects to be 'goody Lawrence' when she marries 'Honest John', but this may be farcical, since their plan to run an alehouse together would probably not qualify her for goodwife status. In addition, the ballad was printed in the later seventeenth century, by which time 'goodwife' probably sounded quite old-fashioned and provincial to English ears. In more than 2000 probate documents from Yorkshire, Lincolnshire, Cambridgeshire, Northamptonshire and Sussex, the title occurs no more than five times – and that includes one unfortunate girl born *c*.1620 and christened Goodwife Morgan.[1] The many married women who do appear in probate documents, usually in connection with debt payments, were referred to as, for example, 'Ann the wife of John Carter', or simply 'Carter's wife'.

In England and Wales today, well over half of all women over the age of 16 are married at any given time.[2] In early modern England, probably only about one third of all adult women were married at any one time.[3] That third were legally under coverture. Sir Henry Finch, in his *Law, or a Discourse Thereof* (1627), explained 'the weakenesse and debilities' inherent in 'femes covert', outlaws, prisoners, infants, 'men unlettered' and 'ideots out of their right minde'.[4] This categorization of married women with criminals and the insane was ostensibly a technical identification of the legal disability of these classes of people: wives were debarred from independent legal action because they were married, rather than because they were women. Still, most women married at some time, and the descriptive terms of association suggest a more contemptuous inference. This contempt becomes apparent after the passage of married women's property law reform in England and many American states, when legal writers fall back on women's 'natural infirmity of judgment' to explain that, while the reforms affected property, they did 'not appear to alter the legal *status* of married women'.[5] The association of married women, idiots and criminals was satirized to great propagandistic effect in late nineteenth- and early twentieth-century England and America by campaigners for female suffrage.

The basis of coverture was ostensibly an economic exchange. The bride's portion was exchanged for her maintenance during marriage, for the groom's responsibility for her contracts (since without property she could not contract) and for a guarantee of subsistence in her widowhood, in the form of dower or jointure.[6] The fundamental difficulty with this exchange was that a woman had no legal remedy if her husband failed to meet his obligations at any time during coverture. He had only an obligation to pay any 'reasonable' debts she contracted in his name, for household necessities, and she could not be sued personally for debt. However, in the words of the anonymous author of *The Hardships of the English Laws*, 'Exemption from debts is not a recompense for divesting of property'.[7] The groom, on the other hand, had received most if not all of his material benefits immediately upon marriage, and if for any reason his bride's portion were not paid he could sue for breach of contract.

In order to evade the disabilities imposed by coverture on the bride and on her natal and future families, marriage settlements were ubiquitous among the aristocracy and gentry. A marriage settlement was a legal evasion of the law of coverture and dower, in the same way that a will was the evasion of the law of intestate inheritance of real and moveable property. One made a will if one did not want one's property to be divided according to the law of intestacy; and one made a marriage settlement in order to avoid the property law incidents which accompanied marriage. Both wills and marriage settlements have been described as deviations from custom, but especially in some segments of the population the deviation was so common as to have become custom itself.

Either a woman or a man might make their fortune by marriage. But a man did not also risk financial ruin, as a woman did, since he did not face the legal constraints on property ownership inherent in early modern coverture. How women managed economically both during and after marriage was determined by two factors: first, their husbands' good will; and second, the type of property arrangements they had made before marriage. Chapter 6 establishes what a marriage settlement was and something of its history. Chapter 7 assesses settlements litigated in the Court of Chancery by the gentry, wealthy yeomen and merchants. And Chapter 8 discovers settlements in probate documents, providing evidence for the first time that ordinary women also made arrangements at marriage to avoid the more onerous aspects of coverture.

6   The nature of marriage settlements

Two specific kinds of marriage settlement have received extensive attention by historians. The first is strict settlement. The principal feature of strict settlement was the 'entail', the settling of an estate upon the yet-unborn eldest son of a man's own eldest son, usually on the occasion of the son's marriage. The entail – or settlement 'in tail male' – thus reinforced the practice of primogeniture from the seventeenth through the nineteenth century.[1] It is generally agreed that the use of strict settlements was confined to the aristocracy and the upper gentry, partly because no others survive, and partly on the assumption that no one else had so keen an interest in the entail of estates, or had cash to pay for the necessary conveyances. The sources used to study these settlements are private family papers, among which the actual conveyances survive. Strict settlements (not always so identified) also occur in literature, including Mary Hays's *Memoirs of Emma Courtney* (1796), Jane Austen's *Pride and Prejudice* (1813), Charles Dickens's *Nicholas Nickleby* (1838–9), Charlotte Bronte's *Shirley* (1849), George Eliot's *Felix Holt* (1866) and Elizabeth Barrett Browning's *Aurora Leigh* (1890).

In addition to the entail on the son and future grandson, strict settlements could also set the portions of the settlor's other children, and of his prospective grandchildren besides the eldest male. The effect of strict settlement on the portions of these younger sons and daughters is hotly disputed. Lloyd Bonfield argues that strict settlement provided greater security for the portions of younger sons and daughters, and so improved on previous practice. Eileen Spring believes that daughters' share of family wealth was reduced by having their portion fixed by their grandfather before their birth, rather than giving free reign to the natural affection of a father towards his living daughter.[2] Aside from this esoteric but entertaining debate, women are largely absent from the literature on strict settlement. The possibility of land passing from father to daughter to grandson, or in the case of widows and sonless families from mother to daughter, is, if not over-looked, at least not discussed. A strict settlement could be made by the groom's father alone, and did not necessarily involve the bride's family. Perhaps for this reason, provisions for wives which could be included in marriage settlements, such as jointure and pin-money, are only mentioned briefly in passing. The focus is rather on the primogenitural aspects of strict settlement as 'a remarkable and unique phenomenon of British society'.[3]

The second type of marriage settlement, less well known than strict settlement, at least for early modern England, is the trust for a married woman's 'sole and separate estate'. These trusts, like strict settlement, were usually established just prior to marriage. A woman contemplating marriage could only establish her own trust before she married, but one could be made for her by someone else at any time. A trust for sole and separate estate preserved a woman's right to specified property during her coverture. The drawback of such a trust was that it was defensible only in equity.

'Separate estate', as it is known, has been studied in eighteenth- and nineteenth-century America, as well as in early modern England.[4] It is also important as the basis of the late nineteenth-century reform of married women's property law in both England and America. Separate estate is generally agreed to have originated at the end of the sixteenth century.[5] It could take the form of capital, in either real or personal property, or of an annuity. From the later seventeenth century the annuity was also known as pin-money.[6] By the mid-nineteenth century pin-money had dwindled to its present meaning of 'a small sum of money for incidental minor expenses',[7] but in the early modern period pin-money could consist of very large sums: £50, £300 or even £1000 p.a.

Literary examples of separate estate or pin-money are less common than examples of strict settlement, and separate estate features as an object of derision, while strict settlement is presented as a fact of life.[8] Like strict settlements, all historians agree that separate estate was employed only by the wealthiest segments of society, those who had substantial property to protect, who would pay to draw up the necessary documents and who could afford to enforce the terms of the trust in the Court of Chancery if necessary. Separate estate has never been studied in documents 'on the ground' for early modern England, but only for colonial America. In the colonies, separate estates were limited to the wealthiest families, and so the natural assumption is that they were also restricted to the upper classes in England and not in use among that segment of the population likely to emigrate.[9]

Both strict settlement and separate estate were important types of marriage settlements, but neither was what most people meant by a 'marriage settlement' in early modern England. Among the collections of upper-class family papers which contain strict settlements, Lloyd Bonfield also found some twenty-eight marriage settlements in Kent and Northamptonshire which relate to ordinary people, copies of which were kept by the male members of the wealthy families because they acted as trustees. These settlements, made primarily by yeomen but also by tradesmen, two husbandmen and two labourers, did not include the provision of entail – they arranged the widow's jointure and transferred land to children.[10] Another source altogether – conveyancing manuals – demonstrate that what was commonly meant by a marriage settlement in early modern England was a document which neither entailed property in the male line nor established a separate estate as such, but rather preserved different aspects of the wife's property rights, which might or might not involve an equitable trust for separate estate.

CONVEYANCING MANUALS

Conveyancing manuals throughout the early modern period demonstrate that the primary purpose of a marriage settlement was to preserve the wife's property rights. The sample forms of settlement presented incorporated any one or more of the following features: setting the amount of the wife's jointure; allowing her to make a will under coverture; obliging her husband to leave her worth so much money at his death; or binding him to pay portions to her children by a previous husband. The sample forms in Thomas Phayer's *Newe Boke of Presidents* (1543) include the following forms of settlement to be made upon marriage:

> 'An indenture of maryage' contracted between the groom and the bride's mother, a widow, including the provision that the bride, herself also a widow, might marry her own daughter to whomever she pleased, with whatever portion she pleased, and might make a will of up to £100 disposing of the groom's goods;

and

> 'A condicion in a joynter, to give astate in certayne landes to the wyfe, where there is none other indenture made betwene the partyes', appointing a trustee to the wife's use for lands worth £40 p.a.[11]

This last sample clause must refer to separate estate. If it were jointure she would not need the trustees. A woman could not enter into a pre-marital contract with her intended husband directly, since her subsequent marriage annulled the contract, so trustees had to be interposed if she was to enjoy property during coverture.

William West's conveyancing manual *Symbolaeography* (1594) also included sixteen sample forms for various conditions in a settlement: to leave a wife worth £80 or £100, or certain goods; to allow a wife to make a will of £40 or £100; to convey to the wife a lease and goods in trust (that is, separate estate) in lieu of a jointure. For widows remarrying, there was 'A conveyance in trust . . . of a lease given unto her by her first husband, that her second husband should not sell it away, as commonly it happeneth'. (As a 'chattel real', a wife's lease could be sold without her consent, unlike real property.) Like Phayer, West also included a sample covenant reserving to a remarrying widow the right to marry her daughter to whomever she please and to set the daughter's portion without hindrance from the second husband.[12]

Nearly two centuries after these early conveyancers, *A Treatise of Feme*

Coverts or, The Lady's Law (1732) proclaimed that 'the fair sex are here inform'd, how to preserve their lands, goods, and most valuable effects, from the incroachments of anyone'.[13] Despite its bold advertisement, the sample settlements in *The Lady's Law* actually only offered the same choices as the earlier conveyancers:

A common marriage-settlement, or jointure of lands.

A settlement by fine and recovery of manors and lands, on the husband for life, remainder to the wife for her jointure, etc. and terms upon trust, for the separate use of the wife, to raise money to buy her cloaths, etc. and for raising portions for younger children.

A marriage settlement made by the wife of her own estate, so as to be entirely at her disposition after marriage; except a part for the husband, etc.

A settlement of a wife's real and personal estate to her own separate use, with a covenant from the husband to permit her to make a will thereof, as she shall think fit.

Marriage articles to place the wife's fortune out at interest, in nature of a settlement; and a covenant for the husband to lay out £1000 on a purchase, and settle the lands on his wife, etc.[14]

The sample settlements in *The Lady's Law* involve large sums of money: £400, £4000 and £12,000 portions; £1000 land purchase for jointure; £500 jointure; and £1500 p.a. separate estate. The portions in Gilbert Horsman's massive three-volume *Precedents in Conveyancing* (1744), at the upper end of the conveyancer market, are even higher, starting at £6000 and rising to £40,000. (The sample forms compiled by Horsman all date from ten to thirty years prior to publication.) More than one third of the total number of pages in *Precedents in Conveyancing* were taken up with marriage settlements, and every one of these settlements involved the wife's property rights. In addition, some also settled land in tail male.

These sample forms illustrate the interrelatedness of settlements, jointure and separate estate, although no one of these devices was necessary to any other. Each form contains many pages of dense legal terminology, and the increase in Chancery litigation over the early modern period is paralleled in the increasing complexity of sample marriage settlements. Settlement forms in Phayer's and West's conveyancers never exceeded nine pages, whereas those in Horsman's conveyancer sometimes extended to twenty-eight pages.

Conveyancing manuals were written for a fairly wealthy readership, but while some sample settlements referred to aristocratic parties to the agreement, many forms involved untitled people without so much as 'Mr' or 'Mrs' before their names. The conveyancers' marriage settlements in the wife's interest might, but usually did not, include strict settlements in tail male. Since settlements to protect the wife's interest in property were central to conveyancing manuals from 1543 to 1744, this type of settlement clearly both pre-dated and survived the late seventeenth-century development of the strict settlement in tail male.[15]

ORIGINS OF SEPARATE ESTATE

The sample settlements in conveyancing manuals do not usually use the term 'separate estate', yet that is their effect. The earliest date currently ascribed to separate estate is the 1580s and 1590s. This attribution is based on the fact that cases in the Court of Chancery involving arrangements which were effectively separate estate are reported from the late sixteenth century. However, legal case reports of *any* kind only began in the late sixteenth century, and what is newly recorded is not necessarily new.

Phayer's mid-sixteenth-century conveyancing manual shows that the practice of separate estate was certainly not new, although its name may have been. Another earlier reference is Sir Thomas Smith's *De Republica Anglorum*, written in the 1570s, which ended its chapter on the common law of 'Wives and marriages' with this specific clarification:

> This which I have written touching mariage and the right in moveables and unmoveables which commeth thereby, is to be understoode by the common law when no private contract is more particularly made.[16]

A private contract appears to refer to a marriage settlement, enforceable in equity rather than common law, and such contracts could not have been extraordinary in the 1570s.

The earliest reported cases in Chancery evince a distinctly matter-of-fact tone in their discussion of separate estate. There is no hint of novelty here. In the first case, from 1582, the report is brief and unrevealing: prior to her marriage, Mrs Kitchin arranged a trust whereby she might dispose of all her jewels and £500 worth of goods by will.[17] Five years later, 'a widow, before marriage, makes a conveyance to the use of herself to friends, because her husband shall not have the benefit'.[18] In 1595, 'a husband is not intitled to a term granted to another in trust for the use of his wife'.[19] The existence of separate estate itself was not at issue in these cases, but rather some dispute arising out of the arrangement, involving a trustee's or husband's misuse of the property.

The first explicit statement of a woman's right to a trust for her separate use was not made until 1673, in the case of Doyly v. Perfull: a woman might assign 'her term in trust for her self before marriage', and 'since Queen Elizabeth's time it hath been the constant course of this Court to set aside and frustrate all incumbrances and acts of the husband upon the trust in the wife's term'.[20] No earlier case had stated this rule outright, but it had clearly been assumed. The reporter in Doyly v. Perfull confirms the origins of separate estate in the reign of Queen Elizabeth, apparently relying on the late sixteenth-century case reports. However, another case reporter in the later eighteenth century claimed that a woman's right to make a pre-nuptial agreement enabling her to make a will during coverture, a form of separate estate, was only established in the mid-eighteenth century.[21] Neither reporter is to be trusted.

The earliest suggestion of separate estate that I know of is a case from 1479 which concerned a woman who 'conveyed lands to her own use and then married'. This case appears in the Year Books, the only earlier source comparable with the reports, but which recorded notes on cases, rather than decisions. After her marriage this woman made a will giving the lands to her husband, and the will was held to be invalid – but whether because it was made by a married woman, because she devised the lands to her husband rather than someone else (in which case the court tended to assume duress) or because her pre-marital conveyance had not included specific provision for disposition by will is not clear. The conveyance to her own use itself appears to have been upheld; it is the details of her actual control over it that are unclear.[22] The proposition that separate estate pre-dated the later sixteenth century might be determined by further research in the Year Books.

The most popular 'cause' of the growth of separate estate is the increasing importance of personal property (which women lost upon marriage, at common law) relative to real property (of which wives retained nominal ownership). But this shift from real to personal property may be ascribed to the fifteenth, the sixteenth, the seventeenth or the eighteenth century.[23] If trusts for separate estate pre-dated the 1580s, then there is no need for legal historians to find something distinctive in the circumstances of late sixteenth-century England to account for the sudden appearance of married women's property rights. Nor is there reason to be surprised at what Courtney Kenny called the 'remarkable rapidity' with which separate estate spread 'among the wealthier classes', or to fall back upon W. S. Holdsworth's lame explanation that common law restraints 'naturally appeared more and more unsatisfactory to the women of the wealthier classes and their relations'.[24]

Separate estate does not necessarily have to do with women's emancipation or independence, as such.[25] It may be a means of removing marital property from liability for the husband's debt. It may also allow a woman's natal family to secure its property descent through her to her children, as well as relieving them of financial responsibility for her in the event her marriage should collapse or her husband prove an 'unthrift'. The laws governing separate estate certainly did not improve women's economic position steadily or consistently. As Holdsworth delicately put it, Chancery decisions on the subject were 'not uniform'.[26]

EARLY MODERN ATTITUDES TOWARDS SEPARATE ESTATE

There is little evidence of popular attitudes towards separate estate in seventeenth-century literature. However, by the eighteenth century most writers viewed separate estate in an extremely negative light, on the grounds that it was 'unromantic'. The *Spectator* and the *Tatler*, Richard Steele's and William Addison's periodicals of the early eighteenth century, were vigorous opponents of pin-money. Romance forbade consideration of any economic aspects of marriage, including portions and jointures, but separate estate in particular was singled out as divisive and destructive of true love.[27]

The only hints of real women's attitudes towards separate estate come from gentry and aristocratic sources, and they are oblique. The shortcomings of the English marital property laws in general were dealt with in Mary More's essay 'The woman's right', which was circulated privately in the 1670s and caused sufficient stir to engender rebuttals. The impressive subtitle of 'The woman's right' was

> Or her power in a greater equality to her husband proved than is allowed or practised in England. From misunderstanding some scriptures, and false rendring others from the originall, plainly shewing an equality in man and woman before the fall, and not much difference after.[28]

In the essay More cautioned her teenage daughter that 'the laws of our country give a man after marriage a greater power of their estate than the wife, unless the wife take care before hand to prevent it (which I advise thee to doe)'.[29]

When Mary Astell proposed an institution for gentlewomen's education, also in 1694, one of her reasons for doing so was that 'here heiresses and persons of fortune may be kept secure from the rude attempts of designing men; and she who has more money than discretion, need not curse her stars for being expos'd a prey to bold, importunate and rapacious vultures'.[30] The strength of these women's language illustrates the depth of their concern over the economics of marriage, although they do not deal specifically with separate estate.

Women writers who compared the restrictions of English marital property law with the relative freedom in other European countries were probably proponents of whatever ameliorations the English system could offer, notably separate estate. Lady Mary Wortley Montagu remarked rather wistfully in 1716 on the freedom of Austrian women, who kept their property in their own possession and disposal, and the following year that Turkish women did the same and took all their property with them again upon divorce.[31] The anonymous author of *The Hardships of the English Laws in Relation to Wives* (1735) expounded on the virtues of Roman civil law and the custom of Portugal that a wife could dispose of half her husband's estate by will, even if she had brought him no portion.[32]

Men writers who observed the contrast between the severity of English marital property law and the more egalitarian continental systems did so only to remark on the singular difference between law and practice. Fynes Morison in 1617 noted that while German wives had large portions, the power to make wills and 'many like priviledges', their husbands, although 'provoked with these injuries', still kept their wives 'within termes of duty'.

May not we then justly marvel, that Englishmen having great power over their wives so as they can neither give anything in life, nor have power to make a will at death, nor call anything their owne, no not so much as their garters, yea, the law (I must confesse too severely) permitting the husband in some cases to beate his wife, and yet the husbands notwithstanding all their priviledges, using their wives with all respect, and giving them the cheefe seates with all honours and preheminences, so as for the most part, they would carry burthens, goe on foote, fast, and suffer any thing, so their wives might have ease, ride, feast, and suffer nothing, notwithstanding no people in the world . . . beare more scornes, indignities, and injuries, from the pampered sort of women.[33]

Edward Chamberlayne in 1669 admitted that a wife in England 'is *de jure* but the best of servants', but her

condition *de facto* is the best in the world; for such is the good nature of Englishmen towards their wives, such is their tenderness and respect, giving them the uppermost place at table and elsewhere . . . and putting them upon no drudgery and hardship.

Chamberlayne maintained that in fact England was the 'paradise of women'.[34] This insistence that English women were in practice treated with extraordinary kindness despite their legal disabilities is entirely absent from the writings of women.

The ubiquity of marriage settlements among the upper classes also belies any widespread belief in husbandly charity and tolerance. Four women can be seen in their own writings dealing directly with their own marriage settlements. For two of them – Dorothy Osborne in the 1650s and Mary Pierrepont in early years of the eighteenth century – the settlement establishing portion, jointure and separate estate was a matter of distaste in the eager, anxious days of courtship with William Temple and Edward Wortley, respectively. These women saw the pre-marital arrangements not as protection but as an obstacle imposed by their fathers between their own persons and the men they loved – not unrealistically since both fathers were opposed to the proposed matches. (In Mary Pierrepont's case, her father insisted that Wortley settle his estate, including Mary's portion, on a future eldest son, which Wortley refused to do – wisely, as his eldest son turned out indeed an 'unthrift'.)

The bridal irritation of Dorothy Osborne and Mary Pierrepont is in sharp contrast to the more mature reflections of Mrs Alice Thornton and Lady Anne Clifford. Alice Thornton is seen by posterity as a widow rather than a bride, and in that situation she had more reason to be grateful for her own separate estate, which had been established by her mother's will rather than by settlement at the time of Alice's marriage. When Mr Thornton died heavily indebted in 1668 Alice declined to administer his estate, in order to protect her own from liability. On the day the appraisers came to the house at East

Newton, in north Yorkshire, her brother-in-law Mr Denton (who, with his wife, lived with the Thorntons) told Alice

> That it was the law . . . the widow was to have her widdow-bed first out of all her husband's goods, . . . and commonly they chose the best . . ., and if I pleased I should have one.

By her own account, Alice handled the subsequent interview in a particularly feminine and highly effective manner:

> I thanked him for his advice, and telling me of it; I knew it was my right and due, as I was his sorrowful widdow; butt in regard there was soe many and great debts of my deare husband's, which could not be scarcely paid, I would deny myselfe of that right and priviledge, . . . wishing that his goods would pay all the debts; and by my deare mother's kindness to me she had given me beds enough for myselfe and family, or else I should be but in a sad condittion, but thanked him for his respect to me in that kinde offer. . . . Affter this passage, before the apprisement begun, my good brother Denton came to me in a freindly way, that perhaps I did not know as much, but he thought fitt to tell me of it, that he knew my mother had given me her personall estate and goods by her will and testament; but whatever was soe given to the wife will fall due to Mr Thornton my husband . . . for the property was in him and not in the wife, beeing under covert barr; and therefore all my ladie's [mother's] goods and personall estate would fall due to be praised amongst the rest of his goods. . . . Uppon which discourse I was much surprized to heare this sad newes; which it had bin all along harped after . . . but now the bottom was laid oppen, it beeing all along a decine to have had the property of her estate to have paid his debts, which was my blessed mother's intention to secure for myselfe and my children, which she foresaw would be left poore enough. Butt, after some pause, I gave him thanks for his kindness in acquainting me with the matter of law in this thing and perticuler, and withall tho' my mother had given her estate and goods to myselfe and children, as I see cause, yett, rather than just debts should not be paid, I would quitt my right in them. . . . 'Butt, Sir, I must now lett you know the reason why my deare mother did settle her estate personall in the manner she has don; to prevent what she otherwise see might come to passe; as 'tis, God knowes, come to passe too true.' . . . she had, by advice of an able lawyer, made a deed of guift to feefees in trust [trustees] of all her estate personall [amounting to £1000] . . . for to secure it to myselfe during life, and at my death to such child or children as I should see best deserving. . . . [Brother Denton] having read [my deare mother's writtings and deeds], was much surprized, and said that he had never seene them before; but I thought I had shewed them to him . . . then he said, that my ladye's goods could not be touched, and that he had never seen anything better don in his life, and that the property was not in Mr Thornton, nor could they be made liable to Mr Thornton's debts or disposall.[35]

Alice's mother, Alice Wandesford, had taken care to mark with her name most of her goods – which comprised *all* of the goods in the Thornton household – 'who like a wise and prudent parent did thus to prevent any disturbance might fall out afterwards'.[36]

Much of Alice's autobiography is taken up with the financial dealings of her widowed mother. These included attempting to recover her jointure in Ireland and England, relieving her son (the heir) while his estate was sequestered by parliament, bringing up Alice and negotiating her marriage. When the time came in 1672 for Alice's own daughter, also Alice, to marry, her suitor agreed 'that whatever her fortune was, it should be wholey for her use and her's' – that is, at young Alice's disposal. The autobiography does not mention at whose behest this condition was made, but undoubtedly Alice Thornton had learned well at her mother's knee.

Lady Anne Clifford wrote of her marriage settlement without the remove of widowhood, but from the battlefield of her marriage. Her extended campaign on two fronts – with her male cousins for the lands in Westmorland given her in her father's will, and with her husband, the Earl of Dorset, for her jointure – was the most celebrated marital property dispute of the seventeenth century. Her cousins claimed the land was settled in tail male and so could not descend to her as her father's only child. Her husband wanted her to come to a cash settlement over the matter, since he needed the money (which, unlike the land, would immediately have been his) to pay his gambling debts. Her opponents connived among themselves. Dorset drew in the king and the archbishop of Canterbury, among others, to cajole or threaten Anne into giving up title to her lands in Westmorland. On her own side, her mother was her sole constant ally, although she hints of further support for her cause, especially among women. A certain Lady Selby in 1616 reported to Anne that she 'heard some folks say that I have done well in not consenting', and the following year, 'The Queen gave me warning not to trust my matters absolutely to the King lest he should deceive me.'[37] Anne's distress throughout the fifteen years of her marriage to Dorset, torn between her inheritance and her duty and desire toward her husband, is heartrending.

> Sometimes I had fair words from him and sometimes foul, but I took all patiently, and did strive to give him as much content and assurance of my love as I could possibly, yet I told him that I would never part with Westmorland upon any condition whatever.

> This night my lord should have lain with me, but he and I fell out about matters,

and shortly after another episode in the ongoing argument,

> my eyes were so blubbered with weeping that I could scarce look up.[38]

The strength of Anne's defiance was matched, perhaps oddly to twentieth-century eyes, by the depth of her wifely devotion. In February 1619, after having been at different times hounded, threatened, deprived of her daughter and banished from her marital home (Knole, in Kent), all at the instigation of her husband, she could still write,

> My lord should have gone to London the 24th of this month, but I entreated him to stay here the 25th, because on that day ten years I was married, which I kept as a day of jubilee to me, so my lord went not til the 27th.[39]

In 1643, after thirty-eight years and a second marriage, Lady Anne came peaceably into possession of her lands in accordance with her father's will, at the death of her male cousin. She enjoyed them for another thirty-three years, dying at the age of 86, survived by two daughters (none of her three sons lived), seventeen grandchildren and nineteen greatgrandchildren.[40] While her property disputes had been spectacular, they were hardly unique. Her own mother and father had separated, requiring a property settlement, in 1603 when Anne was 13. In the middle of Anne's marriage with Dorset, his sister separated from her husband and, to compound Dorset's troubles, his own mother sued him for her 'thirds' out of his inheritance.[41]

Divorce as we know it (that is, with the possibility of remarriage) was extremely rare in seventeenth-century England, because it was only available at great expense by Act of Parliament. The only grounds were non-consummation, affinity, adultery by the wife or adultery plus systematic brutality by the husband. Divorce by mutual consent was mooted in Thomas More's *Utopia* (1516) and John Milton's *On the State of a Divorceless Society* (1644), but both met with failure except for the brief period of the Commonwealth. Short of parliamentary intervention, divorce without the possibility of remarriage was available in the ecclesiastical courts until 1857.

Marital separation, however, was not at all uncommon. Anne Clifford's mother and sister-in-law are by no means isolated cases; her diary mentions other husbands and wives being 'discontented' with each other and living separately. At a social level where a separate house was available for each spouse, the arrangements could be relatively amicable. When Margaret Verney and her husband, a Northamptonshire gentleman, were separated in the 1650s, Margaret received £160 p.a. as a separate maintenance. (By contrast, the jointure agreed in her marriage settlement had been £500 p.a.)[42]

In the event of an unamicable separation a wife could sue for separate maintenance or alimony in either the ecclesiastical courts or in equity. Some of the earliest reported cases of separate estate in Chancery involved estranged couples.[43] Although the word 'alimony' is attributed to the mid-seventeenth century, it may well be older. *The Ladies' Dictionary* (1694) was airily familiar with the term, as that 'portion or allowance, which a married woman sues for, upon any occasional separation from her husband, wherein she is not charged with elopement or adultery'. *The Lady's Law* (1732) repeats this definition almost word for word.[44] In the later middle ages the bride's portion, both land and moveables, may have been returned to her upon marital separation.[45] This system prevailed in continental Europe through the early modern period, but in England the bride's portion was not returned to her upon separation from at least the sixteenth century. Instead, she could ask to receive an allowance, or alimony. Clearly a high-risk option, especially by the later seventeenth century when the ecclesiastical courts were weakened and the Court of Chancery massively inefficient, court-decreed alimony might be avoided by the establishment of separate estate in a marriage settlement, to try to assure the wife's maintenance in the event of marital separation.

A husband's alternative to alimony, of course, was desertion. Daniel Defoe's fictional Roxana learned only after her husband's desertion had left her penniless that 'the very nature of the marriage-contract was, in short, nothing but giving up liberty, estate, authority, and every-thing, to the man'.[46] Most early modern wives would hardly have formulated such a bitterly incisive gloss on the nature of the marriage contract. But a surprising number of them did take action to avoid 'giving up liberty, estate, authority, and every-thing, to the man', by making a marriage settlement.

The marriage settlements of early modern England were far more complex and varied than simple strict settlement or the equitable trust for separate estate. The origins of marriage settlements are unclear, but they certainly pre-date the late sixteenth century. While the literary opinion of any variety of married women's property, notably separate estate, was negative and dismissive, particularly from about 1700, individual upper-class women's diaries express powerful gratitude for their separate property and considerable tenacity in preserving it.

While personal comments on marital property disputes are rare, mention of marital property settlements which did not come into serious disagreement is even rarer. Harmony is not something that people feel it necessary to record in writing. The common type of marriage settlement protecting women's property usually appears in the historical record only in passing, in the context of some other, more immediately pressing, issue. For example, when the gentleman Tom Verney, settling in Barbados in 1638, wrote to his mother to ask for 'household stuff, plate, spoones, and the like, then pewter and brass of all sorts, and linnen of all sorts, both for mee and my servants', he did not ask his father 'becaus this does not belong to him'.[47]

In addition to these occasional offhand remarks, common attitudes towards marriage settlements become clearer by looking at who made marriage settlements, and what provisions those settlements normally involved. This is done first in sources arising from disputes – the case records of litigation in the Court of Chancery – and then in non-contentious sources – probate accounts and wills made by married women.

7 Marriage settlements in the Court of Chancery

WOMEN IN THE COURT OF CHANCERY

There has until now been no study of marriage settlements in the Court of Chancery, and very few studies of anything in Chancery. The records are extremely difficult to work with. Initial bills of complaint and the defendants' answers are filed separately from depositions, and both are separate from decrees, so it is inordinately time-consuming to locate successive documents dealing with the same case. The indexing of each type of document is different, but in general alphabetization is limited to the first letter of the last name, and since the indices are contemporary, entries are often arranged first by the three legal terms of the year, making it necessary to know when a particular document was likely to be filed. Each of the six divisions of Chancery – cases were assigned randomly to one or another division – are indexed separately. Few of the indices to bills of complaint make any reference to the subject under dispute. The indices to five divisions are handwritten, and the listing practices vary over time and in different divisions: in Elizabeth's reign, for example, a married man was often specified as suing 'in the right of his wife', which indicates that the subject matter was land which was hers before marriage, but this form of words was abandoned in the seventeenth century. The index to one division, the Bridges Division, in the period 1613–1714, is printed and gives an indication of the cause of the suit. In this division it is possible to locate marriage settlement cases.

Before looking specifically at marriage settlement cases, it will be helpful to assess how often women appeared at all in Chancery, whether they did so when married or unmarried, and with whom they joined in suits. Despite the corruption and dilatoriness of Chancery, the proportion of women litigants before the court increased over the period 1558–1714 (Table 7.1). In the second half of the sixteenth century women were involved in initiating suits in 17 per cent of all cases, and this proportion rose to 26 per cent in the seventeenth and early eighteenth centuries. Table 7.2 assesses more than 1000 women plaintiffs in Chancery in the period 1558–1714, by their marital status and by their co-plaintiffs. Approximately half of all women plaintiffs sued in conjunction with their husbands. The other half – whether single,

Table 7.1 Sex of plaintiffs in the Court of Chancery 1558–1714

Plaintiff	1558–1603		1613–1714	
	%	n	%	n
One or more men	80	1953	69	1663
Women	17	411	26	621
Indeterminate/corporate	3	82	5	116
Total	100	2446	100	2400

Note: 'Indeterminate' are names whose gender, without further evidence, is unclear (including Bennett, Clement and Francis/Frances); 'corporate' are towns, colleges and manorial tenants.

Table 7.2 Marital status and co-plaintiffs of women in the Court of Chancery 1558–1714

Plaintiff	1558–1603		1613–1714	
	%	n	%	n
Wife with husband	57	233	44	271
One or more widows	11	44	33	203
One or more women, status unspecified	23	96	15	96
Women and men, relation unspecified	9	37	8	51
Wife alone	–	1	–	–
All women	100	411	100	621

wives or widows – sued alone or with other people, usually with other women. Less than 10 per cent of all women sued in conjunction with a man who was not their husband. Only one woman sued as a wife on her own.

At common law, a married woman had to sue jointly with her husband, and it was clearly prudent to do so in Chancery too, although it was not mandatory. Between one quarter and one third of all women plaintiffs did not specify their marital status, and it is possible that these included some married women, although it seems more likely that they were single and widowed. The threefold increase in widows appearing before the court, from 11 per cent to 33 per cent, is particularly striking. In all likelihood, this rise represents not so much an increasing litigiousness among women as their absorption from other courts. In the common law courts of King's Bench and Common Pleas, which were procedurally more complex and charged higher fees than Chancery, it appears from a small sample that the proportion of widows dropped by half (from 6 per cent to 3 per cent of all litigants) between 1560 and 1640.[1] Cases which might have been heard in the Courts of Requests and Exchequer before their abolition in the mid-seventeenth century – and women were prominent among the litigants in these courts – probably found their way into Chancery after that date. Curtailment of ecclesiastical jurisdiction over wills and trusts in the sixteenth century may also have channelled female litigants into the fast-developing equity courts. The increase in female plaintiffs in Chancery between the mid-sixteenth and the early eighteenth centuries from 17 per cent to 26 per cent, and the tripling of the proportion of widows among women, is not necessarily an indication of increasing access to the court for women.[2]

While the number of women plaintiffs illustrates the extent of women's involvement with matters of property and business, the women themselves were not necessarily pleased to be exercising their right to appear before the court; probably most would rather not have been there. Some female defendants in the Court of Requests and in the palatinate court of Chester used the common law of coverture in their defence, to plead that at the time the offence occurred they were 'covert baron' and therefore could not be sued. At the same time, male defendants claimed that a female plaintiff was married and therefore could not sue them.[3]

MARRIAGE SETTLEMENT CASES

The frequency of marriage settlement litigation in the period 1613–1714 can be estimated from some 2400 cases entered under 'A' in the Bridges Division. Approximately 2 per cent of all these bills of complaint pertained to marriage settlements. More precisely, 2 per cent identified the subject in dispute as such. It is possible that cases whose subjects were listed as 'money', 'land', 'performance of a trust', 'personal matters', 'relief upon contract' and so on sometimes dealt with a marriage settlement, but this cannot be determined without reference to every original document. The Bridges Division index lists 61,020 cases. If 2 per cent of these involved marriage settlements, that makes 1220 cases in one division. There were six divisions of Chancery, so there are probably more than 7000 surviving bills of complaint from the plaintiff and/ or answers from the defendant which are specifically about a marriage settlement in the seventeenth century. Only about one third of these 7000 cases would have got any further than the initial bill of complaint, and even fewer would have eventually culminated in a judgement or decree.[4]

However, owing again to indexing chaos it was not possible to match bills and answers with the relevant decrees, so this assessment of marriage settlements concentrates on the initial pleadings. Detailed analysis of seventy bills and answers whose specified subject was a marriage settlement (the fruit of searching through roughly 5000 index entries) is taken to be representative, since all analysis on this size of sample produced exactly the same results as from a preliminary sample of thirty cases.

It is possible that the ecclesiastical courts may also have dealt with trusts and marriage settlements. The ecclesiastical lawyer Henry Consett in the late seventeenth century explained the subtleties of jurisdiction: if a 'father promises to pay a sum of money to a man on marriage with his daughter' then the case may be brought to the ecclesiastical court, but 'if he specifies the day, or some days after marriage' then the case must go to common law.[5] Studies of church courts up to 1640, however, have found few or no property suits among cases of marital litigation.[6] It is more likely that marital property cases were taken to the equity sides of the Courts of Exchequer and Requests (until 1642) in London, and to the equity courts in the palatine counties of Chester, Durham and Lancaster.

Analysis of the Court of Requests (whose filing chaos exceeds even that of Chancery) is currently under way.[7] Unpublished work on the palatinate court of Durham shows that a case in equity there cost only between one tenth and one fifth what a case in the Court of Chancery at Westminster would cost, and a slightly higher proportion of cases involving marriage settlements occurred at Durham than came before the Court of Chancery. In two sample five-year periods, between 3 and 4 per cent of all equity cases in Durham involved a marriage agreement (amounting to thirty-six cases in the space of ten years), and these cases formed an even higher proportion, 4–5 per cent, of all those which ultimately reached a determination.[8] Unfortunately, the equity courts in the three palatine counties are even more difficult to research than Chancery, since no subject indices at all exist.[9]

While cases came to the Court of Chancery from the country, they came from relatively wealthy litigants, and the bulk of them originated in what would become the 'home counties'. The initial costs of suing in Chancery were not especially high. According to *The Country-Man's Counsellor*, the total cost of an injunction to stop proceedings at common law, for example, was not out of the reach of most yeomen or even husbandmen, at only £1 1s. 6d.[10] But initial costs multiplied quickly with commissions to take evidence in the country,[11] complications in the pleadings, extended delays and bribes.

The social standing of the litigants in marriage settlement suits is illustrated in Table 7.3. More than half of these seventy cases involved members of the gentry or higher ranks, and nearly half involved well-to-do yeomen, tradesmen and husbandmen. All but two cases identified at least one party's social status, a much higher rate of identification than that found in probate records. The number of gentlemen and farmers involved in marriage settlement suits dropped over the course of the seventeenth century, but their place was more than filled by the dramatic increase in wealthier tradesmen. Chancery litigants throughout the early modern period may well have been the same people for whom the conveyancers and handbooks on the law relating to women were written.

Most marriage settlement cases in the Court of Chancery were extremely complex, both as to the parties' relation to one another and as to the terms of the settlement itself. The passage of time – and the settlement in question had sometimes been made decades prior to the suit – exacerbated the tangle of issues and interests. The parties to the suit were never as simple as Wife *v.* Husband. The case of John and Ann Bennet *v.* Robert and Elizabeth Saunders, from London in 1683, illustrates the intricacy of litigant relationships: the pair for whom the marriage settlement in question was made were Thomas and Elizabeth; they had one child and then Thomas died; Thomas's father had

Table 7.3 Social status of marriage settlement litigants in the Court of Chancery 1603–1712

| | 1603–1624 | | 1647–1712 | |
	%	n	%	n
Gentry	*44*	*31*	*36*	*25*
Knight		3		1
Esquire		10		8
Gentleman		18		16
Professions	*4*	*3*	*3*	*2*
Clerk		3		1
Physician		–		1
Agricultural	*23*	*16*	*16*	*11*
Yeoman		12		10
Husbandman		4		1
Trades	*3*	*2*	*16*	*11*
Butcher		–		1
Chandler		–		1
Draper		–		1
Joiner		1		–
Maltman		–		2
Merchant		–		4
Shipwright		–		1
Tailor		–		1
Tanner		1		–
Unidentified	*26*	*18*	*30*	*21*
Total	100	70	101	70

Note: Total percentages do not sum to exactly 100 because of rounding to the nearest whole number, in this and all subsequent tables.

given money to Elizabeth's father to buy lands to settle in jointure on Elizabeth, but her own father died without making the purchase, leaving his son, Elizabeth's brother, executor; this son had also since died, leaving his wife Ann executrix; Elizabeth and Ann, then, were sisters-in-law, they had both since remarried, and it was these two now-unrelated couples who were party to the suit.[12] In other marriage settlement cases sisters sued brothers, or husbands alone and couples together sued either her or his parents or their parents' heirs or executors.

Lacking the decision in any given case, it is difficult to determine from the bills and answers which side is telling the truth, or at least more truth than the other side. Like all litigation, the viciousness displayed is depressing, the more so here because the animosity is marital or familial, rather than just neighbourly. A yeoman of Devon, for example, filed a tremendously long and involved bill of complaint in 1670 alleging that his stepdaughters and their husbands had not only destroyed part of the marriage settlement between himself and their mother Susan, but had also instigated Susan to convey away from him goods which, by the standards of most Chancery cases, were a very small matter indeed: a mere £20 worth of 'corn, grain, milk, butter, cheese, wool, apples, roots, and other garden fruits'. He covered the meat of his complaint in a small space, then degenerated into a lengthy and sordid description of the defendants' threats to cut off his ears, and other information which might sway the Court in his favour.[13]

PORTIONS AND JOINTURES

Paring away the layers of litigational complexities, the principal issues in Chancery marriage settlement cases were either the payment of portion to the groom or the settling of jointure on the bride. The ratio of portion to jointure, set out in a marriage settlement, was clearly important to the economy of married women in a system of coverture. This ratio has been studied and calculated at the level of the aristocracy, whose marriage settlements survive among family papers. At this social level the average portion:jointure ratio was approximately £5 of portion to £1 of jointure in the early seventeenth century, declining to 10:1 by 1700.[14] This means that in 1700 the jointure a woman enjoyed as a widow was only 10 per cent of what she had brought to her marriage in portion, whereas her jointure had amounted to 20 per cent of her portion a century earlier. The sample settlement forms in Gilbert Horsman's *Precedents in Conveyancing* (1744) confirm a ratio of 10:1. Not all marriage settlements followed these proportions. For example, in one Star Chamber case in the reign of James I, a portion of £200 was matched by a jointure of £50 p.a., a ratio of 4:1.[15] But in general, most settlements tended to follow the average.

The halving of the average portion:jointure ratio among the aristocracy over the seventeenth century appears on the face of it to be to women's disadvantage, and it has been interpreted that way.[16] But it is necessary to look at the ratios which prevailed at the somewhat lower level of society which took their marriage settlements to the Court of Chancery before accepting simple explanations.

First, a qualification about annuities must be made in any discussion of portion:jointure ratios. The portion specified in a marriage settlement was an actual figure, while the jointure was only notional. Aristocratic jointures usually took the form of annuities, so the actual value of the jointure depended entirely upon how long a woman survived her husband, if she survived him at all. The portion:jointure ratio is better expressed in human terms as the number of years a woman had to survive as a widow in order to get full value out of the portion paid to her husband at marriage. In Lloyd Bonfield's study of late sixteenth- and early seventeenth-century marriage settlements, peers' widows survived their husbands by a mean of almost twelve years in Northamptonshire, and of over sixteen years in Kent.[17] Even at a portion:jointure ratio of 10:1 then, these women, especially the Kentish ones, reaped more in their jointures than they sowed in their portions. (These calculations cannot, of course, take account of inflation over the course of an individual marriage, in proportion to which a widow's jointure would have been of marginally less value than a bride's portion.)

Peers' widows may have survived their husbands longer than ordinary widows, since brides were younger and the age difference between spouses greater among the aristocracy than among the population as a whole. Between the late sixteenth and the early eighteenth century the median age at first marriage for wealthy brides was 19–23 and for grooms 24–9, whereas for the whole population the median age at first marriage was 26–7 for women and 28 for men.[18] On the other hand, an aristocratic woman's earlier marriage put her at greater risk of death in more frequent childbirth.

Even where a wife survived to receive her jointure in the form of an annuity, her enjoyment of it may have been jeopardized by her remarriage. In the later middle ages, jointure was commonly enjoyed for life; this was comfirmed by a mid-sixteenth-century statute, and it was still the arrangement in, for example, the marriages of the upper gentry Verney family in the middle of the seventeenth century.[19] Not only the bride, but also her natal family, had a strong interest in making jointure a lifetime rather than a widowhood right, since it was the direct result of her own marriage portion and since jointure from the first marriage would have to become portion for the second. But the jointures of early modern peers' daughters appear to have been usually limited to widowhood. Horsman's *Precedents in Conveyancing* has early eighteenth-century examples of both jointure for life and jointure for widowhood, but a limitation to widowhood is more common.[20] It would appear that the falling portion:jointure ratio at the highest levels was accompanied by increasing pressure to limit the duration of jointure.

Another factor in the falling portion:jointure ratio was a rising level of portions. Contemporary complaints about aristocratic portion inflation were omnipresent throughout Europe. In England, for example, Sir Edward Coke waxed nostalgic over the reign of Edward I, when 'it appeareth, that small portions preferred in mariage the daughters of good families, when vertue and good blood was more esteemed than great portions'.[21] Elsewhere in Europe the inflation of portions in later medieval and early modern centuries prompted the imposition of legal maximum levels, but proposals for a portion limit consistently failed in England.[22] But while there was a great deal of concern among the upper classes about rising portions, the actual increase relative to prices is problematic.

Among the marriage settlements of the English peerage – which numbered fifty-five families in the late sixteenth century and 160 families in the late seventeenth century – average portions multiplied four to five times over that period, substantially more than the increase of most contemporary prices.[23] However, the same was not true of litigants in Chancery over the same period, who were predominantly gentry, wealthy yeomen and merchants. The median portion in the settlements at issue in Chancery (where it was specified) multiplied less than three times, from £200 in the late sixteenth and first half of the seventeenth centuries to £500–£600 in the second half of the seventeenth century.[24] An increase of 300 per cent is just within the calculations of inflation generally over that time, although like the aristocracy the social levels represented here would also have had access to easier borrowing methods and have felt pressure to dower their daughters as a reflection of their social status.

Moreover, the portion:jointure ratio did not fall as dramatically at this level as it did in aristocratic marriages. Among the gentry litigants in Chancery, the median length of time that a woman had to survive her husband in order to recoup her portion in her jointure rose from five to only seven and a half years over the century. This drop in value over time of 50 per cent was only half as drastic as that at the higher aristocratic levels.[25] It should be noted that settlements litigated in Chancery were not in court because of an unusual portion:jointure ratio. In seventy Chancery bills and answers, there is not one allegation of disproportion, only disagreements over the exact terms of the original agreement. Nevertheless, Chancery records are qualitatively different from collections of family papers, and anyone wishing to be absolutely sure of the differences in portion:jointure ratios at these two social levels will have to study both the gentry and wealthy merchants, on the one hand, and the aristocracy, on the other hand, in either one source or the other.

The cause of the fall in the value of peers' daughters' jointures relative to their portions is complex. A thorough discussion of the relative contribution of falling interest rates and the increasing ease of mortgaging, which facilitated large amounts of borrowing in order to satisfy the small and shrinking groom market, is available from Brian Outhwaite.[26] This explanation fits the case of the aristocracy, and possibly Chancery litigants, but is less satisfying at lower social levels which would have been less able to borrow cash. If the rate of portion inflation among the peerage affected any substantial part of the population, one would expect a fall in the marriage rate, as more and more people could not afford to marry. This decline in marriage did occur at upper social levels. English aristocratic parents preferred to keep their daughters unmarried rather than overextend themselves financially. They thereby produced an extraordinarily high number of upper-class women who never married, a group whose economic circumstances and whose thoughts about their situation ought to be investigated. But in the population as a whole the rate of marriage rose over the period at issue.

Both the rise of portions and the fall in the ratio of portion to jointure, at differential rates, can be partly explained by the use to which portion money was put at different social levels. Among the wealthiest, cash portions were almost invariably used to purchase freehold land which then raised an income for the purpose of, first, sustaining the new marriage and, second, providing an annuity for the bride's jointure. This is the most common type of arrangement in conveyancing handbooks. However, freehold prices rose consistently faster than other commodities, as agricultural prices and rents fell, producing a lower relative income from land.[27] The slower rise in portions among the gentry, wealthy yeomen and merchants in Chancery may reflect the fact that some, but not all, of the portions at this social level were used to buy land to produce an annuity. The larger rise in portions at aristocratic levels than among Chancery litigants is also consistent with the growing economic gap between large landlords and the gentry as a whole over the seventeenth century.[28]

Other cultures besides early modern England, of course, have experienced inflation of marriage portions. In some, like medieval Dubrovnik and sixteenth-century Paris, upper-class portions only kept pace with other prices and with increasing wealth.[29] Two cases are comparable with that of the early modern English aristocracy in so far as the rise of marriage portions far outstripped other rates of inflation: fifteenth-century Florence, at least among the upper classes, and India in the second half of the twentieth century. In both Florence and India, as in early modern England, portion inflation appears to have largely resulted partly from economic developments which facilitated easier borrowing and mortgaging, but also partly from the social importance of dowry as a status symbol.[30] The significance of early modern bridal portions as symbols of social status has not been directly addressed in previous studies, but that must surely be one reason why truly massive inflation was limited to the highest echelons.

Even at the level of Chancery litigants, still a tiny minority of the population at large, a continuing relationship between portions and jointures, rather than rampant inflation, can be identified in those occasional jointure arrangements in Chancery suits which involved a lump sum rather than an annuity. In all eleven of these cases, between 1613 and 1706, the amount of the cash jointure was approximately equivalent to the value of the portion.[31] It would appear that despite the dramatic fivefold rise in aristocratic portions and the more moderate threefold rise in gentry portions, brides in the latter half of the period were not necessarily disadvantaged in their jointures in comparison with their mothers and grandmothers, nor were grooms better off. (The interchangeability of the words 'dowry' and 'dower' is apt.) The expectation that a woman took out of marriage what she took into it seems remarkably consistent over time. However, the question of the intervening years remains.

SEPARATE ESTATE

As well as portions and jointures, separate estate was also, though less frequently, at issue in Chancery marriage settlements. References to pin-money and paraphernalia, which appear regularly in conveyancing manuals, do not occur in these Chancery cases. Most of the settlements which appear in Chancery had been negotiated between a parent or relative of the bride, on the one side, and the groom together with his father on the other side, in the same way that aristocratic marriages were negotiated. Settlements of this type only once incorporated separate estate for the bride, and that one settlement was conspicuous for having been made by the bride's widowed mother acting alone. In the negotiations for the marriage of Dorothy Whittington to a Somerset gentleman in 1601, her mother Phillipp (not an uncommon female name at this time) insisted on a certain amount, unspecified in the pleading, which was to be 'speciallie putt in truste' for Dorothy by the groom's father and mother.[32]

Separate estate was more common in settlements which had been negotiated by the bride on her own behalf, usually on the occasion of her second marriage. A second-time bride was older, perhaps wealthier, and wiser at least in the ways of legal coverture than she had been the first time round. The reason these separate estates appeared in Chancery was not ordinarily trouble with the husband who signed the agreement. Although there is no such thing as a typical Chancery case, in suits over separate estate, as in suits over portions and jointures, it was usually men who sued men. The following case may serve as an example. Around 1600 the widow Janevive Deane, prior to her second marriage to the Wiltshire esquire Charles Pressye, placed a great stock of money in trust with her son-in-law. When Pressye came to live in Janevive's London house she imprinted her own goods with a mark, 'that soe shee might still keep hir owne stock and goodes whole, in apparancie to the worlde'. Pressye avowedly had no objections to either the trust or the marking of the goods until after Janevive's death, when he sued her executor-grandson over the details of the agreement.[33]

In a few suits over separate estate, duplicity on the wife's part was alleged. The gentleman Stuckley Lewis of Anglesey claimed he knew nothing of his wife's pre-marital arrangements in 1603 at the time of his marriage. Twenty-one years later he complained to the Court that his wife Alice, a widow at the time he married her, 'was perswaded the same night before her intermaridge with your orator to make some secrett deede of guifte, bills, bonds or obligacions to . . . her daughters . . . to defraude and defeate your orator of all the personall estate'. Alice's side of the story we shall never know, as she was dead by the time Lewis sued her daughter.[34]

A subtler reason for separate estate than mere fraud was attributed – also by her husband, also after her death – to Thomasine Skinner of London. Unlike most women, Thomasine made her own settlement on the occasion of her first marriage in 1654. Perhaps specifically because she was marrying her brother's apprentice, Thomasine wanted £200 of her £700 portion secured so that in case she died leaving no children she might dispose of the £200 as she thought fit at her death. According to her husband, who subsequently became a merchant, Thomasine was 'intending thereby to have some hand on your orator that he might be the more loveing and respectfull to her and that shee might still thereby keep some moneys in her own power'. This the groom judged 'very unreasonable', at least in retrospect. But he consented, and a bond was drawn up with Thomasine's unmarried sister Mary, in trust. The bond initially had no clause about childlessness, so the groom interlined the provision that the £200 was to be considered separate estate only in the absence of children. Legal conflict over the arrangement did not arise until eighteen years after the marriage, and seven years after Thomasine's death leaving one daughter, when the now-married Mary put the bond into suit at common law, demanding payment and claiming that the interlined words were illegal.[35]

Litigation records, while they are abundant and in some respects conveniently quantifiable, cannot indicate how often people established separate estates. Their frequency can only be estimated where public registration of marriage settlements was required, as in some of the American colonies from the eighteenth century and especially after 1800. With some regional variation, the creation of any kind of marriage settlement in America was infrequent. The north relied most heavily on the common law: in Pennsylvania separate estate was rare; in Connecticut it was illegal. Even in the south, which adopted more of the English system of equity, less than 2 per cent of all marriages in the period 1730–1830 registered a settlement in South Carolina and Virginia.[36]

However, a separate estate could be established by deed of gift or by will during the course of the marriage, as well as by pre-marital settlement. And in Petersburg, Virginia, in the late eighteenth and early nineteenth centuries only one fifth of all separate estates were established by marriage settlement.[37] Comparable in-depth studies of all documents relating to a single English community might also show that separate estates were established less often in marriage settlements than in deeds and wills. The bequest of Alice Wandesford to her daughter Alice Thornton, noted in Chapter 6, is one example of a separate estate established by will. Another well-to-do recipient of a separate estate by bequest was Sarah Fielding, mother of the novelists Henry and Sarah. In the early eighteenth century she received £3000 from her father, a Justice of the King's Bench, for 'the purchase either of a church or colledge lease, or of lands of inheritance'. This money was to be for her sole use, her husband permitted 'nothing to doe with it'.[38] The language used to establish a separate estate may suggest to later readers some animosity between father and son-in-law – this is the interpretation made by Henry Fielding's biographer, for example – but such was not necessarily the case, since the vigorous phrasing was legally required to achieve the desired effect of a daughter's security.

MARITAL SEPARATION

That security was desired more to indemnify a woman's natal family against her maintenance in the event that her marriage broke down than to enable her financial independence. A married woman had difficulty forcing her husband to support her financially during marriage. If she was still cohabiting with her husband she had no recourse if she and her children were ill-provided for. A wife could not desert her husband because she then not only forfeited any right to alimony, but she could not pledge her husband's name to obtain credit for necessaries. As Courtney Kenny quipped in the late nineteenth century, a woman lost her money by marrying her husband, and her credit by leaving him.[39]

Nor could a wife secretly provide for herself while living with her husband. In a formative Chancery case in about the year 1639 (still before cases were regularly reported), a woman with 'an unprovident husband had, unknown to him, by her frugality raised some monies for the good of their children, . . . being otherwise unprovided for'. Her action was initially upheld, but upon review the decision was reversed, 'as being dangerous to give a feme power to dispose of her husband's estate'.[40] The Court thereafter refused to sanction any action by the wife not made on the basis of a pre-marital agreement or trust.

The case history of separate maintenance in equity, like that of separate estate, is fickle. But even the existence of a trust was no guarantee of financial security for a woman abandoned by her husband. The Lancashire merchant William Stout in his autobiography tells the story of a young woman in the first years of the eighteenth century who had a £100 portion held in trust by Stout. She married a man who wasted her fortune, thinking it was his by right of marriage. When he found out about the trusteeship, he was ruined by his creditors and fled the country. With £30 from Stout, the destitute mother of five undertook to make candles and soap in order to maintain her family. She was successful in this business, but four years later her husband returned, took her trade and wasted it, and then left her again. She turned to keeping an alehouse and made a success of that as well, but he returned again, lived off her industry, and abused her and her friends for several years until he died. Finally, in her old age, the original £100 estate was sold by the Stout and the other trustees for her support.[41] It was grotesque cases similar to this one which were publicized in order to sway public opinion in favour of reforming the married women's property law in the mid-nineteenth century.

A few marital separations found their way into Chancery. Mrs Anne Bodvell had obtained a parliamentary decree of £500 p.a. alimony and custody of her two daughters after her father, Sir William Russell of Cambridgeshire, sued on her behalf. She claimed that her husband, John Bodvell, esquire, had frequented lewd women from whom he had got the pox, which he in turn gave to Anne two years after their marriage in 1638. After a cure she returned to him, was infected with another venereal disease five years later, and at the time of the suit (nine years after the first infection) she was in France for costly but unsuccessful cures. John Bodvell was now suing Anne's father, challenging that the amount of alimony was excessive and that he had a lawful right to the custody of his children, to which end he had his own mother lock up his two daughters and deny Anne access. The advantage of a parliamentary decree was that parliament could, and in this case did, order sequestration of the husband's lands for non-payment of alimony.[42] Whether the action was successful here is not known, but as Anne Clifford, whose husband employed some of the same tactics as John Bodvell, eventually came into a peaceful and prosperous widowhood, it is to be hoped the same good fortune came to Anne Bodvell.

A very few maintenance agreements at the level of yeomen are tossed up on the waves of Chancery records. Inevitably, in this source, they are the agreements which ended in discord. John and Ann Layfield, a Westmorland yeoman and his wife, 'some variaunce and discontent' growing between them, separated in 1607. According to him, she was 'unwilling and refused to cohabite', and 'went her waie from him, as at divers times before she had done'. As a result, 'ther fell to some speeches of agreement' between John and his brother, on the one side, and Ann's two grown sons, on the other, by which John was bound to pay Ann £4 p.a. maintenance during his lifetime. (Note the discrepancy in annual maintenance between a woman of the upper gentry/lower aristocracy and a yeoman's wife: Ann Layfield's alimony was less than 1 per cent of Anne Bodvell's.) Some six months after this agreement, again according to John, the couple were reconciled and Ann 'contented and pleased to come home . . . and to take uppon her the charge of keepinge thereof'. But she subsequently 'did ymbezall and put out divers of [John's] goods, chattles and howshold stuffe', before leaving again.

Ann's sons, the defendants in the case, presented her version of the story: John was most

> uncivill, not onelie in beatinge woundinge and evill intreatinge . . . that shee hath recieved three most greeveous maymes *viz* one on her eye, one other in her mouth and the third upon her hucklebone [hipbone] by the vyolence and outragious usage of [John, who] alsoe did for the most parte followe the company of whores and lewed weemen and maynteyned and kept them in his owne house to the apparent showe of all the cuntrie.[43]

The defendants knew of no reconciliation between the pair, as John had alleged, and pointed out that John had just been convicted of manslaughter and branded at Kendal, which information did not appear in John's complaint.

John's Chancery suit against Ann's sons was in response to their suit against him at common law for payment of Ann's annual £4 maintenance. Ann's sons had to act for her because she was still technically under coverture and could not have sued on the bond. Obviously, this case illustrates that alimony was even more difficult to enforce in the seventeenth century than it is today. It also illustrates that, despite the tremendous hostility between Ann and John Layfield, they did arrange a formal contract for alimony. Despite the level of violence, it would appear that there was an expectation of proper separation procedures among their neighbours and kin which a legal agreement alone would satisfy.

Relatively non-contentious separations at the level of yeomen and below appear occasionally in diaries and autobiographies. The Shropshire yeoman Richard Gough relished tales of wife desertion in the country round about Myddle, referring to at least six cases, but he also spoke of at least one agreed separation, in which the husband returned his wife's £100 portion and she went off to keep an alehouse.[44] Adam Eyre, a Yorkshire yeoman and ex-captain in the parliamentary army, very nearly separated from his wife Sarah in 1647. They came to serious strife when he was in debt and she insisted on keeping some property in her own name. The crisis passed when he conceded defeat.[45]

Separation agreements at yeoman level and below which ultimately came to litigation may be found in the ecclesiastical courts, although in general studies of provincial ecclesiastical courts in Norfolk and Wiltshire separation or divorce proceedings were extremely rare.[46] Cases were not particularly numerous in the eighteenth-century London church courts either. But those that exist, when analysed in detail, give a striking and invaluable, if gruesome, insight into domestic violence – and one of its common causes, disagreements over property.[47] The same careful study could usefully be applied to provincial courts in earlier centuries in order to uncover details of the dissolution of marriage and property arrangements at an ordinary social level.

The sensational 'wife-sale', touted as the popular form of divorce before it became legal in the twentieth century, in fact appears to have been virtually non-existent in the sixteenth and seventeenth centuries, only becoming at all common in the late eighteenth.[48] The final means of dissolving marriage, desertion, was the only one open to poorer people. Most deserting spouses were husbands, and their wives, like widows, were frequently thrown onto poor relief. It is difficult to estimate how often women were deserted, but two studies of individual parishes in Devon and Gloucestershire in the eighteenth century suggest that as many as 10 per cent of all marriages ended in separation, mostly for reasons of limited employment and poverty.[49]

We must assume that the vast majority of marriage settlements and separate estates were never litigated. Some means of resolution short of a Chancery suit was available in most areas. Private arbitration could be arranged locally, and unlike judges, arbitrators might be female.[50] For the Somerset widow Ann Murden, Chancery was the last resort in her fight with her brother, a joiner, for a marital maintenance payment due to her by marriage settlement. Together with her husband, Ann had first sued in the 'spiritual' court, then at common law. In 1615, after her husband's death at the age of 80, she resorted to Chancery.[51] Ann Murden's case illustrates simultaneously the alternatives available to Chancery prosecution, and the potential hardship and expense involved in enforcing a marriage settlement against an especially obstinate adversary.

Access to familial and community pressure, to arbitration and to local courts help explain why marriage settlement cases in the Court of Chancery were so infrequent. On the other hand, the relative scarcity of historical records of marital contention – the fact that only 2 per cent of all Chancery cases dealt with marriage settlements of any kind, for example – must be seen in the context of the unquantifiable 'self'-imposed emotional constraints on women not to contest and not to speak out, particularly against their husbands. Observe, for example, the near-universal apologies of seventeenth-century writers for being female and publishing. Since marked tendencies towards verbal concession and silence in mixed-sex conversation are demonstrable in late twentieth-century English and American women,[52] there is good reason to think these tendencies were at least as marked – if wholly unmeasurable – three centuries ago, when overt injunctions to be silent and subservient were far more acceptable than they are today. No amount of evidence that early modern women did speak out, and did contest, and were listened to, is meant to deny that undercurrent of restraint on their behaviour.

It is remarkable that so many women did take their grievances to court, either in conjunction with a male relative or as widows on their own. But many more than these made marriage settlements which, within emotional and financial limits, may have been conducted in a relatively cooperative manner. Such settlements only appear in the historical record after the husband has died, or in the event that a married woman made a will.

8 Marriage settlements in probate documents

TYPES OF SETTLEMENT

The words 'jointure' and 'dower' were used only by men of yeoman status and above. Susan Gaunt, of the city of Lincoln, was married to a prosperous man, perhaps a merchant. According to her husband's will of 1624, Susan was to have in her widowhood 'that which I formerly set out to be for and in lew of her joynter and thirds of all my lands in Yorkshire', plus the messuage in Lincoln where they dwelt, 'according to a former writing'.[1] The Yorkshire yeoman Henry Best wrote a section in his *Farming Book* of 1642 headed, 'Concerninge our fashions att our country weddings', placed in between comments on harvesting barley and rye and 'observations concerninge beasts'. Best noted that as 'soone as the younge folks are agreed and contracted' then their fathers meet 'to treate of a dower [dowry], and likewise of a joynture or feoffment for the woman'.[2] The sister of the Shropshire yeoman Richard Gough had a jointure of unspecified amount.[3] A much more modest yeoman than Best or Gough, in the Sussex weald, bequeathed to his unnamed but 'welbeloved' wife in 1631 'in full recompence of her dower (according as by a certeyne bond I am bound) £3 yearely to bee yssuing out of my lands in Pulborough, paid half-yearly for her life'.[4]

Most of the marriage settlements which are glimpsed in probate accounts were concerned with the bride's property rights in her widowhood, but these were not called 'jointure' or 'dower', and they did not take the form of either a cash annuity or lands for her life. Usually, it was a lump sum of cash that was at issue. She therefore had complete control over it, as she would not over a lifetime arrangement. This type of settlement appeared in probate accounts mainly as the widow's deduction from her dead husband's estate. It is only this partial exposure of the settlement, and not the original agreement itself, which survives.

But the instrument by which an agreement was made is sometimes mentioned, including bonds, covenants, securities and trusts. These marriage settlements were not as complex as those found in conveyancing manuals and Chancery litigation. A simple bond – of the type that the Sussex rector Giles Moore bought pre-printed by the dozen – obliged a man to provide his wife with certain specified property. His obligation took one of three forms: to pay a certain amount to the wife upon his death, which property (or the equivalent value thereof) the wife had brought into marriage; to pay the portions of her children by a previous marriage, since the property she brought to marriage incorporated her previous husband's estate; or to pay to a third party a sum of money for the wife's use, and/or allow her to make a will while married. This last condition in effect constituted separate estate during marriage, but that term was never used.

Bonds were secured by a penalty of double the amount at issue. The penalty could be recovered straightforwardly in common law courts if necessary, by the signatories to the bond on the wife's behalf. The bond was signed by the husband, plus the men or unmarried or widowed women who acted as securities for both husband and wife. A wife herself could not sign the bond. A bond for payment of money upon widowhood or to children of a previous marriage could be sued by a wife only when she became a widow, since the bond, although a moveable good, was a 'chose in action' for the duration of the marriage, and as such reverted to the wife on the husband's death.[5] Even where apparently more complex instruments like 'covenants' and 'trusts' occur in probate accounts, they probably refer only to this simple type of bond.

Such 'settlements' to protect the property rights of the wife or her children by a previous marriage appeared in approximately 10 per cent of all married men's probate accounts.[6] In view of the assumption that only the aristocracy and upper gentry made marriage settlements, and they constituted only 2 per cent of the population, an overall rate of 10 per cent among ordinary people is astonishing. By contrast, the marriage settlement whose purpose was to set the bride's portion appeared very infrequently. All three sets of families involved were relatively wealthy, and the settlements were made between the groom and/or his parents and the bride's parents, but not the bride. One settlement set the portion of the groom (see Chapter 5).

Table 8.1 lists thirty-seven marriage settlements in probate accounts whose specific intent was to preserve the wife's property, and in which the amount of money so protected is specified. All but three of the identified settlements were made by people below the level of the gentry. In addition to these gentlemen, the social status of fourteen men is known: there were ten yeomen, three husbandmen and one weaver. Among all the men who made these settlements, the median value of a husband's moveable estate at the time of his death was £160.[7] Their wealth suggests that roughly half of the women who made these settlements were married to yeomen or wealthier men, and half to yeomen or poorer men. (Refer to Table 2.3 for status–wealth correlations.) Four of the women in Table 8.1 were married to men poorer than the median labourer, and so the habit of making a settlement was not unknown at low levels of society.

At a social level normally thought of by historians as 'propertyless', the importance of small amounts of personal property to ordinary people is

Table 8.1 Marriage settlements in probate accounts

Date	Beneficiary	Instrument	Status	Value (£)	County
To benefit the wife upon widowhood					
1597	Elizabeth Wisdome	Obligation	H	10	S
1617	Agnes Lambe	a.d.		5	C
1624	Grace Righton	Bond	Y	100	L
1627	Helen Minshawe	Bond		17	C
1669	Sarah Graves	Bond		50	C
1672	Isabell Collis	Bond	H	60	N
1676	Elizabeth Kimbell	Bond		12	N
1677	Dorothy Cooke	a.d.		10	N
1678	Joan Hawgood	Trust	Y	80	N
1679	Rebecca Naull	Contract		100	L
1681	Anne Broadbury/Johnson	a.d.		5	L
1683	Hannah Tapp	Covenant		300	N
1683	Elizabeth Fisher/Brewer	Bond	Y	180	L
To benefit the wife's child(ren)					
1606	Alice Taylor	Composition		38	L
1611	Elizabeth Doughty/Baine	Bond		20	L
1611	Suzanne Paule/Barne	Bond		30	L
1616	Margery Farrar/Bentley	Gift		12	C
1618	Joan Bennet/Stone	a.d.	H	20	S
1624	Mary Dawson/Samson	Bond		6	L
1624	Prudence Kay/Ellwards	Security	W	5	L
1624	Dorothy Facy/Vinsent	Bond	G	317	L
1624	Margaret Ashmore/Abraham	Bond	Y	40	L
1624	Audrye Winfrey/Phillopps	Bond		13	L
1670	Mary Feaver/Brampton	Security		50	N
1671	Bridgett Gudgin/Fellowes	Articles	Y	50	N
1672	Cicilie Bankes/Clarke/Marston	a.d.		40	N
1672	Mary Mace/Yeoman	Trust		150	N
1674	Anne Stacke/Taylor	a.d.	Y	14	L
1679	Elizabeth Slow/Jeys	Trust		6	N
1681	Bridget Newton/Wright	a.d.		35	L
1683	Jane Harris/Hodgson	a.d.	Y	75	L
1683	Suzanne Kelke/Holmes	a.d.	Y	100	L
Separate estate					
1611	Alice Coolinge/Paternoster		Y	133	L
1635	Margaret Edmonds/Taylor		G	528	S
1673	Mary Jupp/Mersh		Y	200	S
1662	Margaret Sumner			350	S
1682	Elizabeth Medley		G	25	L

Notes: Instrument: 'a.d.' stands for account deduction, by the accountant from her husband's estate, where the instrument was not specified.

Status: H, husbandman; Y, yeoman; G, gentleman; W, weaver.

County: C, Cambridgeshire; L, Lincolnshire; N, Northamptonshire; S, West Sussex.

illustrated by the size of these settlements. The median amount of money involved was a mere £40 (range £5–£528). Fully one quarter of these settlements secured less than £13, sometimes in goods rather than cash. Three quarters secured less than £100.

Thirteen women made pre-marital settlements for payment directly to themselves upon widowhood, and in several cases it was well they had thought ahead. The estates of one quarter of the husbands who made marriage settlements ended in debt (the same proportion of all men's estates which ended in debt), and in anticipation of that fact the debt to herself was often the first item the widow deducted in her account of the estate. Hannah Tapp in Northamptonshire was not only her husband's administratrix, but also his principal creditrix: he died possessed of £588, of which £300 was due to her. His other debts were large, and the estate went into debt for £88, but Hannah had taken care of herself and her small daughter first.[8] A settlement nullified a woman's right to her 'reasonable part' or 'thirds' in ecclesiastical law, but it offered more security because it constituted a debt like any other, to be deducted from a man's estate, whereas reasonable parts were only allocated after his debts were paid.

Eighteen women made a marriage settlement to benefit their children from a previous marriage. A widow in possession of her former husband's property would lose that property again upon remarriage, leaving her children at the mercy, or forgetfulness, of their stepfather. If a woman's first husband had bequeathed a portion to their minor child (as opposed to dying intestate) and the widow, as executrix, then remarried, technically that bequest remained the property of the executrix, even though she was now under coverture. But several of the women among these eighteen had first husbands who made wills, and they still took out bonds to ensure payment of their children's portions when they remarried.

Regardless of the degree of trust a widow had in her prospective second husband, it was apparently prudent to contract for her children's portions. The frequency with which women had to concern themselves with such matters is illustrated by Cicilie Bankes in Northamptonshire, who upon her second marriage required bonds of the groom to pay portions, at his death, to her two sons by her first husband. By the time she administered her second husband's estate in 1672, deducting her sons' portions herself, she had already married a third time, no doubt with another settlement to protect the property she had acquired from her first two 'ventures'.[9]

If a remarrying widow had not taken appropriate precautions herself, the ecclesiastical court might do so. When John Stone of the Sussex weald married Joan Bennet (widow of John Bennet), who had two young children, John and Joan, he was bound by an obligation for the rent he took in from young John Bennet's lands, but there was no such obligation for young Joan's cash legacy from her father. Nevertheless, the probate court noted in 1618 that Stone 'by reason of their said marriage did possesse and convert to his owne use all the goods, chattells and credits of John Bennet [the elder] and therefore was bound by law and conscience to perform the will of John Bennet'.[10]

In the case of fathers who did not make a will, the 1670 Act for the Better Settling of Intestates' Estates required that any person having charge of an estate for the benefit of minor children was required to give bonds for the children's portions. The language of the Act is neutral. What it actually meant was that any person *not the children's mother* had to give bonds for their portions. In the case of her remarriage, because – and only because – she lost all moveables, any new husband had to give bonds. In practice, remarrying widows and the ecclesiastical courts seem to have been requiring such security long before they were required by parliament to do so. Even in the matter of such small portions as Richard Kay's (£2) and Mary Kay's (£3), allocated out of their intestate father's goods in the Lincolnshire wolds in 1624, their mother Prudence Kay *als* Ellwards told the court that her new husband 'hath given security for the payment of the said portions'.[11] The number of people – usually men – involved in the security of children's portions remained constant regardless of the size of the portion. When the widow Mary Dawson remarried in 1624 in the vale of Lincoln, she secured the portions of her two sons, only £3 each, by binding her new husband and his brother to two other men of neighbouring villages.[12]

If the portions of children allocated from their father's estate were reasonably secure, a widowed mother contemplating remarriage did not have to leave her children's portions as their father's will or the probate court had ordained. She could augment them, either equally or unequally, at her discretion. In the Lincolnshire marsh in the early seventeenth century Elizabeth Doughty's husband John made a will giving a bequest to their daughter, who would also inherit lands of £4 p.a. after her mother's death. But when Elizabeth remarried she required bonds of her second husband, also named John, to give her daughter, at her age of 21 or day of marriage, £20 over and above her bequest and inheritance.[13] An Isle of Ely widow, Margery Bentley, gave her four children £12 from their father's goods before she remarried to Richard Farrar. It is not clear whether or how she secured the gifts, but after Farrar's death in 1616 the court approved her deduction of the £12 from his estate.[14]

In very rare instances the actual document augmenting portions survives. Katherine Trusse, on the edge of the vale of Lincoln, made her bond in anticipation of impending remarriage (Figure 1). Her first husband, a 'waterman', had died in 1624 leaving her with £42, out of which each of their four minor children were assigned £4 10s. by the court. Before remarrying the following year she drew up an obligation specifying that she had augmented each child's portion with an extra 10s. to bring it to £5. In addition, she also gave her daughter Mary a chest with a pair of linen sheets, a pair of pillowbears, a towel, a face cloth and a swaddling band, all of which might have been worth another 15s., and had sentimental value as well. Katherine bound her husband-to-be John Boyne 'to educate and bringe up the sayd foure

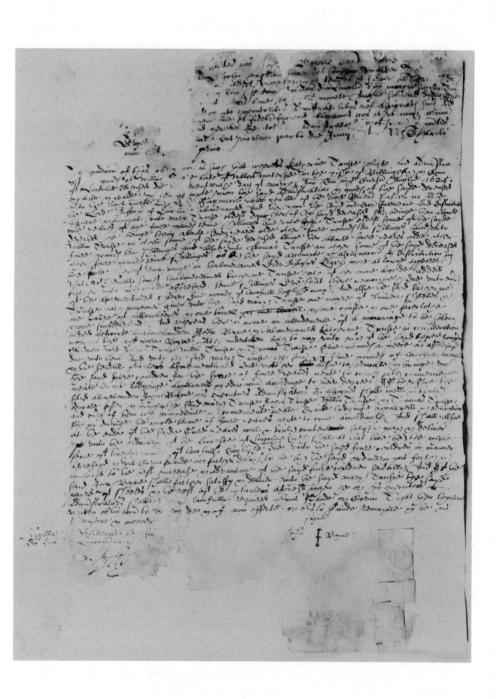

Figure 1 Trusse–Boyne contract

The condic[i]on of this obligac[i]on is such that whereas Katherine Trusse relicte and administra[trix] of [the] goods of Will[ia]m Trusse late of Walcot Waterside in the p[ar]ishe of Billinghay & Coun[ty] of Lincolne deceased did the seventeenthe day of Marche An[n]o d[omi]ni iuxta cursu[m] Angliae 1624 exhibite and yealde up her accompte upon the sayd administration & goods of the sayde deceased unto the right wor[shipfu]ll Mr d[octor] Farmerie vicar gen[er]all of the right Rev[er]end father in God the Lord Bishop of Lincolne above named And thereupon the said Mr Dcor Farmerie did distribute assigne & appoynte unto Mary Trusse eldest daughter of the sayd deceased she beinge then aboute nine yeares of age foure pounds tenne shillinges and unto John Trusse eldest sonne of the sayde deceased he beinge then aboute seven yeares olde other foure pounds ten shillinges and unto Willm Trusse an other sonne of the sayde deceased beinge then aboute foure yeares olde other foure pounds ten shillinges and also unto Thomas Trusse an other sonne of the sayd deceased other foure pounds tenne shillinges as by the sayd accompte & assignacon & distribution in the foote thereof remayninge in thabovenamed Lorde Bishops Reg[ist]ry more at large appeareth Unto w[hi]ch sev[er]all somes thabovenamed Katherine Trusse hath of her owne accorde added farther unto ev[er]y childe aforesayd tenne shillings Soe that there remayneth due unto ev[er]y of the aforementioned children five pounds of lawfull Englishe mony And alsoe the sayd Katherine Trusse hath moreover given unto the sayd Mary Trusse one payre of linnen sheetes & one payre of pillowbeeres & one towell & one chiste & one faceclothe & one swaddlebond: And whereas there is nowe an intendemente of a marriage to be solemnized betwixte thabovebounden John Boyne & thabovenamed Katherine Trusse in consideration whereof the sayd John Boyne hath undertaken both to pay unto ev[er]y of the sayd three yonger children viz John Trusse Willm Trusse & Thomas Trusse five pounds a peece as aforesayd due unto them and unto the sayd Mary Trusse the some of five pounds of lawfull mony & the sevall pticulers aforementioned due unto her and alsoe to educate & bringe up the sayd foure children for the space of foure yeares nexte to come w[i]th conveniente meate drinke lodginge apparrell & educacon accordinge to their degrees If therfore the sayd abovebounden John Boyne his executors admi[ni]strators or assignes shall well & truly educate foster & bringe up the sayd Mary Trusse John Trusse Willm Trusse & Thomas Trusse and ev[er]y of them w[i]th competente & conveniente meate drinke lodginge apparrell & education for & duringe the whole terme of foure yeares nexte to come accordingly And shall alsoe at the ende of the sayde foure yeares well & truly content satisfy pay & deliver up unto the ordinary of the diocese of Lincolne (w[hi]ch shall at that time be) the whole some of twenty pounds of lawfull Englishe mony due unto the sayd foure children in manner aforesayd without Covin fraude or farther delay to be by the sayd ordinary put forth & imployed to the best encrease & advantage of the sayd foure children sevally And if the sayd John Boyne shall farther satisfy & deliver unto the sayd Mary Trusse the sayd payre of sheetes & the rest of the pticulers aforesd when he or his executors or administrators shalbe [thereunto] lawfully required without fraude or Covin That then thabove written obligac[i]on to be voide & of non effecte or els to stande remayne & be in [full] force & power.

children for the space of foure yeares nexte to come with conveniente meate, drinke, lodginge, apparell and educacion', and at the end of that period he was to pay them their portions with the interest earned. The deed, witnessed by four men, was in standard form, that is, enforced by a payment to Katherine, which would be cancelled when Boyne fulfilled the conditions of the obligation on her children's behalf.[15]

The third and final type of marriage settlement to protect a wife's property was a contract for separate estate during coverture, and not surprisingly these are the least common. They can be presumed wherever a married woman made a will or had an inventory or account filed for her estate. Four of the five women for whom inventories or accounts were filed in Table 8.1 were considerably wealthier than most of the other women listed. Even the smallest separate estate, of £25, belonged to Elizabeth Medley, who was married to a gentleman of the Isle of Axholme. This £25 was a miscellaneous assortment of goods, consisting mostly of featherbeds, bedding and linens, plus brass pots and pans and some silver plate, books worth £1, and some hogsheads, barrels and trunks.[16]

Three Sussex women had much more valuable separate estates, in the form of financial assets rather than household goods. Mary Jupp *als* Mersh, a yeoman's wife, owned a 10,000-year lease[17] of land in her own name worth £200, but she owed £200 worth of legacies from her first husband's will when she died in 1673. Her second husband administered her estate, and after her other debts was left with a £47 deficit. (He apparently sustained the loss without difficulty, since when he died some twelve years later his estate was worth £640.)[18] Margaret Edmonds had acquired a substantial £528 due 'upon divers specialties from divers persons' while she was single, and she retained that property at her marriage to John Taylor, a gentleman. When he administered her estate in 1635, he suspected that £128 of that amount was in fact desperate debt, but the expenses of the estate were negligible and Margaret had not made a will, so the residual £518 all accrued to him.[19] But Margaret had been prepared, in case of financial emergency. Although these two women had been married previously, in neither case does it appear that the reason for holding separate estate was the benefit of children from a previous marriage.

The third Sussex wife, Margaret Sumner, died in 1662 holding £350 in the form of a bequest from her father. His will does not survive, but Margaret's bequest was presumably made with the express condition that her husband not intermeddle with it.[20] Separate estates established by will were by no means uncommon among ordinary people – as well as among the likes of Alice Thornton's mother and Sarah Fielding's father (see Chapter 7) – although the terminology sometimes goes unrecognized because it seems so unremarkable. For example, the widowed Yorkshire yeoman Thomas Hall in 1649 left to his second daughter Alice Furbanke his dwelling house for her life, and upon her death to her daughter and son, equally divided. But Alice's husband George was expressly 'debarred and excluded' from claiming or enjoying the said house.[21] These words were sufficient to establish a separate estate for Alice.

In probate documents filed for married women there is no explanation of separate estate, and it may have been that only informal arrangements about property had been made. In the Lincolnshire fen Alice Coolinge, mother of six young children, married the yeoman Richard Paternoster shortly before her death in 1610. But in his account of her estate Alice's administrator makes only one mention of Richard, reimbursing him for part of her funeral feast (two loins of beef, one breast of beef, a quarter of beef, one sheep, white bread, sugar, almonds, fruit, and spices). Alice's residual estate was divided among her five younger sons and daughters; her eldest daughter received only a token share because she would inherit land worth £10 from her father (see Chapter 4).[22] Richard Paternoster was by no means impecunious, but Alice apparently chose not to contribute to his financial well-being at the expense of her children.

The three types of settlement (for the wife in widowhood, for children's portions and for separate estate) were not mutually exclusive. The will of a Kentish innkeeper left his wife and her three daughters by a previous marriage, all together, £40 'according to the security I gave her therefore upon our contract in marriage'.[23] Suzanne Barne *als* Paule of the Lincolnshire marsh held separate estate – her own inventory and account were filed by her second husband in 1612 – in order to protect the legacies of her two minor sons from her first husband's will, of which she was executrix, as well as to protect the gifts she herself had made to them by bond in her widowhood.[24]

Other women did not mention specific marriage settlements, but still expected to take out of marriage the amount that they had brought in. The Northamptonshire widow Dorothy Cooke was left with nothing after paying her husband's debts in 1678. Without reference to any legal instrument, she asked for and received an allowance out of her husband's inventory of those goods 'which were the proper goods of the administratrix before her intermarriage with the defunct'. These items, worth £10 in total, consisted entirely of bedding and linens, including an unusually large quantity (two dozen) of flaxen and diaper napkins.[25] Like Dorothy Cooke, Agnes Lambe of Cambridgeshire apparently had no formal security, but in her account of her husband's estate in 1617 the court allowed 'deduction to be made out of the goods of the deceased for that she brought £5 unto her husband at the tyme of theire marriage which was her owne'. Agnes was awarded her full third of the residual goods, which amounted to £10, over and above her £5 deduction. She gave up the education of her five stepchildren, aged between 7 and 17, to the minister and 'chiefe inhabitants' of Little Shelford, and apparently went her own way, £15 in hand.[26]

For Agnes Lambe and Dorothy Cooke, on the edge of poverty, it was vitally important to mark out their own goods. For someone like Anne Boulton of the Lincolnshire fens, whose yeoman husband's inventory included items which had fairly evidently been hers at their marriage, such as 'child bedd linnen', it was not so important to identify her own 'proper goods'. Anne was left with £861 even after her husband's debts were paid, so even if some of the goods in his inventory did belong to her, she was under no financial pressure to point out the fact.[27]

Because there appears to have been a rough equivalence between the amount of money a woman took into her marriage and the amount of money she took out of it, and because her property in widowhood only rarely took the jointure's typical form of an annuity, the portion inflation and concomitant devaluation of jointure which is so important a feature of the marital economy of early modern peeresses is irrelevant to ordinary women.[28] Because there was no annuity, there was no purchase of land with the bride's portion, which removed the necessity for a disproportionate rise in portions like the one which occurred at upper social levels. There is no observable rise over time either in parental bequests to unmarried daughters, or in probate accounts with a settlement for payment to the wife in widowhood. Complaints from the well-to-do about the rising costs of their daughters' portions were never echoed at an ordinary level.

For ordinary brides the late sixteenth- to early eighteenth-century increase in marriage portions – fourfold among the aristocracy and threefold among the gentry – would have been simply impossible. Over the same period, the wages of skilled craftsmen and labourers in southern England rose by only 50 per cent, and average agricultural labourers' wages throughout England increased by a mere 9 per cent between 1640 and 1749, or a penny a day more at the end of the period than at the beginning.[29] At this level of society, where portions were usually less than £50, income was a more immediate determinant of portion size than among those who could mortgage and borrow to endow their daughters with three times their annual income (see Chapter 5). Both the inordinate inflation of portions and the fall in the relative value of jointures appear to have been phenomena of the wealthiest 5 per cent or so of the population, but the issue of portion inflation at an ordinary level will be settled only by an exhaustive search of probate documents.

It has been suggested, and it seems reasonable, that women would have had greater financial expertise and exercised greater control over property in those parts of the country where they were most involved in market production, particularly in dairying, but also clothmaking and other cottage industries.[30] Although the number of ordinary women's marriage settlements examined here is small, it may be significant that there is no clear variation in the occurrence of marriage settlements in areas of pastoral dairying and woodland, as opposed to arable regions.

The eighteen Lincolnshire settlements do originate disproportionately in the northern fenland and the marshland, as opposed to the arable vale and wolds. But settlements are conspicuously absent in the southern fenland and the Isle of Axholme where dairying and other industries were prominent. While Cambridgeshire had substantial investment in dairying, settlements (as such) appear much less often there than elsewhere, although this may result from the general taciturnity of Cambridgeshire accounts. More than any other area of England, the Ely Diocesan accounts tend to be of the pre-written, fill-in-the-blank variety.[31]

Two areas may possibly suggest particular concentrations of marriage settlements. All of the marriage settlements from Sussex in Table 8.1 – although there are only five – came from the weald and downs, where dairying was important. None of the ten settlements from Northamptonshire originated in the dairying areas of Salcey or Whittlewood Forest, but several did originate in the glovemaking towns. If glovemaking were women's work, as seems possible since it was run largely on a putting-out basis, this should be further investigated.[32] Unfortunately, there are no more probate accounts from Northamptonshire in which to pursue this question. Sussex, and more particularly Lincolnshire, offer an excellent place to pursue the relation between marriage settlements and women's production for market, each having several thousand probate accounts and a good range of agrarian economies within the county.

So far, wives everywhere appear to have been equally concerned to protect what property they had. It is likely that isolating dairying and clothmaking regions as areas of female prominence limits our perception of the range of women's market production. In all agrarian regions, with the possible but as yet unproven exception of strictly arable economies, there were opportunities for women to earn money which have not been sufficiently explored.

WIVES' WILLS

The clearest indication of an uncontested separate estate is the survival of a married woman's will. The ability of married women to make wills in the early modern period was restricted because, in the words of Henry Swinburne, they lacked 'freedom and full liberty'.[33] This had not always been the case. An Anglo-Saxon or early medieval wife had apparently been free to make a will of what was then considered her own property. The earliest evidence of this is the fact that nine of the thirty-three surviving Anglo-Saxon wills made by an individual were made by women, and at least some of these women were married – although they did not routinely specify their marital status, which further suggests that it was irrelevant to their capacity to make a will.[34]

The medieval ecclesiastical law followed Roman civil law, which in the rest of Europe allowed a married woman to make a will of moveable goods. But from the Norman conquest the rule came under dispute in England, conflicting as it did with the common law insistence on coverture. After long dispute, and in the face of strong ecclesiastical resistance, parliament in the mid-fourteenth century objected that a wife could not make a will without a pre-marital agreement with her husband to do so.[35] Even then a husband could revoke his consent at any time up until his wife's will was proved in court.

Some towns apparently allowed a married woman to devise borough land without her husband's consent in the middle ages and a few perhaps even into the sixteenth and seventeenth centuries.[36] The possibility of wives making wills must have remained alive. In 1540, when the Statue of Wills (32 Hen. VIII c.1) enabled the majority of freehold land to be devised by will, it was felt necessary to include a clause explicitly prohibiting such action by married women. The intriguing question of whether wives made wills of borough land – along with questions about feme sole trader status and partibility or impartibility – must await further studies of local, and particularly borough, customs.

It is possible that married women may have resorted to transferring land by court roll or by deed during their lifetime more frequently than men, who always had the option to make a will instead. Evidence of transfers by deed is exceedingly rare. For example, the only reason that anyone now knows of the deed made by the wife of Selby yeoman William Richardson is that in his will of 1681, made after his wife's death, he altered the conditions of her gift: to his daughter Elizabeth, £50 'In lew of one close lyeing within the Lordship of Thorpwilloby, which was surrendered to hir by hir mother'.[37]

The number of wives making wills declined markedly after the mid-fourteenth century, albeit with a certain delay, due perhaps to popular and ecclesiastical resistance. This diminution has been clearly charted in Yorkshire where, in a total of 1500 wills, the proportion made by women fell from 23 per cent to 14 per cent of the total between the late fourteenth and mid-fifteenth centuries, a drop attributable entirely to the disappearance of wives' wills.[38] In the fourteenth century one quarter of all women's wills in Bishop's Lynn, Norfolk, and fully one half of women's wills in the Diocese of Rochester (western Kent) were made by wives.[39] But over the early modern period, as wills survive in increasing numbers, only a handful of wives appear. Their proportion rarely rises above 3 per cent of women's wills, and never above 8 per cent (see Table 12.2). While the proportion of wives' wills filed in the Prerogative Court of Canterbury doubled over the seventeenth century, it remained less than 1 per cent of all women's wills.[40] Clearly it was to married women that the proverb referred: 'Women must have their wills while they live, because they make none when they die.'[41] First recorded in the later seventeenth century, the origins of this phrase are tantalizingly unknown.

Despite stringent legal requirements for the conditions under which a wife could make a will, the exact arrangements which had been made were not always specified in the document itself. Anne Ballard, wife of a Cambridgeshire yeoman, wrote her will 'with my said husbonds lycence and consent' in 1603. But Anne Coates of Sussex recorded only that her husband's name was Matthew in her will of 1714, and she gave him nothing, nor mentioned his permission or lack thereof.[42]

Wives who made wills had often been married before, and this was reflected in their burial requests. A wife making a will could – like Alice Cayster of the Isle of Ely, married to a yeoman who was himself a widower –

choose to be buried by the grave of her first husband instead.[43] The physical memorials survive to wealthy women who made the same choice. One such plaque in Ely Cathedral commemorates

> Dame Martha, daughter of Mr Penington of Suffolke, relict of Robert Mingay Esq., and wife of Sr Roger Jenyns who put up this for her. She dyed in Anno 1707 and according to her desire interred in the vault here with her first husband.

The wills of twice-married men, too, sometimes asked second wives to bury them near to first wives.[44] But the option of Francis Leek, buried in Southwell Minster in 1670 flanked by his first wife on his left and his second wife on his right,[45] was unthinkable for a twice-married woman. Her transferability from one to another man throughout her lifetime did not permit her to integrate her marriages in death in the way that a man could. But at least she could choose at whose side she wished to rest permanently, which in an age of less intently romanticized marriage was a more reasonable request than it would be today. A monument in the church of St Mary Magdalene at Gedney in the Lincolnshire fens commemorates Adlard Welby, esquire, who died in 1570, and Cassandra his wife, who died twenty years later at the age of 60. This monument was erected fifteen years after Cassandra's death 'at the coste and charges of Sr William Welbie Knight of the honourable order of the Bath [their eldest son, now in his fifties], together with Robart Carr, of Aswerbye Esquire, the last husband of Cassandra'. Such accord between stepson and stepfather in honour of Cassandra and her first husband seems stranger to the twentieth century, with a high incidence of divorce and a low incidence of young widowhood, than it did to the seventeenth century. Perhaps the monument was erected voluntarily; perhaps Cassandra asked for it.

The problem in assessing wives' wills is amassing enough of them to analyse. Mary Prior has compiled the largest collection of wives' wills: 1068 wills proved in the Prerogative Court of Canterbury in the period 1558–1700.[46] These women enjoyed a considerable level of wealth, since normally only those who owned property in more than one county had their estates probated in the prerogative court. But it is possible to distinguish the social status of these women very crudely by the presence or absence of a title. It is also possible to make a minimum estimate of how many of these wives had made a will in the course of their first marriage and how many in the course of a subsequent marriage by the presence of an *alias* or a 'formerly' attached to their name.

While the Prerogative Court of Canterbury was the highest court in which to prove a will, nevertheless untitled women – that is, those without even 'Mrs' before their name – made up approximately half of all wives represented (Table 8.2). In the period 1650–60, when probate was not available in lower courts, the proportion of untitled women jumps to 70 per cent, which suggests that wives' wills should be present in the lower courts before and

Table 8.2 Social status in wives' wills proved in the Prerogative Court of Canterbury 1558–1700

	1558–1604		1605–1649		1650–1660		1661–1700	
	%	n	%	n	%	n	%	n
Titled	51	46	45	118	30	72	41	193
Untitled	49	45	55	142	70	172	59	280
Total	100	91	100	260	100	244	100	473

Table 8.3 Serial marriage in wives' wills proved in the Prerogative Court of Canterbury 1558–1700

	1558–1604		1605–1649		1650–1660		1661–1700	
	%	n	%	n	%	n	%	n
1st marriage	66	60	74	193	81	197	82	389
2nd marriage	34	31	26	67	19	47	18	84
Total	100	91	100	260	100	244	100	473

after the interregnum. While the proportion of titled willmakers in Table 8.2 should be taken as a minimum, and untitled willmakers as a maximum figure, it appears that untitled women may have been as likely as gentry and aristocratic women to make a marriage settlement preserving to themselves the right to make a will.

Table 8.3 distinguishes those women who clearly made wills during the course of a second or subsequent marriage from those who appear to have made wills in their first marriage. At least two thirds of the wives who made wills did so in the course of their first marriage, and this proportion rose steadily from 66 per cent to 82 per cent over the period 1558–1700. It is possible that this increase is only apparent and not real if, for example, a change in indexing practice occurred whereby the use of *alias* or 'formerly' was abandoned. If, on the other hand, this high and increasing proportion of women contracting to make wills on the occasion of their first marriage represents a real trend, then the ability to make a will is unlike other types of separate estate which were more likely to be negotiated upon a second marriage, as appeared in Chancery litigation on marriage settlements. It might be expected that upper-class brides would have a higher incidence of first-marriage will-making as a result of larger personal fortunes. But in fact the proportion of wives contracting to make a will at their first marriage is virtually identical among titled and untitled women in the period 1605–60 (Table 8.4). In the later part of the century even more untitled than titled women made a settlement upon the occasion of their first marriage, although the smaller proportion of remarriage settlements may reflect declining remarriage rates in the population as a whole (see Chapter 11).

Table 8.4 Social status and serial marriage in wives' wills proved in the Prerogative Court of Canterbury 1558–1700

	1558–1604		1605–1649		1650–1660		1661–1700	
	%	n	%	n	%	n	%	n
Titled								
1st marriage	72	33	75	88	81	58	74	142
2nd marriage	28	13	25	30	19	14	26	51
Total	100	46	100	118	100	72	100	193
Untitled								
1st marriage	60	27	74	105	81	139	88	247
2nd marriage	40	18	26	37	19	33	12	33
Total	100	45	100	142	100	172	100	280

The wills of the Prerogative Court of Canterbury were made by wealthy people, whether titled and untitled. Only further studies in the wills of lower courts will tell how frequently more ordinary wives made wills. Mary Prior's study of wives' wills in Oxfordshire courts is at present the only one of its kind. While these women were not all wealthy, only five yeomen's, husband-men's and labourers' wives' wills survive in all of Oxfordshire in the century and a half between 1558 and 1700. At the level of the Prerogative Court of Canterbury it is possible to trace connections between the women making wills, and both religion and family tradition appear to have influenced a wife's chance of making a will.[47] This suggests that the practice might vary regionally, and Table 12.2 does show that some parts of England had a much higher incidence of wives' wills than other places. But individual will studies have widely differing beginning and end dates, and so to examine whether these variations were regional rather than chronological it will be necessary in the future to compare different locations over time.

SHADOWS OF SETTLEMENTS

I have mentioned that some women filing probate accounts and some wives' wills do not make clear that a marriage settlement was ever made, although assumptions are made that, legally, would have had to rest on a settlement. So the estimate that 10 per cent of ordinary couples made marriage settlements, based on their occurrence in probate accounts, does not approach a complete reflection of their frequency because there was no requirement that a settlement be mentioned in an account. They were sometimes mentioned almost incidentally. Grace Righton, for example, barely made it into Table 8.1. In her 1624 account of her yeoman husband's estate, £40 of the residual £42 was allocated to her six children, which left Grace with an extraordinarily small share of £2. (She should by the law of intestacy have received one third, or £14.) But as a postscript, the Lincoln ordinary added that he 'hopeth this accomptant will add £2 a peece to the last five portions [that is, the portions of all children except the eldest son] in regard as that £100 owing upon bond to Mr Blowe which £100 she challengeth to be due unto her by reason of that bond'. The bond to Mr Blowe, clearly a marriage settlement, was not mentioned anywhere in the body of the account.[48]

A more elusive settlement may be inferred from the account filed by Margaret Hall of the Isle of Ely. Her husband, although styled 'gent' in an accompanying acquittance, left her with only £32 before debts in 1604, plus a lease valued at £7. Her expenses in the account of his estate amounted to £64, on top of which she submitted a supplementary list of forty-two bonds and four bills which were 'desperat debtes in my consyens nothing worth', amounting to £155. Nevertheless, the account balance was listed not as a negative figure, as the normal procedure was, but simply 'nil'.[49] It seems likely that Margaret had her own separate means of support. A similar suggestion occurs in the Lincolnshire case of Thomas Dalby, whose £26 estate in 1624 included only four items of household furniture – one table, one pan, one brass pot and three kitts (baskets). But the widowed Sarah Dalby and her six children continued to live in this house and work what may have been 15 acres of land. It defies belief that Sarah did not have property which was omitted from her husband's inventory, whether formally or informally.[50]

The most frequent way in which settlements are suggested without being specified is in the case of substantial discrepancies between a husband's and his widow's subsequent estate value. Ann Smith of the Isle of Axholme had had two daughters with her first husband Tayler, of whom one was married and one single. She also had a toddler son (he needed a pair of leading strings costing 4d.) by her second husband William Smith, a husbandman. When William died in 1682 his inventory amounted to £36, and included only 8s. worth of goods in the house; the remainder was in corn, animals, hemp and flax, and husbandry gear. Ann died only three weeks later and her inventory came to £66, including all of William's items (valued slightly higher) plus £18 worth of household furniture, including £2 10s. worth of brass and pewter alone. Ann even signed her will as Ann Tayler, although she is declared as Ann Smith at the beginning. But no mention appears anywhere of a contract to keep her goods separate.[51]

One of the more spectacular widowhood recoveries was that of Elizabeth Dethe, whose optimistically named husband Welcome (Dethe is an old Lincolnshire name) died in 1674. His account identified him as a gentleman with £131, but after paying his debts Elizabeth was left £28 out of pocket. Other widows whose husbands died in debt made it plain to posterity that they were poor and helpless, or 'weake and verie aged', but Elizabeth Dethe made no complaint or plea of any kind to the probate clerk about being left in debt. Seven years later at her own death, Elizabeth's inventory amounted to £106, including such niceties as two carpets, two flowerpots and a 'seeing glass'.[52] It is reasonable to conclude that women whose husbands died in debt, and who themselves died a few years later with a healthy inventory, had made some kind of arrangement for separate property. This arrangement may have been informal, or it may simply not be extant. If it was written down but does not happen to survive, the frequency with which property settlements are implied without being specified suggests that such settlements were sufficiently common not to need careful documentation in subsequent probate records.

The practice of appraisers in listing husbands' and wives' property was not at all consistent and complicates attempts to disentangle marital property, since it is clear that goods considered the wife's were not always included in her husband's inventory even though he technically owned them. Some men's inventories included linens down to the childbearing sheets. But others, like the 1680 inventory of Robert Bettison, of the vale of Lincoln, included no sheets, pillows, napkins or tablecloths, which the household of a prosperous husbandman like himself certainly contained.[53] His widow Susannah's inventory does not survive, but would undoubtedly have listed the linens. In the case of Sarah and William Foxe, of the Lincolnshire marsh, her inventory included items which were not in his. In 1603 William's household goods amounted to only £8 of his £33 inventory; most of his wealth was in animals and husbandry gear. Three years later, Sarah had divested herself of all the outdoor goods, but her householdments totalled £35 in a £40 inventory. Since such a large acquisition in her widowhood is unlikely, these were probably items she had had all along, like her separately itemized 8s. Bible, but which had somehow not been included with her husband's goods.[54]

Sometimes these goods came from a previous husband. For example, when Mary Constable in 1677 had the appraisers in to her Selby house to take the inventory of her recently deceased husband Isaac, his goods came to less than £5. According to the appraisers, 'the remainder of the goods in the said house . . . belonged to a former husband and was by him given in his last will and testament . . . as was the above said day creidably declared to us'.[55] But in most cases a previous husband does not appear. There was clearly at least an informal agreement between the wife, the husband and the appraisers that certain goods – which amounted to considerably more than her 'paraphernalia' (see Chapter 10) – belonged to the wife.

Large, secured debts to family members are another clue to marriage settlements. In Anabell Gilson's account of her husband's estate in Cambridgeshire, his principal debt was £70 on bond to Anabell's brother. Although the money was not specified as being for Anabell's benefit, such large debts – Anabell's husband had only £27 worth of goods – secured on bond, and to a member of the wife's immediate family, may well have been a part of a marriage settlement.[56]

The early seventeenth-century puritan preacher William Perkins mentioned in passing that a woman might retain certain goods during marriage because 'either they were reserved upon the match between them, or else were particular unto her by their mutual consent'.[57] This comment suggests that informal agreements, like those of Dorothy Cooke (page 137) who claimed certain items out of her husband's inventory on the grounds that they were her own 'proper goods' before her marriage, may have been at least as common as formal settlements.

Some kind of informal agreements were essential on a purely practical level in a society in which most married women earned income, and in which debts appear to have been regularly paid to married women in their own right. One of many examples appears in the account of an unmarried Northampton maltster, who died in 1670. His two married sisters administered his estate – with no mention of their husbands – and one of the larger debts paid out was to 'John Clerks wife at the Blew Anckor', due on bond. Northampton may possibly have been one of the towns which treated married women traders as single women in respect of their business, and as a 'feme sole trader' John Clerk's wife could have signed her own bond.[58] On a less professional level, the Sussex rector Giles Moore regularly paid married women for work (weeding and other gardening, spinning wool and flax, sewing, and carrying bricks) and for goods (cloth, beer, butter, seeds). In some cases single or widowed women may have loaned money which was subsequently repaid – directly to them – after they had married. This was the case with Catherine Williams of Northamptonshire, who administered her husband's estate in 1682 and paid a bond for £5 to Mary Williams, now wife of John Holliard, with twelve years' interest.[59]

It has been suggested in the past that women might have avoided common law coverture and preserved their legal independence by means of an irregular marriage.[60] There were three types of irregular marriage: clandestine marriage, performed by a 'hedge priest' or some other unofficial person; 'common law' marriage, or co-residence following an exchange of vows before witnesses, but not in a church; and 'smock' marriage, where the bride came to the ceremony dressed only in her smock or shift. The custom of smock marriage was noted by antiquarians of the last century, who pointed out that the belief in its preservation of a woman's financial independence was in fact wrong.[61] Nevertheless, the idea of smock marriage was at least symbolic of the husband not getting any money with his bride from the early seventeenth century, when Sir John Villiers protested that he would take the heiress Frances Coke, daughter of Sir Edward Coke, 'in her smock', implying (speciously) that he loved her for her person and not her money.[62] In fact, it was he who insisted on her £10,000 portion.

The actual incidence of smock marriage is unknown, but the incidence of clandestine marriage certainly grew during the seventeenth century. Whereas in the sixteenth century no more than a fraction of a per cent of all marriages were clandestine, by the 1690s almost half of the marriages in one market town were clandestine.[63] But the primary reason was probably to avoid the posting of banns in order to hide an inequality between the fortunes of bride and groom, or an illegal remarriage, or to avoid one party's liability for the other's debt.[64] Unfortunately there is no evidence to support the interesting claim that clandestine, common law or smock marriage was used for the purpose of preserving a woman's economic integrity. A common law husband may well have received less sympathy in a court when claiming his right to his wife's earnings or other property, but the people who entered into common law marriages did so primarily from poverty, and so were unlikely to take their grievances to court. How many women took advantage of irregular forms of marriage in the belief that doing so preserved their personal property rights remains unknown. In all probability, the number was negligible, particularly in the light of the evidence presented here that women at all social levels did establish some kind of 'separate estate', but in the form of simple bonds rather than equitable trusts.

COOPERATION AND CONFLICT

If a remarried widow outlived her second husband as well, and *if* the second husband's estate could cover the portions of the first husband's children, and *if* the second husband recognized his obligation to the first husband's children, *then* a contract to protect children's portions became redundant. Such a happy coincidence of circumstances occurred in the marital history of Agnes Rose of the Lincolnshire fenland. Agnes was married to three men, probably all labourers, and appears to have made no formal contract with any of them. By her first husband she had a son, Robert Drinkwater, and by her second a daughter, Agnes Inmom. Both were still minors when she married Christopher Rose, who himself had two grown sons and grandchildren. When Christopher Rose made his will in 1606 he scrupulously re-bequeathed to his stepson Drinkwater the £3 and a 'redd starred kow with whit spotes of her which was geven him' in the will of his own father, and to his stepdaughter Inmom he gave again the £1 from her own father's will. The cow and the pound to his stepchildren were Christopher's principal bequests, since his own sons were already established. Agnes Drinkwater *als* Inmom *als* Rose died only two weeks later, leaving her own will with bequests to all three of her marital families as well as to her own natal family. (Neither the Drinkwater nor the Inmom will survives, but all four of these labourers made wills.)[65]

In marriages less cooperative than Agnes Rose's settlements were a potential cause of strife, but where that strife fell short of actual litigation it is extremely difficult to uncover. One unusually detailed case is reported from late seventeenth-century Massachusetts. Beatrice Plummer's third husband Edmund Berry had contracted to reserve to Beatrice ownership of her first husband's estate, as her second husband had done before him. But Edmund soon changed his mind, hounded her to tear up the contract and denied her provisions until she should give him her property. Beatrice finally did take her case to the Salem Quarterly Court in 1677, although it is easy to imagine that another woman might not have. There Edmund was fined for his 'abusive carriages and speeches' toward his wife, but the judgement seems unlikely to have restored marital harmony.[66]

Similar histories of discord in individual English marriage settlements can undoubtedly be found in litigation. Indications of discontent with a settlement are extremely rare in probate documents, but that is hardly surprising, since in most cases the husband, who was most likely to cause trouble, had recently died. A reversal of the expected conflict occurred in the case of Thomas Goodriche of the Isle of Ely. Thomas had given as 'jointure' to his wife Mary the copyhold house and land which his widowed mother still occupied. In his will of 1582 Thomas wanted to leave the same copyhold, upon Mary's death, to their only daughter, but was stymied by his wife's (unexplained) obstinacy:

> concernyng my house and land at Pidley, . . . I did never meane to geve unto Mary my wyfe any further ryght therin, then for the terme of her lyfe, and after her dissease to remayne unto my heyers but nowe, seing that she thinkethe her state therin so good that she may do her owne will therwithe, and therfore will nott (at my ernest desyer, and at the request of my other frendes, to my comfort and rejoysing) take into coppye withe her myne and her only chylde, Jane. . . . But veary unkyndly towards me, and unnaturally toward oure chylde (to my great greefe) dothe sett her selfe agaynst my request, by reason wherof my owne chylde . . . is lyke to be disherited of that land whiche my father did leave unto me.

In this case, Thomas could do nothing in the face of Mary's resistance but refuse to give her any further bequest in his will, leaving his daughter Jane all moveables and an acre of land with the windmill.[67]

Either spouse who wished to could find a means for abuse of the marital agreement, but the opportunities for husbands like Edmund Berry to exert their will were greater than those for wives like Mary Goodriche. Husbands had more legal and moral resources to call upon in a dispute, in the form of biblical injunctions to wifely obedience and an expectation of discipline exerted by the head of household over unruly members.

While it is possible to find evidence of disagreement, it is unlikely that husbands invariably resented their wives' property claims at this time, as they appear to have done with separate estate in later eighteenth-century literature. Even in real-life eighteenth- and nineteenth-century South Carolina and Virginia, it is suggested, 'to demand a separate estate at the outset was to insult the groom'.[68] The marriage settlements in early modern probate accounts seem to have been comparatively peaceably agreed to and carried out, whether they involved a widow administering her husband's goods or a widower acting as executor for his wife, whom he had agreed in a pre-marital contract might make her own will. We shall never know the number of couples agreeing in this manner.

The most apparent reason for women's failure to take advantage of the settlement possibilities available to them was well phrased by the anonymous married woman, born at the end of the seventeenth century, who published *The Hardships of the English Laws. In Relation to Wives*:

if we reflect how extreamly ignorant all young women are as to points in law, and how their education and way of life, shuts them out from the knowledge of their true interest in almost all things, we shall find that their trust and confidence in the man they love . . . leave few in a condition to make use of that precaution.[69]

That youthful mixture of love and ignorance – partly natural, partly cultivated by those with an interest to protect – is extremely powerful. Many of the voiceless ordinary women who made marriage settlements undoubtedly had personal experience of the legal disadvantages of wifehood from their own or a female relative's previous marriage. At least twenty-three of the thirty-seven women who made the settlements in Table 8.1 had been married before, although this proportion may be inordinately high, since widows with children of a different name are readily identified in probate accounts, whereas the marriage settlement of a first-time bride, if she did not specify that a certain bond payable to another was for her own use, could easily go unrecognized. Among those women who contracted for separate estate in the form of the right to make wills during coverture, and whose wills were duly filed in the Prerogative Court of Canterbury, perhaps two thirds appear to have done so as first-time brides. These, though, may well have been influenced by their female kin.

If this group of marriage settlements in probate accounts is representative – in so far as slightly over one third of settlements were made for a first-time bride and slightly less than two thirds by a widow remarrying, and if between one quarter and one third of all marriages throughout the seventeenth century were remarriages (see Chapter 11) – then it seems that widows remarrying were roughly twice as likely to make a settlement as were maids marrying for the first time. Delarivier Manley, in 1707, did suggest that there was a certain stereotype when she referred to a man in debt who had married in high hopes of cash but whose 'lady, like a right widow, had secured the greatest part of her fortune to her own use'.[70]

Fitzherbert's *The Boke of Husbandry* (1550) detailed at great length the responsibilities of the farming wife and husband, and how each ought to account to the other for their finances.[71] The good housewife could not reasonably be expected to manage the household, the dairy, the garden, and the orchard and beehives, and then take her produce to market and return with necessaries for her family, without some access to resources and to credit. For Fitzherbert the family economy was entirely a mutual affair, but actual examples of cooperation will inevitably be rare in the extreme, since documentation is traditionally produced by conflict, not by peace and harmony. One accidental example in the historical record occurs in a late seventeenth-century Chancery plea, in which a young woman, daughter of a London merchant, happened to mention that a certain transaction (incidental to the one at issue) had taken place in the presence of her mother Elizabeth, since Elizabeth 'managed all her said husband's business in his house and provided for his family'.[72]

As 'primogeniture' does not reflect the reality of inheritance practices, 'coverture' is likewise an inadequate description of marital property relations. The prevalence of early modern marriage settlements qualifies any simple idea of women's legal 'annihilation' within marriage. Whereas strict settlements to preserve property in the male line were used only by the wealthy, different types of pre-nuptial settlements to preserve the wife's property interests were implemented by all levels of society, albeit often without the technical legal terminology. It is this type of provision which most people – including the readers of conveyancing manuals, the litigants in Chancery and the ordinary people who filed probate accounts – meant by a marriage settlement.

Probate account sampling finds that at least 10 per cent of ordinary women – the wives of yeomen, craftsmen, husbandmen and labourers – made marriage settlements to protect their property rights. But the frequency with which property settlements are implied in probate documents of all kinds without being set out in detail suggests that such settlements were actually far more common. Most of these settlements had to do with the rights of widows, rather than separate estate during coverture, but when the amount a woman brought into marriage was equivalent to the amount she took out of it – and that property was more likely to consist in physical goods than in impersonal cash – the distinction between widowhood provision and separate estate is blurred. It is unlikely that wives stopped thinking of certain property as theirs simply for the duration of the marriage.

At upper levels of society the relationship between the portion a bride took into marriage and the jointure a widow took out of it was more complicated. At this level, grooms' families' interest in agglomerating wealth encouraged maximizing control over brides' portions while at the same time minimizing the claims of widows on the patrimony. But brides' families were interested in a certain level of economic security for their female members. There are reasons other than simply the fact of their wealth why the aristocracy made marriage settlements protecting the wife's interest with more regularity than ordinary people did. Aristocratic wives' lower age at marriage and larger spousal age difference increased the likelihood of their being left widows. And the aristocracy was more likely to have freehold land, which if allowed to devolve to the eldest son placed the fortunes of a widow and the other children more at risk.

In the event of marital breakdown before the death of either party, an equitable trust for separate estate was one of the more secure ways in which to ensure wives' maintenance. Separate estate was not new in the seventeenth century. Its traditional origin in the late sixteenth century is based on the inaccurate assumption that what was newly written down was in fact new. To judge from scattered and offhand references in court records, the idea of separate estate is at least medieval. What did develop, particularly from the later seventeenth century, was legal discussion of the particular ramifications of separate estate. However, the legal principles governing separate estate were at no time during the early modern period clearly established. Chancery decisions on the subject are blatantly inconsistent.

If the common law regarded baron and feme as one person, 'one individed substance', as *The Lawes Resolutions of Women's Rights* put it, nevertheless society 'must always consist among two or more'.[73] Familial interests at all social levels were not limited simply to dynasty-building. In the case of a first-time bride, her parents might be particularly concerned about a profligate son-in-law, or suspect his motives if his bride's fortune were substantially larger than his own; they would want to protect her in her widowhood, and entail property on her children in order to avoid its passing to her husband's children by another marriage. A widow remarrying was likely to negotiate her own settlement with her intended, having first-hand experience of legal coverture and because part of her property probably came to her from her previous husband(s). She would want to avoid the possibility of the current husband squandering – well within his marital right – the inheritance of her children by previous marriage(s). She might also want to ensure her own right to make a will in the event she died while under coverture.

Most women, even those with a marriage settlement, were largely at the mercy of their husbands' good will, both during and after marriage. The women who survived coverture are the subject of the next section.

Part IV

Widows

A woman hath understanding, and speech, firme memorie, love naturall, and kindnesse, desire of glorie and reputation, with the accomplishment of many meritorious vertues: But alas, when she hath lost her husband, her head is cut off, her intellectual part is gone, the verie faculties of her soule are, I will not say, cleane taken away, but they are all benummed, dimmed and dazled, so that she cannot thinke or remember when to take rest or refection for her weake body. ... Why mourne you so, you that be widdowes? Consider how long you have been in subjection under the predominance of parents, of your husbands, now you may be free in liberties, and free *proprii iuris* at your owne law.

The Lawes Resolutions of Women's Rights (1632: 232)

John Gay a century later was more satirical than the author of the *Lawes Resolutions*. In *The Beggar's Opera* (1728), Mr Peachum admonished his love-sick daughter Polly, 'The comfortable estate of widow-hood, is the only hope that keeps up a wife's spirits. Where is the woman who would scruple to be a wife, if she had it in her power to be a widow when ever she pleas'd?'[1] Widowhood was the most often caricatured state of female existence, usually in the form of the merry widow. The wealthy, sex-hungry widow as male fantasy was a stock-in-trade of early modern dramatists. Both economically and sexually independent, she was a loose, free electron in a society of coupled atoms, with all its potential – and all its danger.

There have been only two analyses of the early modern merry widow stereotype. Lu Emily Pearson concluded fifty years ago that the popular suspicion of widows, which sometimes flared into abuse, sprang from a fear of women who were not under the governance of husbands, women who controlled their own property and who might run amok with their new-found power.[2] This analysis need not apply only to 'propertied' in the sense of 'wealthy' women, but could include any woman who was self-sufficient. Ten years ago Charles Carlton offered the more psychological interpretation that widows embody 'two of the most fundamental tensions within the male psyche – the contemplation of their woman's sexuality (perhaps with someone else), and their own death'.[3] Both the materialist and the psychological explanations are convincing, and mutually reinforcing.

The merry widow's antithesis was the poor widow of biblical injunctions, the object of worthy charities and the subject of pathetic law suits. 'Poor' in this sense seems to have referred as much to a widow's deprivation of a husband as to her economic state, and it is naturally this archetype that was drawn on by any widow suing in court, regardless of her financial condition. The widowed Mrs Anne Henshaw in 1654 published her petition to recover a cash annuity due from the Earl of Carlisle which had been sequestered by parliament 'for supply of the publick necessities'. She did so as a 'distressed widow', in dire need of the £2000 p.a. without which she and her seven children were 'reduced to a very mean condition'.[4]

In a more plausible, unpublicized case in Chancery in 1647 Elizabeth Cripps, widow of a Gloucestershire yeoman, claimed she was 'destitute' and 'like utterly to perish for want of meanes of livelyhood shee being an aged woman . . . and having small children to maintaine'. On the contrary, the defendants in the case averred that Cripps was actually childless and in receipt of £13 6s. 8d. annually in jointure.[5] If widow litigants' claims of poverty were ambivalent in point of fact,[6] they were a useful means of arousing judicial sympathy as well as providing some defence against any possible suggestion that the plaintiff was rather merrier than she should be.

Since archetypal widows abound, it is fortunate that in real life, too, widowhood is the female condition most visible to posterity. For the purpose of the historical record, a woman steps out from the penumbra of her husband upon widowhood. While women who never married are also visible, there were simply fewer of them, and in many cases the reason a woman appears in the record at all is because her husband has died.

It has often been assumed that women died more often than men in the early years of marriage due to the hazards of childbirth.[7] Among the elite, where brides were younger and had more children and so ran more risks, wives did indeed die more often than husbands.[8] However, among the majority of the population women usually did not bear children until their late twenties, and female mortality was probably only very slightly higher than male mortality during the childbearing years.[9] So if 80 to 90 per cent of adult women married at least once, then up to 45 per cent of all women could expect to be widowed at some time in their lives. Slightly more men than women would have been widowed at least once, as a result of slightly higher female mortality. But since men remarried more than twice as often as women, there were sub-stantially more widows than widowers in the population.[10] One estimate suggests that more than 70 per cent of all widowed persons in the population at any time between the late sixteenth and the early nineteenth centuries were women.[11]

The caricature of the merry widow is belied by widows' usual lack of wealth and low remarriage rates. The economic circumstances of ordinary widows in the year after their husbands' death are examined here in probate documents under two circumstances: where the husband personally granted his estate in a will; and where the widow was left to the vicissitudes of the laws of intestate distribution. Previous local studies of wills have assessed the bequests that husbands left to their widows, any restrictions on those bequests, and the rate at which wives were appointed executrix. In Chapter 9 these are compared with my own analysis of wills from Yorkshire, Lincolnshire and Sussex. This chapter also looks specifically at the implementation of the widow's entitlement to her 'reasonable part' in the northern province, which has not been addressed before because work on women's inheritance in their husbands' wills has so far been limited to the southern province.

Most men died intestate, without having made a will. Chapter 10 evaluates widows' position as estate administrators for the first time, with the use of probate accounts. The generosity that men exhibited towards their wives in their wills has been remarked upon by most students of wills. But this behaviour was matched by the ecclesiastical courts in their distribution of intestate men's estates, at least until the statutory changes of 1670, and possibly later.

In Chapter 11, wills, inventories and accounts together suggest how lone women lived, whether comfortably, independently or in poverty. While both widows and women who never married are discussed in this and the next chapter, more information can be discovered about widows than about single women. Widows' inventories are compared with those of their husbands, showing that a woman was as likely to improve as to dissipate her husband's estate in her widowhood. Probate documents can also add another angle to the debate over the conditions under which widows remarried.

Finally, Chapter 12 discusses the wills made by widows and single women. Although women's wills comprise a minority of the total number which survive, widows seem to have made wills even more often than men, relative to their number in the population. Widows made wills under different circumstances than their husbands had – most obviously, widows did not leave a spouse to manage financial affairs – but both widows' and single women's wills exhibit distinctly different patterns of property distribution from those found in men's wills.

9   Widows of men who made wills

APPOINTMENT AS EXECUTRIX

Legal treatises referred to the executor of a will as a person with great
responsibility. He arranged and paid for the funeral and burial; he paid
all legacies and ensured that the heir inherited land according to conditions
specified in the will, a process often lasting over many years, waiting
until legatees came of age or fulfilling contingent bequests in the event of a
legatee's death; in those areas which legally required it, he apportioned
reasonable parts to the widow and children; and he discharged the deceased's
debts and collected his credits.[1] But the most common early modern executor
was not an executor at all – she was an executrix. The feminine form appears
in legal treatises only in reference to a specifically female appointment, but it
was used consistently in probate documents themselves. In fact it was so
common that pre-written account forms and absent-minded scribes sometimes used it to refer to men in the same position. Thus, for example, the
Lincolnshire will of Isabel Uting in 1684 refers to her son as her executrix.[2]

It was not uncommon for a widow to be executrix of more than one will at
a time. Jane Sowton, in 1635 in the Sussex downs, was already executrix of
her own father's will when her husband died, and as executrix of her
husband she also became responsible for her father-in-law's will, made ten
years previously.[3] Lidia Johnson in the vale of Lincoln was not actually
named executrix by anyone, but in 1670 she found herself responsible for
the will of her brother-in-law, the labourer Charles Johnson. Charles had
made a will disposing of his £27 worth of goods in which he named his
brother William, Lidia's husband, executor. But William died shortly after
Charles, leaving a will in which he named his own minor son, also William,
executor. Lidia, as her husband's executor's mother, undertook responsibility for both wills.[4]

In addition to wills, two contemporary treatises bear witness to the fact that
a married man normally named his wife executrix. *The Lawes Resolutions of
Women's Rights* (1632) initially asserts that a wife 'is not made an executor,
because the office is troublesome', but it later approvingly quotes Sir Thomas
Smith's *De Republica Anglorum* (1583):

Though our law may seem somewhat rigorous toward wives, yet for the most part, they can handle their husbands so well, and doucely, specially when they bee sicke, that where the law gives them nothing, their husbands at their death of their good will give them all, and few there be that be not either made sole, or chiefe executors of their husbands last will and testament, having for the most part the government of their children and their portions.[5]

Table 9.1 ranges studies of wills in fourteen English locations chronologically, and confirms that most men between the fourteenth and the early eighteenth centuries named their wives either sole or joint executrix. In early modern England between 63 per cent and 89 per cent of married men did so (lines 5–13).

It appears from Table 9.1 that in the mid-sixteenth century a man became more likely to appoint his wife sole executrix, whereas earlier she had been joint executrix. This shift is probably due to the nature of the document pool. There is a much smaller number of surviving wills prior to 1550,[6] and these were made by relatively wealthier people. From the more numerous wills which survive in the later centuries it is observable that a wealthy man named his wife executrix significantly less often than an ordinary man, and the wealthier she was the more likely she was to be joint, rather than sole, executrix. The most specific calculations of this disparity have been made for the town of Petersburg, Virginia, in the period 1784–1860. There 80 per cent of poorer men, but only 33 per cent of wealthier men named their wives executrix. Three fifths of the poorer women, but none of the wealthier, were appointed sole executrix.[7] The same patterns prevailed in early modern Terling, Essex, and in three Norfolk parishes, where even among ordinary men, yeomen were less likely than husbandmen, craftsmen and labourers to name their wives executrix.[8]

Ordinary men were apparently not only more egalitarian in distributing their property among their children (see Chapter 4), they also put greater faith in their wives as business partners. Perhaps no one else was available, but probably at an ordinary level women were more closely involved in family financial matters during marriage. Greater financial cooperation in marriage was possible because property was less crucial from a dynastic point of view; it was essential because there was less money to spare. Ordinary women tended to be closer in age to their husbands, giving them more decision-making weight in the household. They were also more likely to have lived independently from their own parents prior to marriage, as servants and apprentices. And as wives their own labour visibly sustained a substantial proportion of the family economy. Wives were commonly referred to in their husbands' wills as 'dear and well-beloved'; the adjectives were formulaic, but they nonetheless suggest affection and trust.[9]

Table 9.1 illustrates the range of practice in appointing wives as executrix in different parts of the country, and should serve as a warning against

Table 9.1 Proportion of wives named executrix 1414–1710

	Place (N)	Sole	Joint	Overall
1	Lincoln (n.a.) 1280–1500	<30%	>50%	c.80%
2	Bristol (n.a.) 1381–1500	<32%	>50%	82%
3	Canterbury (116) 1414–43	<28%	>50%	78%
4	Suffolk and Norfolk (97) 1372–1540	8%	38%	46%
5	King's Langley, Herts (74) 1523–1659	51%	18%	69%
6	Salisbury (362) 1540–1639	72%	9%	81%
7	Abingdon, Berks 1540–1720	–	–	74%
8	Bungay, Suffolk (83) 1550–1600	49%	24%	73%
9	South Elmham, Suffolk (163) 1550–1640	35%	28%	63%
10	London (n.a.) Late 16th century–1603	80%	–	>80%
11	Sussex and Lincolnshire (76) 1579–1689	71%	7%	77%
12	Selby, Yorks (156) 1634–1710	67%	29%	96%
13	Rural Yorkshire (70) 1640–90	60%	29%	89%
14	Sevenoaks, Kent (39) 1660–85	67%	–	–

Sources: Lines 1–3, Ann Kettle, '"My wife shall have it": marriage and property in the wills and testaments of later medieval England', in R. B. Outhwaite (ed.) *Marriage and Society* (1981) p. 100; line 4, Nesta Evans, 'Inheritance, women, religion and education in early modern society as revealed by wills', in P. Riden (ed.) *Probate Records and the Local Community* (1985) p. 66; line 5, Lionel Munby (ed.) *Life and Death in King's Langley: Wills and Inventories, 1498–1659* (1981) my calculation; line 6, Susan Wright, 'Family life and society in sixteenth and early seventeenth-century Salisbury' (Leicester PhD thesis, 1982) p. 250; line 7, Barbara Todd, 'Widowhood in a market town: Abingdon 1540–1720' (Oxford PhD thesis, 1983) pp. 81–6; lines 8 and 9, Evans, 'Inheritance', p. 66; line 10, Vivien Brodsky, 'Widows in late Elizabethan London: remarriage, economic opportunity and family orientations', in L. Bonfield, R. M. Smith and K. Wrightson (eds) *The World We Have Gained* (1986) p. 145; line 11, WSRO and LAO wills; line 12, *Selby Wills* (1911); line 13, BIHR wills; line 14, H. C. F. Lansberry, 'Free bench see-saw: Sevenoaks widows in the late seventeenth century', *Archaeologia Cantiana* 100 (1984) p. 284.

drawing conclusions from any one locality. Earlier this century Alice Clark, apparently on the basis of Worcestershire, Hertford and Middlesex records, found a decline in wives appointed executrix in the later seventeenth century and deduced an erosion of women's status. But in 1979 Richard Vann found an increase in the same proportion in the town of Banbury, and deduced a rise in the status of English women generally.[10] 'Changing attitudes to women' has afforded a too-easy explanation of any patterns involving women. The evidence in Table 9.1 supports neither theory of a rise or theory of a fall over time in the proportion of wives named executrix, but suggests that regional variations were more significant than chronological ones.

For example, in Suffolk in the sixteenth century more women were appointed executrix, and more often sole executrix, in the town of Bungay than in rural South Elmham (lines 8 and 9). This discrepancy between urban and rural areas is supported by the extremely high proportion of widows named sole executrix in Salisbury (line 6) and in London (line 10). In Yorkshire, in the market town of Selby (line 12) a woman was more likely to be appointed executrix than she was in the rural areas of the north and east ridings (line 13). More urban couples may have shared in business enterprises, or perhaps in towns fewer men had male kin close at hand to serve as executors.

On the other hand, the rate in rural Yorkshire (89 per cent) was still higher than in urban Salisbury (81 per cent) and Bungay (73 per cent) in the south, so regional factors other than urbanisation must have been involved. Chronological variations also need to be looked into more closely. In colonial America the proportion of wives named executrix was comparable with that in England in the late seventeenth and early eighteenth centuries, at between 75 per cent and 89 per cent, but this proportion fell dramatically over the course of the eighteenth century. More studies of eighteenth-century English wills are needed to know if the same decline occurred there.[11]

If a man's failure to appoint his wife executrix appears to posterity as ungenerous, it may have been perceived by the testator as sparing his wife a burdensome responsibility. This hypothesis is borne out in the case of Salisbury, where it was precisely older women who were not made executrix.[12] The obvious choice for executor aside from a man's wife was his son – especially if he was grown, but it was also possible to appoint a minor as executor, and some men did. In this case the boy's guardian took responsibility until he came of age; if no guardian was specifically appointed then the boy's mother – or his father's wife – was responsible, as in the case of Lidia Johnson, above. In sixteenth- and early seventeenth-century King's Langley, Hertfordshire, 37 per cent of men who made wills named a son sole executor while their widow still lived (26 of 70 men who left both a wife and a son).[13] These men were the wealthier ones, who were probably most afraid of their widows' remarriage.

By contrast, Lincolnshire and Sussex men named a child (of either sex) sole executor in preference to a wife – who may or may not have been the child's mother – at a rate of only 13 per cent (7 of 56). Yorkshire men did so in a mere 2 per cent of cases (5 of 226). Even in the southern province (Lincolnshire and Sussex), most older widows with adult sons were still named executrix. Of the fifty-four women (including childless women) appointed sole executrix in Lincolnshire and Sussex, 26 per cent had at least one adult son.

The appointment of overseers or supervisors has been seen as an infringement on the freedom of the widow executrix. In Banbury the proportion of men's wills naming overseers fell from half prior to the mid-seventeenth century to one quarter after that, and Vann correlated the decline in overseers with the increasing incidence of widows named executrix, and with a later seventeenth-century improvement in women's status.[14] In Terling, too, overseers vanished over the course of the seventeenth century. But the practice of appointing overseers varied drastically both over time and by region, as can be seen in Table 9.2.

Table 9.2 Proportion of men appointing overseers 1523–1710

		%	n	N
1	King's Langley, Herts 1523–1659	44	44	99
2	Terling, Essex 1550–1700	37	71	192
3	Banbury, Oxon 1550–1724	24–49	–	603
4	Sussex 1579–1682	75	49	65
5	Lincolnshire 1591–1682	52	16	31
6	Selby, Yorks 1634–1710	4	10	224
7	Rural Yorkshire 1640–90	5	5	100

Sources: Line 1, Munby (ed.) *King's Langley*, p. xiv; line 2, Keith Wrightson, 'Kinship in an English village: Terling, Essex 1550–1700', in R. M. Smith (ed.) *Land, Kinship and Life-Cycle* (1984) p. 330 (*n.b.* this figure includes women's wills); line 3, Richard Vann, 'Wills and the family in an English town: Banbury, 1550–1800', *JFH* 4:3 (1979) pp. 364–5; line 4, WSRO wills; line 5, LAO wills; line 6, *Selby Wills*; line 7, BIHR wills.

In Sussex 75 per cent of men's wills appointed overseers, and in Lincolnshire 53 per cent (lines 4 and 5), much higher proportions than in the three earlier local studies of King's Langley, Terling and Banbury (lines 1–3). In contrast, in Yorkshire overseers were almost completely absent from men's wills throughout the seventeenth century (lines 6 and 7), not exceeding 5 per cent. Joint executors were appointed instead (see Chapter 4). But overseers became more popular, rather than less, by the end of the century in Yorkshire. Lincolnshire men, on the other hand, showed no change over time in their appointment of overseers. In Sussex the number of overseers appointed did drop over time, but this corresponded to a drop in the number of women appointed executrix, since in Sussex overseers were appointed specifically where the widow was executrix. Overseers were appointed in exactly the opposite case in Lincolnshire – where someone other than the widow was executor – and the same is true, although to a lesser extent, of the appointment of overseers in King's Langley.

Whatever the explanation of these regional differences – and despite the fact that overseers were invariably men – cooperation and assistance, rather than control, were usually the stated purposes of appointing an overseer. The nature of both executrix's and overseer's jobs were elucidated by Richard Irelande of the Sussex coast, described by his neighbours as a yeoman in his inventory, but by himself as a husbandman in his will of 1634. Richard named his wife Joan executrix, 'hoping that shee will faythfully performe the trust committed unto her as a loving wife ought to doe', and then appointed a 'loving neighbour' and a cousin as overseers, 'desiring them to bee assistant unto my wife'. Joan made her own will less than four months later, naming one of her husband's overseers as her executor and two 'welbeloved frends' as overseers, 'desiring and meaning them to see that my children bee well delt with'.[15] Overseers were commonly described as 'trusty and well beloved friends', which could have been meant to encourage the overseer to do right, rather than by way of affectionate remembrance, but it is significant that very few overseers were described as men in authority, like clergy, for example.[16] The patterns of overseer appointment are not at all clear, but the varying circumstances in which overseers were appointed and the language used to describe them suggest that their presence or absence was not closely related to female autonomy.

As executrix, a widow had virtually complete control over her former husband's estate. Although in general her authority was assumed, her husband occasionally further fortified her position in situations where she was to enjoy property which was subsequently given to a child on her death or remarriage. One who thought this extra protection important was a husbandman of the Sussex downs. Henry Smyth in 1594 bequeathed the bulk of his goods to the daughter and son left at home and to his wife Agnes. Each of the children received a long list of household goods, but Agnes retained a right in a certain joined press (a large cupboard for clothes) in the bedchamber and in all of the husbandry tools, for the duration of her widowhood. Henry's bequests were made on condition that if the children 'behave them unreverently or unnaturally towardes there saide mother and doe not live quietly nor naturally togeathers as lovinge and obedient childeren oughte to doe towardes there mother', then their portions were to be divided between the overseers and the children were to 'departe from the molestinge of there saide mother any further and to take suche chance and fortune as god hath appoynted for such disobedient children'. As it happened, the children did not have long to be disobedient. Their mother died the following year.[17] In a similar vein nearly a century later, a north Yorkshire yeoman declared that if anyone – but in particular the three nephews who would inherit 'all my reall freehold estate, houses, houseing, garthes, landes, meadowes and pasturegates' on his wife's death – 'shall disturbe, molest or sue my deare wife Ellis or her tennants' for their inheritance, then they should forfeit that inheritance to the poor of Pickering.[18]

BEQUESTS

All studies of wills in early modern England agree that in general widows were the principal beneficiaries of their husbands' wills, almost invariably receiving much more than their legal entitlement of one third.[19] The most common bequest to the executrix was 'all the rest of my goods moveable and unmoveable left unbequeathed', in addition to any specified bequests. The substantial value of the residual moveables – if not the unmoveables – can be verified by reference to the inventory, where it survives. When a child was made executor, whether adult or minor, then the residual goods were either not given to the executor, or the willmaker calculated his bequests so that the residual goods accruing to the child-executor worked out to be comparable with the other children's shares. But where the widow was executrix the residual goods generally comprised the bulk of the estate.

A husband who did not plainly give his wife the bulk of the estate often returned to her the goods she had brought with her to the marriage. Two such examples in Sussex are Jane Bartholomew and Mary Challen. In 1677 Jane Bartholomew's bricklayer husband left her £12, the furnished bed in the outer chamber worth £2, and two pairs of sheets not the best, in addition to 'all the goods she had when I married her'. Mary Challen in 1670 got from her yeoman husband all of his household stuff 'in house, gate, and lands' for life, plus the right to 'give and dispose of all such goods and household stuff which shee brought with her at the time of our marriage or since from her father's house'.[20] The return of a wife's portion may have been a substitute for the administration of the estate, since neither of these two women were appointed executrix. But the Challen estate went into debt, partly as a result of paying legal fees, and the simple return of a portion was probably preferable to dealing with an impoverished or embattled estate.

Alternatively, women like Jane Bartholomew and Mary Challen may have made some kind of agreement about property with their husbands prior to marriage which their husbands did not elaborate upon in their wills. Two Essex widows who had their bridal possessions returned in their husbands' wills had been careful to make inventories of these goods at the time of their marriage.[21] Even in the absence of an inventory, women who survived their husbands clearly knew what goods were theirs, and they were in a position (since their husbands did not make a list) to tell the appraisers and the family, if necessary, what did and did not belong in their husbands' inventories.

It is of course possible to find completely opposite examples of widows who were virtually cut out of their husbands' wills, and of widows who were given every last penny of their husbands' estates. Both of these cases are unusual, but one of each occurs in Sussex. Joan Wheatley in 1675 was cut off with the proverbial shilling from the £182 estate of her yeoman husband Richard. Richard named as executrix his minor daughter, and gave her tuition to an apparently unrelated yeoman, who sent the girl off to a schoolmistress in nearby Chichester (referred to in Chapter 3).[22] There may have been animosity between Joan and Richard; equally plausibly, Joan may have been Richard's second wife, not the girl's mother, and have made a contract for her own jointure or separate property at the time of their marriage. If Joan's own inventory had survived, the condition of the Wheatley marriage would be clearer. (The will of either of her parents would also be useful, but of course their name is unknown.) The only thing certain is that not enough information survives to discern the cause of Joan's exclusion.

At the opposite extreme from Richard Wheatley was the husbandman William Wooles. His will of 1629 named his wife Alice executrix and did 'freely, clerely and absolutely give her all my goods, chattells, personall estate and substance'. This was William's only bequest, despite the fact that he and Alice had four unmarried daughters. His 'substance' amounted to a substantial £149, most of which Alice still had when she died four years later, although she kept fewer animals and had 4 instead of 5 acres sown. Alice did make a will herself, in which she undoubtedly provided for her daughters, but it is not extant (see Chapter 3, for the girls' putting out).[23]

Even where a man failed to mention his wife at all in his will, it is very difficult to interpret the family situation. Callisthenes Brooke, esquire, of Selby, actually appears from his will to have been a widower. He left no bequest to a wife; the tuition of his four youngest children was given over to two in-laws; and his inventory was exhibited in court by his married daughter. But ten years later Callisthenes' widow Anne died, with an inventory of £142. She had not been isolated from the family – her will mentions all the same children that her husband's will did, plus new sons-in-law and grandchildren – but apparently she had made other arrangements with her husband about her maintenance in widowhood.[24]

The principal piece of property a man had to give to his wife was usually his house and land. Approximately half of all men who made wills mentioned land (see Chapter 4), but only one quarter specifically mentioned their dwelling house. The widows of the 75 per cent of men who did not mention a house probably continued to occupy the conjugal house during their lifetimes. If the house was copyhold or freehold, they had a right to freebench or dower, respectively. It may have been held in joint tenancy, or it may have been transferred by deed. If the house was leased, it may have been leased for specified lives beyond the testator's own, which almost invariably included the widow's life, or leased for a term of years, in which case it would have been included in the residual goods given to the executrix.

Among that quarter of male willmakers who mentioned their dwelling house, more than three quarters gave it to their wife, at the very least for the near future, and usually for the duration of her life (restrictions are discussed below). Ten men gave the house away from their wives. (All of these cases occurred in the second half of the century, eight in Yorkshire, two in Sussex and none in Lincolnshire.) Only one will actually smacks of malice: Thomas Kirkupp, in Yorkshire in 1650, gave his wife Isabell nothing but 'one brasse kettle', while his brother got the 'mansion house' in which the couple lived.[25] The other nine men clearly did not expect that their wives would be homeless, since feelings of animosity would not prompt a husband to refer to his wife still as 'dear and loving', as these men did. In these cases, a widow was usually given houseroom and/or an annual maintenance instead.

MAINTENANCE AND HOUSEROOM

Annual maintenance payments, in the style of a jointure, were rarely mentioned in wills in any place so far studied in England. Where they do occur, they were made by yeomen, and the amount was usually only £3 or £4 p.a., insufficient for an adult's annual maintenance requirements.[26] Since yeomen were not in the habit of impoverishing their wives, this annuity was clearly supplementary. It is to be assumed that these widows had other income – in the form of separate property, or from their own real estate over which they recovered control upon widowhood, or as a result of some other arrangement with their husband established during his lifetime by deed, contract or other conveyance.

Bequests of houseroom were slightly more common than annual maintenance arrangements. Isabel Ellyott in east Yorkshire in 1645 was to have £2 p.a. from her son John, who received the family house and farm, and was to be allowed 'dirt [presumably in which to plant a garden], housframe, bedding, washeing, and such necessaries as shee hath had formerly . . . dureing her naturall life if shee continue' to live with John.[27] Bequests like this one of room in a son's house suggest that, while her husband was clearly concerned for her well-being, the widow lacked autonomy. In the words of one early dictionary, she lacked 'libertie to live after ones owne law'.[28]

Table 9.3 charts the proportion of houseroom or maintenance bequests to wives in nine separate locations. With the sole exception of Orwell, Cambridgeshire (line 5), where virtually every widow was given houseroom, instead of all or most of the holding for her lifetime, the highest rates of houseroom or maintenance bequests anywhere else so far studied only reached 14–15 per cent in King's Langley, Salisbury and Kibworth Harcourt (lines 1–3). The rates in Abingdon and in Sussex, Lincolnshire and Yorkshire were negligible, not exceeding 3 per cent (lines 4, 6, 7, 8 and 9). In Terling, too, there was only a 'handful' of maintenance or annuity arrangements, and Cambridgeshire parishes other than Orwell also had a low incidence of such provisions.[29]

The distribution of maintenance and houseroom provisions does not correspond to agrarian economies. In Orwell the arable economy necessitated the preservation of large landholdings, which may have been a reason to give land to a son rather than to a wife. But the same should have been true of Abingdon, King's Langley and Kibworth Harcourt, all of which had much lower rates of houseroom provision. In Yorkshire, Lincolnshire and even to some extent Sussex, holdings were partible into smaller pieces, making it

Table 9.3 Bequests to wives of houseroom or maintenance

	Location	%	n	N
1	King's Langley, Herts 1523–1659	15	11	70
2	Salisbury, Wilts 1540–1639	14	55	392
3	Kibworth Harcourt, Leics c.1550–c.1750	15	28	193
4	Abingdon, Berks 1540–1720	3	12	398
5	Orwell, Cambs c.1550–c.1700	c.100	–	–
6	Sussex 1579–1682	3	2	58
7	Lincolnshire 1591–1682	0	0	25
8	Rural Yorkshire 1640–90	3	2	70
9	Selby, Yorks 1634–1710	1	1	156

Sources: Line 1, Munby (ed.) *King's Langley*, p. xx; line 2, Wright, 'Family life', p. 250; line 3, Cicely Howell, *Land, Family and Inheritance in Transition: Kibworth Harcourt 1280–1700* (1983) p. 256; line 4, Barbara Todd, 'The remarrying widow: a stereotype reconsidered', in M. Prior (ed.) *Women in English Society 1500–1800* (1985) p. 73, fn; line 5, Spufford, *Contrasting Communities*, p. 116; line 6, WSRO wills; line 7, LAO wills; line 8, BIHR wills; line 9, *Selby Wills*.

possible for a widow to retain the marital house while adult children were provided with smallholdings or cash to rent or buy land and a house.

The provision for widows in early America also varied regionally. Houseroom and maintenance provisions were much more common in colonial Massachusetts (up to 16 per cent in Salem) and Pennsylvania (nearly 25 per cent) than they were generally in England.[30] Maryland, on the other hand, had a very low incidence of houseroom provisions in the eighteenth century. The favourable situation of widows in Maryland has been attributed to its demographic conditions of few women and high mortality.[31] However, early modern England fits the demographic description of the northern colonies, with balanced sex ratios and relatively low mortality, while sharing Maryland's low incidence of widows' maintenance provisions. The relatively high rate of houseroom provision in Salem, Massachusetts, in the early eighteenth century is attributed to economic expansion and a more demanding younger generation,[32] but again this hypothesis does not fit the English case. It is not true of Orwell, with almost total houseroom provision, and would be difficult to test over a span of 150 years in King's Langley, Salisbury and Kibworth Harcourt, which had rates of houseroom provision comparable with that in Massachusetts. Clearly the reason for the restriction of widows to houseroom or maintenance has not yet been found.

LIMITATIONS ON BEQUESTS

A widow's enjoyment of her common law dower, her ecclesiastical thirds and her manorial freebench was limited to her lifetime. Aside from the operation of law, limitations to life, to widowhood or to the heir's minority could also be imposed by will, and they were most often imposed on the widow's bequest.

In the seventeenth century, limiting a wife's bequest to her widowhood was considered the natural result of a man's desire to protect his own and his children's property from the grasp of any future husband of his widow's, or of her children by another man.[33] The other two types of limitation – to life and to a child's minority – may be seen as having ultimately the same justification. In fact, the chances of a future husband or future children gaining control of a man's property unjustly were slim, for two reasons: first, the incidence of women's remarriage was low; and second, widows took evident pains to protect the inheritance of their former husbands' children by settlement in the event they did remarry (see Chapter 8).

Furthermore, both widowhood and lifetime restrictions would have been obviated if women had not been required to forfeit their property upon (re)marriage. But since both types of limitation preserved patrimony in the male line, they were essential to the law-making class's ability to amass and maintain its landed estates intact. With the benefits of hindsight, the use of bequest limitations suggests at least as much about men's jealousy of their wives themselves as property as it does about their jealousy of land and goods. But while sexual jealousy helps explain limitations on bequests to wives at the level of law, at the level of individuals, more than half of all men – and in some places up to three quarters of all men – imposed no limitation at all on their wives' bequests (see Table 9.4).

Less than 10 per cent of the men who made wills in this study limited any part of their wives' bequest to widowhood (lines 1, 2, 3 and 6), which small proportion confirms the situation in early modern Terling.[34] Most of these limitations applied to the family dwelling house, and specifically to provisions of houseroom or maintenance for the widow. The rate of widowhood limitations was slightly higher in Salisbury, at 12 per cent (line 5), no doubt because the incidence of houseroom and maintenance provisions there was also higher than elsewhere, at 14 per cent (see Table 9.3, line 2). A limitation to widowhood was understandably more often placed on houseroom or maintenance provisions than on an outright bequest of house and goods, and the same was true in King's Langley and in Cambridgeshire.[35]

In the American colonies, both northern and southern, restrictions on wives' bequests were more common than they were in England. In Maryland 16 per cent of men with children limited their wives' bequest to widowhood in the late seventeenth century, and that proportion more than doubled in the following century. In Pennsylvania in the late seventeenth and first half of the eighteenth centuries 36 per cent of men limited their wives' bequest to either

Table 9.4 Restrictions on wives' bequests 1540–1710

Location (N)	To widowhood		To heir's minority		To life		Total limited	
	%	n	%	n	%	n	%	n
1 Rural Yorkshire (70) 1640–90	7	4	3	2	23	16	31	22
2 Selby (156) 1634–1710	9	14	3	5	28	44	40	63
3 Lincolnshire (25) 1591–1682	8	2	12	3	24	6	44	11
4 Kibworth Harcourt (193) c.1550–c.1750	–		–		–		26	50
5 Salisbury (389) 1540–1639	12	45	2	7	34	132	47	184
6 Sussex (58) 1579–1682	9	5	3	2	14	8	26	15
7 North province (226) 1634–1710	8	18	3	7	27	60	37	85
8 South province (471) 1540–1682	11	52	3	12	31	146	45	210

Sources: Line 1, BIHR wills; line 2, *Selby Wills*; line 3, LAO wills; line 4, Howell, *Kibworth Harcourt*, p. 256; line 5, Wright, 'Family life', p. 249; line 6, WSRO wills; line 7, combination of lines 1 and 2; line 8, combination of lines 3, 5 and 6.

widowhood or a child's minority, nearly twice the incidence of any location so far studied in England.[36] Studies of eighteenth- and early nineteenth-century English wills are required to compare regional variations in bequest restrictions with chronological variations.

In Abingdon, Barbara Todd observed a chronological shift: while overall little more than 10 per cent of men limited their wives' bequests to widowhood, these limitations increased markedly from about 1570 through the late seventeenth century. Todd suggests that the rise reflects a growing individualism and desire to perpetuate both family name and family wealth, to which a widow's remarriage posed a threat.[37] However, a closer look at some individual limitations to widowhood cannot really support a dynastic motivation on many men's part.

For example, the Sussex butcher Thomas Lidgiter in 1682 gave to his wife Elizabeth £8 p.a. in her widowhood, together with her expenses in the raising of their three children and the use of such goods and household stuff as she liked. Thomas was careful to specify that if Elizabeth 'shalbee weake and sickly soe that the £8 p.a. . . . shall not be thought sufficient' then she was to receive 'what more shalbee fitt'.[38] But even in the event of her remarriage Elizabeth was still to enjoy £4 p.a., which implies more that Thomas Lidgiter thought his wife's new husband ought to contribute towards her livelihood than that he was antagonistic to her remarriage.

One Selby labourer who died in 1668 combined a widowhood limitation with a positive recommendation for a certain potential future husband for his wife. Elizabeth Blythe was to have the part of the house next the garth (garden) in which she and her husband had lived, and half of the garth for her widowhood, 'except she marry with John Browne's sonne of Biggin, linnen webster, and then the said partes of the said house and garth to remaine to ye only proper use and behoofe of the said John Browne's sonne, his heires etc.'.[39]

In another variation on a widowhood limitation, the fenland yeoman John Pyne in 1598 directed that 'my wief and my sonne . . . shall remaine together with the encrease of their stockes and if my wief doe chaunce to mary then my will ys that my sons porcon shalbe putt into thandes of [my overseer] . . . to be put forth', and 'boundes shalbe taken of the parties that shall have my childrens porcons'.[40] This provision in the event of Joan Pyne's remarriage does not have to be seen as an assumption that her interests would shift to those of her new husband, or that a stepfather would necessarily treat the Pyne children badly, or that John Pyne did not want his wife to remarry. The simple operation of the law of coverture would give all a widow's property to her new husband on marriage and this legal process alone may explain many restrictions to widowhood.

It is impossible to overemphasize the effects of coverture upon property practices. Because of coverture, it was not only men who restricted their executrix's benefits to the period of widowhood. A daughter might do the same thing to her mother. Elizabeth Lea of King's Langley in 1652 named her mother Sarah executrix and gave her the bulk of her substantial £157 inventory, to be at her disposal, as long as her mother remained a widow. 'Butt in case Sarah Lea my mother shalbe betrothed and married unto a husband dureinge her naturall life, my will is that then shee shall have but onely the use of my sayd goods, debtes and chattells aforesayd dureinge her naturall life', they going after her death to Elizabeth's brothers and sisters.[41]

The idea of increasing male individualism is further cast in doubt because in areas other than Abingdon the use of widowhood restrictions receded again from the mid-seventeenth century. In rural Yorkshire, Lincolnshire and Sussex, eight of eleven restrictions to widowhood occurred before 1650.[42] Regionally, men in the southern province placed slightly more restrictions on their wives' bequests than those in the northern province (Table 9.4, lines 7 and 8). But chronologically, the southern wills begin nearly a century earlier, and this raises a third possible explanatory factor: the wealth of the man making the will. Men who made wills before the middle of the sixteenth century tended to be wealthier than those who made wills over the ensuing 150 years. And in the seventeenth century the men who imposed widowhood restrictions were the wealthier ones.

Perhaps ordinary men were relatively sympathetic to the pressures on their wives to remarry (see Chapter 12); perhaps they had greater respect for their wives' judgement; or perhaps their concerns were simply less dynastic than those of wealthy men. It may also have occurred to them that restricting a bequest to widowhood was a risky approach in the long term, since in the event that the widow did remarry then the property had to change hands more often *via* trustees and contingent trustees. This process complicated the administrative process and increased the chances of the property being alienated from the children.

Like limitation to widowhood, limitation to the eldest son's minority was a useful dynastic tool. Among large landowners, 95 per cent of men gave the family seat to the heir immediately upon his majority, but in these families another 'dower' house was available for the widow.[43] However, at an ordinary level a restriction of the wife's bequest to the eldest son's minority was rarely employed. Only 3 per cent of men in both northern and southern provinces (lines 7 and 8) restricted even a part of a wife's bequest to one or more children's minority, and then it could be the youngest as well as the eldest child. As with widowhood limitations, all but one of these cases occurred in the first half of the seventeenth century.

Once again, Cambridgeshire offers an apparently isolated exception to the rule: in the parish of Willingham, restricting a widow's holding to her eldest son's minority was the commonest means of bequest.[44] Willingham is in the fen, and fenland areas had very high mortality rates,[45] so it is possible that wives were not expected to live to their children's majority. The discrepancy in restriction to the heir's majority between Lincolnshire, at 12 per cent, and Yorkshire and Sussex, at 3 per cent, is based on very small numbers (Table 9.4, lines 3 and 6), but two of the three Lincolnshire restrictions did come from fen parishes. The explanation of high mortality is not entirely satisfactory. If a widow was not expected to live to the heir's majority, then why bother to write out a clause restricting her bequest, paying the scribe for the extra words? Further research will have to compare more areas to explain the use of limitations to a child's majority placed on widows' bequests.

An absolute bequest to a wife, without limitations on its duration, assumed that she shared the same familial interests as her dying husband. A life grant to a wife protected property from any subsequent husband and preserved it for the children, while still allowing her maximum control. Lifetime use was both the least restrictive and the most common type of limitation. Even so, generally less than one third of married men gave all or part of their wives' bequests for life only, and nearly always the limitation was on land or dwellings.

REASONABLE PARTS

In the northern province a man's widow, like his children, was entitled by ecclesiastical law to one third of her husband's moveables – her reasonable part, or 'thirds'. Only the final third was at his testamentary disposal. This law was used by Yorkshire men to limit the inheritance of daughters who had already married with portions, and of sons who had inherited or would inherit land (see Chapter 4). Few men mentioned their wives' right to thirds. In rural Yorkshire only 9 per cent of men (6 of 70) did so. Mary Foster, for instance, in 1689 received from her husband their bed 'with the strip'd curtaines' and £26 6s. 8d. 'in full consideracion of her third part of my personall estate'. If she did not accept this cash amount then the executor (not Mary, in this case) was to give her 'only . . . what the law will allow and no more'.[46] One yeoman in 1641 desired that

> my beloved wife Dorothe Brigham shall have that share of my personall estate which the law shall conferr uppon her, made worth £100, provided that she procure her son Thomas Mawburne to joyne in passing the estate of the lands sold by me to . . . otherwise she to have but her share and no more.[47]

In these wills the widow's reasonable part appears to have been used as an enforcement mechanism when the value of her bequest exceeded her legal entitlement but either was in a different form than she might have liked or was conditional upon some action of hers. The thirds rule was mentioned only three times in the wills of 156 married men in the town of Selby, and in none of these three was a widow given less than one third. The silence of the other 153 men on the rule of thirds did not mean that they were ignoring it. Rather, it was not an issue because the widow, usually as executrix, clearly had the bulk of the property in her own hands.

The ecclesiastical right to reasonable parts prevailed in the northern province, in Wales and in the City of London in the seventeenth century. Between 1692 and 1725 it was abolished by a series of statutes. The ostensible purpose was to unify the law throughout the land, and to allow 'freedom of testation' (see Chapter 2). In fact, in passing these statutes, parliament was probably influenced by its members' desire to limit the amount of her husband's estate that a wealthy woman – perhaps their own wives – could claim upon widowhood. A woman who had made a good marriage settlement, incorporating a jointure and perhaps separate estate or pin-money, would also have been aware of her additional entitlement to one third of her husband's moveables. This was more than the members of parliament thought reasonable. Perhaps even had they considered the ordinary woman who had failed to make a marriage settlement, they might have thought it no bad thing to place her upon the mercy of her husband in his will. It is significant that the church in the later seventeenth century was in no position to object strenuously to parliamentary interference in ecclesiastical law, as it had done in the fourteenth century when married women's ability to make a will was abolished (see Chapter 8).

The effects of the legislation abolishing reasonable parts have not yet been established. Henry Horwitz has looked at its ramifications in London, on the wealthy citizens whose wills were probated in the Prerogative Court of Canterbury. (In London the rule of reasonable parts applied only to freemen, or citizens.) Horwitz finds that these men had been ignoring the rule of reasonable parts for many years prior to the legislation, but he treats the type of thirds limitation quoted above, on the bequests to Mary Foster and Dorothy

Brigham, as meaning that a woman was actually given less than her legal entitlement.[48] On the other hand, when the entitlement to thirds prevailed in the southern province in the middle ages, Ann Kettle found the same type of phrasing in men's wills (apparently specifically in London), and she interprets it as I have, to mean that more than the legal minimum was being given, but in a form which was not ideal.[49] It will only be possible to settle the question of whether widows with a restriction to thirds were receiving more or less than their legal entitlement by reference to the inventories of the estates of the men who made these wills. In England these inventories are often not available.

However, the correlation has been made in America. There, over the course of the eighteenth century, the proportion of the estate that men gave to their widows fell to less than one third, or less than widows' right in the event of intestacy. Only after 1800 did provision for widows improve, as a means of preserving family assets in a time of economic dislocation rather than as any recognition of women's autonomy.[50] The widow's right to a reasonable part – or one third even if her husband made a will – was transferred only to the southern colonies (where it is referred to as 'dower of personalty'). And in Maryland and Virginia, where they had the choice, many widows who were given less than their reasonable part chose to take their legal entitlement instead of their bequest.[51] In the case of England, a study of testamentary litigation in the church courts will be required to determine how often a wife was denied her thirds in her husband's will – in those parts of England where she was entitled to it – and whether she chose her legal entitlement in preference to her husband's bequest in these cases.

CONTROL OF CHILDREN'S INHERITANCE

In addition to her own bequest, the executrix had the use of her children's portions during their minority. The importance of this sum is clear in the case of one Catharine Milles, of the Sussex weald. Her yeoman husband gave her the use of their nine children's bequests, amounting to £96. Catherine died four years later, still a widow, and her husband's as yet unpaid legacies to their minor children comprised two thirds of the value of her inventory.[52] By contrast, if anyone other than the wife was appointed executor, that person was not allowed free rein with the children's portions, but had to invest the money and use the annual interest for the children's support. John Hardham, a yeoman of the Sussex coast, in 1671 specifically stated that his 'loving wife' Joan was *not* required to render to their two minor sons an account of either their cash portions *or* their free land at their majority.[53]

It was assumed that the widow executrix had not only the children's interests at heart, but also the authority and experience to manage their portions. A gentleman of Selby gave to his wife Ann Rayner one newly purchased house for her life, and afterwards to their son, but also 'all my other houses . . . to the use of her, her heires, . . . for ever, to sell, lett, or sett or otherwise to dispose of, for the use of my six daughters, as she shall see cause and think fitt'.[54] On a more modest scale, Constance Nowell, widow of a husbandman of the Sussex downs, was entrusted in 1579 with the portions of her three daughters, consisting of £15 and a brass pot each. Her husband Anthony provided that his overseers were to take the children and their portions from his wife Constance – with bonds for security – only in the event that 'my wyffe do not bringe upp or cause to be brought upp all my three daughters in good order and state howe to be good membres in the common wealthe'. (Anthony was clearly not familiar with Sir Thomas Smith's exclusion of women from membership in the commonwealth on the grounds that nature made them 'to keepe home and to nourishe their familie'.) Constance fulfilled her commission, since when she died thirty years later, still farming in two separate places with the help of hired labour, she had seen her two surviving daughters to three marriages and was able to bestow generous bequests upon four grandchildren.[55]

GENEROSITY OR JUSTICE?

Large bequests to wives, and the appointment of wives as executrix, are often cast in terms of male generosity. We are surprised and pleased to find that men in the past thought so highly of their wives' management skills and fiscal responsibility. But the interpretation of men's testamentary actions towards their wives is not straightforward. If women's expectations differed from men's, we are left with almost entirely men's point of view, since they are the ones who leave both spouses and wills. The subtleties can only be illustrated with a case which is far better documented than the ones so far discussed. Although this will is not English, there is no particular reason to think that the conditions of testation in Wittenberg were significantly different when Martin Luther made his will in 1542, four years before his death.

Luther gave his wife Katherine 'the little holding at Zulsdorf, the same which I have purchased and made useful', plus another house, both for her to enjoy during her lifetime.[56] This bequest might strike us as magnanimous, as indeed it strikes both of the will's recent editors.[57] However, from other sources it appears that Katherine herself instigated all of Luther's real estate purchases. It was she who negotiated the acquisition of Zulsdorf. She improved it, farmed it and managed it herself, in addition to running the former cloister at Wittenberg in which her much-extended family lived, together with its adjacent gardens and orchard. In this light, Luther's bequest looks less generous and more like the least he could have done.

If we allow, with his translator, that 'Luther was too preoccupied with more important matters and far too generous a man to be much concerned about his material possessions',[58] then we must ask who so kindly relieved him of that responsibility. It was the tremendously efficient Katherine who preoccupied herself with those less important matters of material possessions. After Luther's death Katherine not only kept the cloister-farm and Zulsdorf, she also purchased yet another property in a nearby village and personally farmed that, in addition to her other two holdings, until her death four years later at the age of 51.[59]

While partnership was the working mechanism of this marriage – or rather, while Katherine was the prime economic mover – the language of Luther's will was that of personal bestowal of gifts from a superior to an inferior. That gesture, in whatever spirit Luther meant it, is too easy to read in later centuries as magnanimity. For the vast majority of marriages about which any record at all survives, that will – that gift from husband to wife – is the only record. Martin Luther and Katherine von Bora may serve as a reminder of the perils of that one document.

10 Widows of men who did not make wills

THE OBLIGATIONS OF AN ADMINISTRATRIX

Most men died without having made a will. While a widow was usually named executrix in her husband's will, where her husband died intestate she was legally entitled to administer his estate.[1] Should she choose to renounce her administration, she received a token fee, usually 1s.[2] Of 475 widows of intestate men in Lincolnshire, Northamptonshire, Cambridgeshire and Sussex, only 4 per cent (20) renounced their right to administration.

When male executors renounced responsibility the usual expression was that they 'declined the trouble'. The widows who renounced administration were also declining what they perceived might be trouble in their husbands' estates: in most of the twenty renunciations the husband's debts exceeded his assets, or at least threatened to do so. In the Sussex weald in 1595, Elizabeth Ward received an extraordinary 8s. for renouncing the administration of her copyholder husband's considerable £95 moveable estate. One of her husband's many creditors took over as administrator, paying out the balances due on more than twelve separate bills and bonds, to end up with less than £5 out of the estate.[3]

Widows' renunciation specifically in cases where their husbands' estates were heavily indebted suggests two things. First, the widow who renounced was sufficiently acquainted with the family's financial health to able to predict a balance in the red. And second, she had property of her own to protect from liability for her husband's debts, since otherwise she could not have afforded to abandon the sinking estate.

Most widows did administer their husbands' estates and one fifth of them (97 of 455) were still left with nothing or in debt at the final account. A woman who chose to administer her husband's estate but went into debt as a result may also have had her own property, and enough of it to cover her husband's debts. Or she may have been confident that her own property was secured sufficiently to be safe from his creditors. Or the family real estate, under her management, could be expected to produce profits out of which outstanding debts could be satisfied. Ultimately a person's debts died with them, so if the estate was insufficient to repay in full, creditors had to 'compound', accepting a proportion in the pound as satisfaction. Widows whose own property was entirely bound up with their husbands' could not have afforded to evade the responsibility of administration if there was a chance of any personal property being left over.

Widows chose to take up administration even more often than they were appointed executrix, whether they were administering their husband's, their child's or their in-law's estate, or two at the same time. When Mary Archer, of the city of Lincoln, administered her yeoman husband's £209 estate in 1624, she also 'inherited' the wills of at least two other people for whom he had been executor, and whose legacies she was bound to pay. She also had to deal with ten separate rents and seventeen debts of various kinds; she was arrested upon a debt for £3 6s. 8d. due to a draper from her husband for her son's suit of apparel; she herself sued another woman to recover a debt of £4 8s. Mary must have been glad to be left at length in peace with her relatively paltry £46 of residual goods.[4]

The legal procedure of filing an account, whether as an executrix or an administratrix, and the mechanisms by which that procedure was enforced, were discussed in Chapter 2. In addition to the technical requirements, we can also glimpse a more human side to the process. While the vast majority of those responsible for estates in the probate courts were women, the structure within which they did so was created and maintained entirely by men. The scribe who wrote a will, the appraisers who made the inventory, any guides to show the way to the court, the sureties bound at the time of taking administration, the apparitors who enforced the filing of accounts, the probate clerk who made the fair copy of the account and double-checked the addition of sums, any lawyers to advise on legal suits, the ecclesiastical judge who approved or did not approve the account and allocated the residual goods, and the Overseers of the Poor to which a widow might have to turn for her own or her children's maintenance – all were men.[5]

The first level of enforcement was the apparitor. While the relationship between apparitor and accountant was probably never warm, details are extremely rare. Most women harassed by an apparitor would have vented their anger to their neighbours or their kin. In the case of Sarah Dalby in 1624, she was sufficiently irate to complain to the apparitor's superiors, the men in the probate court at Lincoln, 24 miles from her home in Appleby, near the Humber estuary. Before the court she alleged

> that one Smith th'apparitor of the deanery . . . cited her to appeare at Lincoln on Wednesday the 23th of June last to take administracion of her husband's goods . . . And she on the Monday before her appearance being the 21th of June . . . did obtaine letters of administracion of her said husband's goods . . . and . . . passed her accompt of the same goods, both which she hath under seale. After which done the said Smith brought to the minister of [Appleby] a suspencion for not appearing and he the said Smith then told her that she cold not be absolved unles she kneeled

before the Judge of Assize and told her further that he wold make her come to his Maister Lands office and make her pay him his fees or it should cost her £5. . . .

Sarah succeeded in getting this suspension from the church absolved, but the apparitor persisted, this time using a more bizarre approach, as Sarah related:

> Notwithstanding in the beginning of this August the said Smith came againe unto her to Appleby . . . and told her that she should appeare at his Mr Lands office the 13th of this August . . . and said if she came not this day he would procure her to be excommunicated and bid her come to the leaden well and he wold bring her before such a fine gentleman as she never sawe before . . . . And she fearing to be excommunicate hath now left her harvest work to her great hindrance and six pore fatherles children at home and verily beleiveth hath taken this jorney on purpose and without any cause. And saith that her husband hath left but £10 14s. 4d. towards her and her said six childrens maintenance which small some is like to be weakened by such . . . vexacions and they thereby much impoverished. She humbly prayeth . . . she be discharged from all future molestacions in his behalfe.[6]

Sarah was indeed discharged, but there is no telling how many other countrywomen, ignorant of legal procedures or susceptible to the authority of an apparitor, no matter how mad, were harassed in similar ways. Unsophisticated countrymen, of course, could also be tricked. One John Copledyke, for example, administering his son-in-law's estate on behalf of his grand-children, explained to the court 'that he being ignorant in the lawes' had asked an apparitor to take out letters of administration on his behalf, but the apparitor had taken them in his own name instead, thereby possessing the estate.[7] But women had to face the situation more often, since they were more often accountants, and since they were less likely than men to be knowl-edgeable about legal procedures. Certainly deference to authority was inculcated throughout society, in men as well as women, but men were not also exhorted to silence and obedience towards an entire sex. If most women did not behave silently and obediently, it is nevertheless reasonable to presume that the exhortations took their toll on confidence. Both women and men could be abused through their ignorance, but only women were also abused through their sex.

Despite their vulnerability, the duties of administering an estate required extensive independent action on the part of accountants. Journeys to appear in court and to retrieve and pay debts might be both complex and costly. For example, in Northamptonshire in 1682, Hannah Tapp's husband had at least £95 in credits at his death. Hannah was wealthy enough to hire lawyers and messengers, at a total cost of £5, to gather these in. (Hannah had made a pre-marital settlement with her husband; see Chapter 8.) Of the £283 worth of debts owed by her husband very few were secured by bond, which meant she could not be penalized for non-payment, so her husband's creditors probably had to come to her to collect them.[8]

But Elizabeth Lawrence, the widow of a husbandman of only moderate means, had to undertake the administrative journeys herself in 1679. First, she travelled the 30 miles from her home in the Lindsey fenland to Lincoln to exhibit her husband's inventory and take out letters of administration. Then she had to pay debts out of the £50 estate to twenty-five men and five women in her own and six other villages and towns up to 20 miles distant from her home.[9] The average amount of these debts was only slightly over £1, so if Elizabeth sent messengers with payment rather than going herself, the relative cost in messengers would have been high. Even a labourer's widow, Elizabeth Roweth, was expected to hire horses for herself and her surety to travel from Swineshead to both Boston (6 miles away) and Lincoln (26 miles away) to deal with her husband's estate.[10]

Accountants were allowed to deduct expenses in horsehire or ferrying costs in the fens – Margaret Parkinson had two men row her from her home in Whittlesey to Cambridge to take care of her husband's account in 1604[11] – and sureties' dinners for court appearances. Directions to the court might also be necessary – Anne Horton's accountant paid a shilling to 'a man for goeing with me to shew me the country', in this case the 7 miles from Publow to Bath in Somerset in 1709.[12]

Administrative costs could be affected by legal changes, like the Act to bolster the flagging wool trade, which from 1678 required all bodies to be wrapped in woollen rather than linen for burial. Whether certified by affidavit or, as Elizabeth Daulton did, by giving Goodwife Whitehead a shilling to go to the justice and swear that Elizabeth's husband had been buried in woollen, the proof required a small fee. Failure to comply resulted in a hefty fine of £2 10s., distributed to the poor.[13]

Elizabeth Steevens *als* Cox, the administratrix of her mother's £33 estate in 1639, was granted more than most by the court at Bath when she claimed £8 for 160 days of her husband's travel in his mother-in-law's business.[14] When an accountant's husband assisted with administration, or even filed the account on his wife's behalf, as Elizabeth Browne's husband did in 1612 for the £14 estate of her mother Cassander Bushey, all business had still to be conducted in his wife's (the deceased's daughter's) name.[15] The same was true in the case of a deceased man's account filed by his remarried widow, if her new husband assisted.[16] This insistence on the personal responsibility of the widow is in sharp contrast with the situation in some American colonies, where a widow was legally required to share the administration of her husband's estate with his adult son or with her subsequent husband, if either existed.[17]

ALLOCATION OF RESIDUAL GOODS

When a husband died intestate leaving a wife and children, his widow was entitled by ecclesiastical law to one third of his moveables, after his debts had been paid. The loss of two thirds of the supplies and goods she had been living on and with throughout marriage seems harsh indeed. But examination of the actual division of residual goods in accounts during the late sixteenth and the first three quarters of the seventeenth century shows that the ecclesiastical courts interpreted the rules of intestate property distribution as elastically for widows as they did for children (see Chapter 4).

The allocation of residual goods to a widow with children was almost invariably in excess of the legal requirement of one third. The median portion of goods assigned to the 152 widows with children prior to the Act was 63 per cent, nearly twice the legal allotment. A substantial minority of women – 18 per cent (28 of 152) – were given *all* of their husbands' residual estates (see Figure 2). Some of these widows had minor children, in which case the future costs of upbringing were apparently considered a part of the child's portion and left entirely at the widow's discretion. In other cases the children were all grown, in which case the court clearly must have considered that the previous benefits those children had received from their father's estate were sufficient for their portions. As in the case of unequal allocation of goods among siblings, future research could investigate whether children ever challenged their mother's larger than legal share of their father's moveable goods.

This relatively advantageous situation for widows changed in 1670. The Act for the Better Settling of Intestates' Estates ostensibly merely restated the existing ecclesiastical rule of reasonable parts: one third of their husband's moveables to widows with children. But while we have seen that the ecclesiastical courts continued to adjust the distribution of portions among siblings after the Act (Chapter 4), the restriction of widows to one third appears to have been strictly enforced. The result was that the Act seriously undermined widows' financial position. This incapacitation is vividly illustrated in those accounts which specified the distribution of the residual goods. Whereas the median portion of goods assigned to widows with children prior to the Act was 63 per cent, after the Act, as Figure 2 shows, widows' portions dropped sharply to the one-third statutory level.[18]

Although dramatic, this drop in widows' allocation is difficult to interpret. Only eighteen post-Act accounts quantified the distribution of residual goods. Most clerks, instead of quantifying as they had done previously, henceforth simply wrote 'Distributed according to the Act' under the balance at the bottom of the account. However, those eighteen post-Act cases in which the distribution was quantified are noticeably more consistent than in the earlier period. This suggests that probate clerks were not considering individual circumstances. At the same time, the clerk's comment 'Distributed according to the Act' may have been intentionally vague in order to avoid exact

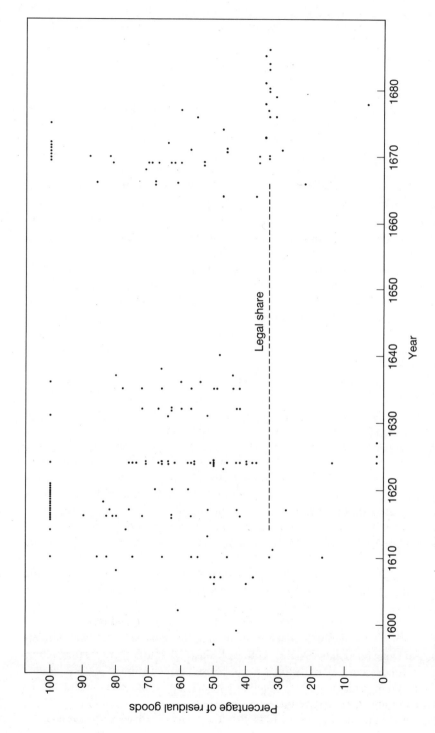

Figure 2 Proportion of men's estates allocated to widows with children by ecclesiastical courts, 1597–1686

quantification, so it is not clear exactly how closely the Act was observed. Nor is it clear to what extent, after 1670, a widow might deduct her expenses in apprenticing or educating a child from that child's portion when she paid it at the child's majority.

There appears to have been no public outcry over the 1670 statute, which argues against a sudden change in practice. Ecclesiastical lawyers, who three hundred years earlier had made strenuous objection to parliamentary rejection of the ecclesiastical rule that a married woman could make a will (see Chapter 8), were silent. Mary More and Mary Astell in the late seventeenth century, and the anonymous author of *The Hardships of the English Laws. In Relation to Wives* in the early eighteenth century, all of whom wrote about women's property, are nevertheless silent on the issue of parliamentary restriction of widows, either in the 1670 statute, or in the later abolition of reasonable parts. All three women were of a social class unlikely to be directly affected by the legislation, since they and their friends would have had marriage settlements instead of relying on the minimal legal provision, but they still might have been expected to mention issues affecting more ordinary women. Even if there was no sudden change in practice at the ecclesiastical courts, there may well have been a gradual one over many years. The financial ramifications of the 1670 Act are unclear, but it can at least be said that it substantially reduced a woman's nominal control of her husband's estate in favour of her children. A widow was left with less legal entitlement to property and less practical authority.

Even before 1670, there were regional differences in the distribution of residual estates. Cambridgeshire (fifty-eight cases) was by far the most generous to widows with children, assigning them a median of 80 per cent of their husbands' goods; more than one third of these women (34 per cent) received 100 per cent of the estate. In contrast, Lincolnshire (seventy-two cases) allotted widows with children a median of only 57 per cent, and less than 6 per cent received all of their husbands' goods. Sussex courts (only fourteen cases) never alloted more than 80 per cent, and usually near 50 per cent. The variations in the distribution of moveable goods may reflect differences in manorial land law. On a manor where freebench consisted of all her husband's holding, for example, a widow might get a smaller proportion of his personal estate than on a manor where freebench was only a fraction of the holding. This hypothesis can only be tested by a comparison of manorial court records and probate accounts in an area where they both survive.

In general, at least until the Act of 1670, the ecclesiastical courts matched the behaviour of men who made wills in that they gave widows a preponderance of their husbands' estates. But ecclesiastical courts went further – they never imposed any penalty for a widow's subsequent remarriage. A widow who had remarried by the time she filed the account of her previous husband's estate did not suffer any reduction in her share of his goods, in relation to his children. In the Lincolnshire wolds, Prudence Kay *als* Ellwards had remarried at the time of filing her first husband's account in 1624. Her two children had between them £5 (42 per cent) of their father's residual £12, for which Prudence's new husband, a weaver, had given security. This left Prudence with only £7, or 58 per cent of her first husband's estate. Although her share was still nearly twice her legal allocation, it was noted by the clerk that Prudence gave her explicit consent to this allocation.[19] The practice of the ecclesiastical courts in this respect remained consistent even towards the end of 1671, just before the Act's implementation. Bridget Gudgin's yeoman husband died in Northamptonshire in 1670, leaving her £234 and four 'small and helplesse' children. Bridget remarried one Edward Fellowes, requiring of him 'articles or covenants of agreement' for the children's portions amounting to £50, and subsequently filed her first husband's account. All of the remaining £87 (64 per cent of her first husband's residual goods) Bridget desired 'to be allowed unto her towards her owne and their maintenance'. Notwithstanding her coverture at the time, the court sanctioned her request.[20]

Figure 2 shows a cluster of cases of residual distribution at 0 per cent in 1624–7, and one case of 3 per cent in 1678. The consent of the widow was usually recorded in writing in those cases where a widow received little or nothing from her husband's residual estate. Where her consent was not recorded it was clear that she had made a pre-marital property settlement with her husband. Several of these cases were the same women who appear in Table 8.1 by virtue of their marriage settlement. A settlement nullified the right to thirds of moveables in the same way that jointure barred the right to common law dower. The reasons for the more minor variations in distribution are obscure, and probably had as much to do with the probate ordinary's personal assessment of the particular woman before him as with the relevant ecclesiastical law.

Nevertheless, the median widow's share of her husband's goods was double that which was allotted her by law for very practical and immediate reasons. In 703 accounts in the period 1572–1711, in Lincolnshire, Cambridgeshire, Northamptonshire and Sussex, the median residual wealth left to be distributed among the widow and children was a mere £33. Had the ecclesiastical court given the widow only her legal £11 out of that £33, and required that the children's portions be put out at interest, it would in most cases have wholly incapacitated the household.

In this respect a widow was disadvantaged compared with the guardian who was appointed for children who had lost both father and mother. These guardians were almost always male and (where discernible) married. With a couple's income and an established household, guardians possessed a critical financial advantage over the children's widowed mother. Guardians could, and did, liquidate the deceased's household in order to raise cash for the children's maintenance. Their mother did not have that option unless she were willing to put forth her children and live as a tenant in another's house. Most widows apparently preferred to live independently and raise their children at a reduced level of comfort (see Chapter 11).

GENEROSITY OF JUSTICE?

As men's testamentary generosity to their wives is qualified by knowing the details of the case of Katherine von Bora Luther, so both large allocations from the ecclesiastical courts to intestate men's widows and large bequests to wives in their husbands' wills are put into perspective by assessing more ordinary women's relative contribution to the marital estate. Some probate accounts allow a detailed comparison of the wealth which a woman brought into a marriage with her husband's wealth at the time of his death. For example, Jane Upperton of the Sussex coast, whose prosperous yeoman husband Thomas died in 1666 worth £668, had brought him more than half of his personal wealth: £340 of his inventory was reserved to pay the legacies of Jane's children by her first husband. Thomas did not mention this fact in his will, and we would know nothing of the composition of his wealth without the account of Jane's estate, filed by her son three years after Thomas's death.[21]

This kind of information is rarely made explicit, but it can be worked out in twenty-one cases either from probate accounts or from inventories filed first for a husband and subsequently for his widow. In these twenty-one cases a woman usually brought to her marriage more than 50 per cent of the total personal wealth of which her husband died possessed. Several wives had brought even more at marriage than the total their husbands were worth at death. These men still had young children at the time of their death, so their estates had not been diminished by the natural attrition of age and the setting up of new households for grown children. This 50 per cent figure is a minimum because it is based on the sums for which women made settlements, either as separate estate or for the portions or legacies of their children by a previous husband, whereas the total amount which a woman brought to marriage was always greater than the amount for which she contracted.

These estimates are approximate and cannot take account of any detail in relative spousal contributions to the marital economy. Probably more of men's wealth lay in land while most of women's wealth consisted of moveables. But the balance is suggestive of far more economic equality in marriage than one would assume from the conventional idea that a man waited to marry until he could 'afford to support' a wife and children. On the contrary, marrying was one way to make ends meet, and might be the quickest way for a man to improve his financial situation.

To extricate a wife's property from her husband's in this way is not an anachronistic enterprise. Early modern women did it themselves. When the time came to divide up her husband's residual goods a widow did not hesitate to point out to the ecclesiastical judge just how much she had brought to the marriage, although what remained of his estate might not cover even that amount. Marie Brice, in the Lincolnshire coastal marshes in 1624, was left with only £6 after she had paid expenses out of her husband Henry's £24 estate, and this whole amount she 'praieth may bee assigned to her, in regard the deceased had £10 in money with this accountant at their intermarriage'. In the same year Sarah Bawtree, widow of the constable of Leake, 'praieth that a favourable respecte may be had to her . . . in regard, [her husband] had in marriage with this accomptant, being a maid, in money and goods, to the value of threescore poundes'. Sarah was awarded £50, just over half her husband's residual estate.[22]

Examples of this special pleading seem to occur only in Lincolnshire. Possibly it did not occur in Cambridgeshire because so many accounts there ended up in debt, in which case there was no benefit to the accountant to plead, or in Sussex because most accounts there were relatively well-off, so the accountant had less need for special consideration. There is no evidence that these women had made property settlements upon marriage. Rather, they simply expected to enjoy the same level of comfort at the end of marriage as they had at the beginning.

One London woman expressed the idea of marital value for money far more assertively than these rural Lincolnshire accountants pleading for the equivalent of their marriage portions. When her husband read her his will in 1593 she did 'find fault that [he] had given her but £400 which was no more, as she then said, than she had brought with her to him, saying that she had deserved more than she had brought with her to him by reason . . . they had lived about three years together'.[23]

The court did not always heed widows' pleas for reimbursement: the young widow Grace Money, in the vale of Lincoln in 1624, was forced to divide her husband's residual estate of only £3 with four nearly grown stepchildren and her own 5-year-old daughter, notwithstanding the fact that she had brought a £24 portion to her husband, 'she being a maide and he a widdower'.[24] On the other hand, Alice Cotton of Northampton was left with £183 after she administered her husband's estate in the later seventeenth century, and the court allowed all of this amount to Alice, specifically because most of these goods had been her own before marriage. But the court also noted that Alice was old and had nothing else to live on, nor did the couple have any children, nor did her husband have any poor relatives. If he had had poor relatives then they might have received a share of his estate, regardless of whether most of it had been Alice's before their marriage.[25] In other cases the court recorded no response to the accountant's plea. Rebecca Checkley, after paying out ten substantial debts within a 10-mile radius of her Northamptonshire home, was left in 1672 with only £35 from her husband's £244 estate, and five children to raise. She made her case plain to the court clerk, who noted, 'And she doth further alledge that she hath not anything left either land or personall estate to mainteyne herselfe and her said children'. The court made no mention of assistance.[26]

Even where a woman had a settlement for separate estate, if her husband died in debt and creditors were at the door, then pressure would be put on her secured property, as Mrs Alice Thornton found to her cost. Alice's mother had carefully marked all the goods she gave to Alice as separate estate (see Chapter 6), but when the appraisers came to take Mr Thornton's inventory

Alice had to rely upon her servant Daphne, servant to her mother before her, to verify the mark.

> I had non in the world which did know which was my mother's, and which was my husband's goods, but she. Soe she went into the house allong with them, and shewed which was my mother's beds, and other goods in every roome belonged to her; for she knew all the markes, and had marked most of them.

But when the appraisers came to the goods

> in the scarlett chamber . . . I tould them that I bought them with my mother's monney, and ought not to be praised, and pleaded they were all her's, bought by me and paid for out of her monney. It was quickly answered me that her monney, beeing converted into goods, and they not expressed in her will and deed of guift, did fall to Mr Thornton's part, and soe must be prized as his.[27]

A less well-off widow without a settlement for separate estate might resort to removing those goods she regarded as her own before the appraisers came to take her husband's inventory. A certain amount of 'her' goods may have been left out of his inventory in any case, in the form of paraphernalia. Before its deterioration into 'accessories or trappings', paraphernalia consisted of 'those goods, which may seem to belong to the wife rather than to the husband, as her apparel, her bed, her jewels, or ornaments for her person' (in the words of the eighteenth-century ecclesiastical lawyer Richard Burn). The ecclesiastical and the common law argued, first, over the exact contents of a woman's paraphernalia, and second, over whether it ought to be included in her husband's inventory. After a good deal of circumlocution on the subject, Burn's *Ecclesiastical Law* (1763) concluded that in general only the wife's 'convenient apparel, agreeable to her degree' should be omitted from her husband's inventory. But then again,

> notwithstanding all that hath been said, if we shall respect what hath been used and observed, such hath ever been the general and ancient custom or rather courtesy of the province of York, as thereby widows have been tolerated, to reserve to their own use, not only their apparel, and a convenient bed, but a coffer with divers things therein necessary for their own persons; which things have usually been omitted out of the inventory of their deceased husband's goods, unless peradventure the husband was so far indebted, as the rest of his goods would not suffice to discharge the same.[28]

Apparently the statutory abolition of reasonable parts in the province of York at the end of the seventeenth century had not swept away a widow's right to paraphernalia. The custom of London, like that of the northern province, allowed a widow to keep her bed out of her husband's inventory. However, apparel and a bed, even with a 'coffer with divers things therein', were insufficient to keep body and soul together. And what was a widow *in extremis* in the southern province outside London to do?

In 1618 in the Isle of Ely Agnes Crow was sued by the new administrator of her husband's £19 estate for her own alleged maladministration of the goods. Among other things, Agnes was charged with leaving out £20 worth of goods from her husband's inventory. These included such peculiarly female objects as 'a bearing blankett of stammell [red woollen cloth] with a velvet lace', used to carry a child to church for baptism and valued at £3, and an old side saddle worth 5 shillings. Along with the more androgynous six pairs of sheets, eight pillowbears, tablecloths, napkins and towels, gold and white money, and fifteen stone (210 lb) of hemp, it is likely that Agnes regarded these goods as her own, either ones she had brought into marriage or acquisitions subsequent to marriage. Perhaps the hemp was the result of her own labour. Since her husband's estate after debts left her with less than £2, it is not surprising that she might have wished to reserve what she could of whatever property was her own. But her husband's creditors, who had initially agreed to take composition of their debts on the understanding that Agnes was 'a poore woeman', challenged her retention of goods when they discovered it. Legally, Agnes had no leg to stand on. (The result in this case is unknown because no findings or decision were filed with the other legal papers, themselves inadvertently folded up with the probate account.)[29]

Widows without children, like Agnes Crow, may have been even more severely affected by the 1670 Act than widows with children. The statute only actually diverged from the pre-existing ecclesiastical rules of division on this one point: a childless widow was to receive only half of her husband's residual goods, rather than all of them, as previously. Henceforth the other half went to his next-of-kin. On the other hand, if a man left children but no wife surviving, the children would still divide all of his goods, as previously. It is not clear if the makers of the Act knew that they were altering existing practice on this point, but there are certainly reasons why they might have wished to do so. In the unlikely event that an aristocratic or gentry heir died without having made a will and leaving a young, childless wife, his younger brothers (and, theoretically at least, his sisters and his mother) might not relish the prospect of the bulk of the moveable estate falling into the hands of a woman unrelated by blood who threatened to live for a good many years and possibly to remarry. The regrettable nature of this situation must have occurred to a fair number of younger sons during the seventeenth century. It is not inconceivable that this scenario described the family circumstance of at least one of the promoters of the Act for the Better Settling of Intestates' Estates.

The effect of this small and unremarked change in the law incorporated in the 1670 Act on an ordinary woman could be to cripple her economically if she had made no other provision for widowhood. Two Lincolnshire examples, before and after the Act, illustrate that the rule was applied regardless of the estate's size: in 1669 Martha Bartrum was assigned all of her yeoman husband's £142 remaining after she had paid his £7 worth of debts; but fourteen years later Rachel Tysedale, widow of a husbandman, received only half of his meagre £11 of moveables remaining, the other half going to his sister as next of kin.[30] Nothing more is known of the life of Rachel Tysedale.

The 'generosity' of men's wills toward their wives – in terms of appointing them executrix and the size of their bequests – could be thought extraordinary as long as a minority of men made wills, in contrast to the common sort of men who died intestate, leaving their surviving families to the vicissitudes of the law. But analysis of the distribution of intestate men's residual goods by ecclesiastical courts, which is found in probate accounts, proves that such is not the case. On the contrary, the widows of intestate men enjoyed at least as many benefits as the widows of men who made wills, in terms of moveable goods. In terms of land and housing for a widow, the probate accounts of intestate men are silent, but then so too are most men's wills. Short of exhaustive parish studies, it is impossible to ascertain which type of land or house any family owned (freehold, copyhold or leasehold), whether this land was allowed to follow the particular legal descent prescribed for its type, or whether the owner transferred its title by any one of the numerous other means available.

There was good reason for both individual men and the ecclesiastical courts to allocate large portions of family property to widows. The comparison of men's inventories with their widows' inventories a short time later strongly suggests that women as wives had brought a very considerable amount of property to their husbands, and usually more than half of the marital estate, at least in terms of personal property. But the widow's allocation from her husband's estate always remained at the discretion of either her husband or the ecclesiastical court. In most cases, these men could be relied upon to treat a widow fairly. Ultimately, they carried a big stick: the courts could always reduce her portion to the legal minimum of one third if her husband died intestate; her husband in his will – if he lived in the southern province or, by the eighteenth century, anywhere in England – could reduce her share to nothing.

If most men did not intentionally impoverish their widows, the intent was clearly to provide them with a reasonably comfortable estate, and not to promote women's economic independence. Up to one third of bequests to widows were limited to their lifetime, without the power of disposal, which meant that they could not sell the property to raise capital. Wealthier men, whose widows might have been in a position to acquire economic power, were least likely to give a widow full control of the estate, and most likely to impose limitations on her bequest.

11 How lone women lived

HOUSEHOLDS

Widows' own probate documents provide glimpses of how some of them lived. As is the case with men's wealth, women's moveable goods are more identifiable than their land. Many widows who headed their own households had personal estates of less than £20, which was unusual for male heads of household. Alice Armeston, for example, died in the vale of Lincoln in 1631 with an inventory of £17. Included in that amount were the lease of her two-room house, worth £1 6s., two cows and eight sheep, at £5 13s., and sufficient household goods to keep herself and four of her five children, aged 4 to 14, the eldest having already been apprenticed. Alice and all the children slept in two beds in the 'parlor'. The two eldest children, a girl and a boy, probably helped their mother work in the fields, since six scythes were also stored in the parlor.[1]

Mary Gladwyne, in the Lincolnshire fenland, also had five minor children at her death in 1611. Her total inventory came to only £11, yet she lived in a three-room house which was either copyhold or freehold, and she paid rents on other lands to four different men. Otherwise Mary's household goods look like Alice Armeston's – with the additional luxury of two cradles for the smallest children. She may have sold the hemp she grew, or spun it herself; that income, plus the basic husbandry tools, two cows, a pig and some poultry kept the family going.[2] A childless widow, Alice Jordane, died in 1621 in Somerset; her father filed the account of her estate. Despite having only £9 worth of moveables, Alice had been part owner of two copyhold tenements, where she grew wheat and beans, and a barn in which to store them. She also paid wages to a servant and a man to help with the harvest.[3]

The living situation of 211 widows is discernible from their own probate accounts or inventories and wills. (Another seventy-seven widows' living arrangements are unclear.) Of the 211 who can be located, only 16 per cent lived in someone else's house, usually that of a married daughter or son. The majority of widows whose estates reached the probate court (84 per cent) headed their own households. This proportion somewhat overestimates the number of widows with their own households, because they are easier to identify than others. However, probate documents do not overrepresent householding women by very much. In parish lists of inhabitants in the early modern period, which are unrelated to wealth, 74 per cent of all widows either headed households or were solitary (in their own house), and only 25 per cent lived in someone else's household.[4] So widows whose estates reached the probate courts were probably somewhat wealthier than the average, but they were not unduly likely to live in their own house.

Certainly women wealthier than Mary Gladwyne, Alice Armeston and Alice Jordane lived in someone else's household. Mary Wright, of the vale of Lincoln, obviously did so: at her death in 1616 she possessed one steer, twenty-nine sheep, and £33 worth of credits owing to her by four men, two from nearby parishes (within 5 miles) and two from parishes 30 miles away on the Lincolnshire coast. She owned no household goods at all. Mary was widowed but childless, in her twenties or early thirties, and had four brothers, with one of whom she might have lived.[5]

An older widow of the Sussex downs, Margaret Wenwright, had £33 when she died in 1629, £30 of which consisted in two debts. The remaining £3 comprised her apparel and ready money, one old book and a chest, two pairs of sheets, two little tubs and two little 'ceelers'. Her estate was administered by her two sons, one of whom she might have lived with.[6] Lady Jane Bury, of the Lincolnshire fen edge, clearly lived in her son's house – probably the one who administered her estate, calling himself 'gent' – since she had no household goods at all. Of her considerable £93 inventory, £52 consisted in arrears of rents owing to her, most of which she in turn owed, probably to another of her sons, styled 'Mr'. But while Lady (or Dame) Jane only had houseroom, she also kept six cows, eleven calves and three swine hogs, one of which had recently been transformed into two flitches of bacon. Her twenty loads of peat stacked in the yard should have been ample to heat her own room, in which were only 'two bibles and some other books' of her own.[7]

In determining how a widow lived from her inventory it is important to remember that women's inventories may be misleading for some of the same reasons that men's are, notably the omission of legacies. The 1634 inventory of the estate of Ann Perrin *als* Saunders of the Sussex downs included only her clothes and ready money, at £1 10s., and £54 10s. worth of credits, owing to her from eleven different men. It would appear, since she had no household goods, that Ann lived in someone else's house. However, in her will of three years earlier it is clear that Ann had her own house and 'backside' which she left, together with all the goods in it, to her seven grandchildren.[8] So the goods that Ann lived with in her house and backside, which would have brought her inventory to much more than £56, vanished before the inventory was taken. Or they were sitting in full view of the appraisers, who did not note them down because Ann's two married daughters, perhaps with their broods, explained that these goods had been bequeathed in Ann's will.

While widows' own probate documents show them most often living in their own house, they rarely reveal who else lived with them, apart from young children. Wills made by men sometimes specified particular housing arrangements for their survivors – either with whom their widow was to live, or who was to live with their widow. John Coltas, a north Yorkshire weaver, left his widow Margaret and a young son when he died in 1683, and arranged in his will for his brother to keep a room in Margaret's house 'soe long as he kepeth unmaryed'.[9] Another north Yorkshire widow, Elizabeth Barrye, also lived with her labourer brother-in-law, William, but it was she who leased a part of his cottage for the term of her own and her daughter Catherine's lives. The two women lived together with the widowed William and his two sons.[10] Had they appeared in a parish list of inhabitants, Margaret Coltas would have been recorded as the head of a household. The status of Elizabeth Barrye is less clear. Was she a 'lodger' even with a lease for two lives? Perhaps two separate households would have been listed within a single cottage. (The legal splitting of even small houses, as opposed to the less formal granting of houseroom for life, appears to have been particularly common in Yorkshire. For example, a Selby labourer in 1654 gave to his widow Jane Constable 'good, right and lawfull power and authoritie to alien and sell the kitchen and chamber over it, with that part of the garth so far as the grip which . . . my brother in law had', while she remained in the rest of the house.[11])

A man who bequeathed houseroom usually provided the alternative of an annuity, in case sharing a house became for any reason inconvenient. The outcome of cohabitation for most ordinary people is unknown, but the case of William Stout's widowed mother is preserved in his autobiography. Mrs Stout kept her own house until the youngest of her six children turned 21, 'and then divided her substance equally among them, but reserving an annueaty suficient for her selfe'. After twenty-five years of self-sufficient widowhood she moved in with her 48-year-old son and his new wife, but 'when the young wife came to house keeping, my mother thought to have some direction in that, more than the young wife . . . would allow'. A year later Mrs Stout moved in with her bachelor son William, to everyone's satisfaction.[12]

It appears that widows may often have lived with other widows, their sisters- and mothers-in-law. Where a man provided in his will for his widowed mother, it was his own widow who carried out the arrangements. A Selby butcher in 1701, for example, simply asked that his 'loveing wife' and his 'honoured and carefull mother' live together after his death.[13] A husband-man of the Lincolnshire marsh was more specific, recording in his own will of 1610 that, by the terms of his father's will, 'I am charged to keepe Anne Barne my mother with meate drinke and lodgings (fitt and beseeming a woman of her estate)'. He passed on that duty to his own wife and executrix Suzanne, who continued to support her mother-in-law in a room in her own house. If the two women lived 'asunder', as they may have done after Suzanne's remarriage the following year, Suzanne was still obliged to maintain Anne.[14]

A Sussex husbandman asked his wife, Elizabeth Aylwin, to keep his widowed sister with 'meat, drink and hearth' by paying her 2s. 6d. per quarter. This may imply that she shared the house, and as Elizabeth had three children of her own and six children of her husband's to bring up, she was probably grateful for another pair of adult hands in the house.[15] More elaborate arrangements were made by a labourer in the Lincolnshire fens, Robert Drenckwater. In 1597 he made his wife executrix 'as my trust is in her', and further directed that

> my mother in lawe shall have her dwellinge in this house and half the ground under the same house and to reape the corne . . . payenge the half of the lord's rent and half the other chardges whatsoever . . . and my wief and my mother to use yt togeather soe longe as the lease lasteth.

Robert's inventory lists only one bed, but his 'mother in lawe' (who was probably his stepmother, rather than his wife's mother) probably had 'hushlements' of her own.[16]

While annuities were rarely used by ordinary husbands for their widows' jointures, they were occasionally employed for the maintenance of aging parents – especially, for some reason, in Northamptonshire – and widows took on responsibility for these just as they did for housing arrangements. The widow Sarah Halford, for example, continued to pay an annuity to her mother-in-law, Joyous Halford, after both of their husbands were dead.[17] A maintenance arrangement was set up by Stephen and Lettice Mace with their yeoman son Stephen and his wife Mary. How the contract was originally established is unclear, but the terms were restated by Mary Mace in her 1680 account of her husband's estate. She was henceforth to pay her parents-in-law £30 p.a. (one and a half years were due in arrears already), and when her father-in-law died, then £10 p.a. to Lettice.[18] Anne Bithery's widowed mother Anne Clarke was maintained by Anne and her husband John, and by Anne alone after John's death, and until Anne Clarke's death within the following year. Such a maintenance arrangement might have been made formally in Anne and John's marriage settlement, or in Anne Clarke's husband's will, or in Anne Clarke's widowhood, between herself, her daughter and her son-in-law.[19]

Only occasionally is a widow visible making her own accommodation arrangements after her husband's death – not because widows did not usually manage these things themselves, but because there is no obvious document in which their actions were recorded, in the way that a man's will records his wishes for his surviving wife, mother or sister. Marie Holland's yeoman husband did not make a will before his death in 1623 in the Lincolnshire fen edge. Marie administered his estate jointly with her married daughter Elizabeth. By mutual agreement they split the residual £36 equally, which gave Elizabeth a larger than usual – although still smaller than legal – portion. In return, Elizabeth and her husband 'promised to Marie . . . during her widdow head her house harbor with out any charge to her the said Marie so convenient as should give her content during all the tyme of her widdow head'.[20]

In the absence of relatives or a house of one's own, widows rented rooms – again, often with other lone women. In Dorset, one 'goody Small' rented a room for 6s. p.a. in the house of another widow, Barbara Barber, who had three of her six children also living with her. Barbara, who owned goods worth £21 at her death in 1632, leased her house and garden from the churchwardens for £1 p.a. When the lease was sold at Barbara's death goody Small may have stayed on, since tuppence was spent for mending the lock of her chamber door.[21] Joyce Jeffries, the unmarried financier of Hereford (see Chapter 5), also rented out 'a litle roome in the back lane' to a widow Golding for 5s. p.a.[22]

In urban areas the historian Olwen Hufton has identified 'spinster clustering': unmarried women sharing housing together, particularly where wages were good for women, largely in textile industries.[23] The same clustering of women occurs in rural areas, with widows as well as single women, and often those who lived together were related by marriage or by blood.

Single women's living arrangements are less clear than widows' because they appear to have been less likely to make a will giving clues. One who did make a will was 20-year-old Elizabeth Ripley, who shared a cottage in Pickering with her widowed sister and a niece in the 1680s.[24] Elizabeth Grainge, of the Yorkshire moors, also clearly cohabited with someone, since much of her 'houshould stufe' was in the houses of two men of nearby villages. A large proportion of Elizabeth's wealth was in cash (£15 worth of debts due from five men), but she had her own stock – four ewes and lambs, and three hogs. These she gave to her brother in her will of 1644 'if they be all livinge', along with all her 'puder dublers' (pewter platters).[25] In general it is necessary to rely on single women's inventories alone.

Slightly less than half of the single women whose estates came before the probate court appear to have lived in someone else's household, although it is rarely clear whose. In the Isle of Axholme, Mary Belfield died intestate in 1632, probably in her thirties. She must have lived in someone else's household since her only domestic goods were one sheet, one pillowbear and one towel. Nevertheless, her £11 inventory shows that she kept sheep – eighteen of them, valued at £5. She had a large amount of yardage, so either wove cloth or sewed for other people. And an unusually high entry for 'purse and apparel' of £5 10s. suggests that she had ready cash in between investments at the time of her death.[26] Whether Mary lived with kin or rented rooms, she clearly supported herself even if she was only worth £11 in goods.

Slightly more than half of the single women who appear in probate documents lived on their own smallholdings. Margaret Hyde, of Romsey in Hampshire, must have been near grandmother age when she made her will, since she gave bequests to married nieces. Margaret died in 1663 with only a £15 personal estate, but she rented her own house and paid another woman, the wife of a heelmaker, to wash her clothes for her. Their relationship must have been based on more than simply employment, since £1 17s. 6d. was deducted from Margaret's estate to pay the washerwoman's wages for the previous fourteen years![27] Another single woman, from a family of often illegitimate labourers in the vale of York, Isabel Beilebie was 'in good health and perfect in minde and memory' in June 1673, but nevertheless thought it appropriate to make her will. Her only bequest was her cottage, in which she lived for another eight years, and this she gave to her sister for life, then to her sister's children.[28] An independent existence for unmarried women was more possible in Yorkshire, where many more girls were given small pieces of land, than it was in Sussex, where landholding women were rare (see Chapter 4).

Women who never married have received even less attention than other women in English history. They formed a larger proportion of adult women in the late sixteenth and early seventeenth century than at any time since, but as marriage is one of the few life events through which ordinary people can be traced, those who did not marry and did not keep an account book – like Joyce Jeffries or Elizabeth Parkin or Sarah Fell – remain shadowy presences, represented by only an occasional will or inventory or probate account. In the absence of much material evidence, and the presence of proverbial and literary antipathy towards unmarried women (see Part II) it has often been assumed that single women were isolated and ostracized. This was un-doubtedly true for some: certainly single women were always more likely to have been stigmatized for their lack of a spouse than single men; and there is some evidence that the women accused of witchcraft tended to be unmarried or widowed.

As for their economic situation, some probate documents show no support network around single women, but this silence is inconclusive, since there are many reasons why relatives or friends might not appear in these sources. On the other hand, the community connections maintained by some unmarried women can be positively substantiated. Two Lincolnshire women (whose age cannot be established) may stand as examples. Geden Longe, a 'virgyn' of the fens, had a personal estate of only £8 in February 1578, but that was apparently sufficient to maintain her independently. She had her featherbed, her painted cloths, 'a little brasse pott and a little bras panne' and a few other dishes, her linens, and abundant apparel (her inventory was itemized in forty separate entries). Nothing about her inventory implies that she was isolated. Several small credits suggest that Geden earned income by spinning wool for various people. She had at one time had three sisters and a brother, all of whom married, although all but one sister had apparently died, leaving behind two nieces and two nephews whom Geden remembered in her will along with a woman friend.[29]

Another single woman, Jane Lison, lived alone in the marshland in a cottage of two rooms and a chamber, with ample goods for comfort: two beds, cupboards and chests, a table and one chair, pewter and brass dishes, a spinning wheel, a milk vessel and some cheeses, four cows, a ewe and a pig. All of this amounted to less than £22 in 1681. Some of the property came from her brother, a labourer, who had died intestate the previous year and whose estate Jane had administered. In her will Jane distributed small bequests to three women friends, one of whom wrote her will for her. She named as her executor a carpenter of a neighbouring parish – he may have been a kinsman, a sweetheart or a friend.[30]

RELATIVE WEALTH AS WIVES AND AS WIDOWS

Widows' moveable wealth can in some cases be compared with that in the accounts and/or inventories of their husbands, and from this it seems that the living conditions of many women probably changed little in the transition from wife to widow. Seventy-five such married couples in which the husband predeceased the wife are available in the documents from Lincolnshire (forty-seven) and Sussex (twenty-eight) examined here.

There were of course discrepancies between husbands' and wives' inventories due to appraisers' inconsistency in valuing many of the same goods at an interval of between two and twenty-four years. But these discrepancies could occur over a matter of weeks too. When John Lockton died in 1623 in the Lincolnshire fenland, the lease of his four-room house and 'all the pullin' (poultry) were valued together at £5. Seven weeks later Protosia Lockton died and in her inventory 'all the pullin' amounted to £1, and the lease of the same house to only £1 6s. 8d.[31]

Occasionally there was also a qualitative difference in the appraisers' approach to husband and wife. Steven Plumtree, a labourer of the Lincolnshire marshland, died in 1604 with a £21 inventory of basic household furniture, bedding, eating utensils, and some cows and pigs. Two years later his widow Magdalen Plumtree died, an old woman with five grown children from two marriages. She had only £12 in total, having sold, lost or consumed some of the cows and pigs, but she still had the table, the napkins (although she had sold or given away the tablecloth) and at least a part of Steven's furnishings. Some of the items that appear only in Magdalen's inventory may have been thought of as hers at the time that Steven's inventory was made – the old cheese press and the spinning wheel, for example. But the appraisers of Magdalen's estate took the unusual step of counting her cheese, her linseed, all the apples, the malt and two 'roops of unyons', plus an acre of wheat. Steven would have had the same alimentary provisions, since he and Magdalen both died in the autumn, but his inventory included none of them.[32]

Bearing in mind the vagaries of appraisal, more than half of these seventy-five widows in Lincolnshire and Sussex died with the same or greater wealth than their husbands had left them. Even this proportion is a minimum, since it relies in a majority of cases on the husband's inventory, where an account is not extant, and his inventory value was inevitably higher than the net estate with which his widow was left after she had paid his debts. (Wherever possible, inventory totals were corrected for debts and legacies.)

Of course, both a widow's wealth and her household position could be affected by how long after her husband's death she herself appeared in the

historical record. One of the problems of tracing these women is that the
closer a husband's and wife's deaths were, the easier it is to identify them.
The longer a widow survived the more likely she was either to remarry and
change her name or to relocate, in either case eluding detection by posterity.
For those who can be identified after a long widowhood, the circumstances in
which they died did not necesarily reflect their living situation throughout
widowhood. Mary Forman, a widow in the Sussex weald, spent the last eight
years of her life (in the 1670s) in her son's household. But having been
widowed for twenty-four years, Mary probably kept the family home and
farm and raised her five young children for sixteen years before moving in
with her son.[33]

Sythe Tokin, of the Lincolnshire fenland half a century before Mary
Forman, also had five children to raise, and her inventory suggests her sources
of income. Three years after her husband's death she lived in the same house,
with almost exactly the same goods, valued at a total of about £27: in the hall
a long table, stools, forms (benches) and chairs, a dishbench and cupboard
with the brass, pewter and wooden utensils; in the low parlour two beds, a
chest, and a kimnell (tub); in the little parlor two chests with the bed linen; in
the milkhouse (probably a lean-to shed) some shelves and bowls. Sythe's
husband may have been a weaver – his inventory had two webs of linen cloth
and a little piece of linsey wolsey, where hers had only hempen and harden
yarn. In addition to spinning, Sythe kept cows (four milk cows and six young
ones, grazing in the fen) and made cheese, of which 42 lb was left at her death.
The children may have helped with spinning or tending the cows, or with
weeding the 2 acres of barley and acre of peas, to which Sythe had added a
half acre of oats before her death.

A widow's possession of a full household was by no means dependent on
her having minor children to raise. Approximately half of the household-
heading widows here were childless or had only adult children. On the Sussex
coast, Elizabeth Kewell kept her entire household together for twelve years
after her yeoman husband died in 1660, leaving her with a substantial £366
inventory and no children. She reduced her outdoor goods by only 37 per
cent, but successfully increased her wealth in credits by 55 per cent, and died
worth £463, leaving everything to her niece and namesake.[34] Elizabeth
Kewell was not unusual in preserving her entire household, including much
of the agricultural goods. Although it might be expected that a widow would
have less livestock, less corn on the ground and fewer husbandry tools than
her husband, widows' wealth in these 'outdoor goods' exceeded the value of
their husbands' outdoor goods almost as often as it dropped.

Both widows and unmarried women held a higher proportion of cash or
credits in their inventories than men. Mary Forman, above, at her death had
at least 75 per cent of the value of her husband's inventory, but more than
half of it consisted of rents, rather than animals and corn, as his had. It has
been proposed that widows were a fertile source of free-floating capital to
fund small rural credit markets,[35] and this is true – always remembering that

single women held a substantially higher proportion of their inventories in credits than widows did, but widows were more numerous and usually had larger sums to lend out. In Lincolnshire, for example, only 18 per cent of widows' inventories (15 of 82) held at least half of their total wealth in credits; whereas 63 per cent of single women's inventories (17 of 27) did so. Only 6 per cent of men (7 of 115) met this standard. What is needed now to understand rural credit is a local study in which it is possible to know the number of single women and the number of widows in the community and the relative size of their inventories, to determine the contribution of each as a group, plus how often children's legacies were 'put out' until their majority, what kinds of securities were used, the mechanism for interest and so on.

Regardless of the form of their property, far more lone women than lone men headed their own household or lived alone. In the earlier seventeenth century nearly three times as many single household heads were widows (13 per cent) as were widowers (5 per cent), and that disparity increased over the century, as widows remarried in fewer numbers.[36] This demographic evidence sits uneasily with historians' stress on the dependence of lone women upon male labour in agricultural societies. Such labour certainly could have been provided by sons and hired hands, as well as by another husband, but it is difficult to avoid the conclusion that men were actually more dependent on women's labour than the reverse. Ellen Stout spent fifty years keeping house in Lancashire, first for her widowed mother and then for her three unmarried brothers in succession. While her brothers would undoubtedly have thought of her as dependent on them, it is clear from her brother William's description of the relationship that the dependence was in fact entirely mutual.[37] Ellen was no more dependent on her brothers than any unmarried man living with his kin – like William Coltas, mentioned on page 189, who lived with his brother, his brother's wife and their child in the vale of Pickering in the early 1680s, and subsequently with his widowed sister-in-law.

Where a lone man headed a household, he was more likely to have a female servant living in. Single men's better economic position enabled them to hire servants. If they could afford it, widows could pay men to do their ploughing and heavy agricultural work, as widowers could pay women to do their cooking, washing, gardening, gathering, childrearing and heavy domestic work. But the relative absence from the demographic record of men who remained widowed and hired help suggests that it was more economical for a man to marry his housekeeper than to pay her. Remarriage, of course, had the added benefits of companionship and intimacy, and many widowed women may also have chosen to remarry, had they had the choice. The statistics of household heading and remarriage certainly make it clear that men were at least as dependent on women's labour as the reverse. What they also show is men's ability to exploit women's labour, a power women in general did not have, either in terms of wages or in terms of remarriage.

REMARRIAGE

Whether in the form of liquid credits or solid husbandry tools and land, widows' wealth has often been regarded by historians from a particularly masculine point of view. Her wealth was her 'chief or only attraction' to a potential suitor, providing 'a channel for relieving the material appetites of ambitious young men', but 'with luck, she might be old enough to die after a reasonably short period of waiting, leaving him free to marry somebody young and attractive'.[38] These historical 'judgements' are remarkably similar to the early modern literary stereotype of the wealthy widow snapped up soon after her husband's demise, for her property rather than her personal attractions.[39] Aside from the breathtaking arrogance of both the contemporary and the historical stereotype, it is wholly untenable in the light of demographic and economic facts.

First of all, wealthy widows were the least likely of all widows to remarry. Second, fewer widows than widowers ever remarried, and even that number was dropping swiftly over the seventeenth century. And third, a substantial proportion of widows were left in poverty, and to suggest otherwise is to wilfully ignore the institutionalized impoverishment of women in general, and widows in particular.

From medieval England to nineteenth-century Virginia, wealthy widows were the least likely of all widows to remarry.[40] This may be simply explained by positing that wealthy women had at least as much say in the matter as would-be snapper-uppers, and the majority were, on balance, content to remain widows. Wealth enabled a widow to weigh conjugal pleasures against legal consequences, and many concluded that to remarry would indeed be 'tempting fortune'.[41] Some wealthy widows obviously did choose to remarry, among them Lady Anne Clifford, whose choice to do so was truly extraordinary, in view of the infelicities of her first 'venture'. But there were, of course, other reasons besides poverty for a woman to remarry, just as there were other reasons besides her wealth for a man to want to marry a widow, as the heir to Sleape Hall in Shropshire testified when he married a widow with many small children, incurring the wrath and disinheritance of his father (see Chapter 5).[42]

A close look at London widows in the late sixteenth and early seventeenth century found that those most likely to remarry were the ones of middling wealth; those least likely to remarry were the gentry widows, who could afford not to, and the widows of poor craftsmen and labourers, who could not afford to.[43] The women in the middle were attractive economic prospects to potential second husbands – perhaps in so far as their financial circumstances counterbalanced the presence of children – and at the same time they were not sufficiently well-off to choose to support themselves and their children comfortably alone.

Poor widows in the countryside may have remarried more often than the urban poor, if they had some rights to land in the form of manorial freebench for life. Local studies suggest that in areas where land was in demand or population was rising and widows had a right to freebench for life, their remarriage was frequent; where land was plentiful or population falling, the remarriage of widows with land was not particularly common.[44] Manorial custom could also limit a widow's freebench to her widowhood or celibacy, although it is impossible to say as yet how many manors did so, and this restriction may further have limited widows' remarriage. One Berkshire manor changed its freebench from a life right to a widowhood right in 1590, at which point widows stopped remarrying.[45]

A low rate of remarriage in areas where a widow's land rights were limited to her widowhood is usually seen as men's lack of interest in a woman without property. It may also be seen as women's refusal to give up property for a man. Where freebench was a lifetime right, in areas where land was scarce a widow would receive many more offers for remarriage than she would in areas where land was plentiful. The more offers that were made, the greater the likelihood that one of them would be acceptable. It is not necessary to interpret landholding widows' higher remarriage rates as their being snapped up by land-hungry young men. In any case, a great deal more work is needed to know whether the limitation of freebench to widowhood was widespread. Barbara Todd's in-depth comparative analysis of freebench and widows' economic activity on two Berkshire manors is an excellent start in opening up a field which cries out for research.[46]

In areas without extensive manorial records, or areas in which manorial freebench customs were not significant, the only way to judge the relative wealth of a widow who remarried and a widow who did not has been by her husband's occupation or status, or by the value of his inventory. Probate accounts make it possible to know what remarrying widows were actually left with by their previous husbands, after his debts had been paid out of his personal estate. This measure of wealth cannot account for factors like the number of children a woman had, her age, or the type of local economy, but while all these factors had some influence on remarriage, they were probably not the determining ones.[47] Although the economic reasons for and against remarriage were more complex than simple wealth, depending on types of land tenure (whether held by rent or by service) and the occupation that a widow had shared with her previous husband (whether it required male labour),[48] a widow's need for a helpmeet was inextricably intertwined with her economic circumstances.

Among the estates of women for whom probate accounts were filed, at least 17 per cent (45 of 261) had been married more than once.[49] At least 14 per cent of 463 widows whose husbands' probate accounts were filed in Lincolnshire, Northamptonshire and Cambridgeshire had remarried by the time of filing, usually one year after his death.[50] Table 11.1 lists the median wealth with which widows were left by their first husbands in four counties, comparing the wealth of those widows who had remarried within one year with the wealth of those widows who were still single at the time of filing their husbands' accounts. The consistency of the median wealth of remarrying widows in Table 11.1 is striking, given the disparity in the median wealth of widows who remained unmarried. The median wealth of remarrying widows was confined to a tight range, between £27 and £35, whereas the median wealth of all widows ranged widely, between £17 and £55. Thus those widows who remarried in the poorer counties of Cambridgeshire and Lincolnshire were wealthier than other widows in those counties; widows who remarried in prosperous Sussex and Northamptonshire were poorer than most. Remarriage within one year suggests some degree of urgency, and these financial figures support the idea of a middle economic level at which remarriage was simultaneously desirable and feasible.

Table 11.1 Median value of husbands' residual estates left to widows remarried within one year and widows still single

	Remarried		Still single	
	£	n	£	n
Cambridgeshire	28	21	15	123
Lincolnshire	30	25	17	170
Sussex	27	3	39	52
Northamptonshire	35	16	55	101

Apart from economic exigencies, it is commonly assumed that the emotional difficulties of remarriage in early modern England were 'immense', or at least caused serious strife.[51] Although it was men who remarried most often, and the evil stepmother occurs occasionally in literature, it was the thought of women's remarriage that provoked antagonism among certain prominent men. In Sir Walter Raleigh's words, 'if she love again, let her not enjoy her second love in the same bed wherein she loved thee'.[52] Such utterances may be best described as individual obessions, rather than as evidence of widespread societal antipathy towards women's remarriage. There is an almost total silence among early modern women on the difficulties of remarriage. Lady Anne Clifford commented freely on every other aspect of social intercourse, but she was not worried about anyone's remarriage, and expressed no misgivings about her own second marriage to the also widowed Earl of Pembroke – even when relations must have been strained during the time that he tried (unsuccessfully) to marry her daughter to his son.

In approximately one quarter of all the marriages which I can identify in probate documents, at least one parent had been married previously. Even this proportion of stepfamilies is underestimated, since the majority of these households are identified by the presence of stepchildren, and while wives' children by previous husbands are identifiable by a different surname, husbands' children by previous wives are not.[53] (This rate of remarriage is the same as that in England today. Since 1976, remarriages as a proportion of all marriages have again attained their sixteenth- and early seventeenth-century heights: 26 per cent in 1986 for women; still slightly more frequent for men, at 27 per cent.[54])

Since remarriage today results predominantly from divorce, whereas early modern remarriage resulted from the death of one spouse, it seems likely that children today experience the greater emotional trauma because they have a continuing relationship with the absent parent. In the wills of ordinary early modern men and women, the relations whom we today would persistently identify as in-laws or half- or step-relations were usually called simply 'mother' or 'father', 'sister' or 'brother', 'daughter' or 'son', with the last name appended. This nomenclature argues against an especially antagonistic atmosphere in mixed-marriage households. Consider the case of Margaret Greave (see Chapter 5). Making her will at the vulnerable age of 18, Margaret's largest bequest went to her new half-sister; she named her elder (full) brother and her stepfather supervisors together, obviously expecting their cooperation, in trust for the rest of her siblings. In assessing societal attitudes towards remarriage and hybrid households,[55] there is no reason to give Margaret Greave's immediate experience of remarriage any less weight than the paranoid speculations of Sir Walter Raleigh.

Attitudes towards remarriage among both women and men at different social levels require more research. Did they shift in the later seventeenth century when unmarried women were increasingly stigmatized in print? At the same time that the proportion of women who ever married was increasing over the early modern period, the proportion of widows who remarried was falling. In Abingdon, Salisbury and the London parish of Stepney the proportion of widows among brides fell by one third to one half.[56] In Stepney the decline in widows' remarriage appears to result from a shift in the sex ratio: in the late sixteenth and early seventeenth centuries there had been a surplus of men in the population, so widows remarried relatively often, whereas by the later seventeenth and early eighteenth centuries a shortage of men in the population reduced widows' opportunities for remarriage.[57] It remains to be seen whether the sex ratio is a contributing factor to the drop in widows' remarriage in Abingdon in the same period, or in Salisbury between the late sixteenth and early seventeenth centuries.

Barbara Todd sees the decline in widows' remarriage at least partly as the result of (men's) growing individualism and desire to perpetuate family and wealth in the seventeenth century.[58] The idea of emerging private property (for men) seems intellectually apt, if not appealing, and there are certainly concrete means by which men's property rights were expanded during the early modern period. The elimination of widows' right to thirds in the southern province before 1500, the 1671 statute which so drastically cut down widows' portion of residual goods in intestacy (see Chapter 10) and the abolition of the right to thirds in the northern province and London at the turn of the seventeenth century (see Chapter 9) all potentially reduced the amount of property a widow had to support herself and her family. It is of course possible that widows were aware of this danger, and made more property

settlements as brides in order to counterbalance the increasingly impoverishing effects of marriage and ensure that they would be comfortable in their
widowhood, but this has yet to be proven. The alternative scenario, which
also needs research, is that increasing numbers of widows were forced onto
poor relief, or simply left without sufficient resources to remarry.

POVERTY

Widows' susceptibility to poverty resulted partly from the deprivation of a
higher-earning partner and partly from their husbands' indebtedness. The
early modern use of 'venture' for 'marriage' is peculiarly appropriate for
women, since they took a serious economic risk by marrying. If women
expected to take out of marriage what they took in, as their requests to the
court in filing their husbands' probate accounts suggest, many were sorely
disappointed.

One quarter of all men left their widows in debt. Men who made wills and
men who did not were equally likely to die indebted. Short of a balance in the
red, many men left their widows with a dramatically reduced estate after their
debts had been paid. The rate of reduction varied by county, but the least
drastic discrepancy between a man's median inventory and his median
account value was still 53 per cent in Sussex (from £81 to £38). Widows in
Northamptonshire were left with 66 per cent less than the value of their
husbands' inventories (£132/£45), in Lincolnshire 76 per cent (£62/£15) and
in Cambridgeshire an astounding 80 per cent less (£43/£8) (for figures see
Table 2.4).

These calculations of estate reduction consider only a husband's debts
(which may have included legacies to his children). If her husband died
intestate, a widow could lose a further one to two thirds of the residual
estate, allocated by the ecclesiastical court as portions for her children (see
Chapter 10).

There were further variations at different social levels. Husbandmen's
widows suffered the most precipitous fall in wealth; yeomen's widows lost a
somewhat smaller proportion (yeomen having more capital and less need to
borrow) and so did labourers' widows (labourers being less able to get credit
in the first place). An enormous 95 per cent drop in the estate value of
Lincolnshire gentlemen and clergy (from £220 to £12) probably reflects the
fact that the wives of these men were most likely to have had separate estate
or guaranteed property in their widowhood, which they might have deducted,
as well as the knowledge of how to make their husbands' estates appear as
small as possible.

But in general, the considerable reduction in the estates left to widows is
clear, and it left them at serious risk of poverty. Quite apart from the
emotional distress of widowhood, the strictly material possibilities for
recovery of a husband and a wife differed dramatically. An early modern
widower could replace his first wife's labour by a second wife, while he

retained all of his first wife's property. An early modern widow, on the other hand, was left legally free by her husband's death, but she lost most of the marital property, in addition to losing his labour and/or income.

Almost everywhere in early modern England (and Europe) women made up the majority of those in receipt of poor relief, and most of them were widows with young children.[59] In the 1980s too, women still constitute 80 per cent of the poor, and single mothers with young children still predominate.[60] Recent discussion of the 'feminization of poverty'[61] must be taken as rhetorical, since poverty has been thoroughly feminized for at least four hundred years. Nor are the statistics skewed by a changing proportion of single parents in the population. Estimates of the percentage of all early modern widows who were on poor relief can only be made in individual parish studies, where it is possible to identify all widows. Of all the widows in the parish of Aldenham, Hertfordshire, in the seventeenth century, more than one third of them were on poor relief.[62] Today, one third of all single mothers of minor children live below the poverty line.[63]

If the emotional effects of early modern widowhood and modern divorce are different, the economic effects are remarkably similar, in terms of downward economic and social mobility. The apparent cause of disproportionate levels of female poverty prior to the late nineteenth century was legal coverture, but while the Victorian and subsequent property law reforms eliminated coverture for most practical purposes, they did nothing to alter the economic imbalances in wage-earning, childrearing and household structure.

The majority of all early modern widows were not reliant upon poor relief. But even gentry widows could find themselves in relative, if not absolute, poverty. In Yorkshire in the later seventeenth century Mrs Alice Thornton was wealthy and had a settlement for separate estate, but even she records in her autobiography

> it was a very pinching consideration to me that I was forced to enter the first conserne of my widdowed condition with bonds, debts, and ingagements for others, whereas I brought so considerable a fortune, and never knew what debt was.[64]

Even a marriage settlement to protect one's property was by no means failsafe. Dorothy Facy, of the Lincolnshire marshland, married John Vinsent, supposedly a gentleman, with a bond in the penal sum of £600, for payment of £317 to her four children from her first husband. But when Vinsent died with only £237 to his name in 1623, Dorothy had little recourse.[65]

Bridget Newton *als* Wright of the vale of Lincoln was a prosperous woman upon her first widowhood in 1672. She was already a joint tenant with her husband Thomas Newton of a toft house (homestead), in addition to which she received by his will the profit of two farm houses and two more toft houses, together with 64 acres, 2 'stongs' (another half acre), and 17 'swaths' (scythe-sweeps) of land, all during their daughter Katharine's minority. After paying Thomas' debts, Bridget and Katharine still had £70 worth of moveables to divide equally. When Bridget remarried to Robert Wright he signed a contract to protect Katherine's half of her father's moveables (see Table 8.1). But when Robert died in 1680 Bridget was left nothing but £33 in debt. The ongoing income from the land and farms carried her through – and Bridget obviously knew how to manage debts and space repayments. She buried Robert handsomely, in the chancel of Hibaldstow parish church, distributing a dozen pairs of mourning gloves at his funeral.[66]

The potential poverty of widows was widely recognized in early modern England, but at the same time most proposals for the relief of the poor addressed the problems of the labouring man with a family, at the mercy of crop failures, disease and unemployment – not the conditions of the widow, at the mercy of the law. Daniel Defoe was one of few to propose a solution to widows' problems, and then he was concerned with relative rather than absolute poverty. His project (never realized) proposed to set up friendly societies for the widows of inferior clergy, shopkeepers and artificers, who married wives with 'only' £300 to £1000 portions and could settle no jointure upon them. Defoe envisioned an insurance office supported by some 2000 married couples, paying small quarterly premiums and contributing to maintenance in the event of any woman's widowhood, provided she had been left less than £2000, clear of debts. Once again, however, those most at risk were left to fend for themselves: Defoe specifically excluded soldiers' and sailors' wives from his project.[67]

Lone women, especially widows, but also those who never married, usually headed their own household. Where they did live in someone else's household the relationship was not normally one of dependence, even if it was couched in those terms at the time because an expectation of female subservience easily elided into female dependence. These women spun or brewed for profit, or they performed domestic work in the household, or they loaned money out at interest, or all three. Widows usually preserved the marital holding after their husbands' death. Where it is possible to trace the estate of a man and the subsequent estate of his widow, she had, more often than not, the same or greater moveable wealth than he had.

The widows whose estates were probated did not remarry, which is why it is possible to trace them. Widows who did remarry may well have been left in more straitened circumstances by their previous husbands. Since the wealthiest widows usually chose not to remarry, a widow's remarriage was not entirely contingent upon her material attractions to men. Clearly both women and men had economic as well as other reasons for marrying. The evidence of probate accounts is still sketchy (a much larger sample size and/or a closer focus on a single location would help) but it supports the idea that widows of middling wealth remarried most often, while both poor and rich widows remarried less often. The personal estates with which widows were left by their husbands, after debts had been paid, ranged widely in value, but the personal estates left to those widows who remarried fell into a much narrower bracket, suggesting a middle band of women who were well-off enough to remarry but not well-off enough not to remarry.

The proportion of widows who remarried declined sharply over the course of the seventeenth century. The reasons for this drop are as yet unclear. Both demographic and ideological shifts have been suggested, but it is also possible that economic factors contributed. The statutes restricting widows' rights in their husbands' property in the later seventeenth century probably had the effect of diminishing their actual ownership of property, which may have hindered their remarriage, although the surviving documents which will settle this question have not yet been found.

Those widows who could not afford to remarry are the ones who swelled the ranks of the poor in such disproportionate numbers. It has been suggested that poor widows are 'less important as a historical phenomenon' than wealthy ones.[68] Certainly they are less important in terms of credit markets, but from the point of view of the Overseers of the Poor, and in terms of sheer numerical preponderance, poor widows are a major historical phenomenon. However, they also formed the bulk of the 'respectable' poor, as opposed to the 'impudent' poor – vagrants and suchlike wandering rogues. It was alright for widows to be poor, and appropriate for them to receive charity. As the archetype of biblical impoverishment, widows' preponderance among the poor was entirely socially acceptable. Widows' poverty appears to have been accepted by men, at any rate. It is a matter of conjecture that women, as potential widows, might have been less complacent about the fact that the vast majority of the poor were widows, and perhaps one third of widows were poor. Women's own wills suggest that they did take notice.

12 Lone women's wills

WHO MADE WILLS AND WHY

Of the 2 million wills which survive from the mid-sixteenth to the mid-eighteenth century, approximately one fifth (or 400,000) were made by women. Existing studies which show the proportion of women's wills in the total made between the fourteenth and the eighteenth centuries are compiled in Table 12.1. This proportion did shift over time. In the sixteenth century the proportion of wills made by women was relatively low, between 12 per cent and 17 per cent of the total (lines 3–7). In the seventeenth century it hovered around 20 per cent (lines 8–13), rising to one quarter of the total in some places by the mid-eighteenth century (lines 14–22). Because various studies focus on different parishes or counties and different time spans, it is difficult to discern clear patterns, but in general it seems that the proportion of all wills made by women grew only slightly over the early modern period.

Because married women were precluded from making a will except by special arrangement with their husbands (see Chapter 8), the vast majority of women's wills were made by widows (about 80 per cent) and single women (up to 20 per cent). The relative proportion of wills made by maids, by wives and by widows in different places at different times is illustrated in Table 12.2. These proportions remained even more constant than the proportion of women among the total throughout the early modern period.

The fact that most wills were made by men suggests that men were more likely to make a will. Three studies of surviving wills, where it was possible to estimate the total population who could have made a will, confirm that a man was up to six times more likely to make a will than a widow or a single woman. In two late sixteenth-century Suffolk parishes, 24 per cent of men but only 4 per cent of widows made a will; in the province of Canterbury in the 1560s and 1620s, roughly 33 per cent of adult men and 5 per cent of adult single and widowed women did so; and in Banbury, 1558–1723, 26 per cent of men and 11 per cent of single and widowed women.[1]

Table 12.1 Percentage of wills made by women, fourteenth–eighteenth centuries

	Location	Dates	%	n	N
1	Diocese of Rochester	1347–8	30	56	186
2	Bishop's Lynn, Norfolk	14th cent.	17	21	125
3	Oxfordshire	1550–90	17	–	254
4	Diocese of Ely	1560–1639	12	1258	10219
5	Willingham, Cambs	1575–1603	13	7	55
6	Norfolk and Suffolk	1550–1640	15	89	600
7	King's Langley, Herts	1523–1659	15	18	117
8	East London	1661–4	19	–	129
9	Worcestershire	1669–70	20	–	275
10	Sevenoaks, Kent	1660–85	20	17	85
11	Norfolk	1590–1750	19	91	471
12	Sussex	1650–1700	21	76	355
13	Selby, Yorks	1635–1710	23	77	333
14	East London	1720s	16	–	177
15	Worcestershire	1720s	22	–	305
16	Banbury, Oxon	1558–1723	19	144	747
17	Banbury, Oxon	1650–1724	25	–	–
18	Banbury, Oxon	1724–1800	33	–	–
19	Lancashire and Cheshire	1660–80	24	868	3593
20	Lancashire and Cheshire	1681–1700	27	970	3551
21	Lancashire and Cheshire	1701–20	21	452	2152
22	Lancashire and Cheshire	1721–40	20	516	2539
23	Diocese of Norwich	1687–1750	24	666	2779

Sources: Line 1, Michael Sheehan, 'The influence of canon law on the property rights of married women in England', *Mediaeval Studies* 25 (1963) p. 122; line 2, Jacques Beauroy, 'Family patterns and relations of Bishop's Lynn will-makers in the fourteenth century', in L. Bonfield, R. M. Smith and K. Wrightson (eds) *The World We Have Gained* (1986) pp. 15–16; line 3, Carole Shammas, 'Early American women and control over capital', in R. Hoffman and P. J. Albert (eds) *Women in the Age of the American Revolution* (1989) p. 140; line 4, Takahashi, 'Number of wills', p. 211; line 5, Margaret Spufford, *Contrasting Communities: English Villagers in the Sixteenth and Seventeenth Centuries* (1974) p. 159; line 6, Evans, 'Inheritance', pp. 56, 61 (with local variations of up to 23 per cent); line 7, Lionel Munby (ed.) *Life and Death in King's Langley: Wills and Inventories, 1498–1659* (1981) my calculation; lines 8–9, Shammas, 'Control over capital', p. 140; line 10, H. C. F. Lansberry, 'Free bench see-saw: Sevenoaks widows in the late seventeenth century', *Archaeologia Cantiana* 100 (1984) p. 283; line 11, Susan Dwyer Amussen, *An Ordered Society: Gender and Class in Early Modern England* (1988) p. 80; line 12, Index to WSRO: STCI/18; line 13, *Selby Wills* (1911); lines 14–15, Shammas, 'Control over capital', p. 140; lines 16–18, Vann, 'Wills and the family', pp. 352, 366; lines 19–22, *Wills at Chester*; line 23, T. F. Barton and M. A. Farrow (comps) *Index of Wills Proved in the Consistory Court of Norwich 1687–1750* (1965).

Table 12.2 Marital status of women making wills, fourteenth–eighteenth centuries

Location Date (N)	Maids		Wives		Widows	
	%	n	%	n	%	n
1 Diocese of Rochester 1347–8 (56)	7	4	55	31	38	21
2 Bishop's Lynn, Norfolk 14th century (21)	10	2	24	5	67	14
3 King's Langley, Herts 1523–1659 (18)	6	1	–	0	94	17
4 Salisbury 1500–1640 (154)	–		5	7	–	
5 Norfolk 1590–1750 (91)	15	14	3	3	81	74
6 Selby, Yorks 1634–1710 (77)	18	14	–	0	82	63
7 North and East Yorkshire 1640–90 (30)	20	6	3	1	77	23
8 Diocese of Norwich 1687–1750 (626)	18	110	8	52	74	464
9 Lancashire and Cheshire 1660–80 (523)	19	99	0	2	81	422
10 Lancashire and Cheshire 1681–1700 (674)	16	106	1	10	83	558
11 Lancashire and Cheshire 1701–20 (387)	19	72	0	1	81	314
12 Lancashire and Cheshire 1721–40 (192)	20	39	–	0	80	153

Sources: Line 1, Sheehan, 'Influence of canon law', p. 122 (conflating his figures for the two
years); line 2, Beauroy, 'Family patterns', pp. 15–16, 25–6 (these figures not listed as
such, but discernible from the text); line 3, Munby (ed.) *King's Langley*, my calculation;
line 4, Susan Wright, 'Family life and society in sixteenth and early seventeenth-century
Salisbury' (Leicester PhD thesis, 1982) p. 119 (all wives' wills date from after 1610);
line 5, Amussen, *Ordered Society*, p. 80; line 6, *Selby Wills*; line 7, BIHR wills; line 8,
Barton and Farrow (comps) *Index of Wills ... Norwich*; lines 9–12, *Wills at Chester*.
Note: In the larger samples from the Diocese of Norwich and Lancashire and Cheshire a handful
of women (less than 1 per cent) were identified by a trade in their wills.

But there are questions which hang about this method of calculating sex-
specific testation rates by comparing surviving wills with population. The
most basic question arises from the differing proportions of women in the
three types of probate documents. In Table 12.1 we see that approximately 20
per cent of all wills were made by women. But a somewhat smaller proportion
(15–20 per cent) of inventories were appraised for women's estates,[2] and
even fewer accounts (10–15 per cent) were filed for women's estates (see
Chapter 2). If women are more prominent among wills than they are among
those for whom inventories and accounts were filed, which included those
who died intestate, it would suggest that those women who were eligible to do
so were more likely than most men to make wills.

The testing of this proposition will have to await the analysis of large quantities of probate accounts, in which proportions of testate and intestate women can be compared with testate and intestate men. The collections of accounts I have amassed are inadequate for this purpose for two reasons: in the case of all the surviving Cambridgeshire and Northamptonshire accounts, there are too few accounts, with too few willmakers; and in the case of the samples from Lincolnshire and Sussex, they tend too much towards women's accounts, for the purpose of matching with their husbands' probate documents.

If widows were particularly likely to make wills, it would not be too surprising. Married men who died without having made a will left wives who had an interest in, and were automatically granted the administration of, their estates. Widows left no such obvious manager for their affairs, however modest those affairs might be. It stands to reason that a will was made precisely if it was not perfectly clear where property was to go. In mid-nineteenth-century Petersburg, Virginia, Suzanne Lebsock found that 'Propertied women who had the legal capacity were more likely than were propertied men to dispose of their assets by will – actively, that is, and with deliberation.'[3] It may well turn out that English widows two hundred years earlier shared the same propensity, at least in some segments of the population.

Which segments of the population were more likely to make a will? One possible encouragement to making a will was the presence of minor children. This was one important reason for a man to make a will – more than half of 200 married or widowed men who made wills in rural Yorkshire, Lincolnshire and Sussex had minor children.[4] But they were not significant for the 100 widows who made wills in the same counties: more than half of the widows had either no children or all their children were grown.[5] In Lincolnshire, probably as a result of high death rates in the fens and the marsh, 82 per cent of widows (23 of 28) who made wills had at least one minor child still at home. But in Sussex the rate was only 32 per cent (16 of 50), and in rural Yorkshire 18 per cent (4 of 22). Women dying with minor children were likely to be married, and so unlikely to make a will or have their estate inventoried. Men whose estates were probated at all, whether or not they left a will, were simply far more likely to have young children. If most men who made a will had minor children, so too did most of the 295 men who died intestate in Lincolnshire and Sussex.

The age profile of women and men making wills was inevitably different. In Sussex and Yorkshire approximately one third of widows making wills were grandmothers, but there were no grandmothers at all in Lincolnshire. Grandfathers making wills, on the other hand, formed a remarkably consistent one fifth of all married men and widowers in all three counties.[6]

Another possible factor in the propensity to make a will was wealth. A correlation between wealth and testation does not mean that in wealthier parts of the country more people made wills. Rather, within any region people who made wills tended to be wealthier than those who did not. The exception to this rule appears to have been the fenland of Cambridgeshire and Norfolk, where willmaking was unusually widespread among poorer men, and in some cases poorer men actually made wills most often.[7] However, in the Lincolnshire fenland those men who made wills were substantially wealthier than those who did not. The median personal estate of those men who made a will was 40 per cent larger than the median estate of those who died intestate. Women in the fenland, however, had the same median wealth whether or not they made a will, although the number of wills at issue here is small.

Table 12.3 charts the median initial wealth of those who made wills and those who did not in Lincolnshire and Sussex, distinguishing between men and women. The median personal estate of all Lincolnshire men and women who made a will, not just those in the fenland, was approximately 40 per cent greater than the median estate of those who died intestate. On the other hand, in Sussex wealth made no difference at all to testation. The median wealth of women who made a will (£66) was only marginally greater than those who did not (£61), and Sussex men who made a will actually tended to have less in personal wealth (£112) than those who did not make a will (£132).

An estate had to be of a certain size to be considered worthy of probate at all, but if wealth were a significant factor in the likelihood of making a will in Sussex a larger discrepancy between testate and intestate inventory values would be expected.[8] When separated by region it appears that Sussex men from the arable south of the county were in fact more likely to make a will if they were wealthier, whereas the pastoral weald followed the east Anglian fenland pattern in that poorer men were more likely to make a will. However, in both arable and pastoral areas, the median wealth of women who made wills slightly exceeded that of women who did not make wills.

The upshot of all these comparisons is that family situation, wealth and local economy seem to have had some impact on men's willmaking (although the relationship is not yet clear), but none of these factors is a good predictor of a widow's likelihood of making a will. Although wealth caused prosperous people to think of making a will more often than poor people, it was also important to many poor people, especially women, to make a will.

The wills of single women and men have not been amassed in sufficient numbers, either here or anywhere else, to analyse potential stimuli to

Table 12.3 Median initial wealth of testates and intestates in inventories and probate accounts 1582–1686

	Intestates		Testates	
	£	n	£	n
Lincolnshire 1594–1686				
Women	35	95	59	32
Men	58	228	92	42
Sussex 1582–1684				
Women	61	61	66	43
Men	132	67	112	39

Sources: BIHR, LAO and WSRO wills.

willmaking. But for single women it is clear that a modest – even a tiny – estate was much less a deterrent to making a will than it was for men. Two single women in the Yorkshire wolds in the 1640s exemplify the meticulousness of single women's wills. Anne Nicholson carefully allocated one green apron, one pair of stockings, one little coffer, and to her uncle one little brass pot and a doubler, but only on condition that he pay part of her burial costs. Should he refuse, then the pot and doubler both went to the executrix. Anne Deane distributed one chest to her aunt, one coverlet to her (also single) sister, and 5s. each to her brother's three children, all of which came to a total value of perhaps £2.[9]

For widows, too, poverty seems to have been much less of an objection to making a will. Elizabeth Skaine, a widow of Chichester, had only £3 8s. 2d. worth of household goods and clothing when she died in 1640, yet she made a will. Elizabeth rented rooms for an exorbitant 10s. p.a., but her landlord had 'layd out for [her] since shee hath bin sick' many small sums for sugar, beer, wine, bread, candles, butter, coals, fish and finally burial. Perhaps freely in gratitude, perhaps reluctantly out of duty, Elizabeth's will gave 1s. to her brother and the remainder to her landlord as executor.[10]

Elizabeth Skaine did direct her property in a direction it would not have gone had she died intestate. Margaret Bankes in 1681 in east Yorkshire named her two married daughters as joint executrices, and as such they split all Margaret's residual goods, just as they would have done had Margaret not made a will. The only material reason she made a will was to give daughter Petronella one red rug, and daughter Margaret 'the bedstead in the parlor of the house wherin I now dwell and the curtain rodds' – but not the mattress or bedding or the curtains themselves.[11] Rather than providing for children or distributing largesse, women made wills out of a need to thank and acknowledge small favours, out of a sense of personal attachment to material goods, in order to help out family and friends in need and from a sense of personal integrity. A woman whose kin, perhaps particularly her female kin, had made a will may have felt that she too ought to do so, regardless of her material standing in the world, as a matter of family responsibility and self-respect.

Mary Dobb, in Selby, had been widowed for many years and had only married children when she made her will just before Christmas 1667. She gave bequests to eleven grandchildren and numerous other kin and friends, then to her daughter Mary Leatham, 'the acre of land I bought of William Warde and the houses I bought of John Gaskinge with garth, gardinge and orchard thereto belonginge, and one litle land at the orchard end', and to her other daughter Ann Tarboton, 'the acre of land I bought of John Marke Beale and the close I bought of Thomas Walker, called Toddhill Layne . . . one land . . . lynge at the end of the orchard that I bought of John Gaskinge'. To three granddaughters, 'three lands in the Lincrofts which I bought of Mr Harebreade'. Mary then went on to a few household goods. This grandmother with £43 in her inventory had recently bought at least ten pieces of land from five different men. Perhaps she did so intentionally because land would remain the property of her married daughters, and of her three granddaughters when they eventually married, as household goods or cash would not without special protection. Both of Mary Dobb's daughters made their own wills as widows – sixteen and twenty-eight years later – in which they devised the lands their mother had given them.[12]

The only reasons for willmaking which were ever made explicit were the occasional negative ones. Ellen Consett *als* Kirkby reluctantly wrote her will in north Yorkshire in 1648, and the task was a burden to her. Ellen's principal asset was a cottage house and garth which she had purchased before her marriage to Robert Consett. She had given him the cottage for his life, and had expected him to perform her bequests 'in consideration of the said house and premisses'. But Robert died, so Ellen – perhaps an old woman and certainly a tired woman since she resented the trouble – was constrained to write a will, giving the house to Margaret Prowd, her young, single half-sister and, while she was at it, 1s. 'apeece to every child that she was aunt to'.[13]

Some women were actively urged to make a will, as can be seen in cases of nuncupative wills, where nothing was written down but witnesses present at the time testified in court to wishes expressed orally. Mary Shucksmith of Chichester, on the 23 August 1625 or thereabouts, 'beinge sicke in body and not like to live', was badgered by one Elizabeth White.

> First beinge asked by Elizabeth White then presente with her howe she meante to dispose of her goods, and advisinge her to dispose thereof, and likewyse beinge advised by Mary Freeman widowe to dispose of her goods tellinge her that they were never the farther from her, first the saide testatrix answeared nothinge, then beinge asked by the saide Elizabeth White againe what her brother Anthony shoulde have, she answeared small and a litle; and then beinge asked by the saide Elizabeth White againe what her brother John shoulde have she answeared he shoulde have nothinge; then beinge asked againe by the saide Elizabeth White whether her Cosens Chambers his sonne sould have yt, (meaning William Chambers) she answeared that he shoulde have that she had, in the presence of Elizabeth White, Mary Freeman, John Chambers, and Elizabeth Chambers his wyfe.[14]

Elizabeth White's advantage in all this is unclear; the Chambers could not press for information in the way that she could since they were presumably immediately related to the principal beneficiary, which would have aroused the suspicion of the probate court. And why the dying woman's goods 'were never farther from her' will remain a mystery. This is the only surviving record of the life of Mary Shucksmith.

In the case of other widows, particularly prosperous ones, it was the clergy who urged the making of a will, for the good of the soul to remember the poor. One gentlewoman, Constance Glemham of the Sussex weald, in April 1634 was 'a verie aged woman but in health of body and minde'. Constance, 'being moved by . . . [the] rector of Trotton to make her will . . . and therein to remember the poore of the parish and her servants', responded obediently, but deviously: she would give everything to her son, 'not doubting but that hee would according to discrecon reward her servants and remember the poore'. This qualification may even have been a later addition of the rector's, since Constance's nuncupative will was not proved until December and the rector was the only witness to that bequest. In the intervening months, Constance was heard by her daughter to say that she also gave to her grandson, her daughter's son, a piece of gold worth £1 13s. Her own son, by a husband prior to Glemham, got the remaining £1017, and he did give his mother an elaborate funeral, spending £126 on black cloth alone.[15]

Aside from external pressure, positive reasons for a woman to make a will must be inferred from family connections, as in the case of Mary Dobb and her daughters, above, or from individual wills' special consideration for female kin and the particularity of bequests of personally significant goods.

DISTRIBUTION

Perhaps the clergy exhorted women more often than men to give to the poor. But if many women were as clever at deflecting these requests as Constance Glemham, then clerical encouragement cannot explain why women actually did make more charitable bequests in their wills. Both women and men gave money to the poor man's box or directed that bushels of wheat be 'beakte in bred' for distribution at their funerals.[16] Widows may have had marginally greater freedom from the necessity to provide for a young family, but their generosity to the poor did not depend on a more advanced stage of the life-cycle. Joan Redwell, widow of a yeoman of the Sussex coast, in 1620 had five bushels (300 lb) of wheat made into bread and bestowed at her burial, enough to provide every poor household in the parish with many loaves. She had four children and three stepchildren to be supported, as did her husband when he died just seven months previously, yet his will made no bequest to the poor.[17] Few willmakers, regardless of their family situation, could not have afforded a shilling or two in charity.

W. K. Jordan's monumental study of charity in early modern England found women less charitably inclined than men in terms of the amount of money they gave. Not only did women have less money to give away in the first place, they were singularly uninterested in high-cost charitable projects like municipal improvements. But in terms of numbers of donors, rather than size of donation, women were much more concerned than men with the care of the poor and with what Jordan called 'social rehabilitation'.[18] In Yorkshire, Lincolnshire and Sussex wills of the seventeenth century too, women consistently made slightly more charitable bequests to the poor than men. Proportions varied regionally and charitable bequests as a whole declined over the early modern period, but 32 per cent of women and 29 per cent of men gave to the poor prior to the mid-seventeenth century, and 17 per cent of women and 14 per cent of men after the mid-seventeenth century.

Jordan did not delve into the causes of women's propensity to personal charity, but this can readily be done with even a small number of wills. Single women were not especially given to charitable bequests. Widows, on the other hand, were particularly aware of other widows in their wills. Mary Forman, the widow of a turner in the Sussex weald, gave the poor widows of the parish £1 in her will of 1677. At the time of her death she had three children and three stepchildren from two marriages, all grown. Mary was comfortably well-off with an estate of £70, and she herself had been widowed for twenty-five years, which may have prompted her generosity towards other less fortunate widows.[19] Another prosperous and long-widowed woman, Mary Stavell, of the Sussex coast, had received £130 from her husband's estate some ten years prior to making her own will in 1680, in which she bequeathed 10s. to the poor widows of Selsey.[20] Anne Toynby, widow of a husbandman in the vale of Lincoln, had been widowed for only seven years, and she owned at the time of her death only £35. Still, she left 6d. to four named widows and 4d. to every widow in Waddington.[21] There were no established almshouses for widows in these parishes at this time. These bequests were gifts to a group of people who must have been well known in the parish, probably to be distributed by the Overseers of the Poor.

In the distribution of possessions among their kin and friends both single women and widows showed a distinct awareness of women's risk of relative poverty, even if their own family members were not at risk of the absolute poverty of the poor rates. It has often been observed that women's wills are more 'diffuse' than men's, meaning that they recognize a wider circle of kin and apparently unrelated legatees.[22] (The only parish in England so far which does not reveal this pattern is Terling, Essex.)[23] Table 12.4 quantifies these general observations, showing the relative proportions of women and men who gave bequests to kin other than their spouse or direct descendants. Women gave bequests to one or more sisters nearly twice as often as men did, and to one or more brothers a third again as often as men. Kin of all kinds – cousins, nieces and nephews, aunts and uncles, and step-relations – all received legacies more often from women than from men.[24]

Women's wider recognition is to be expected, given that they wrote wills usually as widows, when their children were more likely to be adult,

Table 12.4 Bequests to kin and others by sex 1579–1682

Legatee	Women		Men	
	%	n	%	n
Sister	23	24	11	22
Brother	19	20	14	28
Female kin	32	34	25	49
Male kin	30	32	27	53
Friends	26	28	21	42
Total		106		196

Sources: BIHR, LAO and WSRO wills.

previously provided for or dead. The patrimony, in their husbands' name, had already been distributed, either in bequests if he had made a will or in portions by the ecclesiastical court if he had died intestate. Women did not distribute smaller gifts among more people because they had a wider network of kin and friends than their husbands did – although perhaps they were more aware of the importance of those ties, which we call 'extended' only because they reach outside the nuclear family centred on a single male. Rather, women were freer, by the nature of their property and of their concerns, to express personal preference. 'Personalism'[25] is a better description of women's wills than 'diffusion'. The difference between women's wills and men's wills is in large part the difference between matrimony and patrimony. Patrimony suggests property extended vertically or longitudinally through time; matrimony, although significantly it does not mean property in and of itself, implies ties of kinship – and therefore of property – extended horizontally, or latitudinally, in a much more immediate timeframe.

Although women gave bequests to a wider range of people than men did, still most women – between two thirds and three quarters of the total – divided their property exclusively among their children and grandchildren (see Table 12.4). For a widow, the exact nature of her bequests – what she gave and to whom – depended, if she had children, on whether her husband had made a will. Even if he had, it was not uncommon for her own will to compensate for what she perceived as the imbalances of his.

The wills of William and Joan Reymes of the Sussex coast, in August 1605 and January 1606 respectively, have not a single legatee in common. William gave to his daughter Margaret his best cupboard, best coverlet and white cow; to his daughter Lucy £10 and his copyhold estate at her majority; and to his son Henry a table upon stumps with the benches, a pair of sheets, plus 'all the rest' which was coming to him at 21, presumably freehold land by inheritance. Joan gave nothing to any of these three children. She had £51 after debts, and she divided it all equally between her daughter Clarman and her son William, both of whom were small, and neither of whom were mentioned in their father's will. Yet all these children were the offspring of Joan and William together. (The only indications that these people were husband and wife are that William's executrix was a 'Joane', and a single distinctive bequest of William's was mentioned in the account filed for Joan's estate, although not in her will.)[26]

Another Joan and William of the Sussex coast provide a less extreme example of the complementarity of couples' wills. When Joan Michelborne – who gave the poor at her funeral five bushels of wheat – married the yeoman William Redwell, they each had three minor children (two daughters and one son) by a previous marriage. Together they had one further daughter, Joan, before William died in 1620. His will naturally favoured his own children, and gave his son slightly more than his daughters, with a token lamb to each of his wife's children. Joan's will six months later naturally favoured her Michelborne children, and gave the younger daughter more than the elder daughter or the son. Joan was more generous than her husband had been to her two stepdaughters, giving them a 'great chest' and a chest and gold ring which had been William's; but her stepson received nothing by her will. Both parents gave most to their mutual child Joan who, as the youngest, would have had no legacies from grandparents or other provision.[27]

When the husbandman William Toynby died in 1672 in the vale of Lincoln he left to Anne, his second wife – the one who gave 4d. to every widow in Waddington – 'the homestead wherein I now live' for her lifetime, and all household goods 'within and without doors' except the plough and the wain, which were valued at approximately £83. The land went to his two sons after Anne's death, but he gave only 1s. to each of two married daughters. Anne made her own will the following year, although she lived another six years. She had no children of her own, and her will gave each of her four stepchildren a cow and a few specific items of approximately equivalent value. She then divided all the remaining household goods, worth about £20, equally between her stepdaughters, while her stepsons were to divide the winter corn, worth only £3. (Perhaps because of the time that elapsed between her making her will and her death, Anne had bequeathed substantially more than she possessed, so in the event everyone had to take composition of their legacies.[28]) Anne Toynby was more generous to her own nieces and nephews by blood than to her stepchildren, and her behaviour was not uncommon. But what looks like a widow transferring her husband's patrimony to her own natal kin – always in the absence of her own children – should not be surprising in the light of the proportion of the conjugal estate commonly contributed by the wife (see Chapter 10).

In addition to calculating their own bequests to balance their husbands', women's wills also made use of legal devices like contingency clauses to protect certain children. The yeoman Richard Wood, of the vale of Lincoln, in 1681 gave all of his land to Hester his wife – the cottage house for her life only, and after to their eldest son, and the close of meadow for ever. When Hester came to make her own will two years later, she made her youngest son her executor and gave him her close as well. Each of the Woods' unmarried daughters received cash bequests from both their parents, but where their father had used a contingency clause which, in the event of either girl's death, spread the bequest among all of her siblings, their mother used a contingency clause which gave all of each girl's legacy to the other one only.[29]

In later seventeenth-century Yorkshire Alice Wandesford, the mother of Alice Thornton, tried a more complex legal device in her will. First of all she gave her £1000 personal estate (including 'lute, vyoll and virginalls') to her daughter as separate estate, so that it would not come under the control of Mr Thornton. In addition, the elder Alice made the bequest for life only. After Alice Thornton's death the goods were to descend to *her* daughter, and so on in the female line. This bequest was contested by Alice Wandesford's eldest son, unsatisfied with the £4000 p.a. he had from his father, but to no avail.[30]

The will of Ann Succorman's husband does not survive, if he made any.

But it is clear from Ann's own will in 1610 where her interests lay. She gave 3-year-old Rebecca Peartree, probably her granddaughter, her copyhold cottage with 3½ acres 'of the Burlinefee and myne acres of the Welbye fee, and one acre and one roode of the Abbatts fee', all in Gedney, Lincolnshire, in addition to naming Rebecca executrix and leaving her £24 in residual goods. Rebecca's brother received only £1 from his grandmother when he turned 16.[31]

The significance of women's personalism lies not only in the fact that they gave different kinds of bequests to different people, but also in the fact that they favoured female legatees more often than men, whether daughters, nieces, grandaughters or other kin, and even if only in a small way. This distinction is clear in other studies, as well as in the Yorkshire, Lincolnshire and Sussex wills examined here.[32] The actual numbers of female and male legatees in women's wills and in men's wills were only slightly different. Where bequests in thirty men's wills from Lincolnshire (omitting those to overseers and guardians) were given to exactly half women and half men, in twenty-one Lincolnshire women's wills the proportion was approximately 60 per cent female legatees to 40 per cent male. But the amounts given to women by women were consistently greater.

Table 12.5 examines women's principal beneficiaries, whether female, male, or equally female and male. The division by sex refers most often to daughters and sons, but occasionally also to grandchildren and nieces or nephews. A preference for female legatees is most marked in Yorkshire, where 57 per cent of women favoured women in their wills. In the southern province the balance between the three groups is closer, but always less than 40 per cent of women favoured male legatees. If this proportion still seems high, consider that mothers' personal attachment to their sons had as much impact on their property distribution as fathers' individual affection for their daughters (see Chapter 4). The disparity between women's and men's distribution in their wills, and the differing expectations of fairness which women and men clearly had, remains marked.

Because a widow was generally the principal beneficiary of her husband's will or received most of his residual goods from the ecclesiastical court, particularly when she had young children, it fell to her to dispose of those goods again at her death. Household goods, cash and animals were distributed

Table 12.5 Women's principal beneficiaries

	Female		Male		Both sexes		
	%	n	%	n	%	n	N
Yorkshire	57	17	30	9	13	4	30
Lincolnshire	46	11	38	9	17	4	24
Sussex	31	16	40	21	29	15	52
Overall	42	44	38	39	22	23	106

Sources: BIHR, LAO and WSRO wills.

by both women and men equally. Craft tools too appeared equally in women's and men's wills, when items like spinning wheels, skillets and kneading troughs are included in the term along with leatherworking, shoemaking or woodworking tools. Women more often bequeathed clothing than men, and less often land. A widow generally enjoyed her husband's land and its profits in her widowhood, but she could not normally dispose of it because he had given her only a life right, in the same way that her legal entitlement to dower and freebench were limited to life. In the absence of any provision made by her husband, a widow's will begins to look like that of a father with grown or nearly grown children, distributing ploughs and carts, manure and seeds. Equally, in the absence of his wife, a widower bequeathed the goods that had been hers. Thus for example in the 1643 will of William Staggs, a widower and modestly prosperous skinner of north Yorkshire, the first bequest is to his niece Isabel Pillie, 'one new petticoate', followed by individual bequests of his dead wife's coat, ruffs, safeguard and the old petticoat.[33]

The preference for female legatees was not limited to bequests of clothing, which might be expected to go to other women, but extended to all types of household goods, cash and land. Widows and single women did devise land and houses that they themselves owned, generally in smaller amounts than men. Closes, roods, acres, orchards and cottages were inherited (like Rebecca Peartree) or purchased before marriage (like Ellen Consett) or during widowhood (like Mary Dobb). Table 12.6 lists the proportion of women and of men who devised land, in locations between Sussex and Yorkshire. Women devised land in up to one third the proportion in which men did, always remembering that most men did not mention land in their wills either, because there were other means of transferring it. The proportion of women with land increased steadily the farther north the location (lines 1–4). More Yorkshire-women devised land because more of them inherited it (see Chapter 4), but they also seem to have been more active in purchasing land than they were in those parts of Sussex and Lincolnshire where a market in small parcels of land existed. Six of seven women landowners in rural Yorkshire gave their land to a female legatee. In the town of Selby nearly as many women (46 per cent) as men (51 per cent) mentioned land in their wills (line 5), although the women often had part shares of houses and other small pieces of land.

Table 12.6 Proportion of willmakers devising land

		Women			Men		
		%	n	N	%	n	N
1	Sussex	8	4	52	40	26	65
2	King's Langley	11	2	18	42	40	95
3	Lincolnshire	17	4	24	50	15	30
4	Rural Yorkshire	23	7	30	67	67	100
5	Selby, Yorks	46	33	71	51	115	226

Sources: Line 1, WSRO wills; line 2, Munby (ed.) *King's Langley*, my calculation; line 3, LAO wills; line 4, BIHR wills; line 5, *Selby Wills*.

Women who transferred property to their children by deed in their widowhood also preferred their daughters to their sons, probably in compensation for land inheritance. In 1672, the year after her husband died intestate in Northamptonshire, Joyce King put out cash portions at interest with her father-in-law for each of her young children. In addition, she purchased a 'quarterne land' for the use of her daughter Hannah, leaving her son to be content with his cash portion.[34]

In the Lincolnshire marshland Agnes Love, already twice a widow (one of her husbands was a labourer), made a 'deed of gift' in 1611 providing for her children. Like the bond of Katherine Trusse *als* Boyne (see Chapter 8) Agnes Love's document too survives in its original form only through an accident. It was presented to the probate court in lieu of a will, and a fair copy of the deed – minus the full names of the signatories – was subsequently filed among the court's inventories. The original deed is illustrated in Figure 3. This document gave to each of Agnes's three sons £3 plus some ewes and lambs worth 8s., at their attainment of age 18. Daughter Margaret was to have £3 and a cow worth £2 10s., all together 40 per cent more than her brothers' goods. If Agnes should 'go to the world againe or bee married', then her new husband would be required to enter into 'good and sufficient bonds' for payment of the children's portions. Agnes left £18 when she died still unmarried five years later, by which time Margaret had died also; her sons were apprenticed to a miller, a cobbler and a ropemaker.[35]

Single women favoured female legatees even more strongly than widows. Nieces were a particular favourite. At the time of her death in Pickering in 1682, Elizabeth Ripley had one brother and two sisters, one of them also single, but it was the daughter of a third, deceased, sister who was Elizabeth's principal beneficiary. Elizabeth was half-owner with the dead sister of a bedstead and feather bed, and this she gave to her orphan niece Mary Mason, along with £5 and her 'narrow land', or strip in the castle field of Pickering, when Mary reached the tender age of 14, for the heirs of her body forever. Failing such heirs, the narrow land defaulted to Elizabeth's unmarried sister Ellis, who also received her own narrow land in Maltongate field. Elizabeth acknowledged her brother and his two daughters and her married sister and brother-in-law with small bequests.[36] The year previous Mary Widd, also of the vale of Pickering, gave two of her brothers £2 and a measure of malt each – Mary may have been a maltster. A third brother was her executor and her nephew she acknowledged with a ewe and lamb. But her niece was her principal and her most explicit beneficiary, with 'a great spence [cupboard], a bedstead, a chest, a kettle, a buffet [low] stoole, two pewter doublers, a brasse box, and 4s. to change the kettle and buy a pan and a gimmer hog [yearling ewe]'.[37] Wills serve as a reminder that, while ordinary women did not explain their single state to posterity or expound their views on marriage, the sheer number of unmarried women in the population in the seventeenth century meant that girls growing up were likely to have at least one unmarried sister or aunt as an example, and perhaps also as a benefactress.

Figure 3 Agnes Love's deed of gift, Lincolnshire Archives Office, LCC Admon 1616/102.

All men shall knowe by this p[rese]nte deede of gifte that I Annes Love late the wife of Thomas Love deceased of Frampton in the partes of Hollande & in the Countie of Lincoln widowe, do geve unto my Children by vertue of this deede of gifte ev[er]y one of them their porc[i]ons out of my goods & cattells late the aforesaid Thomas Love & to bee paid unto them at the yeres of eighteene or at the age of eighteene yeres olde, And I desire Rob[er]te Stubbs of the same towne & Countie husbandma[n], that if it please almightie god to Call me to his mercy, that hee will see them & ev[er]ly of them have their parts & portions at the age aforesaid truly p[er]formed & paid unto my children. It[e]m I geve unto my eldest boy John Love three poundes & three ewes & lambes wi[i]th the wooll & all profite on May day nexte after the Accomplished yeares of eighteene as is aforemenc[i]oned and to my nexte sonn Humfrey Love three poundes of good and lawfull money of England and two ewes, with their lambes and wooll with their profite on May day nexte after the accomplished yeares of eighteene, and to my yongest sonne Thomas Love three poundes of good and lawfull money of England and three ewes and three lambes and wooll with their profite on the aforesaid May day next after the accomplished yeares of Eighteene, And if the aforesaid John Love Humfrey Love and Thomas Love do not like the aforsaid ewes and lambes, that then they shall have for every Ewe and lambe havinge the chose amongst them then or there shall have for ev[er]ly ewe and lambe, with the profite not liked on eighte shillings of good and lawfull money of England, and if it bee my fortune to go to the world againe or bee married, I geve to Margaret Love

my daughter three poundes of gold and lawfull money of England and one Cow, or fiftie shillings for her Cow to bee paid at May day next after the accomplished yeares of Eighteene, and ev[er]ly one of them to bee others heires if they die without marriage, and if I bee married that then hee which is my husband shall have the use of these aforsaid goods and Cattells for and towards the bringinge upp of the aforsaid John Humfrey Thomas and Margaret, enteringe into good and sufficient bonds for the payment of it at the yeares of eighteene yeares of age of ev[er]ly of them: And if I the above named Annes Love do departe this world before they come to lawfull yeares as is before rehearsed, that then the aforesaid Roberte Stubbes shall take these goods and Cattells into his owne hands at the two yeares end after my departure and take bonds to and for my children use payinge the Rentes of ev[er]ly porc[i]on of goods and Cattells to my husband towards the bringinge upp of my children whilst they and ev[er]ly of them come to the age of Eighteene yeares, dated the first day of July in the nynth yeare of the Raigne of our sov[er]aigne lord James by the grace of god of England Scotland France and Irelande kinge defendor of the faith etc. Anno d[om]in[i] 1611. Annes Love her signe. Seene, subscribed and deliv[er]ed in the p[rese]nce of James Gebson et Thomas

Women's choice of an executor was consistent with their preference for female legatees. Men who made wills usually named an executrix, rather than an executor, because they had wives to undertake the job. Women's choice of executor differed sharply between the northern and southern provinces (see Table 12.7). In the southern province (lines 3–5) between two thirds and three quarters of women appointed a son, a son-in-law or a brother as executor;[38] between one quarter and one third appointed a daughter or other female kin, or joint executors of both sexes. But in Yorkshire (lines 1–2) the majority of women named an executrix or joint executors of both sexes – usually all their children, or all the children except for the eldest son. This habit of excluding the eldest son was also found in men's wills (see Chapter 4). In Selby it is even possible to say that widows only appointed a son executor in the absence of a daughter. In both north and south women who made wills would name a daughter executrix even if they had sons as well, whereas a man never took that step. Wills made by single women named sisters and brothers as executors in approximately equal numbers; often they had only one sibling.

Table 12.7 Women's choice of executrix or executor

		Executrix		Executor		Mixed		
		%	n	%	n	%	n	N
1	Selby, Yorks	54	37	28	19	18	12	68
2	Rural Yorkshire	45	13	45	13	10	3	29
3	Lincolnshire	22	5	65	15	13	3	23
4	Sussex	26	10	72	28	3	1	39
5	King's Langley	28	5	67	12	6	1	18

Sources: Line 1, *Selby Wills*; line 2, BIHR; line 3, LAO; line 4, WSRO; line 5, Munby (ed.) *King's Langley*, my calculation.

The proportions of women appointing an executrix, although not the majority in the south, are still considerable, in light of the risk run to the deceased's estate by the executrix's future marriage. Technically, goods which a married woman possessed by virtue of being an executrix remained her own and did not pass to her husband, but there was the question of enforcement. The practice of marking goods, as Alice Wandesford and Janevive Deane did (see Chapters 6 and 7), may have been much more common than these two cases alone suggest, even among ordinary people – and particularly among women, since the presumption of ownership would always have been against them.

The goods of widows and single women who died intestate were distributed by the ecclesiastical courts with exactly the same consideration that men's goods were divided. Thus when the young Anne Paxton died in Northamptonshire in 1677, her considerable £85 of residual goods were distributed among her siblings: to her single sisters Elizabeth and Susanna, £35 each; to her brother Thomas, only £15, since he had inherited land from their parents. (Inheriting land was, of course, no guarantee of solvency. Thomas Paxton died five years later, leaving his wife Mary in debt.)[39]

The wills people wrote reveal not only what property they owned but also their personal attachments, to goods and to people. The wills of women and men are in many ways similar, both in what they bequeath and to whom. But the significant qualitative differences are, first, women's wider recognition of kin, and second, their preference for female legatees. Future research has yet to determine whether women or men were more likely to make a will, given the legal restrictions women laboured under, and the fact that most of the wills surviving are men's. Women's special provision for and protection of female legatees, as well as their specific charitable bequests for poor widows – and for the poor in general, who were mostly widows – strongly suggest an awareness of women's economic vulnerability, the result of an inheritance system which disadvantaged them and their legal coverture in marriage.

The idea prevails among economic historians that the property rights of widows who persisted in living to a ripe old age presented anything from 'difficulty' to 'years of continuous obstruction and difficulty' for the male heirs awaiting their inheritance. Resentment of widows for detaining property from the next generation is assumed too prevalent even to require evidence.[40] We may assume that a man who was sued by his mother for her dower or jointure – like the Earl of Dorset (see Chapter 6) – probably did resent her. And even more so if she was only his father's widow, not his mother. But that was, after all, only his opinion; her friends undoubtedly thought differently. Economic historians have assumed the primacy of the heir's interest, or the patrimony, forgetting the importance of everyone else in the family – and notably the heir's mother, whose claim derived from matrimony. The male line of descent *through* time is now perceived as more important than the horizontal claims of women and younger sons *at* the time.

There is, in fact, virtually no serious complaint about widows' property rights voiced in the early modern period. At an ordinary level, an atmosphere of marital trust is clearly indicated by the fact that a widow was generally her husband's executrix and principal beneficiary if he made a will. The responsibility taken on by a widow as administratrix or executrix – including paying legacies and portions, collecting and discharging debts, any debt litigation, and accounting to the church courts for all her actions – requires that she must have shared financial responsibilities as a wife too, in order to acquire the skills and assurance necessary to assume administration, and to hold the necessary respect in her own family and community to do so. The ecclesiastical courts too assumed a marital economic partnership by consistently allocating a widow well over the legal portion of one third of her intestate husband's estate.

If ordinary widows were substantially better off than their bare legal rights suggest, remember that the median residual wealth they were left with from their husbands' estates was only £33. And that the behaviour of individual men and probate courts was not strictly a matter of generosity, since in most cases more than half of all moveable wealth in the marital household had been brought there by the wife.

The actual circumstances surrounding widows' property are at complete variance with the statutory abolition of their limited entitlements in the later seventeenth century. The negligible incidence of estate mismanagement can hardly have given rise to the 1670 Act for the Better Settling of Intestates' Estates, which severely impinged upon the justice of ecclesiastical courts' distribution of marital estates by cutting down widows with children to a one-third share and childless widows to one half. As a result of this restriction on intestate distribution, men who made wills too could come gradually to feel justified in giving their wives' less (as indeed they did in the American colonies). Later, the abolition of women's and children's right to reasonable parts in the northern province, Wales and London further undermined the tenuous security of widows. At the very least, the abolition of minimal legal entitlements encouraged men's conception that they were being magnanimous in their wills, rather than that they were only doing the right thing.

The ultimate effect of these laws is not yet known. More research on women's wills in the eighteenth century, on women's predominance among the poor and on remarriage may hold keys. Throughout the early modern period most widows did not remarry. A majority lived on their own holdings – often tiny, but still self-sufficient. This was true whether a widow had children to raise, whether she was childless or whether her children were grown and fully able to take care of their mother. Women's control over property in their widowhood could be limited by their husbands, but the care with which women bequeathed the property that was at their disposal, and specifically to other women, suggests not only close ties of female friendship, but also that women recognized other women's economic vulnerability.

Conclusion

It is relatively easy to compile information on how women as a sex were supposed to act in early modern England, and lists of the legal restrictions placed upon them. It is much more difficult to ascertain exactly how women did behave and how they responded to their legal disabilities.

In the main, women did not write about their own experience. Lady Anne Clifford and Mrs Alice Thornton are fascinating and charismatic, but there is no female equivalent of Henry Best or William Stout or Roger Lowe to offer first-hand insight into the life of a farmer's or merchant's wife or of an apprentice. We know virtually nothing from personal writing about ordinary women's daily lives – what they planted in the garden, how often they went to market and what they bought and sold there, or what they thought about their mistresses and masters, their servants or their families.

Ordinary early modern women's lives are only observable indirectly in impersonal legal documents, and then they are most visible in death – their parents', their husbands' and their own. Attitudes towards people and property have to be painstakingly reconstructed from the skeleton of property transfer, through both an analysis of large quantities of similar material and an in-depth, imaginative reading of each individual document. In probate documents women's voices are muted not because they did not speak at the time, but because the probate court in which those documents were created was operated entirely by men. At the same time, the majority – probably three quarters – of all those coming before the court to exhibit inventories, prove wills and file accounts were women.

The ecclesiastical courts in general were the only ones in which women comprised a majority of the people appearing. They were also the only courts whose business included administration, as opposed to litigation. In manorial and borough courts, in common law courts and in equity courts women comprised a minority of litigants, chiefly because most litigation involved property and women's control of property was severely limited. Women did comprise a considerable minority of litigants even in these courts, because a minority of adult women at any given time were married. But if a woman only appeared in one court in her whole life, it was likely to be the ecclesiastical probate court.

The twin pillars of common law control over women's economic fortunes – primogeniture in inheritance and coverture in marriage – were draconian in theory, but had less impact in practice. They were both unworkable on an everyday level. Throughout the early modern period the common law was still tempered by manorial ideas of partible inheritance and ecclesiastical ideas of community property in marriage and partibility in inheritance, as well as by equitable protection of special settlements in marriage. The actual practice of property distribution has been illustrated here by examining each legal phase of women's life-cycle: before, during and after marriage. The window on the late sixteenth to early eighteenth century opened by probate sources reveals a pattern of women's relation to property which is largely continuous, and probably both pre- and post-dates the survival of the relevant records.

Among the vast majority of the population, girls were raised on equivalent financial terms with their brothers, as far as food, clothing, treatment in sickness and basic education went. Probate accounts in which widowed mothers and guardians detailed their expenses in raising children reveal that both the annual maintenance costs and the apprenticeship premiums of girls were identical to those of their brothers. This equivalent material investment in ordinary children is extraordinary in light of the ideological undervaluing of females in all areas.

In inheritance, the operation of primogeniture – the most commonly identified aspect of inheritance in early modern England – was restricted primarily to freehold land, although increasingly applied to copyhold land too. Even then it was legally applied only in the absence of a will or deed to the contrary. In the early modern period most land was occupied by people who held in leasehold or copyhold, or by virtue of a trust, and not in freehold. However, even manors which practised partibility normally limited the distribution of land to all sons in the first instance. And in practice most fathers chose to favour sons over daughters in the distribution of land. Most men did not actually mention land in their wills, but transferred it during their own lifetime or allowed it to descend by law.

Girls were given land along with their brothers more often in Yorkshire. More importantly, they also regularly inherited land by operation of law in that fifth of marriages which produced only daughters. At an ordinary social level fathers without sons apparently did not choose to divert land away from their daughters in favour of more distant male kin, as they did among the 'landed' classes.

Even where daughters did not inherit land, their parents tended to compensate them with a substantially larger share of moveable goods than their brothers had, in order approximately to balance all children's shares of parental wealth. Where the eldest son was still favoured, he was slightly favoured, not overwhelmingly so. Balancing children's inheritance was possible because moveables were relatively much closer in value to land in the early modern period than they are today. While land certainly had symbolic value in its association with men, probably most people's wealth in moveable goods exceeded their wealth in land, a fact obscured by the frequent application of the term 'propertyless' to people without land. Daughters' larger bequests of moveable goods from their parents were reinforced by technical means: 'filial portions' limitations in the northern province; contingency clauses in the case of a legatee's death in the southern province; and throughout England by requiring that a son with land should pay his sister's cash bequest, upon default of which she was to enter into possession of his land until such time as she was paid.

Where the ecclesiastical courts divided the estates of those who died without having made a will, they too reduced land-inheriting children's share of moveable goods. The courts continued to apply their elastic interpretation of the requirement that each child have an 'equal' share, cutting down or cutting out the heir's share of moveables, even after the 1670 Act for the Better Settling of Intestates' Estates, which specifically prohibited such action.

Inherited portions, which would become marriage portions, or dowries, were important at all social levels, despite the fact that most ordinary young women's portions amounted to considerably less than 5 per cent of the size of gentry women's portions. Orphaned teenage girls managed their own portions, renting out animals and investing cash sums, and they carefully disposed of small goods in their own wills. Upon marriage, the groom's fortune was expected to equal his bride's. Although it is bridal portions that are most discussed – largely because it is men who did and do the discussing and they are the ones who profited financially from marriage – nevertheless in practice an equivalent portion from the groom was essential.

The majority of women married, but a larger proportion of women never married in the early modern period than at any time since. These women who remained 'maids' all their lives are also the only ones who continued on an equal legal footing with men. In theory, the equality of daughters' inheritance was lost to them under coverture. In practice, wives at all social levels – not just the Lady Margaret Hobys and the Dame Anne Filmers – managed finances on their own behalf and jointly with their husbands. For maximum financial security within marriage a pre-marital settlement was essential. Wealthier wives made complex marriage settlements, with the help of attorneys who relied upon the examples provided in conveyancing handbooks. These settlements were enforceable only in equity, and many wives did pursue their interests all the way to the Court of Chancery. Almost invariably a married woman sued in conjunction with her husband (in suits against her natal family for her portion) or with her father or brother (in suits against her husband or his family for separate estate or maintenance, or for her jointure). Widows and single women tended to sue alone, or with other women.

Ordinary women also circumvented the more incapacitating aspects of coverture by means of marriage settlements of a simpler type. This has not previously been recognized because the documents themselves – usually simple bonds which could be sued as any common debt – do not survive. But the shadow of these settlements is cast where a widow filed her account of her husband's estate and deducted the amount of money for which she (or technically, her sureties) had contracted before marriage. Most settlements ensured payment of a certain sum upon widowhood, to either a widow or her children. Some guaranteed a wife the right to dispose of property while under coverture. Whether a settlement stipulated payment to the wife upon widowhood or to her children at their majority, its purpose was the same – to protect the bride's property.

Such marriage settlements among ordinary people are only occasionally mentioned in wills, usually those of yeomen. But probate accounts indicate that, at the very least, 10 per cent of ordinary women employed pre-marital property settlements. These were made especially where widows remarried, since these women had both extra property to protect and experience of the adverse effects of coverture. But even in the case of first-time brides, it should not be surprising that women who brought half of the total marital estate to their husbands might find their minimal legal entitlements to property in the event of widowhood unsatisfactory.

Until now it has been assumed that only the upper classes – the wealthiest 5 per cent of the population – employed marriage settlements. Yet even women who could not write and may have been unable to read, like Katherine Trusse and Agnes Love, the wives of watermen and labourers (Figures 1 and 3), had bonds and deeds drawn up on their behalf, to protect their children's portions in the event of remarriage. We will never know how many marital property agreements were made on faith, without the insurance of legal documents. Nor will we ever know how many men peaceably carried them out; or how many men quietly failed to carry them out, to their wives' disgust or resignation; or how many couples had furious arguments about property arrangements, but stopped short of litigation.

In legal theory, wives were in a radically different condition to unmarried and widowed women. But coverture was – socially at least – a fiction. As *The Lawes Resolutions of Women's Rights* observed, 'society must always consist in two or more'. There is considerable evidence of the continuity of women's property through marriage, even apart from formal marriage settlements. In Chancery Court cases, the value of a bride's portion and of her widow's jointure were equivalent, when jointure took the form of a lump sum rather than an annuity. At ordinary levels a wife was regularly either the principal beneficiary of her husband's will, or she was given back the goods she had brought at the time of marriage and was expected to know which those were. A few women took the precaution of marking their goods, like Janevive Deane, 'that soe shee might still keep hir owne stock and goodes whole, in apparancie to the worlde'.[1]

When young women brought the equivalent amount of property to marriage that their husbands brought, and when they expected to take at least as much away again if they were widowed, it is unlikely that they ceased to regard that property as in some sense theirs for the duration of marriage. This is particularly the case at ordinary social levels where the property consisted largely of tangible goods, not intangible cash. Ultimately, of course, the property was not theirs unless they had legally secured it, and even if they had made a settlement, recovery of the money where a husband had squandered it was difficult. A woman who, as a widow, asked the ecclesiastical court for the equivalent of her bridal portion out of her husband's estate and did not get it – because his estate was insufficient, or because the court decided the supplicant was unworthy, or because the deceased had other needy kin – was sadly disappointed.

In general, however, it has been observed for some time that a man in his will usually named his widow executrix and made her his principal beneficiary. But husbands' generosity to their widows has hitherto been assumed to be distinctive to that minority of men who made wills. Probate accounts, in specifying the distribution of intestate estates, show that ecclesiastical courts were no different from men who made wills in this respect. As administratrix, the widow of a man who died intestate generally received an allocation of 66 per cent of his residual goods from the probate ordinary, approximately double the proportion stipulated by ecclesiastical law.

Widows' double share was not simply a matter of ecclesiastical magnanimity. The median amount left in a man's moveable estate after his debts had been paid was only £33. To assign a widow only her third, or £11, would in many cases have forced her and her children onto the poor rates, which was not in the court's or her parish's interest. During the later seventeenth century, the ecclesiastical 'generosity' towards ordinary widows was exactly opposite to trends among the wealthy. Wealthy men in their wills and wealthy men in parliament were cutting down widows' legal share of one third, because one third of a rich man's estate was far more than his widow required for comfortable subsistence. The Act of 1670 halving a childless widow's entitlement to her intestate husband's moveable estate and the later series of Acts to abolish a widow's ancient entitlement to reasonable parts were meant to trim the financial independence of wealthy widows down to merely an adequate subsistence.

But at an ordinary level the ecclesiastical courts were forced to adapt the laws of intestate distribution in order to prevent large numbers of widows from starving in the streets. Even so, widows still made up the vast majority of those in poverty. Widows poor enough to require parish relief were the objects of pity (and they were safely under control). But the self-sufficient widow – and particularly the well-to-do widow – was sufficiently feared to be popularly mythologized as rapacious and threatening.

The effects of this stereotype on the individual women prosperous enough to have their estates probated is unknown. The great majority of these widows headed their own households. Where the relative wealth of married couples can be discerned, over half of all widows possessed the same or greater moveable wealth at their death than their husbands had left to them. These widows, as also women who never married, distributed property in a different way than men did. First of all, widows may have been more likely than any other group in the population to make wills, which speaks to their determination to make their own choices, even if they had only small personal goods to bestow. The wills of widows and single women favour a wider range of kin than men's, and specifically they favour females. Widows' 'personalism' often compensated for perceived imbalances, either in their husbands' wills or in an ecclesiastical distribution of their husbands' estates. Daughters and younger sons were given more, and contingency clauses in the event of a legatee's death were used to protect that preference. Female favouritism was predominant both for moveables and for land – usually small pieces, perhaps a cottage. Women's particular generosity to the poor in their bequests suggests that an awareness of female susceptibility to poverty and women's legal vulnerability was behind their preference for female kin as well.

This book has only sketched an outline of how property was distributed by men to daughters, wives, and widows, and how women protected property when they had control over it and distributed it at their death. Much more research is needed – to fill in details, to clarify regional and class differences, to develop explanations of why it was all so, and to unravel further the interrelation of law and practice.

The relative upbringing of girls and boys can be further investigated in probate accounts, as well as in school records and accounts of parish Overseers of the Poor. While never-married women are the most difficult group to find out about, their sheer volume in the population merits much more research on where they lived and how they managed financially. The relative marriage portions of bride and groom could be pursued in litigation over broken contracts in the church courts, and marriage settlements should appear both there and in the three palatine equity courts. Did women marrying in different regions of the country have different ideas about their own entitlement to property under coverture, depending on the employment available to them both before and during marriage? Were marriage settlements actually less common in the northern province until the end of the seventeenth century because women knew that as widows they would still enjoy their right to a 'reasonable part' of their husband's estate, regardless of his will? The details of widows' provision requires much more investigation. It would be useful to know, for example, exactly where and when men used restrictions on their wives' bequests. Was the enjoyment of that property limited to the term of their widowhood or to the heir's minority? What kind of property was it? And how did the use of these restrictions vary over region and over time? Did it have any relation to the declining frequency of women's remarriage, in so far as that was affected by widows' choice or poverty? Or was the decline strictly a demographic phenomenon?

Ultimately, the most effective means of restricting a woman's remarriage was the system of coverture and the threat of losing control of her property.

It is impossible to overemphasize the ramifications of coverture upon property practices: women were never appointed overseers of wills, and virtually never trustees of funds or guardians of children – not simply because men were assumed more responsible, but also because if a woman married her legal responsibilities passed to her husband, who, to the man or woman making a will or setting up a trust, was an unknown quantity. It was because of the disadvantages of coverture that women who made their own wills exhibited a different sense of property than men did.

The division of this book into the three traditional segments of female existence – as maids, as wives and as widows – underscores women's enforced dependence in early modern England. Their position was invariably defined in terms of men. No man ever underwent anything like the disabilities of coverture – unless he was convicted of treason.

The maids, wives and widows of early modern England lived and died with an awareness of overlapping economic and emotional influences on their property which the historian can only hope to approximate. These influences were shaped both by different regions and by different laws.

The disadvantage of a geographically wide-ranging survey like this one is its inability to weigh the impact of specific local economies, individual landholding and manorial customs. The advantages of a broad scope are twofold. First, it points up regional differences to be followed up, particularly between northern and southern England. Why was a Yorkshire daughter more likely to be named executrix in either of her parents' wills, and to get more land from them than she would have farther south? At the same time a Yorkshire wife was more often named executrix of her husband's will, and least often with an overseer; she was almost never limited by a maintenance provision, was most likely to receive land, and least likely to have her right therein limited to lifetime or widowhood.

Second, and most importantly, a broad scope allows general patterns of property ownership to emerge, and local aberrations to be identified. In terms of who made wills, for example, it is now possible to see that large numbers of poor men and women in some fenland areas made wills, whereas in general those who made wills were noticeably wealthier than those who did not. The women of King's Langley and Bishop's Lynn were unusual in preferring male legatees in their wills; most women willmakers favoured female legatees. Terling was unique in its lack of different bequest patterns between women's and men's wills. Abingdon men's use of restrictions to widowhood on their wives' bequests increased while elsewhere the practice was dying out. And Orwell men's provision of annual maintenance or houseroom, as opposed to giving their wives the main holding for life, was radically different from anywhere else in England so far discovered. Sweeping generalizations about women's 'status' in early modern England on the basis of will patterns in specific parishes or counties – for example, the presence or absence of overseers, or the proportion of women named executrix by their husbands – are premature.

Despite the long-term continuity in women's relation to property, the shifting legal balance of power over a period of several hundred years – but particularly in the seventeenth century – cut serious inroads into women's already severely restricted entitlement to property. The ecclesiastical and manorial courts which had been the principal resort for women were, for a variety of reasons, falling into disrepute. As for equity courts, which usefully recognized the existence of married women, the three palatine jurisdictions were fading over the seventeenth century, and the Court of Chancery was far out of the reach of most people.

As the common law rode the tide of centralization and 'rationalization', it came to affect more people than ever before. In the middle ages the common law had been the law of the rich. By the nineteenth century the situation was reversed. With manorial and ecclesiastical protection eliminated, rich women turned to equity, leaving others at the mercy of the common law. One of the principal arguments of the Victorian campaigns for the reform of married women's property law was that the injustice of the common law fell hardest on working-class women.[2] These campaigns were cast by reformers in the light of an awakening of unwitting prisoners to their age-old oppression. A historical perspective suggests rather a resistance to long-tightened screws.

From the later seventeenth century parliament intervened in probate administration with statutes which appear to be merely procedural, but which in fact substantially undermined women's entitlement to personal property. The 1670 Act for the Better Settling of Intestates' Estates and the gradual abolition of reasonable parts for the widow and children of a man who made a will seriously undermined women's legal position, even if it had little immediate effect on their practical position. Few men, after all, were inclined to disinherit their wives and children wholly. But the legal changes allowed a man to make subtle adjustments in his distribution of family property at his discretion; the statutes therefore specifically increased men's control over women and children. In eighteenth-century America, men's wills regularly gave their daughters less than their sons and their wives less than their right in the event of intestacy. More research is needed on eighteenth-century England to know whether the same were true here.

There are several possible reasons why these changes took place in the late seventeenth century, including a general climate of conservatism and re-trenchment following the restoration of the monarchy, and the overt identif-ication of 'the individual' with the male individual in the burgeoning number of publications on political and property theory. The incremental 'rational-ization' of the legal system succeeded simultaneously in creating a consistent theory of private ownership and in excluding women from that theory by virtue of their marriage.

But conflict between differing legal views of women's condition did not start in the seventeenth century. As early as the mid-fourteenth century the ecclesiastical right of wives to make a will was eliminated. The widows of men in the southern province lost their right to a reasonable part of their husbands' moveables before 1600, by means as yet unknown. More and more manors came to apply primogeniture to the inheritance of copyhold land in place of partible inheritance, which may have affected some daughters as well as younger sons.

Nor did the progressive limitation of women's property cease with the statutory abolition of reasonable parts. If marriage settlements in the wife's interest did not originate in the sixteenth century, their number probably increased from that date, as protection from manorial and ecclesiastical courts declined. Marriage settlements for separate estate probably increased in the late seventeenth and eighteenth centuries, since cases were more frequently recorded in the Court of Chancery and more wives were making wills. But as marriage settlements relieved some of the statutory pressure on women's property rights, settlements themselves came under attack. Towards the end of the eighteenth century the Court of Chancery imposed increasingly contorted phraseological criteria on the establishment of a separate estate. In 1590, no express power of disposal was necessary to create a separate estate as long as the intent was clear,[3] but by 1800 the phrases 'to her own use', 'absolute use' and 'sole control' were all insufficient to establish a separate estate.[4] In addition, separate estate was hedged about with ludicrous restrictions on the control women had over them, with the device known as a 'restraint on anticipation'.

In addition to legal changes there were demographic, economic and cultural changes over the course of the seventeenth and eighteenth centuries which affected women's control of property. A late age of first marriage gave women a degree of economic and social independence while single which must have shaped their attitudes for the rest of their lives. But the median age of first marriage gradually declined, until in the mid-eighteenth century women married three to four years younger than they had a hundred years earlier. Earlier marriage not only limited women's pre-marital autonomy, but also increased the number of children they bore, which in turn intensified their domestic labour. The rate of widows' remarriage dropped rapidly from the seventeenth century, but the proportion of female-headed households also declined, so more widows were dependent on more relatives.[5] And by the eighteenth century the number of women never marrying had dropped to less than half its previous level,[6] so more women fell under the shadow of an even harsher coverture.

Economic changes brought down the relative value of daughters' inheritance. In the sixteenth and seventeenth centuries the value of the parcels of land that sons inherited could be balanced by moveable goods given to daughters. But over the eighteenth century new materials – soft woods for furniture, china for dishes, thinner fabrics for clothing and household linen – brought down the value of moveable goods relative to the value of land to such an extent that it would no longer have been possible for a parent to balance siblings' inheritance had they been so inclined.

Cultural changes may be measured by language, like the invention in the late seventeenth century of new ways to stigmatize unmarried women. Male resentment of women who insisted upon separate property in marriage was fanned in the eighteenth century by the literary representation of marriage in sentimental terms of romantic love and surrender, rather than in the terms of economic partnership and religious companionship which had prevailed in the sixteenth and seventeenth centuries. Expectations about the purpose of marriage and rights within marriage were shifting.

Expectations played an enormous but largely incalculable role in property distribution. In marriage, for example, the expectations of the bride, the groom, their fathers and mothers were formed by local practice, family practice and personal experience of misfortune, as well as by laws. The question of husbands' expectations being shaped by laws was raised above. It seems the expectations of mothers and older female kin of the bride, if not the bride herself, might have rather different origins. Women in certain upper-class families set an example for their kinswomen to make wills or settlements for separate property. There was clearly a tradition of securing women's property rights in the families of Lady Anne Clifford and Mrs Alice Thornton, for example. The possibility that widows were particularly likely to make wills and the preference of women's wills for female legatees suggest that female kin may also have played an important role in property transmission among ordinary women. But expectations among women in individual ordinary families are extremely difficult to trace because of the lack of established genealogies and family memoirs, and because of women's change of name upon marriage.

In spite of legal, demographic, economic and social shifts, an underlying continuity ties the women of 1550 and earlier to the women of 1750 and later. Men's perceived need to restrict women legally within marriage is as constant as their need to persuade women to think in terms of marriage as the natural female state. Certainly the appeal to men of maximum power within marriage pre-dated the sentimental attacks of *The Spectator* on pin-money in the early eighteenth century, just as it survives into our own century. In terms strongly reminiscent of early twentieth-century objections to women's suffrage, the preacher Jeremy Taylor in 1653 expressed an almost pathetic desire for the fictional unity of husband and wife:

> Let the husband and wife infinitely avoid a curious distinction of mine and thine; for this hath caused all the lawes, and all the suits, and all the wars in the world; let them who have but one person, have also but one interest.

So far Taylor may have been alluding to the strife of the civil war (analogies between the king and people, on the one hand, and husband and wife, on the other, were not uncommon). But he clearly had a real-life wife in mind when he directed that she was to say to her husband – but not he to her – 'I have nothing of my own, my goods, my portion, my body and my minde is yours'.[7]

Many men would have liked to regard women as property in and of themselves; but while married women's legal disabilities put them in the same category with idiots, convicted criminals and infants, they were never legally classed with chattels. Nonetheless, there are ways in which women were treated as a form of property. The specious theory of the 'unity' of husband and wife, and the constant threat of legal incapacitation; the association of a woman's marriage portion with her sexual honour; the view of rape as a form of theft, not from the victim but from her husband or male relatives; the prosecution of adultery only in cases where the woman was married; and the implications of even a practice as apparently innocuous as losing one's name upon marriage – all these smack of men's ownership of women. Certainly in the seventeenth century a number of women (and a very few men) protested that women were treated little better than slaves.

Concurrent with increasing legal restrictions, the later seventeenth and eighteenth centuries also saw a rapid rise in the number of women who wrote for private circulation and for publication. Several of these wrote critically about women's legal position. Mary Astell, Mary, Lady Chudleigh, the anonymous author of the much reprinted *Essay in Defence of the Female Sex*, and the pseudonymous 'Sophia', among others, vociferously objected to women's subjugation within marriage. The Gloucestershire clergyman's wife who wrote *The Hardships of the English Laws. In Relation to Wives. With an Explanation of the Original Curse of Subjection Passed Upon the Woman. In an Humble Address to the Legislature* excoriated the common law for going far beyond the biblical curse of subjection. Daniel Defoe's fictional Roxana acquired the breadth of experience to discern love from marriage only in her middle years. In refusing the offer of a suitor whom she had already bedded to make her (as he thought) an honest woman, she explained, 'It is not you . . . that I suspect, but the laws of matrimony puts the power into your hands; bids you do it, commands you to command; and binds me, forsooth, to obey'.[8] Not one of these eloquent defences of women and attacks upon the legal system make reference to specific statutory changes, but then their authors belonged to social groups unlikely to have been personally affected.

English men's use of coverture to control women economically was unique. Seventeenth-century legal theorists justified the system by the practical needs of household debt and credit management, but this explanation pales in view of the failure of the rest of Europe to employ the fiction of the unity of husband and wife. Other European countries, which went through their own jurisdictional disputes in the sixteenth and seventeenth centuries, used variations on the Roman civil law system of community property in marriage and partible inheritance. In practice, there were probably many similarities in property distribution between Europe and England.[9] The most striking difference was in the event of marital breakdown. Widows and women abandoned by their husbands in England were among the least protected anywhere in the world, let alone in Europe, where a restitution of dowry was legally required.

The peculiar English system of coverture was taken to extremes in the American colonies, particularly the northern colonies. There widows had to share the administration of their husbands' estates with their eldest son if adult; they enjoyed a right to a reasonable part only in southern colonies; fewer widows were named executrix by their husbands; many fewer women made wills; fewer brides made settlements; daughters' bequests were smaller, and not commensurate with their brothers' land.

In England, legal theory continued at some variance with actual practice. This discrepancy was in part the conflict between a social ideal of patrimony and the social importance of matrimony. Virtually all men believed in some degree of female subjection, but that was not inconsistent with a particular attachment to – even a passionate fondness for – their mothers, daughters and wives. An approach of 'divide and rule' accommodated both legal subjugation and individual generosity. In the words of the Duchess of Newcastle, it allowed men to 'rail of all women generally, but praise every one in particular'. Men could exercise their discretion in setting their children's portions, in allowing their wives to make a will, to some extent in agreeing to a marriage settlement, and in the amount they left to their widows. The ecclesiastical courts, as well as individual men, had ample leeway throughout most of the early modern period to allocate the residual goods of an intestate man as they saw fit – in order to balance children's portions or in order to keep widows and children off the poor rates. Male beneficence usually prevailed, but if it did not there were fewer and fewer remedies. Both the common law ideals of coverture and primogeniture and the ecclesiastical division of intestates' moveables strictly into thirds were impractical rules to implement in general practice, but they were capable of being invoked in principle at any time. The benevolence of husbands and ecclesiastical courts remained informal and unofficial, conditional upon women's good behaviour. As the incisive Roxana pointed out to her suitor, 'all that you call oneness of interest, mutual affection, and the like, is curtesie and kindness then, and a woman is indeed, infinitely oblig'd where she meets with it; but can't help herself where it fails'.[10]

Probably many women shared the double view – the two concepts of women – which inhabited men's minds. Many women would have joined with Margaret Cavendish in condemning their own sex, without having themselves in mind. Lee Holcombe, discussing nineteenth-century reforms of the married women's property law, observes that 'the language and underlying assumptions of the common law were a powerful psychological depressant to women'.[11] This sounds like a particularly twentieth-century judgement until it is placed beside Richard Allestree's comments in his preface to *The Ladies Calling* (1673): 'the world is much governed by estimation: and as applause encourages and exalts, so an universal contemt debases and dejects the spirit'.[12] Allestree was assuring his readers that they were not 'foolish and scandalous' or 'silly and vicious' – as men were wont to tell women they were. The legal attitude to women – in particular the common law's insistence on coverture, which later came to be called by reformers women's 'civil death' – may not unfairly be described as 'an universal contemt'. From the point of view of a legal system in which property was controlled by men, a woman was a conduit – nothing but the intervening stage between her father's and her husband's and her son's ownership.

Debasement and dejection are not easily susceptible to historical observation. Only occasionally does a sense of betrayal and incomprehension cry out, as in the epigraph to *The Hardships of the English Laws*, taken from the Psalms:

> For it was not an enemy that reproached me, then I could have born it; neither was it he that hated me, that did magnifie himself against me, I then would have hid myself from him. But it was thou, a man, mine equal, my guide, and mine acquaintance. We took sweet counsel together, and walked into the house of God in company.

The author went on to quote the anguished Job: 'Tho' I speak, my grief is not asswaged; and tho' I forbear, what am I eased?'

Less well-read women can occasionally be seen retaining a strong sense of self-preservation within a potentially incapacitating environment. The connection between property and self-respect was unwittingly exposed by Thomasine Skinner's husband when he complained that she wanted to 'keep some moneys in her own power', 'intending thereby to have some hand on [her husband] that he might be the more loveing and respectfull to her'.[13] Women of all social classes – from Lady Anne Clifford to the Lincolnshire labourers' widow Agnes Drinkwater *als* Inmom *als* Rose – leave remarkably little indication that they perceived of themselves either as property or as conduits for men's property.

The pressure of ordinary people on the laws of property is now more clearly visible than ever before. Chancery Court records represent a sort of middle ground, somewhere in between the lawmakers and the 'rascabilitie', but the people of probate accounts are distinctly ordinary: women whose husbands were yeomen, husbandmen, labourers, tradesmen and craftsmen. The transfers of property made by these people – between parents and children, and between married couples – when taken together represent a communal habit, a kind of quiet collective action. As such, their actions are as much comments on the legal structure as the *Lawes Resolutions* or *The Hardships of the English Laws*, albeit inarticulate. They were not refusing outright to follow the common law system of inheritance and of marital property law. It was the limitation of the early modern legal mind and remains our own limitation to identify the common law with *the* law in early modern England. Ordinary people saw multiple and overlapping legal structures and chose those elements of each which suited them.

As ordinary people treated their property differently from 'landed' families, so ordinary women took different decisions about their property than ordinary men, according to their perceptions of self-interest. Women had different ideas about moral desert, about who was in need and about what was important – if these did not constitute a different culture, they were certainly distinct economic values, and deserve to be further investigated.

It is often complained that sources for the study of women in the early modern period are so few. Yet it is remarkable how much detail is recoverable when marriage portions are investigated not just for their value to husbands, jointure not just for its ratio to portions, widows' financial position not just for the opportunities it presents for young cads, and the inheritance of daughters and provision for widows for their effects upon women's own position rather than for their depletion of male heirs' estates.

An ideological view of women is readily available in didactic literature instructing them how to behave and in legal treatises, both of which abound in early modern England. These views undoubtedly affected women in some degree, but they are not, by any stretch of the imagination, a reflection of real life. The relationship between theory and practice where women are concerned is an 'insidious blend'.[14] The discrepancy between the two can easily be identified in the twentieth century. Legal reform in the late nineteenth and early twentieth centuries lifted all of the strictly legal disadvantages under which early modern women suffered. And yet in practice, women today earn the same relatively low wages and constitute the same majority of the poor and the same majority of single parents as women in early modern England, living in a radically different ideological world.

Legislative reform left intact the less immediately obvious aspects of economic control, like unequal responsibilities for unpaid domestic work and childrearing. Women retain their historical responsibility for the household in a world which offers equal employment opportunities but no longer regards housewifery as an 'art, trade and mystery'. A materialist assessment of economic conditions in early modern England is possible, and must be placed alongside the ideological outpouring that seems to accompany female existence anywhere it goes. Only together do theory and practice approximate anything like lived experience.

Glossary

administratrix   feminine form of administrator, in charge of the estate of one who has died without making a will (an 'intestate')

alias   in a woman's name, indicates a previous marriage, or occasionally a maiden name and married name

alienate   to sell, lease or otherwise dispose of real property

alimony   annual allowance paid to a wife from her husband, living separately

annuity   annual cash payment

apparitor   informant to the ecclesiastical court

aquittance   release from debt, signed by creditor

bawdy court   litigation side of ecclesiastical court, dealing with defamation, drunkenness and sexual offences, among other things

bequeath   to dispose of moveable property in a will

borough   town with a municipal corporation and right to self-government

borough English   ultimogeniture, the custom on some manors by which the youngest son inherited land

chapbook   small, cheap book or pamphlet sold by chapmen

chattel   moveable good or piece of personal property

chattel real   lease of land

conveyancer   conveyancing manual or handbook, listing sample forms of settlements, deeds, wills, land transfers etc.

coparcenary   joint ownership; in English land inheritance, in the absence of sons all daughters inherit together equally in coparcenary; each daughter is a 'coparcener'

copyhold   land held of the lord, either at will or according to the custom of the manor

coverture   the common law fiction that a husband and wife were one person and that one was the husband; she being figuratively covered by him, she had no independent legal identity at common law for purposes of civil, and to some extent criminal, suits

demurrer   plea for the dismissal of a law suit as insufficient

devise   to dispose of land in a will

dower   generally, the property a woman enjoys in her widowhood;

specifically, a widow's common law entitlement to one third of her husband's real property for her lifetime

dowry   a marriage portion, property a bride takes into marriage

entail   settlement of property on a succession of heirs who are themselves unable to alienate that property, so preserving an estate

executrix   feminine form of executor, in charge of the estate of someone who has made a will; plural is executrices

feme covert   a married woman, in law French

feme sole trader   status of married women in some (and perhaps many) boroughs whereby they are treated as unmarried to the extent of any business they run separate from their husbands

filial portion   any individual child's share of the 'reasonable part' or third of their father's goods to which all children together were entitled; used in Yorkshire

freebench   a widow's entitlement to her husband's manorial land, in amount ranging from one third to all of the land, and in duration either for her widowhood or for her lifetime, depending on the manor's custom; also 'widow's bench', or simply 'bench'

gavelkind   custom of inheritance on some manors, especially in Kent, by which land is divided equally among all sons

heir   the person who stands to inherit freehold or copyhold land, according to the canons of descent (primogeniture in the first instance, coparcenary among daughters in the second instance etc.)

inherit   used technically of heritable land only (see 'heir'); used also in this text in its more generic sense of receipt of property by bequest or devise

intestate   the condition of having died without making a will, or the person having done so

inventory   list of goods owned, made soon after death and exhibited in ecclesiastical court by the executrix or administratrix

joined   furniture made by a joiner, finer than simple planks

jointure   joint tenancy of land, the widow's right to receive the income from specified land for her life/widowhood, usually settled in a marriage settlement

law French   the Anglicized language of the Normans, used in English law from the twelfth to the seventeenth centuries

leasehold land   land rented for a term of years or lives

legatee   recipient of a legacy

legitim   the medieval term for 'reasonable parts' or 'thirds'

manor   originally, the district subject to the jurisdiction of the lord's court, changing over the early modern period into a landed estate with residual feudal characteristics

mark   13s. 4d., archaic by the seventeenth century

messuage   dwelling house with outbuildings and land (of indeterminate extent)

moveable goods   personal property, chattels

noble 6s. 8d.

nuncupative a will made orally but not written down, sworn to in court by witnesses

ordinary officer of the ecclesiastical probate court

oxgang a measure of land anywhere between 10 and 18 acres; also a 'bovate'

palatine county county having independent jurisdiction for certain purposes; in England these were the counties of Durham, Lancashire and Cheshire

paraphernalia property a woman could claim from her husband's estate upon widowhood, consisting of her clothes, jewels, plate, and sometimes her bed

personal estate/property moveable goods, chattels

pin-money in the seventeenth century, a married woman's annual income for her own use, a kind of separate estate; over the ensuing two hundred years it deteriorated to mean small change, or 'butter-and-egg money'

poor rates from the later sixteenth century, taxes to support the deserving poor, assessed, collected and distributed on a parish basis

portion used here to mean both the property a child inherits from a parent (filial portion) and the property a bride takes into marriage (marriage portion), also called a dowry

primogeniture the eldest son's right to inherit land

probate ordinary the official of the probate court

real property freehold land

reasonable parts widow's and children's right to one third each of their husband/father's moveable goods, in ecclesiastical law; same as 'thirds' and '*legitim*'

recognisance bond or obligation to a court to either appear in court at a later date or to keep the peace

rejoinder the fourth plea in a law suit, the second from the defendant, after the plaintiff's complaint, the defendant's answer and the plaintiff's replication

relict the legal term for the widow of a specific, named man

residual estate/goods property remaining after debts have been paid out of an estate

rood one quarter of an acre, a stong

separate estate property a married woman held despite her coverture, by virtue of a trust

stong one quarter of an acre, a rood

surety guarantor of an oath, used on bonds and to prove wills or administrations

testate the condition of having made a will, or the person having done so

testator man who made a will (the feminine form is testatrix)

tail male the settlement of property on successive generations of male heirs

thirds widow's and children's right to one third each of their husband/father's moveable goods, in ecclesiastical law; same as 'reasonable parts' and '*legitim*'

tithe   tax on land or produce to support the clergy
trencher   plate
victualler   supplier of food, innkeeper
wainscot   wall panelling, often oak
waste   to destroy, ruin or spend
weald   wild, open country, formerly forested
wold   treeless, rolling plain

Notes

1 INTRODUCTION

1 Edward Chamberlayne, *Angliae Notitiae, or the Present State of England* (1669) pp. 501–2. *Baron and Feme: A Treatise of the Common Law Concerning Husbands and Wives* (1700) p. 4. *A Treatise of Feme Coverts or, the Lady's Law* (1732) p. 81, quoting Sir Edward Coke's *The Institutes of the Laws of England* (1628–44). William Alexander, *The History of Women, from the Earliest Antiquity to the Present Time*, 3rd edn (1782) p. 486. Courtney Stanhope Kenny, *The History of the Law of England as to the Effects of Marriage on Property and on the Wife's Legal Capacity* (1879) p. 98.

2 Technically 'inheritance' refers only to the heir's right to real property, but throughout I adopt the present common usage, meaning transfer of any property at death, in preference to the strictly correct but cumbersome 'devolution'. Even today the majority of all wealth is inherited rather than earned, although the wealth of most people is earned, not inherited. Carole Shammas, Marylynn Salmon and Michel Dahlin, *Inheritance in America from Colonial Times to the Present* (1987) p. 3.

3 Carole Pateman, *The Sexual Contract* (1989). Susan Moller Okin, *Women in Western Political Thought* (1979) chs 9–11.

4 This apt description is J. Z. Titow's, in 'Some differences between manors and their effects on the condition of the peasant in the thirteenth century', *AgHR* 10 (1962) p. 7.

5 The adjective is Susan Staves's, in *Married Women's Separate Property in England, 1660–1833* (1990) pp. 9–10.

6 Lawrence Stone, *The Family, Sex and Marriage in England 1500–1800* (1977) p. 8. See also Lloyd de Mause (ed.) *The History of Childhood* (1974), Jean-Louis Flandrin, *Families in Former Times: Kinship, Household and Sexuality* (1979), Michael Mitterauer and Reinhard Sieder, *The European Family: Patriarchy to Partnership from the Middle Ages to the Present* (1982), Mark Poster, *Critical Theory of the Family* (1978), Edward Shorter, *The Making of the Modern Family* (1975), Miriam Slater, 'The weightiest business: marriage in an upper-gentry family in seventeenth-century England', *P&P* 72 (1976) pp. 25–54, Randolph Trumbach, *The Rise of the Egalitarian Family: Aristocratic Kinship and Domestic Relations in Eighteenth-Century England* (1978), and Eli Zaretsky, *Capitalism, the Family and Personal Life* (1976).

7 Ruth Perry, 'Radical doubt and the liberation of women', *Eighteenth-Century Studies* 18:4 (1985) p. 475.

8 Michael MacDonald, *Mystical Bedlam: Madness, Anxiety and Healing in Seventeenth-Century England* (1981) p. 73. Alan Macfarlane, *The Family Life of Ralph Josselin, a Seventeenth-Century Clergyman* (1970) p. 165. For other sensible treatments of early modern familial emotion see Ralph Houlbrooke, *The English Family 1450–1700* (1984), Alan Macfarlane, *Marriage and Love in England 1300–1840* (1986), Linda Pollock, *Forgotten Children: Parent–Child Relations from 1500 to 1900* (1983), J. A. Sharpe, 'Plebeian marriage in Stuart England', *TRHS* 35 (1985) pp. 69–90, and Stephen Wilson, 'The myth of motherhood a myth: the historical view of European child-rearing', *Social History* 9 (1984) pp. 181–98.

9 Interesting comments on the management of each school, in terms of the relative effect of

their publishers on popularity, are found in Chris Middleton, 'Women's labour and the transition to pre-industrial capitalism', in L. Charles and L. Duffin (eds) *Women and Work in Pre-Industrial England* (1985) p. 202, and Ferdinand Mount, *The Subversive Family: An Alternative History of Love and Marriage* (1982) p. 9.

10   Barbara Harris, 'Marriage sixteenth-century style: Elizabeth Stafford and the third Duke of Norfolk', *Journal of Social History* 15:3 (1982) pp. 371–2. Suzanne Lebsock, *The Free Women of Petersburg: Status and Culture in a Southern Town, 1784–1860* (1984) p. 53.

11   Respectively, Eileen Spring, 'Law and the theory of the affective family', *Albion* 16:1 (1984) pp. 1–3, and Steven Ozment, *When Fathers Ruled: Family Life in Reformation Europe* (1983) pp. 162, 177.

12   Sir Thomas Smith, *De Republica Anglorum* (1970, facsimile of 1583 edn) pp. 12–13.

13   Introduction by Paula Barbour to Bathsua Makin's *An Essay to Revive the Antient Education of Gentlewomen* (1980) *passim*. Margaret George, 'From "goodwife" to "mistress": the transformation of the female in bourgeois culture', *Science & Society* 37 (1973) pp. 152–77. David Latt, 'Praising virtuous ladies: the literary image and historical reality of women in seventeenth-century England', in M. Springer (ed.) *What Manner of Woman: Essays on English and American Life and Literature* (1977) p. 40. Robert Michel, 'English attitudes towards women, 1640–1700', *Canadian Journal of History* 1 (1978) p. 35.

14   *Population Trends* 61 (Autumn 1990) Table 7, p. 55.

15   Linda Pollock, '"Teach her to live under obedience": the making of women in the upper ranks of early modern England', *C&C* 4:2 (1989) pp. 231–58.

16   Gouge, *Of Domesticall Duties*, quoted in Susan Amussen, *An Ordered Society: Gender and Class in Early Modern England* (1988) p. 44. On further opposition to Gouge's ideas of wifely submission see Elspeth Graham, 'Authority, resistance, and loss: gendered difference in the writings of John Bunyan and Hannah Allen', in A. Laurence, W.R. Owens and S. Sim (eds) *The Pulpit Guarded: Confrontations Between Orthodox and Radicals in Revolutionary England* (1990) pp. 118–19. Margaret Ezell, *The Patriarch's Wife: Literary Evidence and the History of the Family* (1987) ch. 3. *The Diary of Roger Lowe of Ashton-in-Makerfield, Lancs. 1663–74* (1938) p. 55.

17   *The English Gentleman and the English Gentlewoman*, 3rd edn (1641), dedication to the Countess of Pembroke and preface (no page numbers).

18   *Queen-Like Closet*, quoted in Ada Wallas, *Before the Bluestockings* (1929) p. 51. Elaine Hobby, *Virtue of Necessity: English Women's Writing 1649–88* (1988) p. 175.

19   John Ray, *A Collection of English Proverbs* (1670) p. 17.

20   *Some Proposals for the Imploying of the Poor*, quoted in Alice Clark, *Working Life of Women in the Seventeenth Century* (1992) p. 135, and Michael Roberts, '"Words they are women, and deeds they are men": images of work and gender in early modern England', in L. Charles and L. Duffin (eds) *Women and Work in Pre-Industrial England* (1985) p. 135, with further comments on the unsuitability of markets for women, p. 154.

21   *The Journeys of Celia Fiennes* (1949) 'preface to the reader' and p. 94.

22   *The Boke of Husbandry* is reprinted in *Certain Ancient Tracts Concerning the Management of Landed Property* (1767) pp. 88–92, and also quoted at length in Clark, *Working Life*, pp. 46–9. Long attributed to Anthony Fitzherbert, it is now ascribed to his brother John. *The Merry Conceits and Passages of Simon and Cisley* (17th century), in MCC: Samuel Pepys's *Penny Merriments* I, pp. 1226–47. *Robert Loder's Farm Accounts 1610–20* (1936) p. 133. *The Journal of Giles Moore* (1970) pp. 25, 47, 132, 315–19. *The Household Account Book of Sarah Fell of Swarthmoor Hall* (1920). For other tradeswomen see Susan Wright, '"Churmaids, huswyfes and hucksters": the employment of women in Tudor and Stuart Salisbury', in L. Charles and L. Duffin (eds) *Women and Work in Pre-Industrial England* (1985), and Margaret Spufford, *The Great Reclothing of Rural England: Petty Chapmen and their Wares in the Seventeenth Century* (1984).

23   I am grateful to Tessa Watt, author of *Cheap Print and Popular Piety, 1550–1640* (1991), and Helen Weinstein, editor of *A Catalogue of the Pepys Ballad Collection* (1992), for performing a mental check on this literature for me.

24   *Narrative of the Persecution of Agnes Beaumont in 1674* (n.d.) *passim*. *Diary of Roger Lowe*, p. 45, for example.

25   *The Life of Adam Martindale, Written by Himself* (1845) pp. 6, 17.

26   Proverbs 7:11–12; 31:10–31.

27   For the origins of the debate with Christine de Pisan (1365 to after 1429) see Beatrice

Gottlieb, 'The problem of feminism in the fifteenth century', in J. Kirshner and S. F. Wemple (eds) *Women of the Medieval World* (1985) p. 356.

28 Reprinted in Simon Shepherd, *The Women's Sharp Revenge: Five Women's Pamphlets from the Renaissance* (1985). See also Katherine Usher Henderson and Barbara McManus, *Half Humankind: Contexts and Texts of the Controversy About Women in England, 1540–1640* (1985).

29 Barbour, introduction to Makin's *Antient Education*, p. x. Gottlieb, 'Problem of feminism', p. 357. Felicity Nussbaum, introduction to *Satires on Women*, Augustan Reprint Society Series 180 (1976) pp. ii–iii. Shepherd, *Sharp Revenge*, p. 160.

30 Iain MacLean, *The Renaissance Notion of Woman: A Study in the Fortunes of Scholasticism and Medical Science in European Intellectual Life* (1980) p. 7.

31 Quoted in Sara Heller Mendelson, *The Mental World of Stuart Women* (1987) p. 17.

32 See for example Patricia Crawford, 'Women's published writings 1600–1700', in M. Prior (ed.) *Women in English Society 1500–1800* (1985), Moira Ferguson (ed.) *First Feminists: British Women Writers 1578–1799* (1985), Hobby, *Virtue of Necessity*, and Janet Todd (ed.) *Dictionary of British and American Women Writers 1660–1800* (1984).

33 *The Diary of Lady Margaret Hoby 1599–1605* (1930). Rachel Weigall, 'An Elizabethan gentlewoman: the journal of Lady Mildmay, circa 1570–1617', *Quarterly Review* 215:428 (July 1911) pp. 119–38.

34 *Letters of the Lady Brilliana Harley* (1854). *Memoirs of Lady Fanshawe* (1905). *The Letters of Dorothy Osborne to William Temple 1652–54* (1928). *Letters from the Right Honourable Lady Mary Wortley Montagu 1709 to 1762* (1906).

35 *Two Elizabethan Women: The Correspondence of Joan and Maria Thynne 1575–1611* (1982).

36 E. M. Symonds, 'The diary of John Green (1635–57)', *English Historical Review* 43 (1928) pp. 385–94, 598–604, and 44 (1929) pp. 106–17.

37 Mendelson, *Stuart Women*, pp. 15, 41–2. For excerpts from the writing of Anne Clifford, Margaret Cavendish, Alice Thornton and others see also E. Graham *et al.* (eds) *Her Own Life: Autobiographical Writings by Seventeenth-Century English Women* (1989).

38 *Antient Education*, p. 26.

39 More is printed in Ezell, *Patriarch's Wife*, pp. 191–203. Mary Astell, *The First English Feminist: Reflections upon Marriage and Other Writings* (1986) e.g. p. 102. 'Sophia', *Woman's Superior Excellence over Man: Or, a Reply to the Author of a Late Treatise, Entitled 'Man Superior to Woman'* (1740) p. 69. On Sophia's lifting of material from Poulain de l'Barre's *De l'égalité des deux sexes* see Alice Browne, *The Eighteenth-Century Feminist Mind* (1987) pp. 122–3, and Felicity Nussbaum, *The Brink of All We Hate: English Satires on Women 1660–1750* (1984) p. 8.

40 *Roxana* was first published in 1724, but the heroine appears to have been only slightly younger than her author, who was born in 1660 (1987 edn, pp. 37–8) so she was modelled on his contemporaries, rather than on any distinctively new woman of the 1720s.

41 *The Ladies Library* (1714) introduction to vol. 1. Daniel Defoe, *An Essay upon Projects* (1697) pp. 282–302. For other references to female institution proposals see Browne, *Feminist Mind*, p. 97, and Ruth Perry, *Women, Letters and the Novel* (1980) p. 43.

42 See further, Patricia Higgins, 'The reaction of women, with special reference to women petitioners', in B. Manning (ed.) *Politics, Religion and the English Civil War* (1973), and Hobby, *Virtue of Necessity*, pp. 13–16. I am grateful to Sandy Harrison for bringing petitions to my attention.

43 *De Republica*, p. 31. On the term 'middling sort' see Keith Wrightson, 'The social order of early modern England: three approaches', in L. Bonfield, R.M. Smith and K. Wrightson (eds) *The World We Have Gained* (1986).

44 Amussen, *Ordered Society*, pp. 172–3.

45 Quoted in Mildred Campbell, *The English Yeoman under Elizabeth and the Early Stuarts* (1942) p. 217.

46 For more on work see my introduction to the 1992 edition of Clark's *Working Life*.

47 Amy Erickson, 'An introduction to probate accounts', in G. Martin and P. Spufford (eds) *The Records of the Nation* (1990) p. 286, and Peter Spufford, 'A printed catalogue of the names of testators', in ibid., pp. 169–70. In referring to administrators' and executors' accounts together as 'probate accounts' I follow the only previous study to make detailed use of this source, Clare Gittings's *Death, Burial and the Individual in Early Modern England* (1984).

48 Rowena Archer and B.E. Ferme, 'Testamentary procedure with special reference to the

executrix', *Reading Medieval Studies* 15 (1989) pp. 3–34. Caroline Barron, 'The "golden age" of women in medieval London', ibid., pp. 35–58. Ann Kettle, '"My wife shall have it": marriage and property in the wills and testaments of later medieval England', in R.B. Outhwaite (ed.) *Marriage and Society* (1981). Kay Lacey, 'Women and work in fourteenth- and fifteenth-century London', in L. Charles and L. Duffin (eds) *Women and Work in Pre-Industrial England* (1985). Maxine Berg, 'Women's property and the industrial revolution', in *Journal of Interdisciplinary History*, 24:2 (1993), 233–50.

49 See the summary of A. D. M. Forte, 'Some aspects of the law of marriage in Scotland: 1500–1700', in E. Craik (ed.) *Marriage and Property* (1991).

50 R. W. Unwin, 'Tradition and transition: market towns in the Vale of York, 1660–1830', *Northern History* 17 (1981) p. 75.

51 The courts examined are the lower church courts in which ordinary people's estates were probated: the consistory court of Lincoln; the archdeaconry of Chichester, the Dean of Chichester's peculiar, and the deanery of Pagham and Tarring; the archdeaconry of Ely and the Bishop of Ely's peculiar; the archdeaconry of Northampton; the archdeaconries of Taunton, Bath and Wells; the archdeaconry of Canterbury; the peculiar court of Wimborne Minster in Dorset; the archdeaconry of Winchester; the deanery peculiar, the deaneries of Rydall and Harthill, and the peculiar court of Selby in Yorkshire.

52 Christopher Clay, 'Landlords and estate management in England', in *AHEW* V:ii (1985) pp. 162–3.

53 John Bullokar, *An English Expositor* (1616).

54 Clay, 'Estate management', pp. 171, 174. Pearl Hogrefe, 'The legal rights of Tudor women and their circumvention by men and women', *Sixteenth-Century Journal* 3 (1972) pp. 97–105. W. K. Jordan, *Philanthropy in England 1480–1660* (1959) pp. 354, 355 fn. Keith Wrightson, 'Kinship in an English village: Terling, Essex 1500–1700', in R. M. Smith (ed.) *Land, Kinship and Life-Cycle* (1984) p. 329.

55 Typically, the baldest statement is Lawrence Stone's 'first commandment' of women's history: thou shalt not study women except in relation to men and children. 'Only women', *New York Review of Books* 32:6 (11 April 1985) p. 21. He ignores the obvious inverse, that men should be studied only in relation to women and children.

56 *Fisher Row: Fishermen, Bargemen, and Canal Boatmen in Oxford, 1500–1900* (1982) p. 235.

57 Alan Ryan, Oxford, Blackwell, 1984.

58 Edwin Ardener, 'Belief and the problem of women', in S. Ardener (ed.) *Perceiving Women* (1977) p. 3.

59 For published uses of 'venture' see Richard Gough, *The History of Myddle* (1981) pp. 91, 123.

2 LAW, SOCIETY AND DOCUMENTS

1 *Lawes Resolutions*, Sect. 1, p. 3, also quoted in Doris Stenton, *The English Woman in History* (1957) p. 61. A late sixteenth-century compilation, the authorship of this work is generally attributed to Thomas Edgar. For both authorship and readership see Wilfred Prest, 'Law and women's rights in early modern England', *The Seventeenth Century* 6 (1991) pp. 172–80.

2 *Eighteenth-Century Short Title Catalogue* (microfiche, London, The British Library Board, 1990).

3 Laurel Phillipson, 'Quakerism in Cambridge before the Act of Toleration (1653–1689)', *Proceedings of the Cambridge Antiquarian Society* 76 (1987) p. 21. I owe this reference to Bill Stephenson. For Docwra's publications see Patricia Crawford, 'Women's published writings 1600–1700', in M. Prior (ed.) *Women in English Society 1500–1800* (1985) p. 242.

4 *The Woman's Prize or the Tamer Tamed* (1966) pp. 56–7. Italics mine.

5 Nottingham Drama Text (1977) p. 34. I am grateful to Cosmo Corfield for this reference.

6 The popularity of *Symbolaeography* and the extent to which conveyancers borrowed from each other are discussed in Eric Poole, 'West's *Symboleography*: an Elizabethan formulary', in J. A. Guy and H. G. Beale (eds) *Law and Social Change in British History* (1984) pp. 97–106.

7 Extended title of the *Conveyances*, 2nd edn (1689). *The Letters of Dorothy Osborne to William Temple 1652–54* (1928) pp. 183, 186, 189–90.

8 *The Diary of Roger Lowe of Ashton-in-Makerfield, Lancs. 1663–74* (1938) p. 14, and pp. 17,

29, 35, 73, 81, for example. Margaret Spufford, *Contrasting Communities: English Villagers in the Sixteenth and Seventeenth Centuries* (1974) p. 182.

9   *The Journal of Giles Moore* (1970) p. 184.

10 James Craig Muldrew, 'Credit, market relations and debt litigation in late seventeenth-century England, with specific reference to King's Lynn' (Cambridge PhD thesis, 1990).

11 Copyhold tenure is the origin of the terms 'landlord' and 'landlady', both of which meant a large landowner prior to the pejoration of 'landlady' into a woman who runs a boarding house.

12 Peter Bowden, 'Agricultural prices, wages, farm profits and rents', in *AHEW* V:ii (1985) p. 74. Eric Kerridge, *Agrarian Problems in the Sixteenth Century and After* (1969) p. 48. An exhaustive discussion of leases is found in Christopher Clay, 'Landlords and estate management in England', in *AHEW* V:ii (1985) pp. 212–30.

The same piece of land might be held by one person in freehold, by another from the first in copyhold, and by a third from the second in leasehold, so one person might be both landlord of one holding and tenant of another. The introduction by Marie Clough to Bartholomew Bolney's *The Book of Bartholomew Bolney* (1964) illustrates how Bolney, whose 'small' estate in Sussex of 900 acres was acquired piecemeal in the fifteenth century, was always in the middle of a tenurial chain:

> at every intervening stage the land had been sold, rented, or leased in one of a dozen different ways, often by groups of trustees, and each transaction might add considerably to the number of individuals with a legal interest in the same piece of land.
>
> (p.xxviii)

13 *Lawes Resolutions*, p. 120.

14 For permutations in the interpretation of dower in medieval England see George Haskins, 'The development of common law dower', *Harvard Law Review* 62:1 (1948) pp. 42–55, and Janet Senderowitz Loengard, '"Of the gift of her husband": English dower and its consequences in the year 1200', in J. Kirshner and S. F. Wemple (eds) *Women of the Medieval World* (1985). For examples of negotiated Anglo-Saxon dowers see Dorothy Whitelock (ed.) *Anglo-Saxon Wills* (1930) pp. 25, 83.

15 The most common types of customary tenures were gavelkind, with a freebench of one half, and Borough English, with a freebench of anywhere between one half and all of the land. George Meriton, *The Touchstone of Wills, Testaments, and Administrations* (1668) p. 118. Particular manors' freebench and inheritance customs are discussed by the following: Judith Bennett, *Women in the Medieval Countryside: Gender and Household in Brigstock Before the Plague* (1987) p. 14; Clay, 'Estate management', pp. 198–212; Christopher Dyer, 'Changes in the size of peasant holdings in some west midland villages 1400–1540', in R. M. Smith (ed.) *Land, Kinship and Life-Cycle* (1984) p. 280; B. A. Holderness, 'Widows in pre-industrial society: an essay upon their economic functions', in ibid., p. 432 (*n.b.* 'dower' in this article means 'freebench'); Alan Macfarlane, 'The myth of the peasantry: family and economy in a northern parish', in ibid., pp. 336–8; Peter Franklin, 'Peasant widows' "liberation" and remarriage before the Black Death', *EcHR* 39:2 (1986) p. 189; Cicely Howell, *Land, Family and Inheritance in Transition: Kibworth Harcourt 1280–1700* (1983) pp. 239, 255; Kerridge, *Agrarian Problems*, Pt 1, ch. 2; Spufford, *Contrasting Communities*, pp. 88–90; R. H. Tawney, *The Agrarian Problem in the Sixteenth Century* (1967) Pt 1, ch. 2, Sect. D; Barbara Todd, 'Freebench and free enterprise: widows and their property in two Berkshire villages', in J. Chartres and D. Hey (eds) *English Rural Society 1500–1800* (1990). See also Mary Bateson (ed.) *Borough Customs* II (1906) pp. cviii–cxi.

16 On the manorial use of jointures at different social levels see Peggy Jefferies, 'The medieval use as family law and custom: the Berkshire gentry in the fourteenth and fifteenth centuries', *Southern History* 1 (1979) pp. 51–3, 57–9, and R. M. Smith, 'Women's property rights under customary law: some developments in the thirteenth and fourteenth centuries', *TRHS* 5th series 35 (1985) pp. 190, 193.

17 Rowena Archer, 'Rich old ladies: the problem of late medieval dowagers', in A. J. Pollard (ed.) *Property and Politics: Essays in Later Medieval English History* (1984) p. 19. John Baker, *An Introduction to English Legal History*, 2nd edn (1979) pp. 229–30.

18 See discussions in *Baron and Feme*, p. 113, and Courtney Kenny, *The History of the Law of England as to the Effects of Marriage on Property and on the Wife's Legal Capacity* (1879) p. 52.

19 Dower could also be brought before equity, according to Maria Cioni, 'The Elizabethan

Chancery and women's rights', in D. Guth and J. W. McKenna (eds) *Tudor Rule and Revolution* (1982) p. 174.

20 Edmund Snell, *The Principles of Equity* (1868) p. 295.

21 *Lawes Resolutions*, p. 129.

22 The custom of the manor was not so time-honoured as to be immune to population and economic pressure. For arguments over customs see Dyer, 'Peasant holdings', p. 292 and Tim Stretton, 'Women, custom and equity in the Court of Requests', in J. Kermode and G. Walker (eds) *Women, Crime and the Courts in Early Modern England* (1994).

23 John Day, 'On the status of women in medieval Sardinia', in J. Kirshner and S. F. Wemple (eds) *Women of the Medieval World* (1985) p. 306. The tension between partibility and impartibility is analysed by Cicely Howell, 'Peasant inheritance customs in the midlands, 1280–1700', in J. Goody, J. Thirsk and E.P. Thompson (eds) *Family and Inheritance: Rural Society in Western Europe 1200–1800* (1976) pp. 113–22.

24 Joan Thirsk, 'Industries in the countryside', in F. J. Fisher (ed.) *Essays in the Economic and Social History of Tudor and Stuart England* (1961) p. 77.

25 From the Statute of Wills (1540) most freehold (two thirds of that in military tenure and all of that in non-military tenure) could be disposed of by will. After 1645 all freehold was disposable either during the owner's lifetime or by will.

26 The middle ages distinguished between a will of land and a testament of moveables, but by the sixteenth century the two instruments were invariably combined in one. Henry Swinburne, *A Treatise of Testaments and Last Wills* (1590) pp. 2–3.

27 3rd edn (1674) preface.

28 The average Bible in the mid-seventeenth century cost 7s., and newspapers 2d. Tamsyn Mary Williams, 'Polemical prints of the English revolution, 1640–60' (London PhD thesis, 1986) pp. 32–3.

29 The phrase is Sir Thomas Smith's in *De Republica Anglorum* (1970, facsimile of original 1583 edn) p. 101, but other writers are equally ambiguous.

30 Another medieval name for reasonable parts was *legitim*. On jurisdictional shifts and conflicts see Baker, *English Legal History*, p. 321, and Michael Sheehan, 'The influence of canon law on the property rights of married women in England', *Mediaeval Studies* 25 (1963) p. 123. For early comments see Sir Henry Finch, *Law, or a Discourse Thereof* (1627) p. 175. Today the southern 'freedom of testation' is often misleadingly presented as the norm, and the preservation of reasonable parts as a deviation. Haskins, 'Common law dower', p. 47. Ann Kettle, '"My wife shall have it": marriage and property in the wills and testaments of later medieval England', in R. B. Outhwaite (ed.) *Marriage and Society* (1981) p. 93. Lawrence Stone, *The Family, Sex and Marriage in England 1500–1800* (1977) pp. 195–6.

31 Swinburne, *Testaments*, pp. 105–6.

32 The province of York was deprived in 1692 (4 Wm. & Mary c.2), except for the families of freemen of the cities of York and Chester. Apparently at their own request, freemen of York were included in the ban in 1704 (2 & 3 Anne c.5). Wales followed in 1696 (7 & 8 Wm. 3 c.38) and the City of London in 1725 (11 Geo. I c.18). Chester was the only place in England to retain the custom.

33 C. W. Brooks and Kevin Sharpe, '"History, English law, and the renaissance', *P&P* 72 (1976) pp. 133–42. J. G. A. Pocock, *The Ancient Constitution and the Feudal Law: a Study of English Historical Thought in the Seventeenth Century* (1957) especially pp. 30–1, 45–6, 239. Donald Veall, *The Popular Movement for Law Reform 1640–1660* (1970) ch. 3.

34 Sir Frederick Pollock and F. W. Maitland, *A Concise History of the English Law Before the Time of Edward I* II (1898) p. 402.

35 *The Dialoges in Englishe, betwene a Docter of Divinitie, and a Student in the Lawes of Englande* (1st edn 1528–31) p. 15. For dating see Baker, *English Legal History*, p. 164.

36 J. S. Cockburn, *A History of English Assizes 1558–1714* (1972) map 2, p. 26 and pp. 139–40. Richard Hunt, 'Quarter sessions order books', in L. M. Munby (ed.) *Short Guides to Records* (1972) no page numbers. B. C. Redwood (ed.) *Quarter Sessions Order Book 1642–9* (1954) introduction.

37 J. H. Bettey, 'Land tenure and manorial custom in Dorset 1570–1670', *Southern History* 4 (1982) pp. 51–2.

38 Charles Gray, *Copyhold, Equity and the Common Law* (1963) chs 1 and 2.

39 The operation of manorial courts is detailed in Kerridge, *Agrarian Problems*, p. 24. For medieval borough courts see Bateson (ed.) *Borough Customs* I and II.

40 Legal texts do not specify which boroughs these were, but they certainly included Fordwich, Lincoln, Torksey, Winchelsea and Worcester, according to the records collected in Bateson (ed.) *Borough Customs* I, pp. 227–8, and recent research shows Chester and Southampton also had the custom of feme sole traders (personal communication from, respectively, Jane Laughton and Siân Jones).

41 Marcus Knight 'Litigants and litigation in the seventeenth-century Palatinate of Durham' (Cambridge PhD thesis, 1990).

42 In the period 1558–1603 only 5 per cent of 2445 plaintiffs were clearly members of the gentry or aristocracy. PRO: *Chancery Bills and Answers, Elizabeth* III: S–Z (calculation made from all cases under S, T, U and V). In the period 1613–1714, 15 per cent of 1588 plaintiffs were gentry or above. *Index of Chancery Proceedings, Bridges Division, 1613–1714* I (1913). These figures are minimums because the indices do not always list titles, particularly the 'Mr' of a mere gentleman, but it is extremely time consuming to sample the bills of complaint themselves.

43 C. W. Brooks, *Pettyfoggers and Vipers of the Commonwealth: The 'Lower Branch' of the Legal Profession in Early Modern England* (1986) p. 281 (*n.b.* the King's Bench proportion is based on a relatively small sample of litigants).

44 *The Journeys of Celia Fiennes* (1949) p. 307.

45 Baker, *English Legal History*, p. 95.

46 Jurisdictional details for the counties discussed in this book are found in the *Phillimore Atlas and Index of Parish Registers* (1984).

47 Robert Mason (1596) Moulton, LAO: LCC Will 1596/115. See preface for full explanation of manuscript references.

48 *The Guardian* 26 October 1991, p. 19.

49 M. W. Barley, 'Farmhouses and cottages 1550–1725', *EcHR* 7 (1955) p. 292. Lloyd Bonfield, 'Normative rules and property transmission: reflections on the link between marriage and inheritance in early modern England', in L. Bonfield, R. M. Smith and K. Wrightson (eds) *The World We Have Gained* (1986) p. 172. Stephen Coppel, 'Wills and the community: a case study of Tudor Grantham', in P. Riden (ed.) *Probate Records and Local Community* (1985) p. 78. Nesta Evans, 'Inheritance, women, religion and education in early modern society as revealed by wills', in ibid., p. 55. Margaret Spufford, 'Peasant inheritance customs and land distribution in Cambridgeshire from the sixteenth to the eighteenth centuries', in J. Goody, J. Thirsk and E. P. Thompson (eds) *Family and Inheritance: Rural Society in Western Europe 1200–1800* (1976) p. 172. Richard Vann, 'Wills and the family in an English town', *JFH* 4:3 (1979) p. 352. Susan Wright, 'Family life and society in sixteenth and early seventeenth-century Salisbury' (Leicester PhD thesis, 1982) p. 247.

50 They rest on surviving wills or will registers, but it is apparent from administration bonds and probate accounts that wills were made which do not survive, neither in an original nor in the court's register. An *inventory* reference to the 'testator' or 'intestate' has been used to measure testation in Banbury, by Vann, 'Wills and the family', p. 354. This measure is probably unreliable. At least in Sussex, 'testator' and 'intestate' were used haphazardly in inventories. The erratic variation of both will and inventory preservation over time can be seen for a single parish in J. A. Johnston, 'The probate inventories and wills of a Worcestershire parish 1676–1775', *Midland History* 1:1 (1971–2) p. 21.

51 Robert Brentano, *Rome Before Avignon: a Social History of Thirteenth-Century Rome* (1974) p. 274.

52 Hodgeson, Wood Enderby, LAO: LCC Admon 1641/92.

53 Procter (1616) Weston, LAO: LCC Admon 1616/288. William Violett (1670) Oving, WSRO: EpI/33/1670.

54 Swinburne, *Testaments*, p. 218. Meriton, *Touchstone*, pp. 118, 137. William Nelson, *Lex Testamentaria* (1714) pp. 211–13. For a more easily accessible summary see Richard Burn, *Ecclesiastical Law* II (1763) pp. 645–9.

55 H. C. F. Lansberry, 'Free bench see-saw: Sevenoaks widows in the late seventeenth century', *Archaeologia Cantiana* 100 (1984) p. 292. David Vaisey, 'Probate inventories and provincial retailers in the seventeenth century', in P. Riden (ed.) *Probate Records and the Local Community* (1985) pp. 100–1.

56 Prices are taken from *The Household Account Book of Sarah Fell of Swarthmoor Hall* (1920) p. 75, and Moore, *Journal*, pp. 24, 28, 30, 135–6, 143–4, 259.

57 The only full-length study of these accounts is Clare Gittings's *Death, Burial and the Individual in Early Modern England* (1984). They have been used in smaller numbers and recommended for further research by Margaret Spufford, *The Great Reclothing of Rural England: Petty Chapmen and their Wares in Seventeenth-Century England* (1984), Barbara Todd, 'Widow-hood in a market town: Abingdon 1540–1720' (Oxford PhD thesis, 1983) p. 217, and Vaisey, 'Provincial retailers'. Two accounts are included without comment in Lionel Munby (ed.) *Life and Death in King's Langley: Wills and Inventories, 1498–1659* (1981). See also Jacqueline Bower's 'Probate accounts as a source for Kentish early modern economic and social history', *Archaeologia Cantiana* 109 (1991) pp. 51–62.

    Occasionally, in the event of a minor orphan not yet able to inherit, an account was delayed up to ten years or more after the estate came to the accountant: for example Alice Hobbs, £21/7 (1619) Othery, SRO: D/D/Ct/H64, and Susannah Keen, £142/–67 (1711) Bleadon, SRO: D/D/Ct/K9.

58 The highest proportion of executors' accounts among the total occurred in Sussex, at 34 per cent (66 of 194). In Lincolnshire only 19 per cent of accounts (76 of 401) and in Cambridgeshire only 11 per cent (25 of 224) were filed by executors. Whether these figures reflect actual differences in regional rates of testation or merely variations in court practice remains to be seen.

59 I owe a preview of the Kent data to Peter Spufford and Jacqueline Bower. This material will be published in an index with analysis by the British Record Society.

60 The accounts which survive in Cambridgeshire and Northamptonshire all originated within a fairly close radius of the courts at Cambridge or Ely and Northampton, so the median administrative costs were lower. Those from the Lincolnshire and Sussex samples spread further throughout the county, so accountants spent more in conducting administrative business.

61 For fees in the Province of York see Henry Consett, *The Practice of Spiritual or Ecclesiastical Courts* (1685) pp. 422–3, or Ronald Marchant, *The Church under the Law: Justice, Administration and Discipline in the Diocese of York 1560–1640* (1969) pp. 111–12. The balance of the account was not always negative in cases of abatement, and there was no standard cutoff point; the ordinary charges of accounts with comparable or even lower balances might not be abated. Decisions about fees appear to have been subjective, depending on individual circumstances in each case which do not survive in the documents – perhaps the accountant's own wealth, other sources of income, the number and age of any children, and the personal reputation of the accountant. The amount due might be reduced by as little as 3s. or cut to half the normal fees.

62 Swinburne, *Testaments*, pp. 228–9.

63 For example, Lloyd Bonfield, 'Contrasting sources: court rolls and settlements as evidence of hereditary transmission of land amongst small landowners in early modern England', *University of Illinois Law Review* 3 (1984) p. 652, or 'Normative rules', p. 170, or Conrad Russell, *The Crisis of Parliaments 1509–1660* (1971) p. 60. Dismissal of church courts is also common from Americanists, as for example Lois Green Carr, 'The development of the Maryland Orphans' Court, 1654–1715', in A. C. Land, L. G. Carr and E. C. Papenfuse (eds) *Law, Society and Politics in Early Maryland* (1977) pp. 42, 45.

64 (1685) Epistle to the Reader.

65 Martin Ingram, *Church Courts, Sex and Marriage in England, 1570–1640* (1987) chs 1 and 11. Earlier discussions include R.H. Helmholz, *Marriage Litigation in Medieval England* (1974) pp. 113–23, and Marchant, *Church under the Law*, pp. 108–9, 243–5. See also Amy Erickson, 'The property ownership and financial decisions of ordinary women in early modern England' (Cambridge PhD thesis, 1990) pp. 54–7. The most recent published critique of the persistent claim of ecclesiastical inefficacy is John Bossy's entertaining review 'In the sight of God', *Times Literary Supplement* (23–9 September 1988) p. 1036.

66 For the practical effects of the upheaval, see Christopher Kitching, 'Probate during the civil war and interregnum', Parts 1 and 2, *Journal of the Society of Archivists* 5:5 and 5:6 (1976) pp. 283–93, 346–56. For lack of complaint about the probate side of ecclesiastical courts see Veall, *Law Reform*, especially p. 193.

67 A copy of the proclamation survives attached to the account of Robert Hilton, £4/2 (1617) Elm, CUL: EDR A12/1/1617/33.

68 William Chaundler, Midhurst, WSRO: STC1/15/219b. John Vincent, WSRO: EpI/33/1607. Elizabeth Vincent, WSRO: EpI/33/1607. The abbreviation '*als*' for '*alias*' designates the

multiple names of a woman who has been married more than once, or occasionally her maiden name and married name.

69 Parkinson, £81/52 (1604) Whittlesey, CUL: EDR A12/1/1604/15. See also the above John Vincent.

70 Robert Hill, £46/25 Petworth, WSRO: EpI/33/1635. Other examples are the accounts of Anne Holwell (1622) Weston Zoyland, SRO: D/D/Ct/H31, and Anne Elliott, £55/-24 (1728) Bridgewater, SRO: D/D/Ct/E18, each of which has attached a four-page list of items disposed of on the day of the sale.

71 Alexander Crow, £19/2 (1618) Elm, CUL: EDR A12/1/1618/4.

72 Onn, £9/-2 (1632) Wigtoft, LAO: Ad Ac 23/76.

73 There were between one and two hundred cases a year in the Exchequer Court of York. Marchant, *Church under the Law*, pp. 90, 110. The Salisbury consistory court saw eighteen cases in one year. Ingram, *Church Courts*, p. 68. See also Ralph Houlbrooke, *Church Courts and the People During the English Reformation, 1520–70* (1979) ch. 4.

74 Meriton, *Touchstone*, p. 250. Nelson, *Lex Testamentaria*, p. 19. Michael Sheehan, *The Will in Medieval England: From the Conversion of the Anglo-Saxons to the End of the Thirteenth Century* (1963) pp. 214, 218.

75 *Testaments*, pp. 232–3.

76 W. S. Holdsworth, *A History of English Law* III, 3rd edn (1923) pp. 558–60. Marchant, *Church under the Law*, p. 112. This view appears to derive from Nelson, *Lex Testamentaria*, p. 18.

77 The decline is sharp in Lincolnshire, Northamptonshire, Sussex and Hampshire, but appears more gradual in Kent and Somerset. A complete picture must await the indexing of probate accounts throughout England, currently being conducted under the auspices of the British Record Society.

78 Two similar but unsuccessful bills were introduced in 1662 and 1667. The latter proposed to extend the benefits of the City of London's intestate division into thirds to all of England, which was already ecclesiastical law throughout England. Anchitell Grey, *Debates of the House of Commons* I *1667–94* (1769) pp. 121–2. The successful Act of 1670 originated in the House of Lords, but no record survives in the *Journals of the House of Commons* or *Journals of the House of Lords* of who proposed it or why. *Historical Manuscripts Commission, 8th Report and Appendix* (1881) Pt 1, p. 118, n.145, and p. 122, n.167; *9th Report and Appendix* (1883) Pt 2, p. 3, n.18. The background of this bill and its unsuccessful predecessors might be further pursued in the private diaries of Members of Parliament.

79 Robert Richardson, £566/-192 (1674) Chesterton, CUL: EDR A12/2/1673/1.

80 Tillington, WSRO: M Dean 1614/16.

81 Pepper, £167, LAO: Inv 220a/119. Agnes Parsons, £776/130 SRO: DD/SP/442. On women's occupational identification see comments of Michael Roberts, '"Words they are women, and deeds they are men": images of work and gender in early modern England', in L. Charles and L. Duffin (eds) *Women and Work in Pre-Industrial England* (1985) pp. 130–1, 139–41.

82 *Selby Wills* (1911) p. 18.

83 *De Republica*, p. 30.

84 See Edward Chamberlayne, quoted by David Cressy, 'Describing the social order of Elizabethan and Stuart England', *Literature and History* 3 (1976) p. 30, and Alice Clark, *Working Life of Women in the Seventeenth Century* (1992) especially pp. 56, 65.

85 Bettey, 'Manorial custom in Dorset', p. 33ff. Kerridge, *Agrarian Problems*, p. 23. Tawney, *Agrarian Problem*, p. 24. The proportion of total acreage held in this manner was smaller than the proportion of the population so holding. Clay, 'Estate management', p. 199.

86 The sizes of farms in various counties are estimated by Carl Bridenbaugh, *Vexed and Troubled Englishmen 1590–1642* (1968) p. 205; Clark, *Working Life*, p. 57, who does not specify where the smallholdings are, but on the basis of her bibliography they must have been in Devon, Hertfordshire, Middlesex, Sussex, Wiltshire or Worcestershire; David Hey, 'Yorkshire and Lancashire', in *AHEW* V:i (1984) p. 70; Brian Short, 'The south-east', in ibid., p. 292; Spufford, *Contrasting Communities*, pp. 38, 161, 165–6; Keith Wrightson, *English Society 1580–1680* (1982) p. 31.

87 Alan Everitt, 'Farm labourers', in *AHEW* IV (1967) pp. 401–3.

88 *Journeys*, p. 136. Sixty new knights were created in Raleigh's 1596 expedition to Cadiz (Scales).

89 J. D. Marshall, 'Agrarian wealth and social structure in pre-industrial Cumbria', *EcHR* 33:4 (1980) p. 521. Keith Wrightson, 'The social order of early modern England: three approaches', in L. Bonfield, R. M. Smith and K. Wrightson (eds) *The World We Have Gained* (1986) p. 189.

90 The same is true of Powick, Worcestershire (Table 2.3, line 7). Johnston, 'Probate inventories', p. 24.

91 *Selby Wills*, pp. 50–1. See also Spufford, *Contrasting Communities*, p. 37.

92 In identifying the economy of some 500 parishes I have relied on the regions defined in *AHEW* V:i (1984), including Hey, 'Yorkshire and Lancashire', G.E. Mingay, 'The east midlands', and Short, 'The south-east'. For further clarification I have consulted the following: J. Ellis's 'Modern map of Lincolnshire' (1790) BL: 3355.(19); John Jones, *A Human Geography of Cambridgeshire* (1924); Philip Pettit, *The Royal Forests of Northamptonshire: A Study in Their Economy 1558–1714* (1962–3); Alan Rogers, 'Three early maps of the Isle of Axholme', *Midland History* 1:2 (1971–2) pp. 25–7; Spufford, *Contrasting Communities*, maps 1 and 2; Joan Thirsk, *English Peasant Farming* (1957) map 4, p. 50; and David Hey and Margaret Spufford in person.

93 G. E. Mingay, in *The Gentry: The Rise and Fall of a Ruling Class* (1976) p. 14, estimates that these men had an annual income of £250, but it is not possible to compare annual income with total moveable wealth.

94 Everitt, 'Farm labourers', pp. 397–9. Hey, 'Yorkshire and Lancashire', p. 82.

95 Nesta Evans, *The East Anglian Linen Industry: Rural Industry and Local Economy 1500–1800* (1985) p. 74. Marshall, 'Agrarian wealth', pp. 517–19. Carole Shammas, *The Pre-Industrial Consumer in England and America* (1990) p. 161.

96 Susan Dwyer Amussen, *An Ordered Society: Gender and Class in Early Modern England* (1988) p. 17, on Cawston, Norfolk. Macfarlane, 'Myth of the peasantry', p. 347, on Killington, Cumbria. W. Newman Brown, 'The receipt of poor relief and family situation: Aldenham, Hertfordshire 1630–90', in R. M. Smith (ed.) *Land, Kinship and Life-Cycle* (1984) p. 409. Keith Wrightson, 'Kinship in an English village: Terling, Essex 1550–1700', in ibid., p. 321.

97 For example the children of William Lilley, £29/–3 (1682) Morton, LAO: Ad Ac 44/4, and of Thomas Smith, £20/12 (1624) Spalding, LAO: Ad Ac 19/68.

98 Barley, 'Farmhouses and cottages', p. 293, referring to the mid-sixteenth to early eighteenth centuries. Marshall, 'Agrarian wealth', p. 508, on the period 1661–1750. Michael Roberts marks the increase in occupational designation over the same period, which is generally equated with increasing wealth. 'Words they are women', fn. 77.

99 D. C. Coleman, *The Economy of England 1450–1750* (1977) pp. 21, 100, Figs 2 and 6. R. B. Outhwaite, *Inflation in Tudor and Early Stuart England* (1969) p. 10, Table I.

100 Barley, 'Farmhouses and cottages', p. 293. Shammas, *Pre-Industrial Consumer*, pp. 36–8, 147.

101 M. W. Barley, 'Rural building in England', in *AHEW* V:ii (1985) pp. 653–4, 657–8. F. G. Emmison, *Elizabethan Life* (1976) pp. 1–3, 7. Rachel Garrard, 'English probate inventories and their use in studying the significance of the domestic interior, 1570–1700', in A. van der Woude and A. Schuurman (eds) *Probate Inventories* (1980). Shammas, *Pre-Industrial Consumer*, pp. 36–8, 163.

102 William Lowick (1606) Baston, LRO: LCC Admon 1606/98, and Helen Lowick (1607) Baston, LRO: Ad Ac 7/3. See also Munby (ed.) *King's Langley*, p. xxvii.

103 For an excellent review of the literature on medieval women and the law see Janet Senderowitz Loengard, 'Legal history and the medieval Englishwomen: a fragmented view', *Law and History Review* 4:1 (1986) pp. 161–78.

104 For the nineteenth century see Lee Holcombe, *Wives and Property: Reform of the Married Women's Property Law in Nineteenth-Century England* (1983), and Mary Lyndon Shanley, *Feminism, Marriage, and the Law in Victorian England, 1850–1895* (1989) especially chs 1, 2 and 4, and on America, Norma Basch, *In the Eyes of the Law: Women, Marriage and Property in Nineteenth-Century New York* (1982) especially chs 2 and 3.

105 *An Introduction to the History of the Land Law* (1961) preface.

PART II MAIDS

1 *Lawes Resolutions*, p. 6.

2 *Poetical Recreations*, Pt I, quoted in Bridget Hill (ed.) *Eighteenth-Century Women: An Anthology* (1984) p. 123. The age of 25 as the brink of old-maid-hood may reflect the expected marriage of gentry daughters, of whom Jane Barker was one, at a younger age than more ordinary women. Statistically, 25 was only the *median* age of all women at first marriage, so half of all women would have been older.

3 Quoted in Hill (ed.) *Eighteenth-Century Women*, p. 125.

4 *A Woman of No Character: An Autobiography of Mrs Manley* (1986) p. 129.

5 E. A. Wrigley and Roger Schofield, *The Population History of England, 1541–1871: A Reconstruction* (1981) p. 260, Table 7.28, reworked in Roger Schofield, 'English marriage patterns revisited', *JFH* 10:1 (1985) pp. 9–10. This estimate assumes no difference in celibacy rates by sex, but similar high rates of female singleness also occur in probate accounts, which would not be expected to overestimate the number of unmarried among the women for whom accounts were filed, both testate and intestate: in a sample of thirty-nine Somerset accounts filed for women, at least 18 per cent appear never to have married; in fifteen Northamptonshire accounts, at least 26 per cent; and in sixteen Cambridgeshire accounts, 13 per cent.

6 Katherine O'Donovan, 'The male appendage – legal definitions of women', in S. Burman (ed.) *Fit Work for Women* (1979) p. 135. Susan Staves, *Married Women's Separate Property in England, 1660–1833* (1990) p. 217.

3 UPBRINGING

1 Amartya Sen, 'More than 100 million women are missing', *New York Review of Books* 37:20 (20 December 1990) pp. 61–6. Anne Winter, 'Girl child', *Everywoman* (March 1991) 20–1. See also Barbara D. Miller, 'Female infanticide and child neglect in rural North India', in N. Scheper-Hughes (ed.) *Child Survival: Anthropological Perspectives on the Treatment and Maltreatment of Children* (1987).

2 John Boswell, *The Kindness of Strangers: The Abandonment of Children in Western Europe from Late Antiquity to the Renaissance* (1988) pp. 100–2, 186, 258–9, 261–4.

3 Keith Wrightson, 'Infanticide in the early seventeenth century', *LPS* 15 (1975) pp. 10–22. See also discussion in Richard Wall, 'Inferring differential neglect of females from mortality data', *Annales de Demographie Historique* (1981) pp. 122–5.

4 *The Autobiography of Mrs Alice Thornton of East Newton, Co. York* (1873) pp. 98, 126. Patricia Crawford, 'Katharine and Philip Henry and their children: a case study in family ideology', *Transactions of the Historic Society of Lancashire and Cheshire* 134 (1984) p. 45. Ann Haskell refers to daughters in the middle ages as a 'partial disgrace', and notes that the bitterness of medieval women was greatest when dealing with their daughters, in 'The Paston women on marriage in fifteenth-century England', *Viator* 4 (1973) p. 470. That bitterness, however, undoubtedly involved more psychological complexity than simple shame at having borne a daughter.

5 Respectively, Alan Macfarlane, *Marriage and Love in England 1300–1840* (1986) p. 69, although he does point out (p. 53) that English son-preference was slight in relation to other societies, and Lloyd de Mause, introduction to *The History of Childhood* (1974) p. 37.

6 Olwen Hufton, 'Women in history: early modern Europe', *P&P* 101 (1983) p. 130. Wall, 'Inferring differential neglect', pp. 125–6. Maud Pember Reeves, *Round About a Pound a Week* (1914) pp. 97, 112, for example. Margery Spring Rice, *Working Class Wives: Their Health and Conditions* (1939) pp. 156–7, 170.

7 Various pieces of evidence are presented in Alice Clark, *Working Life of Women in the Seventeenth Century* (1992) pp. 69, 72–3, Bertha Putnam, 'Northamptonshire wage assessments of 1560 and 1667', *EcHR* 1st ser. 1 (1927–8) pp. 131, 133, and Elizabeth Waterman, 'Some new evidence on wage assessments in the eighteenth century', *English Historical Review* 43 (1928) p. 400.

8 The estimates are American, and variations depend on age, pregnancy and lactation. Food and Nutrition Board, National Academy of Sciences, *Recommended Daily Allowances* (1974).

9 Young William Lockin of Lincolnshire, whose father was described by himself as a husbandman, but as a gentleman by his gentleman administrator, was given money 'to have in his purse' and 'at a cocking'. Thomas Lockin, £625/449 (1666) Langton by Partney, LAO: Ad Ac 32/65. Martha Mayhew of Horsted Keynes, Sussex, was given by her uncle and guardian, the rector, 6d. 'for a fairing' or just 'to spend', and later a shilling 'to play withall'

or 'to spend at dancings'. *The Journal of Giles Moore* (1970) pp. 71, 73, 79.

10   BL: Harleian MS 1957, p. 46 (family account book of Randle Holme, genealogist and heraldic painter in the city of Chester).

11   Helen Lowick, £28/0 (1607) LAO: Ad Ac 7/3. William Lowycke, £28 (1606) LAO: LCC Admon 1606/98.

12   *The Autobiography of William Stout of Lancaster 1665–1752* (1967) p. 72.

13   I am grateful to Keith Wrightson for his reference to, and microfilm of, the Terling Overseers' accounts, 1694–1706. According to Wrightson and David Levine, in *Poverty and Piety in an English Village: Terling 1525–1700* (1979) p. 40, a pauper child cost only £1 10s. p.a., or 6d. a week. I am unable to substantiate this figure in the sources. My sum agrees with those of Alice Clark, who found children receiving poor relief of 1s. to 1s. 6d. per week for food alone. *Working Life*, pp. 70–2. It is confirmed by Overseers' accounts from Linton and Gamlingay (Cambridgeshire) in the 1670s and 1680s, where children had between 1s. 6d. and 1s. 10d. per week, exclusive of clothing (kindly communicated to me by Margaret Spufford).

14   K. D. M. Snell and J. Millar, 'Lone-parent families and the welfare state: past and present', *C&C* 2:3 (1987) pp. 387–422.

15   W. Newman Brown, 'The receipt of poor relief and family situation: Aldenham, Hertfordshire 1630–90', in R. M. Smith (ed.) *Land, Kinship and Life-Cycle* (1984) p. 418. Clark, *Working Life*, p. 72. Barbara Hanawalt, 'Childrearing among the lower classes of late medieval England', *Journal of Interdisciplinary History* 8:1 (1977) p. 22. Ann Kussmaul, *Servants in Husbandry in Early Modern England* (1981) p. 72. Alan Macfarlane, *The Family Life of Ralph Josselin, a Seventeenth-Century Clergyman* (1970) p. 92–3. The distinction in types of putting out is discussed in Jocelyn Dunlop, *English Apprenticeship and Child Labour* (1912) pp. 151–4.

16   Anne Chalke, £96/–7, Pulborough, and Alice Wooles, £84/1, Barnham, both WSRO: EpI/33/1633. The exact ages of the Wooles children other than Ann are not given. Premiums were also found to vary by age, but not by sex, in several hundred pauper apprenticeships analysed by Pamela Sharpe, in 'Poor children as apprentices in Colyton 1598–1830', *C&C* 6:2 (1991) p. 256.

17   Michael Mitterauer and Reinhard Sieder, *The European Family: Patriarchy to Partnership from the Middle Ages to the Present* (1982) p. 98. Edward Shorter, *The Making of the Modern Family* (1975) p. 26. Lawrence Stone, *The Family, Sex and Marriage in England 1500–1800* (1977) pp. 468–72.

18   Thomas Healey, £471/342 (1683) Burringham, LAO: Ad Ac 44/44.

19   Stout, *Autobiography*, pp. 73, 99, 154, 172.

20   Vivien Brodsky, 'Widows in late Elizabethan London: remarriage, economic opportunity and family orientations', in L. Bonfield, R. M. Smith and K. Wrightson (eds) *The World We Have Gained* (1986) p. 141. Clark, *Working Life*, pp. 175–7. Dunlop, *English Apprenticeship*, p. 151. Michael Roberts, '"Words they are women, and deeds they are men": images of work and gender in early modern England', in L. Charles and L. Duffin (eds) *Women and Work in Pre-Industrial England* (1985) p. 142. K. D. M. Snell, *Annals of the Labouring Poor: Social Change and Agrarian England 1660–1900* (1985) p. 294.

21   Sue Wright, '"Churmaids, huswyfes and hucksters": the employment of women in Tudor and Stuart Salisbury', in L. Charles and L. Duffin (eds) *Women and Work in Pre-Industrial England* (1985) p. 103.

22   *Guide* (1669) p. 167.

23   *Narrative of the Persecution of Agnes Beaumont in 1674* (n.d.) pp. 35, 41. John Chamberlain, *The Chamberlain Letters: A Selection of the Letters of John Chamberlain Concerning Life in England from 1597 to 1626* (1966) p. 59.

24   *The History of Myddle* (1981) pp. 92, 114, 129.

25   Thornton, *Autobiography*, p. 101. Rachel Weigall, 'An Elizabethan gentlewoman: the journal of Lady Mildmay, circa 1570–1617', *Quarterly Review* 215:428 (July 1911) p. 138.

26   *Five Hundred Pointes of Good Husbandrie...*, preface to *Booke of Huswiferie*, 4th edn (1580) pp. 66a–b.

27   Title page of the 9th edn (1683).

28   Wiliam Blaby £20/9 (1682) Butterwick, LAO: Ad Ac 44/50. Jonas Mabbutt £291/146 (1684) Sutton St Edmunds, LAO: Ad Ac 44/134.

29   *The Gentlewomans Companion: or, a Guide to the Female Sex* (1675) p. 179. Commonly

attributed to Hannah Wolley, this book is rather a pirated compilation of her previous works. Elaine Hobby, *Virtue of Necessity: English Women's Writing 1649–88* (1988) pp. 172–4. Scald head, very common among pauper children, may have been ringworm of the scalp. A. L. Wyman, 'The surgeoness: the female practitioner of surgery 1400–1800', *Medical History* 28 (1984) p. 30.

30 Snell, *Labouring Poor*, ch. 6.

31 Laurel Thatcher Ulrich, *Good Wives: Image and Reality in the Lives of Women in Northern New England 1650–1750* (1982) pp. 43–4.

32 Martha Howell, *Women, Production and Patriarchy in Late Medieval Cities* (1986) p. 173. Merry Wiesner, 'Guilds, male bonding and women's work in early modern Germany', *Gender and History* 1:2 (1989) especially pp. 126–7.

33 Thomas Bickley and Christiana Bickley *v.* Barsheba Dynes (1694) PRO: C5/144/6.

34 On Wolley see Ada Wallas, *Before the Bluestockings* (1929) pp. 19–22, 28, and Hobby, *Virtue of Necessity*, pp. 166–75. *Compleat Servant-Maid* (1700; 1st edn 1677) pp. 16–20. Bathsua Makin, *An Essay to Revive the Antient Education of Gentlewomen* (1673) pp. 42–3, in an advertisement for her school at the end of the tract. *The Household Account Book of Sarah Fell of Swarthmoor Hall* (1920) p. 113. On *Advice to the Women and Maidens* see Hobby, *Virtue of Necessity*, p. 176, and Keith Thomas, 'Numeracy in early modern England', *TRHS* 5th ser. 37 (1987) p. 113. For the education of aristocratic women in housewifery see Ivy Pinchbeck and Margaret Hewitt, *Children in English Society* I (1969) pp. 29–30.

35 Moore, *Journal*, pp. 116, 180.

36 Dorothy Gardiner, *English Girlhood at School: A Study of Women's Education Through Twelve Centuries* (1929) pp. 214, 304–5, 313.

37 John Seamor, £61/8 (1665) Caythorpe, LAO: Ad Ac 43/39.

38 Jean Vanes, *Apparelled in Red: The History of the Red Maids School* (1984) pp. 11, 17–19, 26, or her *Education and Apprenticeship in Sixteenth-Century Bristol*, Bristol History Association Local History Pamphlet 52 (1982) pp. 18, 26.

39 Stout, *Autobiography*, p. 68. See also Patricia Crawford, '"The only ornament in a woman": needlework in early modern England', in *All Her Labours* II: *Embroidering the Framework* (1984) and references in Mildred Campbell, *The English Yeoman under Elizabeth and the Early Stuarts* (1942) p. 274; Gardiner, *English Girlhood*, pp. 310, 313; Gough, *Myddle*, p. 61; and Margaret Spufford, *Contrasting Communities: English Villagers in the Sixteenth and Seventeenth Centuries* (1974) p. 203 fn. 32. On colonial America see Ulrich, *Good Wives*, p. 44, and Lois Green Carr and Lorena Walsh, 'The planter's wife: the experience of white women in seventeenth-century Maryland', *WMQ* 3rd ser. 34 (1977) p. 558.

40 Richard Wheatley, £182/132 (1678) Sidlesham, WSRO: EpI/33/1678 and STCI/26/138b.

41 'A possession of one's own: women and consumer behaviour in England 1660–1740', *Journal of British Studies* 25:2 (1986) p. 142.

42 BIHR: John Stapleton (1642) Cottingham, Harthill.

43 Pell, £173/49 (1606) Silk Willoughby, LAO: Ad Ac 7/60 and LCC Will 1606/95. For schools information, see *Victoria County Histories*.

44 David Cressy, *Education in Tudor and Stuart England* (1975) pp. 75, 110. M. H. Curtis, 'Education and apprenticeship', *Shakespeare Survey* 17 (1964) p. 59. Macfarlane, *Josselin*, p. 91. C.V. Wedgwood, *The King's Peace 1637–41* (1955) p. 81. Helen Weinstein, 'Religious preconceptions in the mind of the just-reading public in the seventeenth century', forthcoming. On the problems of measuring female literacy and the discrepancy between ability to read and ability to write see Margaret Spufford, *Small Books and Pleasant Histories: Popular Fiction and its Readership in Seventeenth-Century England* (1981) pp. 22–4, 34–5.

45 Victor Skipp, *Crisis and Development: An Ecological Case Study of the Forest of Arden 1570–1674* (1978) pp. 83–4.

46 Moore, *Journal*, p. 72.

47 John Webb (ed.) *Poor Relief in Elizabethan Ipswich* (1966) pp. 126, 128, 133–5, 138.

48 *Victoria County History, Lincolnshire* II, pp. 442–3.

49 F. G. Emmison, *Elizabethan Life* (1976) p. 122.

50 Pinchbeck and Hewitt, *Children*, pp. 24–5. R. W. Unwin, 'Tradition and transition: market towns in the Vale of York 1660–1830', *Northern History* 17 (1981) pp. 106–7.

51 *Robert Loder's Farm Accounts 1610–20* (1936) pp. 45, 68, 87, 107, 122, 172. Gregory King, 'Natural and political observations', in P. Laslett (ed.) *The Earliest Classics: John Graunt and Gregory King* (1973) p. 250.

52 Quoted in Sara Heller Mendelson, *The Mental World of Stuart Women* (1987) p. 17.
53 *Appeal to the Men of Great Britain on Behalf of Women* (1974; 1st edn 1798) p. 260.
54 Juliet du Boulay, *Portrait of a Greek Mountain Village* (1974) p. 106.

4 INHERITANCE

1   Alan Macfarlane, *Marriage and Love in England 1300–1840* (1986) p. 266. Lionel Munby (ed.) *Life and Death in King's Langley: Wills and Inventories 1498–1659* (1981) p. xxii. Margaret Spufford, *Contrasting Communities: English Villagers in the Sixteenth and Seventeenth Centuries* (1974) p. 111.
2   BIHR: James Raynes (1648) Appleton, Rydall.
3   Suggested by Keith Wrightson, *English Society 1580–1680* (1982) p. 108.
4   *Lawes Resolutions*, p. 73. Ann Kettle, '"My wife shall have it": marriage and property in the wills and testaments of later medieval England', in R. B. Outhwaite (ed.) *Marriage and Society* (1981) pp. 89–90. Eleanor Searle, 'Freedom and marriage in medieval England: an alternative hypothesis', *EcHR* 29 (1976) p. 482.
5   Barbara Crawford, 'Marriage and the status of women in Norse society', in R. B. Outhwaite (ed.) *Marriage and Society* (1981) p. 84.
6   Gregory Musgrave, Haxey, LAO: Stow Will 1669–71/144. James Musgrave, £106/–119 (1682) LAO: Ad Ac 44/10 and Stow Will 1681–3/22. For all land measures see Ian Adams, *Agrarian Landscape Terms* (1976).
7   R. M. Smith, 'Some issues concerning families and their property in rural England 1250–1800', in R. M. Smith (ed.) *Land, Kinship and Life-Cycle* (1984) pp. 40–6, based on the work of E. A. Wrigley and J. Goody.
8   Childless couples are underrepresented in probate documents (only 9 per cent of the total) because in this source the presence of a child may be the only way of identifying a marriage.
9   'The heiress-at-law: English real property law from a new point of view', *Law and History Review* 8:2 (1990) pp. 273–96.
10 John King, £51/31 (1635) Tillington, WSRO: EpI/33/1635, and STCI/18/370. The wainscot, bench, glass and safe would have been considered part and parcel of the freehold (see Chapter 2).
11 John Perlebine, £103 (1592) Sibsey, LAO: Inv 81/728 and LCC Will 1591/i/448. Agnes Perlebine, £38/30 (1612) (died 1593) LAO: Ad Ac 11/20 and LCC Admon 1591/197. Thomas Perlebine, £74 (1612) LAO: Inv 112a/324 and LCC Admon 1612/260.
12 For example, the introduction by Miranda Chaytor and Jane Lewis to Alice Clark, *Working Life of Women in the Seventeenth Century* (1982) pp. xxx, xxxvi.
13 M. W. Barley, 'Rural building in England', in *AHEW* V:ii (1985) p. 677. F. G. Emmison, *Elizabethan Life* (1976) p. 6. Carole Shammas, *The Pre-Industrial Consumer in England and America* (1990) p. 160.
14 R. G. Griffiths, 'Joyce Jeffreys of Ham Castle: a 17th century business gentlewoman', *Transactions of the Worcestershire Archaeological Society* 10 (1933) p. 10.
15 William Bankes, £222/104 (1672) Arthingworth, NRO: Acct 104. I do not think it makes a difference here that the appraisers thought they were valuing a leased house, while a freehold house may have been worth more. The appraisers must have assumed that any lease was very long – they clearly did not ask anyone how long it had to run, or they would have learned that it should not be included in the inventory. On fictive leases for very long periods of time see Chapter 8.
16 Examples of rents and prices are found in the following documents: Barbara Barber, £21/1 (1632) DRO: PE/WM:CP2/4/48; Robert Berry *v.* Mary Burges (1672) PRO: C5/443/20; Nicholas Crabbe, £50/–3 (1617) Littleport, CUL: EDR A12/1/1617/15; 'Diary of Joyce Jeffries of Hereford, 1638–48', BL: Egerton MS 3054, or Griffiths, 'Joyce Jeffreys', p. 21; Robert Sabberton, £8/–8 (1617) Downham, CUL: EDR A12/1/1617/1.

   For examples and estimates of the purchase price of land relative to its annual value in the early modern period, between ten and twenty times its annual value, see the following: *The Chamberlain Letters: A Selection of the Letters of John Chanberlain Concerning Life in England from 1597 to 1626* (1966) p. 276; Mary Finch, *The Wealth of Five Northamptonshire Families 1540–1640* (1956) p. 58; Richard Gough, *The History of Myddle* (1981) p. 96; H. J. Habakkuk, 'The long term rate of interest and the price of land in the seventeenth century', *EcHR* 5:1 (1952) pp. 28–9; Spufford, *Contrasting Communities*, p. 75; Lawrence Stone, *The*

Crisis of the Aristocracy 1558–1641 (1967) p. 245. This ratio is by no means invariable: Joyce Jeffries bought Goulding Hall for £25 10s., but she rented it at £12 p.a. Griffiths, 'Joyce Jeffreys', p. 10.

17 Clark, *Working Life*, p. 78. She also discusses the cheapness of building houses relative to our own century (p.73).

18 BIHR: Thomas Jaram (1649) Middleton, Harthill.

19 My observation of cow costs corresponds with those of Mark Overton, in 'Agricultural change in Norfolk and Suffolk, 1580–1740' (Cambridge PhD thesis, 1980) pp. 243, 245. Peter Bowden, on the other hand, estimates that an average cow cost approximately £4 in the period 1640–99. 'Agricultural prices, wages, farm profits and rents', in *AHEW* V:ii (1985) Appendix D, Table 26, p. 874.

20 Richard Mockford, Steyning, WSRO: S Dean Will 1616/29.

21 BIHR: Anne Levet (1691) Pocklington, Deanery Peculiar. Pocklington parish register.

22 Barber, £21/1 (1632) Wimborne Minster, DRO: PE/WM CP2/4/48.

23 For details of the administration of sales see Mary Thurban, £28/9 (1629) Arundel, WSRO: EpI/33/1629, or Maurice Greenfield, £146/17 (1682) Shipley, WSRO: EpI/33/1682. If an item sold for less than its ascribed value in the inventory, the difference could be claimed as an allowance in the probate account.

24 See also Spufford, *Contrasting Communities*, p. 159.

25 Keith Wrightson and David Levine, *Poverty and Piety in an English Village: Terling 1525–1700* (1979) p. 30. Mildred Campbell notes the frequency with which the phrase 'lately purchased' appears in documents. *The English Yeoman under Elizabeth and the Early Stuarts* (1942) p. 70.

26 Nesta Evans, *The East Anglian Linen Industry: Rural Industry and Local Economy 1500–1800* (1985) p. 80. J. A. Johnston, 'The probate inventories and wills of a Worcestershire parish 1676–1775', *Midland History* 1:1 (1971–2) p. 32. Wrightson and Levine, *Poverty and Piety*, p. 96.

27 Lloyd Bonfield, 'Contrasting sources: court rolls and settlements as evidence of hereditary transmission of land amongst small landowners in early modern England', *University of Illinois Law Review* 3 (1984) pp. 650–2.

28 Lloyd Bonfield, 'Normative rules and property transmission: reflections on the link between marriage and inheritance in early modern England', in L. Bonfield, R. M. Smith and K. Wrightson (eds) *The World We Have Gained* (1986) p. 172. Cicely Howell, *Land, Family and Inheritance in Transition: Kibworth Harcourt 1280–1700* (1983) p. 259.

29 Alice Wilson, £279/0 (1683) Appleby, LAO: Ad Ac 44/38 and Stow Will 1681–3/174. John Wilson, £312 (1679) LAO: Inv 178/425 and Stow Will 1679–80/80.

30 Sergeant, Huttoft, LAO: LCC will 1594/ii/84.

31 In Lupton (Westmorland) and Orwell (Cambridgeshire) girls occasionally got cows, but in Earls Colne (Essex) girls never got either animals or agricultural tools. Macfarlane, *Marriage and Love*, pp. 265–6. Spufford, *Contrasting Communities*, p. 112.

32 Gregory Musgrave, Haxey, LAO: Stow Will 1669–71/144. James Musgrave, £106/–119 (1682) LAO: Ad Ac 44/10 and Stow Will 1681–3/22.

33 *Selby Wills* (1911) p. 76.

34 *The Journal of Giles Moore* (1970) pp. 286–8.

35 *The Mill on the Floss* (1860) Book 1, ch. 8.

36 Will of Richard Robinson, *Selby Wills*, p. 139. See also Spufford, *Contrasting Communities*, p. 159.

37 Miriam Slater, *Family Life in the Seventeenth Century: The Verneys of Claydon House* (1984) pp. 34–45.

38 BIHR: John Walls (1643) Wilton, Rydall.

39 BIHR: Thomas Dry (1645) Bishop Burton, Harthill.

40 Henry Horwitz, 'Testamentary practice, family strategies, and the last phases of the custom of London, 1660–1725', *Law & History Review* 2:2 (1984) pp. 223–39.

41 See, for example, the wills of Arthur Bell or Thomas Catlin, *Selby Wills*, pp. 19, 39–40.

42 BIHR: John Campleman (1680) Allerston, Deanery Peculiar.

43 See also the comments of Cicely Howell, 'Peasant inheritance customs in the midlands 1280–1700', in J. Goody, J. Thirsk and E. P. Thompson (eds) *Family and Inheritance: Rural Society in Western Europe 1200–1800* (1976) p. 141.

44 In rural Yorkshire, 20 of 70; in Selby, 45 of 156.
45 Joan Thirsk, 'The common fields', *P&P* 29 (1974) p. 12, and 'The European debate on customs of inheritance, 1500–1700', in J. Goody, J. Thirsk and E. P. Thompson (eds) *Family and Inheritance: Rural Society in Western Europe 1200–1800* (1976). Donald Veall, *The Popular Movement for Law Reform 1640–1660* (1970) pp. 217–18.
46 *The Life of Adam Martindale, Written by Himself* (1845) p. 23.
47 Mary Bateson (ed.) *Borough Customs* II (1906) pp. xciv–xcv. Rosamond Jane Faith, 'Peasant families and inheritance customs in medieval England', *AgHR* 14 (1966) p. 82.
48 Johnston, 'Probate inventories', p. 33. *Pace* Ralph Houlbrooke, *The English Family 1450–1700* (1984) p. 235, and those historians who subscribe to the 'trickle-down' theory of social development, that all ideas worth having start at the top and gradually seep down to the poor.
49 Peter Laslett, *Family Life and Illicit Love in Earlier Generations* (1977) pp. 57–8, on the hamlet of Wiseton in Clayworth, Nottinghamshire, in 1688.
50 Alice Coolinge, £133/70 (1611) Whaplode, LAO: Ad Ac 10/35.
51 John Lincoln, £54/45 (1607) West Keal, LAO: Ad Ac 8/119.
52 Houlbrooke, *English Family*, p. 237.
53 Matthew Burtoft, £29/6 (1669) Burringham, LAO: Ad Ac 33/26.
54 Edward Stow, £139/70 (1680) Waddingworth, LAO: Ad Ac 34/64.
55 Douglis, £75/70 (1680) Chipping Warden, NRO: Acct 7.
56 Thomas Sanderson, £573/553 (1671) Moulton, NRO: Acct 76.
57 William Gibbs, £488/135 (1680) Blisworth, NRO: Acct 41.
58 Barker, £77/41 (1619) Linton, CUL: EDR A12/1/1618/9.
59 Cooper, £22/17 (1617) Over, CUL: EDR A12/1/1617/3.
60 *The Touchstone of Wills, Testaments, and Administrations*, 3rd edn (1674) p. 110. The other places are as yet unidentified.
61 Ockenden *als* Aylwyn, £73/65 (1608) Felpham, WSRO: EpI/33/1608.
62 Mobbs, £32/20 (1678) NRO: Acct 136.
63 Richard Irelande (1634) East Wittering, WSRO: STCI/18/336. Joan Irelande, £89/16 (1635) WSRO: EpI/33/1635 and STCI/18/350b.
64 For mediation in ecclesiastical litigation, as opposed to administrative probate cases, see Susan Dwyer Amussen, *An Ordered Society: Gender and Class in Early Modern England* (1988) p. 174, Martin Ingram, *Church Courts, Sex and Marriage in England, 1570–1640* (1987) p. 34, and J. A. Sharpe, 'Such disagreement betwyx neighbours: litigation and human relations in early modern England', in J. Bossy (ed.) *Disputes and Settlements: Law and Human Relations in the West* (1983) pp. 173–8.
65 Elizabeth Jackson, £33/28 (1611) Aslackby, LRO: Ad Ac 10/165.
66 John Knightly, £38/24 (1619) Guilden Morden, CUL: EDR/A12/2/1619/1.
67 William Fullshot, £34/11 (1624) Waddingworth, LRO: Ad Ac 19/6.
68 Maria Cioni, 'Women and law in Elizabethan England, with particular reference to the Court of Chancery', (Cambridge PhD thesis, 1974) pp. 91–3.
69 Barbara Diefendorf, *Paris City Councillors in the Sixteenth Century: the Politics of Patrimony* (1983) p. 253.
70 David Narrett, 'Men's wills and women's property rights in colonial New York', in R. Hoffman and P. J. Albert (eds) *Women in the Age of the American Revolution* (1989) pp. 120, 128–9. Gloria Main, 'Widows in rural Massachusetts on the eve of the revolution', in ibid., p. 78. Shammas, *Pre-Industrial Consumer*, p. 208. Carole Shammas, Marylyn Salmon and Michel Dahlin, *Inheritance in America from Colonial Times to the Present* (1987), pp. 32, 64. Jeanette Lasansky, *A Good Start: The Aussteier or Dowry* (1990) p. 11 (on Pennsylvania).

5 PORTIONS AND MARRIAGE

1 Robert Wrinche, £14/–79 (1617) Teversham, CUL: EDR A12/1/ 1617/25.
2 Jane Burnell, £69/–73 (1703) Lilton, SRO: DD/SP/442.
3 William Violett (1670) Oving, WSRO: EpI/33/1670. Jane Violett (1662) WSRO: STCI/23/73.
4 Ann Friend, £41/34 (1672) Bishop's Waltham, HRO: Acct.
5 Whittle (1612) Stapleford, LAO: Ad Ac 11/50 and Inv 1611/305.
6 Susannah Westland, £30/–6 (1672) Freiston, LAO: Ad Ac 43/65 and LCC Admon 1670/230.

Rose Westland, £618 (1684) LAO: Inv 185a/23. The accounts of young girls filed with no expenses except funeral and administration vary widely in assessed value: Anne Lydyward, £8/7 (1619) Wimborne Minster, DRO: Acct 22; Elizabeth Trimme, £8/6 (1639) Wimborne Minster, DRO: Acct 54; Elizabeth Heaton, £300/273 (1679) Great Grimsby, LAO: Ad Ac 43/109 and LCC Admon 1677/34.

7 John Spaldinge £175/141 (1599) Holton Beckering, LAO: Ad Ac 5/395. Susan Spaldinge £20/17 (1602) LAO: Ad Ac 5/45 and LCC Admon 1602/121.

8 Seagrave, £24/21 (1619) Helpringham, LAO: Ad Ac 15/71.

9 Isabel Wharton, £19/4 (1612) Gedney, LAO: Ad Ac 11/7 and LCC Will 1611/ii/199. Charles Wharton, £12 (1610) LAO: LCC Admon 1610/253.

10 *The Journal of Giles Moore* (1970) p. 323.

11 Of the total 113, 66 per cent of wills (75) gave more money to girls than boys, 19 per cent (21) more to boys than girls and 15 per cent (17) to both equally.

12 Of forty inventories for the estates of single people, more than three quarters of whom were female, 70 per cent held at least half the value of their inventories in credit or cash. (All estimates are over and above a generous £5 allowance for 'purse and apparel'; these were almost invariably listed together in inventories, but usually amounted to only £1 or £2.) Further research on debt and credit will profit by looking at debtors' accounts to assess their creditors, as well as at creditors' inventories. See also B. A. Holderness, 'Credit in a rural community, 1660–1800: some neglected aspects of probate inventories', *Midland History* 3:2 (1975) pp. 98–100.

13 Statutory rates of interest were 10 per cent to 1624, 8 per cent to 1652, 6 per cent to 1713 and 5 per cent thereafter. Interest rates in inventories, unlike those in accounts, sometimes varied from the statutes. Holderness, 'Credit in a rural community', p. 97.

14 Julius Kirshner and Anthony Molho, 'The dowry fund and the marriage market in early quattrocento Florence', *Journal of Modern History* 50:3 (1978) pp. 403–38.

15 Ivy Pinchbeck and Margaret Hewitt, *Children in English Society* I (1969) ch. 5. Jean Vanes, *Apparelled in Red: The History of the Red Maids School* (1984) p. 8. See also Charles Carlton, *The Court of Orphans* (1974).

16 Thomas Gaunt, £133/68 (1624) Lincoln, LAO: Ad Ac 19/47 and LCC Will 1621/i/144.

17 BIHR: Hugh Bellard, yeoman (1647) Cottingham, Harthill. Thomas Cowling, husbandman, £52/13 (1624) LAO: Ad Ac 19/58. John Higham, £26/5 (1620) CUL: EDR A12/2/1620/2.

18 Robert Greene, £18/7 (1624) Algakirk, LAO: Ad Ac 19/92.

19 Richard Charles (1668) Aslackby, LAO: LCC Will 1668/I/54.

20 Thomas Hornby, LAO: Stow Will 1675–8/97. Mary Hornby, £429/79 (1684) LAO: Ad Ac 44/127.

21 Henry Bauger, £17/8 (1632) Horbling, LAO: Ad Ac 23/159. For an example of a father giving his daughter the option, see the will of Anthony Collier in 1679, *Selby Wills* (1911) pp. 47–8.

22 CRO: EDR Consist. Ct. Wills, 1603. I owe this reference to Margaret Spufford.

23 Elizabeth Marner, £157/58 (1640) Midhurst, WSRO: EpI/33/1640 and EpI/29/138/30. Elizabeth Marner, £41 (1643) WSRO: EpI/29/138/38 and M Dean Will 1642/6.

24 *Autobiography of Mrs Alice Thornton of East Newton, Co. York* (1873) pp. 49, 75, 181.

25 *The Autobiography of William Stout of Lancaster 1665–1752* (1967) p. 87.

26 *The English Woman in History* (1957) p. 117. Bridget Hill (ed.) *Eighteenth-Century Women: An Anthology* (1984), pp. 129–32. Cynthia Pomerleau, 'The emergence of women's autobiography in England', in E. C. Jelinek (ed.) *Women's Autobiography: Essays in Criticism* (1980) pp. 29–30.

27 Olwen Hufton, 'Women without men: widows and spinsters in Britain and France in the eighteenth century', *JFH* 9:4 (1984) p. 373.

28 *Adam Bede* (1859) p. 56.

29 R. G. Griffiths, 'Joyce Jeffreys of Ham Castle: a 17th century business gentlewoman', *Transactions of the Worcestershire Archaeological Society* 10 (1933) pp. 1–32, or the original account book, 'Diary of Joyce Jeffries, 1638–48', BL: Egerton MS 3054. B. A. Holderness, 'Elizabeth Parkin and her investments, 1733–66: aspects of the Sheffield money market in the eighteenth century', *Transactions of the Hunter Archaeological Society* 10:2 (1973) pp. 81–7.

30 Shakespeare, *King Lear*, Act I, scene i.

31 Linda Campbell, 'The women of Stiffkey' (East Anglia MA thesis, 1985) pp. 31, 41. Cicely

Howell, *Land, Family and Inheritance in Transition: Kibworth Harcourt 1280–1700* (1983) pp. 173–4, Table 17 (my estimation from her figures). Ann Kussmaul, *Servants in Husbandry in Early Modern England* (1981) p. 37.

32   Daye, Spalding, LAO: Inv 127/102. Atkinson, Tetney, LAO: Inv 127/367.

33   William Tysdale, *Tenours and Forme of Indentures* (1546) (no page numbers). Evidence of renting cows is found in John Maxoile, £25/9 (1624) Aisthorpe, LAO: Ad Ac 19/113; Timothy Barton, £168/26 (1709) Downham, CUL: EDR A12/2/misc/31. A larger lease of sheep is mentioned in Mildred Campbell, *The English Yeoman under Elizabeth and the Early Stuarts* (1942) p. 199. My thanks to Eric Carlson for his surprise that three Cambridgeshire servants in the late sixteenth century bequeathed animals in their wills, which made me think about the small-scale possibilities.

34   Lionel Munby (ed.) *Life and Death in King's Langley: Wills and Inventories 1498–1659* (1981) pp. xv–xvi.

35   Abraham Cleave, £110, Waterbeach, CUL: EDR A12/2/1650–99/14. Griffiths, 'Joyce Jeffreys', pp. 14, 22.

36   In one Worcestershire parish in the eighteenth century only 3 per cent of wills mentioned servants. J. A. Johnston, 'The probate inventories and wills of a Worcestershire parish 1676–1775', *Midland History* 1:1 (1971–2) p. 32.

37   Based on 171 wills from Lincolnshire and Sussex. All proportions of legatees are minimum, since their relationship to the willmaker was not necessarily specified.

38   *The Diary of the Lady Anne Clifford* (1923) p. 104. C. V. Wedgwood, *The King's Peace 1637–1641* (1955) p. 261. For Frances Coke see her father's entry in the *Dictionary of National Biography*. Sara Heller Mendelson, *The Mental World of Stuart Women* (1987) p. 76. *Memoirs of Lady Fanshawe* (1905) p. 57.

39   Thornton, *Autobiography*, pp. 100, 213. Lu Emily Pearson, *Elizabethans at Home* (1957) p. 128. Mendelson, *Stuart Women*, p. 21. Margaret Ezell, *The Patriarch's Wife: Literary Evidence and the History of the Family* (1987) p. 18. *The Letters of Dorothy Osborne to William Temple 1652–54* (1928) p. 185. Miriam Slater, *Family Life in the Seventeenth Century: The Verneys of Claydon House* (1984) p. 63.

40   *The Weaker Vessel: Woman's Lot in Seventeenth-Century England* (1984) p. 337.

41   BIHR: John Legard (1646) New Malton, Rydall. *Selby Wills*, pp. 31–2. See also H. C. F. Lansberry, 'Free bench see-saw: Sevenoaks widows in the late seventeenth century', *Archaeologia Cantiana* 100 (1984) pp. 289–90, for the Kentish gentleman steward to the Earl of Dorset who gave his eldest daughter £800, and the other three £500 each. This preference for the eldest daughter at gentry levels – see also Slater, *Family Life*, p. 8 – is almost never seen among ordinary people.

42   Alan Macfarlane, *The Family Life of Ralph Josselin, a Seventeenth-Century Clergyman* (1970) pp. 64–5. Moore, *Journal*, p. 83. William Hinde, £417/173 (1669) Fittleworth, WSRO: EpI/33/1669. Lansberry, 'Sevenoaks widows', pp. 289–90. BIHR: John Robinson (1644) Harthill, and Michael Lamb (1686) Hayton, Deanery Peculiar.

43   Robert and Elizabeth Curtis *v.* Richard Baldwin (1659) PRO: C5/36/17.

44   BIHR: Thomas Craven (1685) Ebberston, Deanery Peculiar.

45   Alan Macfarlane, *Marriage and Love in England 1300–1840* (1986) p. 264. See also, for Cambridgeshire examples, Margaret Spufford, *Contrasting Communities: English Villagers in the Sixteenth and Seventeenth Centuries* (1974) pp. 112, 140, 142.

46   *Selby Wills*, p. 95.

47   Vanes, *Apparelled in Red*, p. 21.

48   William Bennett, Walberton, WSRO: STCI/15/305b. Thomas Lidgiter, £358/59 (1682) Steyning, WSRO: EpI/33/1682 and STCI/27/263b.

49   *Marriage and Love*, p. 264.

50   *Selby Wills*, p. 139.

51   Diane Owen Hughes, 'Domestic ideals and social behaviour: evidence from medieval Genoa', in C. E. Rosenberg (ed.) *The Family in History* (1975) p. 117. Samuel Kline Cohn, *The Labouring Classes in Renaissance Florence* (1980) pp. 44–6. The patriciate are taken here to be 17 per cent of the population, higher than the proportion of English aristocrats and gentry.

52   Barbara Diefendorf, *Paris City Councillors in the Sixteenth Century: Politics of Patrimony* (1983) p. 191.

53   *The Life of Adam Martindale, Written by Himself* (1845) p. 16.

54 *The Diary of Roger Lowe of Ashton-in-Makerfield, Lancs. 1663–74* (1938) p. 45.
55 Stout, *Autobiography*, p. 168.
56 *The History of Myddle* (1981) pp. 92, 99, 124, 128, 161.
57 Gough, *Myddle*, pp. 91–2.
58 *Lawes Resolutions* (1632) p. 72.
59 Ibid., p. 90.
60 Ibid., p. 182.
61 Katharine Browne, £108/–8 (1712) Charlton Mackrell, SRO: D/D/Ct 66.
62 Lewis Hill, £34/32 (1605) Grantham, LAO: Ad Ac 6/25. Mary Hill, £28/24 (1605) LAO: Ad Ac 6/28.
63 For comments on the coexistence of dowry and brideprice see Ursula Sharma, *Women, Work and Property in North-West India* (1980) p. 138.
64 Osborne, *Letters*, pp. 138–9.
65 Thornton, *Autobiography*, pp. 52, 78.
66 *Letters from the Right Honourable Lady Mary Wortley Montagu 1709 to 1762* (1906) p. 1. The *Gentleman's Magazine* is reported as a curiosity by R. Chambers, *Book of Days* I (1863) p. 258, and James Vaux, *Church Folk-Lore* (1902) p. 140.
67 Mary Finch, *The Wealth of Five Northamptonshire Families 1540–1640* (1956) p. 28, fn. 3, and p. 35.
68 See for example Gough, *Myddle*, p. 127–8, and BIHR: Christopher Hutton, husbandman, 1650, Warter, Harthill. Grooms' portions were also equivalent to brides' among artisans in medieval Genoa. Hughes, 'Domestic ideals', p. 127. Grooms' portions are not mentioned by (male) historians of dowries in other Italian cities.
69 John Sowton (father), (1627) South Stoke, WSRO: STCI/17/77b. John Sowton (son), £524/275 (1636) South Stoke, WSRO: EpI/33/1635 and Inv 185/10.
70 E. M. Symonds, 'The diary of John Green (1635–57)', *English Historical Review* 44 (1929) p. 116.
71 For the later eighteenth and early nineteenth centuries see Leonore Davidoff and Catherine Hall, *Family Fortunes: Men and Women of the English Middle Class 1780–1850* (1987) especially pp. 279–80.
72 See for example Jane Lambiri-Dimaki, 'Dowry in modern Greece', in M. A. Kaplan (ed.) *The Marriage Bargain: Women and Dowries in European History* (1985) pp. 165, 177.
73 Alan Macfarlane is only the most recent to discuss portions entirely in female terms. *Marriage and Love*, pp. 263–6. See also the comments of Christiane Klapisch-Zuber, 'The Griselda complex: dowry and marriage gifts in the quattrocento', in her *Women, Family and Ritual in Renaissance Italy* (1985) on the same phenomenon in another context.
74 Respectively, R. B. Outhwaite, 'Marriage as business: opinions on the rise in aristocratic bridal portions in early modern England', in N. McKendrick and R. B. Outhwaite (eds) *Business Life and Public Policy* (1986) p. 29, Ralph Houlbrooke, *The English Family 1450–1700* (1984) p. 244, and Peter Earle, *The Making of the English Middle Class: Business, Society and Family Life in London 1660–1730* (1989) p. 197.
75 Charles Carlton, 'The widow's tale: male myths and female reality in sixteenth and seventeenth-century England', *Albion* 10:2 (1978) pp. 119, 121–3. Vivien Brodsky Elliott, 'Single women in the London marriage market: age, status and mobility, 1598–1619', in R. B. Outhwaite (ed.) *Marriage and Society* (1981) p. 90. Peter Laslett, *Family Life and Illicit Love in Earlier Generations* (1977) pp. 162–3, 169. Macfarlane, *Marriage and Love*, p. 93.
76 Lawrence Stone and Jeanne Fawtier Stone, *An Open Elite? England 1540–1880* (1984) p. 76.
77 Thornton, *Autobiography*, p. 100.
78 Rachel Weigall, 'An Elizabethan gentlewoman: the journal of Lady Mildmay, circa 1570–1617', *Quarterly Review* 215:428 (July 1911) pp. 119–38. *Two Elizabethan Women: The Correspondence of Joan and Maria Thynne 1575–1611* (1982) p. xx. Thornton, *Autobiography*, p. 80.
79 E. M. Symonds, 'The diary of John Green (1635–57)', *English Historical Review* 43 (1928) pp. 388–9.
80 Ezell, *Patriarch's Wife*, pp. 18–25.
81 BIHR: John Flike (Fligg) (1643) East Cottingwith, Harthill.
82 BIHR: John Legard (1646) New Malton, Rydall.
83 Brodsky Elliott, 'London marriage market', pp. 86, 91–7.

84 On Kirby Lonsdale see Alan Macfarlane, 'The myth of the peasantry: family and economy in a northern parish', in R. M. Smith (ed.) *Land, Kinship and Life-Cycle* (1984) p. 343.

85 Lowe, *Diary*, pp. 33–4, 75, 91, for example. Gough, *Myddle*, p. 169. The historian Wallace Notestein was surprised by the 'unconventional' early modern fashion for women to court men. 'The English woman, 1580–1650', in J. H. Plumb (ed.) *Studies in Social History* (1955) p. 75. At least he noticed – most recent historians of marriage and the family have overlooked this point.

86 *A Pleasant Dialogue Betwixt Honest John and Loving Kate* (1685) and *The Merry Conceits and Passages of Simon and Cisley* (n.d.) in MCC: Samuel Pepys's *Penny Merriments* I, pp. 209–32, 1226–47. I am grateful to Margaret Spufford for references and photocopies. Both appear, heavily edited, in Roger Thompson (ed.) *Samuel Pepys' Penny Merriments* (1976) pp. 116–20, 123–7.

87 *Depositions and Other Ecclesiastical Proceedings from the Courts of Durham, extending from 1311 to the reign of Elizabeth* (1845) pp. 226–8, also quoted in John Gillis, *For Better, for Worse: British Marriages, 1600 to the Present* (1985) p. 48. Ralph Houlbrooke, in *English Family*, p. 85, also states that 'quite often' women who had land demanded a portion with their husband. For other examples from court records in Norfolk see Susan Dwyer Amussen, *An Ordered Society: Gender and Class in Early Modern England* (1988) p. 71.

88 Martindale, *Life*, pp. 16, 35.

89 Gough, *Myddle*, p. 190.

90 W. K. Jordan, *Philanthropy in England 1480–1660* (1959) pp. 263, 274, 370–1. Macfarlane, *Marriage and Love*, p. 268. Susan Wright, 'Family life and society in sixteenth and early seventeenth-century Salisbury' (Leicester PhD thesis, 1982) p. 102. The sample form for a will in Thomas Phayer's *A Newe Boke of Presidents* (1543) (unpaginated) includes a bequest in reversion to 'the maryage of poore maydens'.

91 For the history of the saint see David Hugh Farmer, *Oxford Dictionary of Saints* (1987). For his representation in renaissance Italy and Chartres see Michael Taylor, 'Gentile da Fabriano, St Nicholas, and an iconography of shame', *JFH* 4:7 (1982) 321–32.

92 Julius Kirshner, 'Pursuing honor while avoiding sin: the *Monte delle Doti* of Florence,' *Studi Senesi* (1977) pp. 177–258.

93 *Pace* Fraser, *Weaker Vessel*, pp. 38, 97.

94 *Marriage and Love*, p. 69.

PART III WIVES

1 *Journal of Giles Moore* (1970) pp. 14, 23, 51, 72, 81, for example. *Household Account Book of Sarah Fell of Swarthmoor Hall* (1920) p. xxix. Barbara Todd, 'Widowhood in a market town: Abingdon 1540–1720' (Oxford PhD thesis, 1983) p. 230, fn. *A Pleasant Dialogue Betwixt Honest John and Loving Kate* (1685), p. 23 in MCC: Samuel Pepys's *Penny Merriments* I. See also Mildred Campbell, *The English Yeoman under Elizabeth and the Early Stuarts* (1942) pp. 242, 248. CUL: EDR A12/2/1624–34/6. The word almost never appears in seventeenth-century Durham or Essex or Yorkshire, either, according to Keith Wrightson and David Hey.

2 *Population Trends* 61 (Autumn 1990) Table 7, p. 55.

3 Peter Laslett, *Family Life and Illicit Love in Earlier Generations* (1977) p. 87. The figure is for the parish of Clayworth, Nottinghamshire.

4 *Law, or a Discourse Thereof*, p. 26. The same categorization occurs earlier in Henry Swinburne's *A Treatise of Testaments and Last Wills* (1590).

5 Thomas Barrett-Lennard, *The Position in Law of Women* (1983; 1st edn 1883) p. xxvii.

6 Edmund Snell, *The Principles of Equity* (1868) p. 278.

7 *The Hardships of the English Laws. In Relation to Wives* (1735) p. 43.

6 THE NATURE OF SETTLEMENTS

1 For discussions of strict settlement see Lloyd Bonfield, *Marriage Settlements, 1601–1740: The Adoption of the Strict Settlement* (1983); Christopher Clay, 'Marriage, inheritance and the rise of large estates in England, 1660–1815', *EcHR* 21 (1968) pp. 503–18; J. P. Cooper, 'Patterns of inheritance and settlement by great landowners from the fifteenth to the

eighteenth centuries', in J. Goody, J. Thirsk and E. P. Thompson (eds) *Family and Inheritance: Rural Society in Western Europe 1200–1800* (1976); Barbara English and John Saville, 'Family settlement and the "rise of great estates"', *EcHR* 33:4 (1980) pp. 556–8, and *Strict Settlement: A Guide for Historians* (1983); and H. J. Habakkuk, 'Marriage settlements in the eighteenth century', *TRHS* 4th ser. 32 (1950) pp. 15–30.

2 Lloyd Bonfield, 'Affective families, open elites and strict family settlements in early modern England', *EcHR* 39:3 (1986) pp. 346–7, 353–4, and 'Strict settlement and the family: a differing view', *EcHR* 41:3 (1988) pp. 461–6. Eileen Spring, 'The family, strict settlement and historians', *Canadian Journal of History* 18:3 (1983) pp. 381, 396, and 'The strict settlement: its role in family history', *EcHR* 41:3 (1988) pp. 454–60.

3 For example, English and Saville, *Strict Settlement*, pp. 100, 144.

4 For studies dealing principally with separate estate see Maria Cioni, 'The Elizabethan Chancery and women's rights', in D. Guth and J. W. McKenna (eds) *Tudor Rule and Revolution* (1982); Gwen Gampel, 'The planter's wife revisited: women, equity law and the Chancery Court in seventeenth-century Maryland', in B. J. Harris and J. K. McNamara (eds) *Women and the Structure of Society* (1984); Janelle Greenberg, 'The legal status of the English woman in early eighteenth-century common law and equity', *Studies in Eighteenth Century Culture* 4 (1975) pp. 171–81; Suzanne Lebsock, *The Free Women of Petersburg: Status and Culture in a Southern Town, 1784–1860* (1984) ch. 3; Susan Moller Okin, 'Patriarchy and married women's property in England: questions on some current views', *Eighteenth-Century Studies* 17:2 (1983–4) pp. 121–38; Marylynn Salmon, 'Women and property in South Carolina: the evidence from marriage settlements, 1730–1830', *WMQ* 39 (1982) pp. 655–85, and *Women and the Law of Property in Early America* (1986); Susan Staves, *Married Women's Separate Property in England, 1660–1833* (1990).

5 Cioni, 'Elizabethan Chancery', p. 173; Courtney Kenny, *The History of the Law of England as to the Effects of Marriage on Property and on the Wife's Legal Capacity* (1879) p. 14; Basil Lawrence, *The History of the Laws Affecting the Property of Married Women in England* (1884) p. 125; Okin, 'Married women's property', p. 123.

6 Lawrence quotes one mid-nineteenth-century Chancery decision: 'you cannot trace the line that divides [pin-money] from the separate property of the wife with any distinctness'. *Laws Affecting Property*, p. 122. The origins of pin-money – both the term and the practice – are not yet clear. See further Staves, *Separate Property*, pp. 132–3, and Eileen Spring, 'Law and the theory of the affective family', *Albion* 16:1 (1984) p. 10.

7 For example, women factory workers after both world wars were criticized for taking men's jobs merely in order to earn 'pin-money'. The modern derogation limits the credibility of early modern pin-money for Spring, 'Law', p. 10, and English and Saville, *Strict Settlement*, p. 25.

8 See Staves, *Separate Property*, ch. 5.

9 Lois Green Carr and Lorena Walsh, 'The planter's wife: the experience of white women in seventeeth-century Maryland', *WMQ* 3rd ser. 34 (1977) p. 561. Gampel, 'Planter's wife', p. 23. Lebsock, *Status and Culture*, p. 72. Marylynn Salmon, 'The legal status of women in early America: a reappraisal', *Law and History Review* 1 (1983) p. 149.

10 'Contrasting sources: court rolls and settlements as evidence of hereditary transmission of land amongst small land-owners in early modern England', *University of Illinois Law Review* 3 (1984) pp. 656–7.

11 *A Newe Boke of Presidents* (1973 reprint) (no page numbers).

12 *Symboleography*, ss. 221, 222, 165, 223, 81, 285, 286.

13 *The Lady's Law* p. vii. The other two women's legal handbooks, *The Lawes Resolutions of Women's Rights: Or, the Lawes Provision for Woemen* (1632) and *Baron and Feme: A Treatise of the Common Law Concerning Husbands and Wives* (1700), contain no sample settlements of any kind, although both refer to the practice of separate estate.

14 *The Lady's Law*, pp. 209, 217, 229, 236, 243.

15 For even earlier examples of settlements for the wife's jointure, which outnumbered settlements in tail male, see Peggy Jefferies, 'The medieval use as family law and custom: the Berkshire gentry in the fourteenth and fifteenth centuries', *Southern History* 1 (1979) especially p. 53.

16 (1970, facsimile of original 1583 edn) p. 105.

17 Avenant *v.* Kitchin (1582) *Choyce Cases*, p. 154.

18 Fitzjames *v.* Hirsley (1590) *Tothill*, p. 43.

19 Waterhouse *v.* Wytham (1595) *Tothill*, p. 91, and *Croke Eliz.*, p. 466.

20 Doyly *v.* Perfull (1649–79) *Chancery Cases* I, p. 225.

21 Rippon *v.* Dawding (1769), *Ambler*, p. 565, citing Peacock *v.* Monk (1750), *Vesey sen.* II, p. 190, and George dem. Thornbury *v.* Jew (1764), *Ambler*, p. 627. Ambler overlooked the cases of Avenant *v.* Kitchin (1581) and Palmer *v.* Keynell (1637). *Choyce Cases*, p. 154, and *Chancery Reports* I, p. 118. This dating is followed by G. W. Keeton's standard text, *Introduction to Equity*, 6th edn (1965; 1st edn 1938) p. 22, and by George Haskins, 'The estate by the marital right', *University of Pennsylvania Law Review* 97:3 (1949) p. 351.

22 I take this interpretation from the discussion in Kenny, *Effects of Marriage on Property*, p. 144. It is not his interpretation.

23 Respectively, John Baker, introduction to *The Reports of Sir John Spelman* II (1977) p. 209; Kenny, *Effects of Marriage on Property*, p. 90; Okin, 'Married women's property', p. 125, and *Lawes Resolutions*, p. 73; Lee Holcombe, *Wives and Property: Reform of the Married Women's Property Law in Nineteenth-Century England* (1983) pp. 33–5.

24 Kenny, *Effects of Marriage on Property*, p. 14. Holdsworth, *A History of English Law* V (1924) p. 310.

25 Staves's *Separate Property* makes this abundantly clear.

26 *English Law* V, p. 311. See also the excellent discussion in Staves, *Separate Property*, pp. 139–47. Maria Cioni, on the other hand, blithely assumes that women's equitable rights advanced progressively, and nowhere mentions reversals. 'Elizabethan Chancery', *passim*.

27 Ruth Perry, *Women, Letters, and the Novel* (1980) pp. 30, 35. Staves, *Separate Property*, especially ch. 5.

28 In Margaret Ezell, *The Patriarch's Wife: Literary Evidence and the History of the Family* (1987) appendix 2. The 'false rendring' referred to is specifically the inaccurate biblical translation of the Greek word meaning 'obey' into the English 'submit', but only when referring to wives' relation to their husbands, and nowhere else. This translation, More felt, seriously misrepresented women's moral obligation to their husbands.

29 Ibid., p. 192.

30 *A Serious Proposal to the Ladies*, 4th edn (1697) p. 90.

31 *Letters from the Right Honourable Lady Mary Wortley Montagu 1709 to 1762* (1906) pp. 74, 116.

32 *Hardships of the English Laws*, pp. 28–33.

33 *An Itinerary Written by Fynes Morison Gent* (1617) p. 221. I am grateful to Tim Stretton for this reference.

34 *Angliae Notitiae, or the Present State of England* (1669) pp. 496–502.

35 *The Autobiography of Mrs Alice Thornton of East Newton, Co. York* (1873) pp. 246–7, 121.

36 Ibid., p. 249.

37 *The Diary of the Lady Anne Clifford* (1923) pp. xxiii, 32, 49.

38 Ibid., pp. 62, 65, 70.

39 Ibid., p. 88.

40 Ibid., pp. xxx, xlviii.

41 Ibid., pp. 12, 53, 68.

42 Miriam Slater, 'The weightiest business: marriage in an upper-gentry family in seventeenth-century England', *P&P* 72 (1976) pp. 43–5, or *Family Life in the Seventeenth Century: The Verneys of Claydon House* (1984), pp. 97–9.

43 Mary Sankey *als* Walgrave *v.* Golding (1579) *Tothill*, p. 95. Flecton *v.* Dennys (1584) *Monro*, pp. 655–9. Georges *v.* Chancie (1639) *Tothill*, p. 97, and *Chancery Cases* I, p. 118.

44 For attribution see *New English Dictionary on Historical Principles. Ladies' Dictionary*, p. 31. *Lady's Law*, pp. 171–2. For an example of earlier use see the case of John Bodvell *v.* William Russell (1654) Caernarvon and Cambridgeshire, PRO: C5/19/12 (discussed in Chapter 7).

45 Michael Sheehan, 'The influence of canon law on the property rights of married women in England', *Mediaeval Studies* 25 (1963) p. 115.

46 *Roxana* (1987; 1st edn 1724) p. 187.

47 F. P. Verney (ed.), *Memoirs of the Verney Family* I (1892) p. 152. My thanks to Linda Pollock for this reference.

7 MARRIAGE SETTLEMENTS IN THE COURT OF CHANCERY

1 C.W. Brooks, *Pettyfoggers and Vipers of the Commonwealth: The 'Lower Branch' of the Legal Profession in Early Modern England* (1986) p. 281.
2 Maria Cioni found that the number of female Chancery litigants under Elizabeth had risen since the late fifteenth century and concluded that progressive social attitudes to women allowed them to be more legally active. 'The Elizabethan Chancery and women's rights', in D. Guth and J. W. McKenna (eds) *Tudor Rule and Revolution* (1982) p. 159. It is not clear whether this earlier rise was proportional to the total number of cases or merely an absolute increase, but in either case it cannot be ascribed to changing social attitudes to women before the rates of female litigants in other courts are examined.
3 Personal communications from Jane Laughton and Tim Stretton, in connection with their PhD research.
4 James Alexander, 'A study of the Court of Chancery records as a source for economic and social history' (London School of Economics MSc thesis, 1985), 'Initial pleas' chapter.
5 *The Practice of the Spiritual or Ecclesiastical Courts* (1685) p. 20.
6 Eric Carlson, *Marriage and the English Reformation* (1994), ch. 6. R. H. Helmholz, *Marriage Litigation in Medieval England* (1974). Martin Ingram, *Church Courts, Sex and Marriage in England, 1570–1640* (1987).
7 Stretton, 'Elizabethan Court of Requests'.
8 Marcus Knight, 'Litigants and litigation in the seventeenth-century Palatinate of Durham' (Cambridge PhD thesis, 1990) p. 236.
9 I am grateful to Steve Hindle and Andy Wood for information on the palatinate jurisdictions of Chester and Lancaster from their PhD research.
10 *The Country-Man's Counsellor* (seventeenth century) pp. 6–8. The anonymous author of *Considerations Touching the Dissolving . . . of the Court of Chancery* (1653) claimed that the costs of suing in Chancery had not increased in the previous hundred years, while the cost of cloth and victuals had increased more than threefold (p. 20).
11 Alexander, 'Court of Chancery records', pp. 4–6. Maria Cioni, 'Women and law in Elizabethan England with particular reference to the Court of Chancery' (Cambridge PhD thesis, 1974) pp. 37, 43–4. An original commission to take evidence in the country – in this instance, Croydon – is attached to the initial pleas in the case of Robert and Elizabeth Curtis *v.* Richard Baldwin (1659) Surrey, PRO: C5/36/17, together with a miniature copy of the complaint for the use of the interviewers, since the originals measure 1–2 by 2–3 feet.
12 PRO: C5/452/10.
13 William Ball *v.* Richard & Thomasine Clampitt (1670) PRO: C5/445/114. Spelling in the quote is modernized.
14 H. J. Habakkuk, 'Marriage settlements in the eighteenth century', *TRHS* 4th ser. 32 (1950) pp. 20–1.
15 Mildred Campbell, *The English Yeoman under Elizabeth and the Early Stuarts* (1942) p. 287.
16 Habakkuk, 'Marriage settlements', pp. 23–4. Eileen Spring, 'The family, strict settlement, and historians', *Canadian Journal of History* 18:3 (1983) p. 388.
17 Lloyd Bonfield, *Marriage Settlements 1601–1740: The Adoption of the Strict Settlement* (1983) pp. 117–18.
18 Lawrence Stone, *The Family, Sex and Marriage in England, 1500–1800* (1977) pp. 43–4. E. A. Wrigley and Roger Schofield, *The Population History of England, 1541–1871: A Reconstruction* (1981) p. 255.
19 Rowena Archer, 'Rich old ladies: the problem of late medieval dowagers', in A. J. Pollard (ed.) *Property and Politics: Essays in Later Medieval English History* (1984) pp. 19, 23. Joel Rosenthal, 'Aristocratic widows in fifteenth-century England', in B. J. Harris and J. K. McNamara (eds) *Women and the Structure of Society* (1984) p. 37. *A Treatise of Feme Coverts or, The Lady's Law* (1974; 1st edn 1732) p. 71. Miriam Slater, 'The weightiest business: marriage in an upper-gentry family in seventeenth-century England', *P&P* 72 (1976) p. 51, or *Family Life in the Seventeenth Century: The Verneys of Claydon House* (1984) pp. 104–5.
20 R. B. Outhwaite, 'Marriage as business: opinions on the rise in aristocratic bridal portions in early modern England', in N. McKendrick and R. B. Outhwaite (eds) *Business Life and Public Policy* (1986) p. 22.
21 *The Institutes of the Laws of England* II (1797) p. 233.

22 Stanley Chojnacki, 'Patrician women in early renaissance Venice', *Studies in the Renaissance* 21 (1974) pp. 194–5. J. P. Cooper, 'Patterns of inheritance and settlement by great landowners from the fifteenth to the eighteenth centuries', in J. Goody, J. Thirsk and E. P. Thompson (eds) *Family and Inheritance: Rural Society in Western Europe 1200–1800* (1976) p. 223. *Letters from the Right Honourable Lady Mary Wortley Montagu 1709 to 1762* (1906) p. 74. Susan Mosher Stuard, 'Dowry increase and increments in wealth in medieval Ragusa (Dubrovnik)', *Journal of Economic History* 16:4 (1981) pp. 795–811. Donald Veall, *The Popular Movement for Law Reform 1640–1660* (1970) p. 219.

23 Outhwaite, 'Marriage as business', pp. 23–4. The thrust of this article is that between 1525 and 1729 portions increased twelve or thirteen times. However, the sharpest rise occurred in the sixteenth century, and I do not have the data to compare Chancery portions with peeresses' portions for this period.

24 Medians are derived from forty-eight examples, twenty-two in the first half of the century and twenty-six in the second half. Although the Chancery cases themselves date from 1603, the portions which the early cases concern were generally paid in the last decade of the sixteenth century.

25 Nineteen cases quantified both the portion and an annual jointure, and the ratios are consistent within the earlier and the later periods.

26 'Marriage as business'.

27 Christopher Clay, 'The price of freehold land in the later seventeenth and eighteenth centuries', *EcHR* 27 (1974) pp. 173–89. See also discussion in Outhwaite, 'Marriage as business', p. 28.

28 Christopher Clay, 'Marriage, inheritance, and the rise of large estates in England 1660–1815', *EcHR* 21 (1968) pp. 503–18.

29 Stuard, 'Dowry increase', p. 810. Barbara Diefendorf, *Paris City Councillors in the Sixteenth Century: the Politics of Patrimony* (1983) p. 234.

30 Christiane Klapisch-Zuber, 'The Griselda complex: dowry and marriage gifts in the quattrocento', in *Women, Family and Ritual in Renaissance Italy* (1985) especially pp. 213, 245. Ursula Sharma, *Women, Work and Property in North-West India* (1980) pp. 138, 142, 164, 174.

31 For example, Mercy Reynolds *v.* Margaret Reynolds (1613) Hertfordshire, PRO: C2/Jas.I/R8/14, and Anne Brandon *v.* Henry Player (1706) Kent, PRO: C5/594/43.

32 Edward Lancaster *v.* Robert Poyntz (1603) PRO: C2/Jas.I/L16/25.

33 Charles Pressye *v.* Jeremy Bushier (1621) PRO: C2/Jas.I/P19/28.

34 Stuckley Lewis *v.* Robert apHugh apRobert & Ellen his wife (1624) PRO: C2/Jas.I/L2/11.

35 John Berry *v.* Mary Skinner *als* Newton (1672) PRO: C5/60/4.

36 Suzanne Lebsock, *The Free Women of Petersburg: Status and Culture in a Southern Town, 1784–1860* (1984) p. 72. Marylynn Salmon, 'The legal status of women in early America: a reappraisal', *Law and History Review* 1 (1983) pp. 149–50, and *Women and the Law of Property in Early America* (1986) ch. 1.

37 Lebsock, *Status and Culture*, p. 61.

38 Austin Dobson, *Fielding* (1883) p. 2.

39 *The History of the Law of England as to the Effects of Marriage on Property and on the Wife's Legal Capacity* (1879) p. 148.

40 Scot and Brograve's Case, referred to in *Chancery Cases* I, pp. 117–18.

41 *The Autobiography of William Stout of Lancaster, 1665–1752* (1967) pp. 125–6.

42 John Bodvell *v.* William Russell (1654) Caernarvon and Cambridgeshire, PRO: C5/19/12.

43 John & Edward Layfield *v.* Oliver & Richard Chatborne (1609) PRO: C2/Jas.I/L3/23. 'Country' here means county, as when John Chamberlain in 1602 described a Gloucestershire knight convicted of 'diverse foul matters and extortions committed in his country'. *The Chamberlain Letters: A Selection of the Letters of John Chamberlain Concerning Life in England from 1597 to 1626* (1966) p. 31.

44 *The History of Myddle* (1981) accord p. 125, desertions pp. 93, 123, 175, 191, 221, 227.

45 Keith Wrightson, *English Society 1580–1680* (1982) pp. 96–8.

46 Susan Dwyer Amussen, 'Gender, family and social order, 1560–1725', in A. J. Fletcher and J. Stevenson (eds) *Order and Disorder in Early Modern England* (1985) p. 209, fn.44. Ingram, *Church Courts*, pp. 171–2, 181–2.

47 Margaret Hunt, 'Wife-beating, domesticity and women's independence in eighteenth-century London', *Gender and History* 4:1 (1992).

48 Samuel Pyeatt Menefee, *Wives for Sale: An Ethnographic Study of British Popular Divorce* (1981) appendix of cases, pp. 211–59.
49 Mary Fissell, 'Women and families: thoughts on life-cycle and poverty in eighteenth-century England', paper presented to the Cambridge Group for Population Studies, March 1991. Pamela Sharpe, 'Marital separation in the eighteenth and early nineteenth centuries', *LPS* 45 (1990) pp. 66–70. See also Alice Clark, *Working Life of Women in the Seventeenth Century* (1992) pp. 80–9.
50 Cioni, 'Women and law in Elizabethan England', pp. 70–4. I have not personally come across reference to any female arbiters. For a previous attempt at arbitration see the pleas in Anthony Lunde *v.* John & Henry Lunde (1623) Yorkshire, PRO: C2/Jas.I/L2/51.
51 Ann Murden *v.* Richard Weye (1615) PRO: C2/Jas.I/M8/27.
52 Nancy Henley, 'Power, sex and nonverbal communication', Marjorie Swacker, 'The sex of the speaker as a sociolinguistic variable', and Don Zimmerman and Candace West, 'Sex roles, interruptions and silences in conversation', all in B. Thorne and N. Henley (eds) *Language and Sex: Difference and Dominance* (1975). Dale Spender, *Man Made Language* (1980) pp. 41–50, and *Invisible Women: The Schooling Scandal* (1982) p. 58.

8 MARRIAGE SETTLEMENTS IN PROBATE DOCUMENTS

1 Thomas Gaunt, £133/68 (1624) Lincoln, LAO: Ad Ac 19/47 and LCC will 1621/i/144.
2 *The Farming and Memorandum Books of Henry Best of Elmswell, 1642* (1984) pp. 122–3. On Essex yeomen's wives' jointure and dower see F. G. Emmison, *Elizabethan Life* (1976) p. 101.
3 *The History of Myddle* (1981) pp. 87, 169.
4 Edward Duke or Ducke, £52/–5 (1631) Warminghurst, WSRO: EpI/33/1631 and STCI/18/56b.
5 See reported cases in Chancery of 1618, 1620 and 1657, where agreements between wife and husband entered into before marriage remained valid in common law if she survived coverture. W. S. Holdsworth, *A History of English Law* V (1924) p. 311.
6 In a sample of 100 Lincolnshire accounts, 12 per cent mentioned a marriage settlement in 1624 and 6 per cent in 1671–86; in all 105 surviving Northamptonshire accounts, 1669–85, 11 per cent mentioned a marriage settlement. In three counties in Massachusetts in the 1760s, slightly more than 10 per cent of married men's wills alluded to pre-nuptial agreements, but these appear to refer to older widowers requiring their younger brides to relinquish all claims to the estate in return for a cash settlement, and so are not comparable to the settlements at issue here. Gloria Main, 'Widows in rural Massachusetts on the eve of the revolution', in R. Hoffman and P. J. Albert (eds) *Women in the Age of the American Revolution* (1989) pp. 74, 80.
7 The range was £13 to £640, in thirty-two cases where the data were quantifiable. Information on any husband of the woman in question is included, and one man who was a brother, where that was the only estate value available.
8 John Tapp, £588/–88 (1683) Higham Ferrers, NRO: Acct 23.
9 William Bankes, £222/104 (1672) Arthingworth, NRO: Acct 104.
10 John Stone, £196/113 (1618) Nuthurst, WSRO: EpI/33/1618.
11 George Kay, £18/12 (1624) Stixwould, LAO: Ad Ac 19/115.
12 Robert Dawson, £13/7 (1624) Stainfield, LAO: Ad Ac 19/128.
13 Alice Doughty, £41/36 (1611) East Halton, LAO: Ad Ac 10/55. For other examples of women who during widowhood augmented their children's portions see Alice Seagrave, £24/21 (1619) Helpringham, LAO: LCC Admon 1618/184 and Ad Ac 15/71; and Suzanne Barne, £74/9 (1611) Hannah, LAO: Ad Ac 10/149 and Inv 110/241.
14 Farrar, £42/28, Tydd St Giles, CUL: EDR/A12/1/1616/16.
15 William Trusse, £56/42 (1624) Walcot nr. Billinghay, LAO: Ad Ac 19/16. Trusse–Boyne obligation (1625) LAO: LCC Admon 1625/278.
16 Medley, £25/17 (1682) Belton, LAO: Ad Ac 44/16 and Inv 183/366.
17 Such fictive leases – for extremely long terms, at peppercorn rents – were originally employed to avoid the undesirable feudal incidents of outright ownership, but they were not uncommon even at the end of the seventeenth century. In a later example, one north

Yorkshire yeoman in 1689 gave to his wife his part of a farm and a broad field 'duering the terme of tow thousand yeares yett all of them which is un expired'. BIHR: Henry Ness, Deanery Peculiar. Such fictive leases were 'tantamount to purchase'. Mildred Campbell, *The English Yeoman under Elizabeth and the Early Stuarts* (1942) p. 79.

18 Mary Juppe *als* Mersh, £200/–47 (1674) Steyning, WSRO: EpI/33/ 1673 and EpI/29/ 183/100. Richard Juppe (1685) WSRO: EpI/29/168/113.

19 Margaret Taylor *als* Edmonds, £528/518 (1635) Midhurst, WSRO: EpI/33/1635 and EpI/ 29/138/027.

20 Margaret Jewer *ux* John Sumner, Easebourne, WSRO: EpI/29/75/35.

21 BIHR: Thomas Hall (1649) Malton, Rydall.

22 Alice Coolinge *als* Paternoster, £133/70 (1611) Whaplode, LAO: Ad Ac 10/35.

23 H. C. F. Lansberry, 'Free bench see-saw: Sevenoaks widows in the late seventeenth century', *Archaeologia Cantiana* 100 (1984) p. 289.

24 Suzanne Paule *als* Barne, £74/9 (1611) Hannah, LAO: Ad Ac 10/149 and Inv 110/241. Richard Barne (1610) LAO: LCC Will 1610/14.

25 Richard Cooke, £165/–1 (1677) Chipping Warden, NRO: Acct 60.

26 George Lambe, £45/35 (1617) Little Shelford, CUL: EDR/A12/1/1617/1.

27 Henry Boulton, £1094/861 (1632) Bardney, LAO: Ad Ac 44/64 and LCC Admon 1632/15. Anne Boulton, LAO: LCC Will 1638/235.

28 On the rarity of annuities see also Susan Wright, 'Family life and society in sixteenth and early seventeenth-century Salisbury' (Leicester PhD thesis, 1982) p. 103. On the equivalence of portion and widowhood provision see also Margaret Spufford, *Contrasting Communities: English Villagers in the Sixteenth and Seventeenth Centuries* (1974) p. 112.

29 Peter Bowden, 'Agricultural prices, wages, farm profits and rents', in *AHEW* V:ii (1985) Appendix E, Table 28, pp. 877–8. Sheila Hopkins and Henry Phelps Brown, 'Seven centuries of building wages', in H. P. Brown and S. Hopkins, *A Perspective of Wages and Prices* (1981) pp. 4–5.

30 Susan Dwyer Amussen, *An Ordered Society: Gender and Class in Early Modern England* (1988) p. 69. On women's prominence in dairying and clothmaking see Alice Clark, *Working Life of Women in the Seventeenth Century* (1992) pp. 53–4, and David Underdown, 'The taming of the scold: the enforcement of patriarchal authority in early modern England', in A. Fletcher and D. Stevenson (eds) *Order and Disorder in Early Modern England* (1985) p. 135.

31 The few surviving scratch copies of accounts, made by the accountant, give far more detail than the 'fair writing' or official copies. See for example Grace Roise (n.d.) Wisbech, CUL: EDR A12/2/misc/9.

32 While L. A. Clarkson discusses glovemaking in Northamptonshire in some detail, he nowhere suggests who did the work. *The Pre-Industrial Economy in England 1500–1750* (1971) especially p. 101. Women were involved in both glovemaking and shoemaking in the city of Oxford. Mary Prior, 'Women and the urban economy: Oxford 1500–1800', in M. Prior (ed.) *Women in English Society 1500–1800* (1985) pp. 106–7.

33 *A Treatise of Testaments and Last Wills* (1590) p. 29v.

34 Dorothy Whitelock (ed.) *Anglo-Saxon Wills* (1930).

35 Beatrice Wallis Chapman and Mary Wallis Chapman, *The Status of Women Under the English Law* (1909) p. 16. Ann Kettle, '"My wife shall have it": marriage and property in the wills and testaments of later mediaeval England', in R. B. Outhwaite (ed.) *Marriage and Property* (1981) p. 94. Kay Lacey, 'Women and work in fourteenth and fifteenth-century London', in L. Charles and L. Duffin (eds) *Women and Work in Pre-Industrial England* (1985) p. 31. Michael Sheehan, 'The influence of canon law on the property rights of married women in England', *Mediaeval Studies* 25 (1963) pp. 118–21.

36 Mary Bateson (ed.) *Borough Customs* II (1906) pp. civ–cv. See also Courtney Kenny, *The History of the Law of England as to the Effects of Marriage on Property and on the Wife's Legal Capacity* (1879) p. 144.

37 *Selby Wills* (1911) pp. 137–8.

38 Patricia Cullum, '"And hir name was charite": women and charity in medieval Yorkshire', in P. J. P. Goldberg (ed.) *Woman is a Worthy Wight: Women in Medieval English Society 1200–1500* (1992).

39 Jacques Beauroy, 'Family patterns and relations of Bishop's Lynn willmakers in the

fourteenth century', in L. Bonfield, R. M. Smith and K. Wrightson (eds) *The World We Have Gained* (1986) pp. 15–16, 25–6. Sheehan, 'Influence of canon law', p. 122.

40 Mary Prior, 'Wives and wills 1558–1700', in J. Chartres and D. Hey (eds) *English Rural Society, 1500–1800* (1990) p. 208.

41 John Ray, *A Collection of English Proverbs*, 2nd edn (1678) p. 63. This proverb appeared in subsequent editions, but not in the first edition of 1670. My thanks to Mary Fissell for this reference.

42 Great Wilbraham, CUL: EPR Consistory Court Original Will, Ballard, 1603. My thanks to Chris Marsh for this reference. Anne Coates, Shipley, WSRO: STCI/32/28.

43 Wisbech, CUL: EPR Consistory Court Original Will, Cayster 1570. I am again grateful to Chris Marsh for this reference.

44 For example, BIHR: John Robinson, gent. (1644) Beverley, Harthill, and John Titlow, tanner, *Selby Wills*, p. 171.

45 The inscription, in the floor of the south transept, reads '*Fran Leek* prebend de Woodbrow sepultus 17 die Decemb 1670 inter Mariam Flower viduam priorem uxorem ad sinistram et *Margareta Leek* secundam ad dextram. *Resurgemus*'. A similar case from 1373 in Lincolnshire is mentioned in Kettle, 'Marriage and property', p. 96.

46 See her article 'Wives and wills'. I am extremely indebted to her for graciously sharing this painstakingly acquired list.

47 Prior, 'Wives and wills', pp. 213–17.

48 Edward Righton, £178/42 (1624) Potter Hanworth, LAO: Ad Ac 19/117.

49 Michael Hall, £32/0 (1605) Littleport, CUL: EDR A12/1/1604/10.

50 Thomas Dalby, £26/11 (1624) Appleby, LAO: Ad Ac 19/125 and LCC Admon 1624/44.

51 William Smith (1682) Haxey, LAO: Inv 183/313. Ann Smith, £66/10 (1685) LAO: Ad Ac 44/159 and Inv 183/310 and Stow Will 1681–3/148 (*n.b.* Ann's inventory gives an incorrect parish).

52 Welcome Dethe (1674) Spalding, LAO: Ad Ac 34/111. Elizabeth Dethe (1681) LAO: LCC Admon 1680/47.

53 Robert Bettison, £151/101 (1681) Glentham, LAO: Ad Ac 42/84 and Inv/DI/37/2/B/72.

54 Sarah Foxe, £40/25 (1606) Burgh-le-marsh, LAO: Ad Ac 7/26 and LCC Admon 1606/59. William Foxe, LAO: LCC Admon 1603/49.

55 *Selby Wills*, p. 50. For another such case see Keith Wrightson and David Levine, *Poverty and Piety in an English Village: Terling 1525–1700* (1979) p. 39. See also David Vaisey, 'Probate inventories and provincial retailers in the seventeenth century', in P. Riden (ed.) *Probate Records and the Local Community* (1985) p. 101, and Margaret Spufford, 'The misleading nature of the probate inventory', in J. Chartres and D. Hey (eds) *English Rural Society 1500–1800* (1990).

56 Thomas Gilson, £27/–72 (n.d.) Little Abington, CUL: EDR A12/2/misc/23. Other examples of such debts include John Herbert, £149/–56 (1677) Northampton, NRO: Acct 70, and Amy Frampton, £74/49 (1665) Wimborne Minster, DRO: PE/WM:CP2/4/70.

57 Quoted in Lu Emily Pearson, *Elizabethans at Home* (1957) p. 371.

58 Robert Scambler, £165/–15 (1671) NRO: Acct 93. See also Clark, *Working Life*, pp. 51–2.

59 Thomas Williams, £65/–5 Middleton Cheney, NRO: Acct 56.

60 Bridget Hill, *Women, Work and Sexual Politics in Eighteenth-Century England* (1989) p. 211. John Gillis, 'Conjugal settlements: resort to clandestine and common law marriage in England and Wales 1650–1850', in J. Bossy (ed.) *Disputes and Settlements* (1983) pp. 278–9, citing Katherine O'Donovan, 'The male appendage – legal definitions of women', in S. Burman (ed.) *Fit Work for Women* (1979) p. 131. Katherine O'Donovan, *Sexual Divisions in Law* (1985) p. 47, citing Ivy Pinchbeck, *Women Workers and the Industrial Revolution 1750–1850* (1981 edn) p. 285.

61 R. Chambers, *Book of Days: A Miscellany of Popular Antiquities* vol. 1 (London and Edinburgh, W. R. Chambers, 1863) p. 259. *Notes and Queries* 1st ser. 6 (1852) p. 561 and 13th ser. 152:I (1927) p. 169.

62 Antonia Fraser, *The Weaker Vessel: Woman's Lot in Seventeenth-Century England* (1984) p. 15.

63 Eric Carlson, *Marriage and the English Reformation* (1994), ch. 4. Martin Ingram, *Church Courts, Sex and Marriage in England 1570–1640* (1987) pp. 216–18. The figures for the

earlier period may be affected by registration, since the only reason they were noted by the parish clerk in the 1690s was for tax reasons, thanks to the Marriage Duty Act of 1695. E. A. Wrigley, 'Clandestine marriage in Tetbury in the late seventeenth century', *LPS* 10 (1973) pp. 15–21.

64 Roger Lee Brown, 'Clandestine marriages in London, especially within the Fleet Prison, and their effects on Hardwicke's Act, 1753' (London MA thesis, 1972) pp. 29, 164, 170, 178.

65 Christopher Rose, Brothertoft, LAO: LCC Will 1606/68. Agnes Rose, £29/16 (1606) LAO: Ad Ac 7/11 and LCC Will 1606/9.

66 Laurel Thatcher Ulrich, *Good Wives: Image and Reality in the Lives of Women in Northern New England 1650–1750* (1982) p. 24.

67 Thomas Goodriche, Downham (Manor), CUL: EPR Consist. Ct. Will 1583, but filed with EDR A12.

68 Suzanne Lebsock, *The Free Women of Petersburg: Status and Culture in a Southern Town, 1784–1860* (1984) p. 61.

69 *Hardships of the English Laws* (1735) p. 33.

70 *A Woman of No Character: an Autobiography of Mrs Manley* (1986) pp. 122–3.

71 Reprinted in *Certain Ancient Tracts Concerning the Management of Landed Property* (1767) pp. 88–92, and also quoted at length in Clark, *Working Life*, pp. 46–9.

72 Abraham & Susanna Bonnett *v.* James Connill (1695) PRO: C5/116/8.

73 *Lawes Resolutions* (1632) p. 116.

PART IV WIDOWS

1 Act I, scene x.

2 'Elizabethan widows', *Stanford Studies in Language and Literature* (1941) pp. 140–2.

3 'The widow's tale: male myths and female reality in sixteenth and seventeenth-century England', *Albion* 10:2 (1978) pp. 124–9.

4 'The humble petition of Anne Henshaw, widow, late wife and executrix of Benjamin Henshaw, esquire, on the behalf of her self and her seven children' (1654).

5 Cripps *v.* Bridget Clutterbucke *et al.*, PRO: C5/385/42.

6 For the same phenomenon in medieval manorial courts, where the plaintiffs' wealth is ascertainable, see Judith Bennett, *Women in the Medieval Countryside: Gender and Household in Brigstock Before the Plague* (1987) p. 152.

7 For example Doris Stenton, *The English Woman in History* (1957) p. 101.

8 Lawrence and Jeanne Fawtier Stone, *An Open Elite? England 1540–1880* (1984) p. 94.

9 Keith Wrightson and David Levine, *Poverty and Piety in an English Village: Terling 1525–1700* (1979) p. 58. E. A. Wrigley and Roger Schofield, *The Population History of England, 1541–1871: A Reconstruction* (1981) p. 250. On maternal mortality, see Roger Schofield, 'Did the mothers really die? Three centuries of maternal mortality in "the world we have lost"', in L. Bonfield, R. M. Smith and K. Wrightson (eds) *The World We Have Gained* (1986) pp. 259–60.

10 J. Dupaquier *et al.* (eds) *Marriage and Remarriage in Populations of the Past* (1981). Alan Macfarlane, *Marriage and Love in England 1300–1840* (1986) p. 235, on the parish of Earls Colne. Susan Wright, 'Family life and society in sixteenth and seventeenth-century Salisbury' (Leicester PhD, 1982) pp. 233–6.

11 Peter Laslett, *Family Life and Illicit Love in Earlier Generations* (1977) Table 5.9, p. 198. See also Gregory King, 'Observations . . . upon the state and condition of England, 1696', in P. Laslett (ed.) *The Earliest Classics* (1973) p. 39.

9 WIDOWS OF MEN WHO MADE WILLS

1 For an excellent summary, but one that perpetuates the assumption of a male executor, see Michael Sheehan, *The Will in Medieval England: from the Conversion of the Anglo-Saxons to the End of the Thirteenth Century* (1963) pp. 214–19.

2 Uting, Blyborough, LAO: Stow Will 1684–6/31.

3 John Sowton (son), £524/275 (1636) South Stoke, WSRO: EpI/33/1635. John Sowton (father) (1627) WSRO: STCI/17/77b.

4 Charles Johnson, £27/15 (1670) Lenton, LAO: Ad Ac 33/201 and LCC Will 1670/ii/695.

5 *Lawes Resolutions*, pp. 233, 242, quoting *De Republica*, p. 104. The *Lawes Resolutions* is unusual in referring to women with the masculine form of executor.

6 See the graphs of will survival in Motoyasu Takahashi, 'The number of wills proved in the sixteenth and seventeenth centuries', in G. Martin and P. Spufford (eds) *The Records of the Nation* (1990). For further evidence of medieval joint executorship, which was unquantified and therefore could not be included in Table 9.1, see Jacques Beauroy, 'Family patterns and relations of Bishop's Lynn will-makers in the fourteenth century', in L. Bonfield, R. M. Smith and K. Wrightson (eds) *The World We Have Gained* (1986) p. 38.

7 Suzanne Lebsock, *The Free Women of Petersburg: Status and Culture in a Southern Town, 1784–1860* (1984) pp. 36–8.

8 Susan Dwyer Amussen, *An Ordered Society: Gender and Class in Early Modern England* (1988) p. 84. Keith Wrightson, *English Society 1580–1680* (1982) p. 94. See also Diane Owen Hughes, 'Domestic ideals and social behaviour: evidence from medieval Genoa', in C. E. Rosenberg (ed.) *The Family in History* (1975) p. 126. The only study that finds rich men more likely than poor men to appoint their wives executrix is Gloria Main's 'Widows in rural Massachusetts on the eve of the revolution', in R. Hoffman and P. J. Albert (eds) *Women in the Age of the American Revolution* (1989) pp. 77–8.

9 These phrases, along with references to 'trusty and well-beloved friends' (as overseers) appear as early as the fifteenth-century *Paston Letters* (1983) p. 23, for example.

10 Alice Clark, *Working Life of Women in the Seventeenth Century* (1992) p. 39. Richard Vann, 'Wills and the family in an English town: Banbury 1550–1800', *JFH* 4:3 (1979) p. 366.

11 Lois Green Carr and Lorena Walsh, 'The planter's wife: the experience of white women in seventeenth-century Maryland', *WMQ* 3rd ser. 34 (1977) p. 556. David Narrett, 'Men's wills and women's property rights in colonial New York', in R. Hoffman and P. J. Albert (eds) *Women in the Age of the American Revolution* (1989) pp. 117–19. Laurel Thatcher Ulrich, *Good Wives: Image and Reality in the Lives of Women in Northern New England 1650–1750* (1982) p. 38, fn. 6. The only study of eighteenth-century English wills is Maxine Berg's 'Women's property and the industrial revolution', *Journal of Interdisclipinary History* 24:2 (1993) pp. 233–50.

12 Susan Wright, 'Family life and society in sixteenth and early seventeenth-century Salisbury' (Leicester PhD thesis, 1982) p. 250.

13 Lionel Munby (ed.) *Life and Death in King's Langley: Wills and Inventories, 1498–1659* (1981) p. xv.

14 'Wills and the family', pp. 364–6.

15 Joan Irelande, East Wittering, WSRO: STCI/18/350b. Richard Irelande, WSRO: STCI/18/336.

16 Ralph Houlbrooke thought that in sixteenth-century Norwich and Winchester parish priests were 'commonly' named as overseers. *Church Courts and the People During the English Reformation, 1520–70* (1979) pp. 101–2. It is possible that this is correct for the sixteenth century, or for these two areas, but as he was studying church court records it is also possible that wills in which the priest was overseer were more likely to end up in litigation. On the differing early modern uses of the word 'friend' see Naomi Tadmor,'"Family" and "friend" in Pamela: a case study in the history of the family in eighteenth-century England', *Social History* 14:3 (1989) pp. 290–306.

17 Henry Smyth, Bury, WSRO: STCI/14/349. Agnes Smyth, £54/45 (1594) WSRO: EpI/33/235.

18 BIHR: George Conyers (1684) Pickering, Deanery Peculiar.

19 Munby (ed.) *King's Langley*, p. xix. Vivien Brodsky, 'Widows in late Elizabethan London: remarriage, economic opportunity and family orientations', in L. Bonfield, R. M. Smith and K. Wrightson (eds) *The World We Have Gained* (1986) p. 145. Nesta Evans, 'Inheritance, women, religion and education in early modern society as revealed by wills', in P. Riden (ed.) *Probate Records and the Local Community* (1985) p. 67. But see references to eighteenth-century America, below.

20 Thomas Bartholomew, £88/38 (1678) Ford, WSRO: EpI/33/1678 and STCI/26/142. Richard Challen, £45/0 (1671) Cocking, WSRO: EpI/33/1671 and STCI/24/110b. See also Ann Kettle, '"My wife shall have it": marriage and property in the wills and testaments of later medieval England', in R. B. Outhwaite (ed.) *Marriage and Society* (1981) p. 97, and Munby (ed.) *King's Langley*, p. xix.

21   F. G. Emmison, *Elizabethan Life* (1976) p. 102.
22   Richard Wheatley, £182/132 (1678) Sidlesham, WSRO: EpI/33/1678 and STCI/26/138b.
23   William Wooles, £149 (1629) Barnham, WSRO: EpI/29/13/10 and STCI/17/235. Alice Wooles, £84/1 (1633) WSRO: EpI/33/1633 and EpI/29/13/15.
24   *Selby Wills* (1911) pp. 31–2.
25   BIHR: Thomas Kirkupp (1650) Snainton, Rydall.
26   For annual maintenance of an adult see Amy Erickson, 'Maternal management and the cost of raising children in early modern England', in R. Wall and O. Saito (eds) *Social and Economic Aspects of the Family Life Cycle* (forthcoming).
27   BIHR: Thomas Ellyott (1645) Bracken, Harthill.
28   Henry Cockeram, *The English Dictionarie* (1968, 1st edn 1623).
29   Keith Wrightson, 'Kinship in an English village: Terling, Essex 1550–1700', in R. M. Smith (ed.) *Land, Kinship and Life-Cycle* (1984) p. 327. Margaret Spufford, *Contrasting Communities: English Villagers in the Sixteenth and Seventeenth Centuries* (1974) pp. 88–9, and 162, on Chippenham and Willingham. Orwell can hardly be taken as representative of English practice, as it has been by the Americanist Narrett, 'Colonial New York', p. 112.
30   Main, 'Rural Massachusetts', p. 85. Carole Shammas, 'Early American women and control over capital', in R. Hoffman and P. J. Albert (eds) *Women in the Age of the American Revolution* (1989) pp. 142–3. James Somerville, 'The Salem (Mass.) woman in the home, 1660–1770', *Eighteenth-Century Life* 1 (1974) pp. 12–13.
31   Carr and Walsh, 'Planter's wife', pp. 568, 571.
32   Somerville, 'Salem woman in the home', pp. 12–13.
33   Henry Swinburne, *A Treatise of Testaments and Last Wills* (1635 edn) pp. 299–301.
34   Wrightson, 'Kinship', p. 327. Ralph Houlbrooke maintains that 'many' sixteenth-century wills throughout England stipulated that a widow lost her benefits on her remarriage, but he was looking at wills involved in litigation, which suggests that widowhood limitations may often have been contested. *Church Courts*, pp. 106–7. Emmison, looking at uncontested Essex wills, also observes that 'many' men limited bequests to widowhood, but this is not quantified. *Elizabethan Life*, p. 100.
35   Munby (ed.) *King's Langley*, p. xx. Spufford, *Contrasting Communities*, p. 113. King's Langley, Cambridgeshire and Terling are not included in Table 9.4 for lack of specific calculations.
36   Lois Green Carr, 'Inheritance in the colonial Chesapeake', in R. Hoffman and P. J. Albert (eds) *Women in the Age of the American Revolution* (1989) pp. 172, 179. Shammas, 'Control over capital', p. 142.
37   'The remarrying widow: a stereotype reconsidered', in M. Prior (ed.) *Women in English Society 1500–1800* (1985) pp. 72–3.
38   Thomas Lidgiter, £358/59 (1682) Steyning, WSRO: EpI/33/1682 and STCI/27/263b.
39   Will of Mark Blythe, *Selby Wills*, p. 25.
40   Baston, LAO: LCC Will 1598/83. For a similar contingent restriction to widowhood, see the will of Thomas Adam, in Spufford, *Contrasting Communities*, p. 117.
41   Munby (ed.) *King's Langley*, pp. 135–6.
42   Selby cannot be included in the chronological comparison because too few wills survive prior to 1650.
43   Lawrence Stone and Jeanne Fawtier Stone, *An Open Elite? England 1540–1880* (1984) p. 82.
44   Spufford, *Contrasting Communities*, p. 162.
45   Roger Schofield and E. A. Wrigley, 'Infant and child mortality in England in the late Tudor and early Stuart period', in C. Webster (ed.) *Health, Medicine and Mortality in the Sixteenth Century* (1979).
46   BIHR: John Foster (1689) Pickering, Deanery Peculiar.
47   BIHR: Robert Brigham (1641) Holme on Spaldingmoor, Harthill.
48   Henry Horwitz, 'Testamentary practice, family strategies, and the last phases of the custom of London, 1660–1725', *Law and History Review* 2:2 (1984) pp. 223–39.
49   Kettle, 'Marriage and property', pp. 94, 98.
50   Carr, 'Colonial Chesapeake', p. 182. Richard Chused, 'Married women's property and inheritance by widows in Massachusetts: a study of wills probated between 1800 and 1850', *Berkeley Women's Law Journal* 2 (1986) pp. 42–88. Narrett, 'Colonial New York', pp. 110,

115, 119. Shammas, 'Control over capital', pp. 141–3.

51 Carr, 'Colonial Chesapeake', pp. 173, 177–8.
52 Catharine Milles, £117/36 (1619) Pulborough, WSRO: EpI/33/1619. John Milles, WSRO: S Dean Will 1615/51.
53 Yapton, WSRO: STCI/25/20b.
54 Will of Jarvis Rayner, *Selby Wills*, p. 131.
55 Constance Nowell, £42/30 (1609) South Stoke, WSRO: EpI/33/1609 and STCI/15/305b. Anthony Nowell, WSRO: STCI/12/91b. Smith quoted in David Cressy, 'Describing the social order of Elizabethan and Stuart England', *Literature and History* 3 (1976) p. 34.
56 *Luther's Works* XXXIV, transl. Lewis Spitz (1960) p. 295. I am indebted to Richard Wall for reference to this will.
57 Spitz comments patronizingly, 'Although the financial returns from this investment were small, Katie was fond of the estate and Luther delighted in calling her "Lady Zulsdorf".' Ibid. Richard Wall questions 'whether later protestants were always so generous to their wives'. 'The will of Martin Luther', *LPS* 35 (1985) p. 53.
58 Introduction to the will, *Luther's Works*, p. 291.
59 For details of Katherine von Bora Luther see Roland Bainton, *Women of the Reformation in Germany and Italy* (1971) pp. 33–4, 40–1.

10 WIDOWS OF MEN WHO DID NOT MAKE WILLS

1 Stated in 1529 (21 Hen. VIII c.5), although the practice was probably much older. From 1605 (3 Jas. I c.5 p. 10) a recusant woman was denied the right to administer for her husband, in addition to losing two thirds of her jointure and dower, but it is not clear how often either provision was enforced.
2 See for example, Robert Sabberton, £8/–8 (1617) Downham, CUL: EDR A12/1/1617/1, or Robert Hilton, £4/2 (1617) Elm, CUL: EDR A12/1/1617/33.
3 John Ward, West Grinstead, WSRO: EpI/33/1595.
4 John Archer, £209/46 (1624) LAO: Ad Ac 19/90.
5 Women were eligible to serve as Overseers of the Poor. Rose Graham, 'The civic position of women at common law before 1800', in R. Graham, *English Ecclesiastical Studies* (1929) pp. 373–5. None of the overseers in Aldenham, Hertfordshire, in the decade 1674–84 was female. W. Newman Brown, 'The receipt of poor relief and family situation: Aldenham, Hertfordshire 1630–90', in R. M. Smith (ed.) *Land, Kinship and Life-Cycle* (1984) pp. 421–2. Nine women overseers are listed in Alan Rodgers (ed.) *Narrowing the Field: A Study of Local Government in the Parish of Enborne, Bucks* (Reading University Dept of Extended Education booklet, 1990).
6 Thomas Dalby, £26/11 (1624) LAO: Ad Ac 19/125.
7 Chris Kettle, £167/57 (1608) Hatton, LAO: Ad Ac 8/147.
8 John Tapp, £588/–88 (1683) Higham Ferrers, NRO: Acct 23.
9 Thomas Lawrence, £50/–3 Toynton St Peter, LAO: Ad Ac 43/128. The debts were in Toynton All Saints, adjoining Toynton St Peter; Greetham, 8 miles northwest; Horncastle, 10 miles northwest; East Barkwith, 20 miles northwest; Tothill, 12 miles north; and Tattershall, 12 miles southwest (all distances approximate).
10 Thomas Roweth, £34/17 (1670) Swineshead, LAO: Ad Ac 33/178.
11 Richard Parkinson, £81/52, CUL: EDR A12/1/1604/15.
12 Anne Horton, £104/22 (1709) Publow, SRO: D/D/Ct/H93.
13 Robert Daulton, £29/7 (1680) Carlton le Moorland, LAO: Ad Ac 43/101. For a fine see Hester Wood, £117 (1685) Messingham, LAO: Ad Ac 44/139. The Act (30 Car.II s.1 c.3 (1678)) imposed a £5 fine, but this was clearly not imposed in Lincolnshire, as also in Prestwich, where a £2 10s. fine was recovered in 1681, after which date the offence was no longer prosecuted. John Harland and T. T. Wilkinson, *Lancashire Folk-Lore* (1867) pp. 269–70. The procedure to enforce compliance specified in the statute is ludicrously cumbersome.
14 Alice Cox, £33/–14 (1639) Chelwood, SRO: D/D/Ct/C16.
15 Cassander Bushey, £14/10 (1612) Mareham in the Fen, LAO: Ad Ac 11/86.
16 For example, Thomas Pickringe, labourer, £42/36 (1624) Aby, LAO: Ad Ac 19/25.

17   For example, Gloria Main, 'Widows in rural Massachusetts on the eve of the revolution', in R. Hoffman and P. J. Albert (eds) *Women in the Age of the American Revolution* (1989) p. 72.
18   I take as the dividing line the date when the Act appears in accounts, which in Lincolnshire is 1672, and in Northamptonshire 1673.
19   George Kay, £18/12 (1624) Stixwould, LAO: Ad Ac 19/115.
20   Robert Gudgin, £234/87 (1671) Daventry, NRO: Acct 88.
21   Upperton, Littlehampton, WSRO: EpI/33/1669, EpI/29/127/22 and STCI/23/327.
22   Henry Brice, £24/6 (1624) Theddlethorpe All Saints, LAO: Ad Ac 19/89. William Bawtree, £182/98 (1624) Leake, LAO: Ad Ac 19/78.
23   Vivien Brodsky, 'Widows in late Elizabethan London: remarriage, economic opportunity and family orientations', in L. Bonfield, R. M. Smith and K. Wrightson (eds) *The World We Have Gained* (1986) p. 146.
24   Clement Money, £20/3 (1624) Edenham, LAO: Ad Ac 19/104.
25   Thomas Cotton, £206/183 (n.d.) Northampton, NRO: Acct 86.
26   William Checkley, £244/35, Little Preston, NRO: Acct 105.
27   *The Autobiography of Mrs Alice Thornton, of East Newton, Co. York* (1873) pp. 248–9.
28   Burn, *Ecclesiastical Law*, pp. 649–51.
29   Alexander Crow, £19/2 (1618) Elm, CUL: EDR A12/1/1618/4.
30   George Bartrum, £149/142, Pickworth, LAO: Ad Ac 44/118. William Tysedale, £59/11 (1683) Tydd St Mary, LAO: Ad Ac 44/85.

11 HOW LONE WOMEN LIVED

1   Armeston, £17/–3 (1632) Lessingham, LAO: Ad Ac 23/4 and Inv 23/48.
2   Gladwyne, £11/4 (1612) Swineshead, LAO: Ad Ac 10/164 and LCC Admon 1611/88.
3   Jordane, £9/–4 (1621) East Chinnock, SRO: D/D/Ct/J22.
4   Peter Laslett, *Family Life and Illicit Love in Earlier Generations* (1977) p. 198.
5   Wright, £44/25 (1619) LAO: Ad Ac 14/130 and LCC Admon 1616/413.
6   Wenwright, £33/29 (1629) Storrington, WSRO: EpI/33/1629 and EpI/29/188/020.
7   Bury, £93/7 (1680) Linwood Grange, Blankney, LAO: Ad Ac 34/44 and LCC Admon 1678/6.
8   Perrin *als* Saunders, £56/26 (1635) Upmarden, WSRO: EpI/33/1635, EpI/29/135/009 and STCI/18/333.
9   BIHR: John Coltas (1683) Pickering, Deanery Peculiar.
10   BIHR: William Barrye (1680) Pickering, Deanery Peculiar.
11   Will of Ambrose Constable, *Selby Wills* (1911) pp. 49–50.
12   *The Autobiography of William Stout of Lancaster, 1665–1752* (1967) pp. 175, 157.
13   Will of Richard Reame, *Selby Wills*, p. 132.
14   Richard Barne (1610) Hannah, LAO: LCC Will 1610/14. Suzanne Paule *als* Barne, £74/9 (1611) LRO: Ad Ac 10/149.
15   Richard Aylwin (1615) Duncton, WSRO: M Dean 1615/26.
16   Drenckwater (1597) Brothertoft, LAO: LCC Will 1597/61.
17   Francis Halford, £160/62 (1670s) Clipston, NRO: Acct 114.
18   Stephen Mace, £838/562 (1680) Wellingborough, NRO: Acct 17.
19   John Bithery, £155/50 (1672) Irthlingborough, NRO: Acct 107.
20   George Holland, £42/36 (1624) Helpringham, LAO: Ad Ac 19/118.
21   Barbara Barber, £21/1 (1632) DRO: PE/WM:CP2/4/48.
22   'Diary of Joyce Jeffries of Hereford, 1638–48', BL: Egerton MS 3054.
23   'Women without men: widows and spinsters in Britain and France in the eighteenth century', *JFH* 9:4 (1984) p. 361.
24   BIHR: Elizabeth Ripley (1682) Pickering, Deanery Peculiar.
25   BIHR: Elizabeth Grainge (1646) Rosedale, Rydall.
26   Belfield (1632) Belton, LRO: Ad Ac 23/165 and LCC Admon 1632/13. Her own birth does not appear in the parish register but her brother and married sisters were aged between 30 and 45.
27   HRO: Acct of Margaret Hyde, £15/8 (1664) Romsey.
28   BIHR: Isabel Beilebie (1681) Hayton, Deanery Peculiar. The parish registers for Hayton are

patchy and Isabel's own birth does not appear, but three of five male Beilebies are described as labourers and two of four children born are bastards.

29　Geden Longe (1578) Spalding, LRO: Inv 62/66. Her will does not survive, but her inventory is unusual in listing bequests.

30　Lison or Licen, £22 (1681) Ashby cum Fenby, LAO: Inv 182/237 and LCC will 1681/i/217. Thomas Lyson, £33/17 (1680) LAO: Ad Ac /54.

31　Protosia Lockton, £65/3 (1624) Brothertoft, LAO: Ad Ac 19/46 and LCC Admon 1623/156. John Lockton, £70 (1623) LAO: Inv 127/369.

32　Magdalen Plumtree, £12/8 (1606) Fotherby, LAO: Ad Ac 7/146, and LCC Admon 1606/131. Steven Plumtree, LAO: Inv 100/26. These inventories, among many others, show J. A. Johnston was wrong in thinking the niceties of handtowels, napkins and tablecloths were new to the lower orders in 1699. 'The probate inventories and wills of a Worcestershire parish 1676–1775', *Midland History* 1:1 (1971–2) p. 25. One labourer even had 'quishens'. LAO: Inv 111/140.

　　Magdalen Plumtree's spinning wheel, at 1s., is cheap enough not to be itemized in most cases, and wheels may occur more often in women's than in men's inventories, which casts doubt on the attempt to map textile industry by assessing spinning wheels in inventories, most of which are men's. Carole Shammas, *The Pre-Industrial Consumer in England and America* (1990) pp. 31, 36.

33　Mary Forman, £70/–19 (1677) West Chiltington, WSRO: EpI/33/1676 and EpI/29/48/77. John Forman, £94 (1652) WSRO: EpI/29/48/52 and STCI/21/476b.

34　Elizabeth Kewell, £463/360 (1672) Rustington, WSRO: EpI/33/1672, EpI/29/164/44 and STCI/25/52b. John Kewell, £366 (1660) WSRO: EpI/29/164/34 and STCI/22b/10.

35　Most extensively by B. A. Holderness, 'Credit in a rural community, 1660–1800: some neglected aspects of probate inventories', *Midland History* 3:2 (1975) pp. 100–2, 'Credit in a rural society before the nineteenth century, with special reference to the period 1650–1720', *AgHR* 24:2 (1976) pp. 101–2, and 'Widows in pre-industrial society: an essay upon their economic functions', in R. M. Smith (ed.) *Land, Kinship and Life-Cycle* (1984).

36　Peter Laslett, 'Mean household size in England since the sixteenth century', in P. Laslett and R. Wall (eds) *Household and Family in Past Time* (1972) p. 147. Richard Wall, 'Woman alone in English society', *Annales de Demographie Historique* (1981) pp. 303–17. See also Susan Wright, 'Family life and society in sixteenth and early seventeenth-century Salisbury' (Leicester PhD thesis, 1982) p. 235. This proportion of female-headed households is comparable with that in other places in early modern Europe: John Day, 'On the status of women in medieval Sardinia', in J. Kirshner and S. F. Wemple (eds) *Women of the Medieval World* (1983) p. 312; Barbara Diefendorf, 'Widowhood and remarriage in sixteenth-century Paris', *JFH* 7:4 (1982) pp. 380–1; Maura Palazzi, 'Female solitude and patrilineage: unmarried women and widows during the eighteenth and nineteenth centuries', *JFH* 15:4 (1990) pp. 453–4.

37　Stout, *Autobiography*, p. 87.

38　J. Z. Titow, 'Some differences between manors and their effects on the condition of the peasant in the thirteenth century', *AgHR* 10 (1962) p. 7. Holderness, 'Widows in pre-industrial society', p. 428, or, for more, 'Credit in a rural community', p. 101. See also M. M. Postan's 'marriage fugue', in which a widow's function is to pass property from an old man to a young man. *Medieval Economy and Society* (1972) pp. 33, 146.

39　For the stereotype see Charles Carlton, 'The widow's tale: male myths and female reality in sixteenth and seventeenth-century England', *Albion* 10:2 (1978) p. 123.

40　Suzanne Lebsock, *The Free Women of Petersburg: Status and Culture in a Southern Town, 1784–1860* (1984) pp. 26–7. Joel Rosenthal, 'Aristocratic widows in fifteenth-century England', in B. J. Harris and J. K. McNamara (eds) *Women and the Structure of Society* (1984) p. 40. Barbara Todd, 'Widowhood in a market town: Abingdon 1540–1720' (Oxford PhD thesis, 1983) p. 189. Wright, 'Family life', pp. 243, 250.

41　The phrase is Doris Stenton's, in *The English Woman in History* (1957) p. 68.

42　Richard Gough, *The History of Myddle* (1981) pp. 91–2.

43　Vivien Brodsky, 'Widows in late Elizabethan London: remarriage, economic opportunity and family orientations', in L. Bonfield, R. M. Smith and K. Wrightson (eds) *The World We Have Gained* (1986) p. 123.

44 Margaret Spufford, *Contrasting Communities: English Villagers in the Sixteenth and Seventeenth Centuries* (1974) pp. 116–17, 162. Wright, 'Family life', p. 263.

45 Barbara Todd, 'Freebench and free enterprise: widows and their property in two Berkshire villages', in J. Chartres and D. Hey (eds) *English Rural Society 1500–1800* (1990) pp. 178–80. While the Court of Chancery refused to uphold a freebench limitation to chastity or remarriage by the late sixteenth century, if it was challenged (according to Maria Lynn Cioni, 'The Elizabethan Chancery and women's rights', in D. J. Guth and J. W. McKenna (eds) *Tudor Rule and Revolution* (1982) p. 169), such a limitation was probably still enforceable on a local level against freebench holders unable to bring a suit in Chancery.

46 Todd, 'Freebench and free enterprise'.

47 Roger Schofield and E. A. Wrigley, 'Remarriage intervals and the effect of marriage order on fertility', in J. Dupaquier *et al.* (eds) *Marriage and Remarriage in Populations of the Past* (1981) pp. 218–19.

48 For some of the intricacies see Peter Franklin, 'Peasant widows' "liberation" and remarriage before the black death', *EcHR* 39:2 (1986) pp. 186–204, and Todd, 'Widowhood', p. 189.

49 Cambridgeshire, 17 per cent (5 of 29); Lincolnshire, 15 per cent (19 of 124); Sussex, 19 per cent (21 of 108). Northamptonshire has very few surviving accounts of women's estates.

50 Cambridgeshire, 14 per cent (21 of 146); Northamptonshire, 14 per cent (16 of 118); Lincolnshire, 14 per cent (27 of 199). These percentages are minimums, since remarriage was not always specified. In Sussex only 5 per cent of widows (3 of 55) had clearly remarried within a year, but in the light of the high remarriage figures among women whose own estates were probated (see previous note), this is probably a deficiency of recording practice rather than a low rate of remarriage.

51 Ralph Houlbrooke, *The English Family 1450–1700* (1984) pp. 215, 217. Alan Macfarlane, *Marriage and Love in England 1300–1840* (1986) p. 233.

52 *Advice to a Son*, quoted in Todd, 'Widowhood', p. 154, fn. See also Lu Emily Pearson, 'Elizabethan widows', *Stanford Studies in Language and Literature* (1941) pp. 124–42. For a truly spectacular individual case of paranoia over the remarriage of widows, see Richard Trexler, 'In search of father: the experience of abandonment in the recollections of Giovanni di Pagolo Morelli', *History of Childhood Quarterly* 2 (1975) pp. 225–51.

53 Houlbrooke, in *English Family*, p. 217, suggests children were rare in stepfamilies, but this seems unlikely.

54 Equal Opportunities Commission, *Women and Men in Britain: a Research Profile* (1988) p. 5, Table 1.7 (percentage calculations my own).

55 The phrase is Susan Wright's, in 'Family life', p. 280. She too thinks tensions in the hybrid household were probably no greater than in an 'unbroken' home.

56 Barbara Todd, 'The remarrying widow: a stereotype reconsidered', in M. Prior (ed.) *Women in English Society 1500–1800* (1985) p. 60. Wright, 'Family life', p. 232. Jeremy Boulton, 'London widowhood revisited: the decline of female remarriage in the seventeenth and early eighteenth centuries', *C&C* 5:3 (1990) p. 327. The calculations of E. A. Wrigley and Roger Schofield, in *The Population History of England 1541–1871: A Reconstruction* (1981) pp. 258–9, that in the sixteenth century as much as 30 per cent of all marriages were remarriages, but by the first half of the eighteenth century only 20 per cent were so, do not differentiate by sex and are based on two parish registers from Cambridgeshire and Suffolk. See Boulton, 'London widowhood', pp. 324–5.

57 Boulton, 'London widowhood', pp. 341–3.

58 'Remarrying widow', p. 74.

59 David Levine and Keith Wrightson, *The Making of an Industrial Society: Whickham 1560–1765* (1991) p. 355. Todd, 'Widowhood', pp. 5, 228–9. John Webb (ed.) *Poor Relief in Elizabethan Ipswich* (1966) *passim*. Tim Wales, 'Poverty, poor relief and the life-cycle: some evidence from seventeenth-century Norfolk', in R. M. Smith (ed.) *Land, Kinship and Life-Cycle* (1984) pp. 378, 387. The only parish I know of in which more than half of the poor were men was Eccleshall, Staffordshire, in 1697–8 (my thanks to Margaret Spufford for sharing her unpublished research on Eccleshall).

60 Rosemary Bray, 'A special victory', *Ms Magazine* (April 1986) p. 48. This figure refers to the United States. British government figures on low income identify poverty with the receipt of supplemental benefit/income support. Nearly three times as many women as men are in

receipt of pensions, but this still underestimates their proportion among the poor, since family pensions are claimed in the husband's name. Of all single *parents* dependent on relief in Britain, 86 per cent are female, exactly the same proportion as that for the period 1700–1850. K. D. M. Snell and J. Millar, 'Lone-parent families and the welfare state: past and present', *C&C* 2:3 (1987) p. 397.

61 See, for example, Hilda Scott, *Working Your Way to the Bottom: The Feminization of Poverty* (1984), and *Signs* 10:2 (1984) special issue on women and poverty.

62 W. Newman Brown, 'The receipt of poor relief and family situation: Aldenham, Hertfordshire 1630–90', in R. M. Smith (ed.) *Land, Kinship and Life-Cycle* (1984) p. 412 (my calculations from his table).

63 Marianne Takas, 'Divorce: who gets the blame in "no-fault"?', *Ms Magazine* (February 1986) p. 48.

64 *The Autobiography of Mrs Alice Thornton of East Newton, Co. York* (1873) pp. 260–1.

65 Vinsent, £237/surplussage (1624) Withern, LAO: Ad Ac 19/99.

66 Wright, £98/–33 (1681) Hibaldstow, LAO: Ad Ac 34/75. Newton LAO: LCC Admon 1672–4/45.

67 *An Essay upon Projects* (1697) pp. 132–3.

68 Holderness, 'Widows in pre-industrial society', p. 428.

12 LONE WOMEN'S WILLS

1 Nesta Evans, 'Inheritance, women, religion and education in early modern society as revealed by wills', in P. Riden (ed.) *Probate Records and the Local Community* (1985) p. 55. Motoyasu Takahashi, 'The number of wills proved in the sixteenth and seventeenth centuries', in G. Martin and P. Spufford (eds) *The Records of the Nation* (1990) pp. 212–13. Richard Vann, 'Wills and the family in an English town: Banbury, 1550–1800', *JFH* 4:3 (1979) p. 352.

2 For large-scale studies of thousands of inventories see Carole Shammas, *The Pre-Industrial Consumer in England and America* (1990) p. 181, and Lorna Weatherill, 'A possession of one's own: women and consumer behaviour in England 1660–1740', *Journal of British Studies* 25:2 (1986) p. 133. The percentages on a local scale, with only a few hundred wills, are extremely erratic and do not necessarily reflect the proportions which were filed. See J. A. Johnston, 'The probate inventories and wills of a Worcestershire parish 1676–1775', *Midland History* 1:1 (1971–2) pp. 22–3. Estimates of the number of deaths which resulted in an inventory range from 10 per cent to 58 per cent of adult male and widowed female deaths in different areas. Mark Overton, 'English probate inventories and the measurement of agricultural change', in A. van der Woude and A. Schuurman (eds) *Probate Inventories* (1980) p. 209. In some places, such as Terling, Essex, or Chippenham, Cambridgeshire, inventories which were filed with the court have been subsequently destroyed. Keith Wrightson and David Levine, *Poverty and Piety in an English Village: Terling 1525–1700* (1979) pp. 37, 92. Spufford, *Contrasting Communities*, p. 59.

3 *The Free Women of Petersburg: Status and Culture in a Southern Town, 1784–1860* (1984) pp. 130–4.

4 See also Margaret Spufford, 'Peasant inheritance customs and land distribution in Cambridgeshire from the sixteenth to the eighteenth centuries', in J. Goody, J. Thirsk and E. P. Thompson (eds) *Family and Inheritance: Rural Society in Western Europe 1200–1800* (1976) p. 171, on the village of Willingham.

5 Keith Wrightson, *English Society 1580–1680* (1982) p. 112, has suggested that women living until their children were grown were unlikely to make a will. This may have been the case in Terling, since distribution patterns in women's wills did not differ from men's wills there (see below), which is atypical and suggests that men and women may have had the same motives for willmaking.

6 For measurement of men's bequests to grandchildren, nieces and nephews, and cousins, in Essex and Wiltshire, see also David Cressy, 'Kinship and kin interaction in early modern England', *P&P* 113 (1986) pp. 53–7.

7 On Willingham see Spufford, 'Peasant inheritance customs', p. 170. On the Ely Consistory Court, with a primarily fenland jurisdiction, see Takahashi, 'Number of wills', pp. 209–11.

On Norfolk see Amussen, *Ordered Society*, p. 93.

8 Vann, for example, found intestates' personal estates worth less than half those of testates in Banbury. 'Wills and the family', p. 354. See my cautions about the way in which this is measured, Chapter 2.

9 BIHR: Anne Nicholson (1642) Etton, Harthill, and Anne Deane (1644) South Cliffe, Harthill.

10 Elizabeth Skaine, £3 (1640) Chichester, WSRO: EpIII/9/1/1640 and EpI/29/541/044.

11 BIHR: Margaret Bankes (1681) Pocklington, Deanery Peculiar.

12 *Selby Wills* (1911) pp. 56–7, 104–5, 160.

13 BIHR: Ellen Consett *als* Kirkby (1648) Hovingham, Rydall. Ellen may have been married at the time she made her will. Her own birth-name was Prowd, but at what point Kirkby entered her life is unclear. There is no rule for whether husbands take consecutive or inverse order in the *alias* ranking.

14 Mary Shucksmith (1625) Chichester, WSRO: STD II/4.

15 Constance Glemham, £1017/834 (1635) Trotton, WSRO: EpI/33/1635, and STCI/18/341b. Later in the century the rector of Horsted Keynes urged his brother, on his deathbed, to remember their poorer kin in his will. He was rather more successful than the rector of Trotton, eliciting a promise of £10 each. *The Journal of Giles Moore* (1970) pp. 286–7.

16 Thomas Awde, £75 (1614) Selsey, WSRO: EpI/29/166/4 and B Dean Will 1614/12.

17 Joan Redwell, Bosham, WSRO: STCI/16/166. William Redwell, £163 (1620) WSRO: EpI/29/25/18 and STCI/16/89b.

18 *Philanthropy in England 1480–1660* (1959) pp. 354–5.

19 Mary Forman £70/–19 (1677) West Chiltington, WSRO: EpI/33/1676 and STCI/26/121b. John Forman £94 (1652) WSRO: STCI/21/476b.

20 Mary Stavell (1680) Selsey, WSRO: STCI/27/171b. Nicholas Stavell, £423/231 (1671) East Wittering, WSRO: EpI/33/1670. See also Elizabeth Collins (1648) Horsham, WSRO: STCI/21/285.

21 Anne Toynby, £35/0 (1679) Waddington, LAO: Ad Ac 43/121. William Toynby, £86 (1672) LAO: Inv 175/198.

22 Vivien Brodsky, 'Widows in late Elizabethan London: remarriage, economic opportunity and family orientations', in L. Bonfield, R. M. Smith and K. Wrightson (eds) *The World We Have Gained* (1986) p. 148. Gloria Main, 'Widows in rural Massachusetts on the eve of the revolution', in R. Hoffman and P. J. Albert (eds) *Women in the Age of the American Revolution* (1989) p. 88. Spufford, *Contrasting Communities*, p. 115. Vann, 'Wills and the family', p. 366.

23 Keith Wrightson, 'Kinship in an English village: Terling, Essex 1550–1700', in R. M. Smith (ed.) *Land, Kinship and Life-Cycle* (1984) pp. 324–5, or Wrightson and Levine, *Poverty and Piety*, p. 93.

24 The findings of Vann, 'Wills and the family', pp. 364–5, in 750 wills from Banbury over the period 1550–1800, are similar, but the legatees are not distinguished by sex.

25 Lebsock, *Status and Culture*, ch. 5.

26 Joan Reymes, £72/51 (1609) Yapton, WSRO: EpI/33/1609 and STCI/15/231b (1606). William Reymes (1605) WSRO: STCI/15/224.

27 Joan Redwell (1620) Bosham, WSRO: STCI/16/166. William Redwell, £163 (1619) WSRO: EpI/29/25/18 and STCI/16/89b.

28 Anne Toynby, £35/0 (1679) Waddington, LAO: Ad Ac43/121, LCC Admon 1678/138 and LCC Will 1678/61. William Toynby, £86 (1672) LAO: Inv 175/198 and LCC Will 1672/i/30.

29 Hester Wood, £117/70 (1685) Messingham, LAO: Ad Ac 44/139 and Stow Will 1684–6/138. Richard Wood, £237 (1682) LAO: Inv 219b/80 and Stow Will 1681–3/191.

30 *The Autobiography of Mrs Alice Thornton of East Newton, Co. York* (1873) pp. 114, 119–21.

31 Ann Succorman, £42/24, LAO: Ad Ac 10/84, and LCC Will 1610/36.

32 See also Amussen, *Ordered Society*, p. 91, Richard Chused, 'Married women's property and inheritance by widows in Massachusetts: a study of wills probated between 1800 and 1850', *Berkeley Women's Law Journal* 2 (1986) pp. 84–5, and Lebsock, *Status and Culture*, p. 58, on separate estates in late eighteenth- and early nineteenth-century Virginia, both by will and by deed. Many studies do not examine gender preference among legatees, one of the largest being Vann on Banbury. Three studies find no difference in women's and men's preference for sons: Jacques Beauroy, 'Family patterns and relations of Bishop's Lynn will-makers in the fourteenth century', in L. Bonfield, R. M. Smith and K. Wrightson (eds) *The World We Have Gained* (1986) pp. 33, 36, 42; Main, 'Rural Massachusetts', p. 89; Susan Wright, 'Family life and society in sixteenth and early seventeenth-century Salisbury' (Leicester PhD thesis, 1982) p. 289.

33 BIHR: William Staggs, Newmalton, Rydall.
34 Robert King, £132/60 (1671) Woodford, NRO: Acct 102.
35 Agnes Bettison *als* Love, £18/–1 (1624) Frampton, LAO: Ad Ac 19/73 and LCC Admon 1616/102.
36 BIHR: Elizabeth Ripley (1682) Pickering, Deanery Peculiar.
37 BIHR: Mary Widd (1681) Wilton, Deanery Peculiar.
38 See also Amussen, *Ordered Society*, p. 92.
39 Anne Paxton, £106/85 (1677) Sulgrave, NRO: Acct 47. Thomas Paxton, £93/–14 (1683) NRO: Acct 80.
40 The quotes are from B. A. Holderness, 'Widows in pre-industrial society: an essay upon their economic functions', in R. M. Smith (ed.) *Land, Kinship and Life-Cycle* (1984) p. 432, and Rowena Archer, 'Rich old ladies: the problem of late medieval dowagers', in A. J. Pollard (ed.) *Property and Politics: Essays in Later Medieval English History* (1984) p. 20. She later concedes, 'No record survives of contemporary opinion on the existence of dowagers and their effect on succession' (p.26). Janet Senderowitz Loengard cites four secondary but no contemporary works to support the idea of antagonism over dower, and all of her own evidence is of a litigious nature. '"Of the gift of her husband": English dower and its consequences in the year 1200', in J. Kirshner and S. F. Wemple (eds) *Women of the Medieval World* (1985) p. 254. See also Lloyd Bonfield, *Marriage Settlements, 1601–1740: The Adoption of the Strict Settlement* (1983) pp. 117–18, or 'Affective families, open elites and strict settlements in early modern England', *EcHR* 39:3 (1986) p. 344, and Mary Finch, *The Wealth of Five Northamptonshire Families 1540–1640* (1956) p. 28.

CONCLUSION

1 Charles Pressye *v.* Jeremy Bushier (1621) PRO: C2/Jas.I/P19/28.
2 Lee Holcombe, *Wives and Property: Reform of the Married Women's Property Law in Nineteenth-Century England* (1983) p. 148.
3 Henry Swinburne, *A Treatise of Testaments and Last Wills* (1590) p. 156.
4 Edmund Snell, *The Principles of Equity* (1868) p. 282.
5 Richard Wall, 'The household: demographic and economic change in England, 1650–1970', in R. Wall, J. Robin and P. Laslett (eds) *Family Forms in Historic Europe* (1983) p. 505.
6 E. A. Wrigley and Roger Schofield, *The Population History of England, 1541–1871* (1981) p. 260, Table 7.28. Roger Schofield, 'English marriage patterns revisited', *JFH* 10:1 (1985) pp. 9–10.
7 'Married life', in J. Chandos (ed.) *In God's Name: Examples of Preaching in England From the Act of Supremacy to the Act of Uniformity* (1971) pp. 510–11.
8 Daniel Defoe, *Roxana* (1987) p. 190.
9 Compare, for example, the conditions described in Barbara Diefendorf, 'Women and property in *ancien régime* France: theory and practice in Dauphiné and Paris', in J. Brewer and S. Staves (eds) *Early Modern Conceptions of Property* (1995), and Isabelle Chabot, 'Widowhood and poverty in late medieval Florence', *C&C* 3:2 (1988) pp. 291–311.
10 Defoe, *Roxana*, pp. 190–1.
11 'Victorian wives and property', in M. Vicinus (ed.) *A Widening Sphere* (1977) p. 7, fn. 3.
12 *The Ladies Calling*, 5th edn (1677) preface.
13 John Berry *v.* Mary Skinner *als* Newton (1672) PRO: C5/60/4.
14 Eileen Power, 'The position of women', in C. G. Crump and E. F. Jacobs (eds) *The Legacy of the Middle Ages* (1926) p. 400.

Bibliography

MANUSCRIPT SOURCES

Cambridge, Cambridge University Library: Accounts EDR A12/1–2.
Chichester, West Sussex Record Office: Accounts EpI/33, EpIII/9/1 and EpIV/ 10/1–2a; Inventories EpI/29; Wills STCI and Deanery.
Dorchester, Dorset County Record Office: Accounts PE/WM CP2/4.
Lincoln, Lincolnshire Archives Office: Accounts Ad Ac 1–45; Inventories LCC Admon and Inv; Wills LCC, Stow and Dean & Chapter.
London, Public Record Office, Chancery Lane: Chancery Court Bills and Answers C2/ Eliz, C2/Jas I and C5.
Northampton, Northamptonshire Record Office: Archdeaconry of Northampton, Bundle of Accounts and Court Proceedings 1665–85.
Taunton, Somerset Record Office: Accounts D/D/Ct and DD/SP/442.
Winchester, Hampshire Record Office: Accounts.
York, Borthwick Institute for Historical Research: Wills from the Deaneries of Harthill and Rydall (1640s) and the Deanery Peculiar (1680s).

SECONDARY SOURCES

Adams, Ian H., *Agrarian Landscape Terms*, London, Institute of British Geographers, 1976.
Alexander, James M. B., 'A study of the Court of Chancery records as a source for economic and social history', unpublished MSc thesis, London School of Economics, 1985.
Alexander, William, *The History of Women, from the Earliest Antiquity to the Present Time*, 3rd edn, London, C. Dilly, 1782.
Allestree, Richard, *The Ladies' Calling*, 5th edn, Oxford, at the Theatre, 1677 (1st edn 1673).
Amussen, Susan Dwyer, 'Gender, family and social order, 1560–1725', in Anthony Fletcher and John Stevenson (eds) *Order and Disorder in Early Modern England*, Cambridge, Cambridge University Press, 1985.
—— *An Ordered Society: Gender and Class in Early Modern England*, Oxford, Blackwell, 1988.
Archer, Rowena E., 'Rich old ladies: the problem of late medieval dowagers', in A. J. Pollard (ed.) *Property and Politics: Essays in Later Medieval English History*, Gloucester, Alan Sutton, 1984.
Archer, Rowena E. and Ferme, B. E., 'Testamentary procedure with special reference to the executrix', *Reading Medieval Studies* 15 (1989), 3–34.
Ardener, Edwin, 'Belief and the problem of women', in Shirley Ardener (ed.)

Perceiving Women, London, J. M. Dent, 1977; originally published in Jean S. LaFontaine (ed.) *The Interpretation of Ritual*, London, Tavistock, 1972.

Astell, Mary, *A Serious Proposal to the Ladies*, 4th edn, London, R. Wilkin, 1697 (1st edn 1694).

—— *The First English Feminist: Reflections Upon Marriage and Other Writings*, ed. Bridget Hill, Aldershot, Hampshire, Gower, 1986.

Bainton, Roland, *Women of the Reformation in Germany and Italy*, Boston, Massachusetts, Beacon Press, 1971.

Baker, J. H. (ed.) *The Reports of Sir John Spelman* II, Selden Society Series 94 (1977).

—— *An Introduction to English Legal History*, 2nd edn, London, Butterworths, 1979.

Barley, M. W., 'Farmhouses and cottages, 1550–1725', *EcHR* 7 (1955), 291–306.

—— 'Rural building in England', in Joan Thirsk (ed.) *The Agrarian History of England and Wales* V:ii, Cambridge, Cambridge University Press, 1985.

Baron and Feme: A Treatise of the Common Law Concerning Husbands and Wives, London, R. & E. Atkyns for John Walthoe, 1700.

Barrett-Lennard, Thomas, *The Position in Law of Women*, Littleton, Colorado, Fred B. Rothman, 1983 (reprint of original 1883 London edn).

Barron, Caroline, 'The "golden age" of women in medieval London', *Reading Medieval Studies* 15 (1989), 35–58.

Barton, Thomas F. and Farrow, M. A. (comps) *Index of Wills Proved in the Consistory Court of Norwich 1687–1750*, Norfolk Record Society Series 34 (1965).

Basch, Norma, *In the Eyes of the Law: Women, Marriage and Property in Nineteenth-Century New York*, Ithaca, New York, and London, Cornell University Press, 1982.

Bateson, Mary (ed.) *Borough Customs*, 2 vols, Selden Society Series 18 (1904) and 21 (1906).

Beaumont, Agnes, *Narrative of the Persecution of Agnes Beaumont in 1674*, ed. G. B. Harrison, Constable's Miscellany Series 31, Glasgow, n.d.

Beauroy, Jacques, 'Family patterns and relations of Bishop's Lynn will-makers in the fourteenth century', in Lloyd Bonfield, Richard M. Smith and Keith Wrightson (eds) *The World We Have Gained*, Oxford, Oxford University Press, 1986.

Bennett, Judith M., *Women in the Medieval Countryside: Gender and Household in Brigstock Before the Plague*, Oxford, Oxford University Press, 1987.

Berg, Maxine, 'Women's property and the industrial revolution', paper presented to the Colloquium on Women and Development, Harvard University, 3–4 May 1991, *Journal of Interdisciplinary History* 24:2 (1993), 233–50.

Best, Henry, *The Farming and Memorandum Books of Henry Best of Elmswell, 1642*, ed. Donald Woodward, London, Oxford University Press for the British Academy, 1984.

Bettey, J. H., 'Land tenure and manorial custom in Dorset 1570–1670', *Southern History* 4 (1982), 33–54.

Bolney, Bartholomew, *The Book of Bartholomew Bolney*, ed. Marie Clough, Sussex Record Society Series 63 (1964).

Bonfield, Lloyd, *Marriage Settlements, 1601–1740: The Adoption of the Strict Settlement*, Cambridge, Cambridge University Press, 1983.

—— 'Contrasting sources: court rolls and settlements as evidence of hereditary transmission of land amongst small landowners in early modern England', *University of Illinois Law Review* 3 (1984), 639–58.

—— 'Affective families, open elites and strict family settlements in early modern England', *EcHR* 39:3 (1986), 341–54.

—— 'Normative rules and property transmission: reflections on the link between marriage and inheritance in early modern England', in Lloyd Bonfield, Richard M. Smith and Keith Wrightson (eds) *The World We Have Gained*, Oxford, Oxford University Press, 1986.

—— 'Strict settlement and the family: a differing view', *EcHR* 41:3 (1988), 461–6.

Bossy, John, 'In the sight of God', *Times Literary Supplement* (23–9 September 1988), 1036.

Boswell, John, *The Kindness of Strangers: The Abandonment of Children in Western Europe from Late Antiquity to the Renaissance*, New York, Pantheon, 1988.

du Boulay, Juliet, *Portrait of a Greek Mountain Village*, Oxford, Clarendon Press, 1974.

Boulton, Jeremy, 'London widowhood revisited: the decline of female remarriage in the seventeenth and early eighteenth centuries', *C&C* 5:3 (1990), 323–55.

Bowden, Peter J., 'Agricultural prices, wages, farm profits, and rents', in Joan Thirsk (ed.) *The Agrarian History of England and Wales* V:ii, Cambridge, Cambridge University Press, 1985.

Bower, Jacqueline, 'Probate accounts as a source for Kentish early modern economic and social history', *Archaeologia Cantiana* 109 (1991), 51–62.

Brathwait, Richard, *The English Gentleman and the English Gentlewoman*, 3rd edn, London, John Dawson, 1641 (1st edn 1631).

Bray, Rosemary, 'A special victory', *Ms Magazine* (April 1986), 48.

Brentano, Robert James, *Rome Before Avignon: a Social History of Thirteenth-Century Rome*, London, Longman, 1974.

Bridenbaugh, Carl, *Vexed and Troubled Englishmen 1590–1642*, Oxford, Clarendon Press, 1968.

Bridgman, Sir Orlando, *Conveyances*, 2nd edn, London, Richard & Edward Atkins for Wm. Battersby & T. Basset, 1689.

Brodsky, Vivien, 'Widows in late Elizabethan London: remarriage, economic opportunity and family orientations', in Lloyd Bonfield, Richard M. Smith and Keith Wrightson (eds) *The World We Have Gained*, Oxford, Oxford University Press, 1986.

Brodsky Elliott, Vivien, 'Single women in the London marriage market: age, status and mobility, 1598–1619', in R. B. Outhwaite (ed.) *Marriage and Society*, London, Europa, 1981.

Brooks, C. W., *Pettyfoggers and Vipers of the Commonwealth: The 'Lower Branch' of the Legal Profession in Early Modern England*, Cambridge, Cambridge University Press, 1986.

Brooks, C. W. and Sharpe, Kevin, 'History, English law and the renaissance', *P&P* 72 (1976), 133–42.

Brown, Roger Lee, 'Clandestine marriages in London, especially within the Fleet Prison, and their effects on Hardwicke's Act, 1753', unpublished MA thesis, University of London, 1972.

Brown, W. Newman, 'The receipt of poor relief and family situation: Aldenham, Hertfordshire 1630–90', in R. M. Smith (ed.) *Land, Kinship and Life-Cycle*, Cambridge, Cambridge University Press, 1984.

Browne, Alice, *The Eighteenth-Century Feminist Mind*, Brighton, Harvester, 1987.

Bullokar, John, *An English Expositor*, Menston, Yorkshire, Scolar Press, 1967 (1st edn 1616).

Burn, Richard, *Ecclesiastical Law*, 2 vols, London, H. Woodfall and W. Strahan for A. Millar, 1763.

Campbell, Linda, 'The women of Stiffkey', unpublished MA thesis, University of East Anglia, 1985.

Campbell, Mildred, *The English Yeoman under Elizabeth and the Early Stuarts*, New Brunswick, New Jersey, Yale University Press, 1942.

Carlson, Eric, *Marriage and the English Reformation*, Oxford, Blackwell, 1994.

Carlton, Charles, *The Court of Orphans*, Leicester, Leicester University Press, 1974.

—— 'The widow's tale: male myths and female reality in sixteenth and seventeeth-century England', *Albion* 10:2 (1978), 118–29.

Carr, Lois Green, 'The development of the Maryland orphan's court, 1654–1715', in

A. C. Land, L. G. Carr and E. C. Papenfuse (eds) *Law, Society and Politics in Early Maryland*, Baltimore, Maryland, Johns Hopkins University Press, 1977.

—— 'Inheritance in the colonial Chesapeake', in Ronald Hoffman and Peter J. Albert (eds) *Women in the Age of the American Revolution*, Charlottesville, Virginia, University Press of Virginia, 1989.

Carr, Lois Green, and Walsh, Lorena S., 'The planter's wife: the experience of white women in seventeenth-century Maryland', *WMQ* 3rd ser. 34 (1977), 542–71.

Centlivre, Susannah, *A Bold Stroke for a Wife*, ed. Thalia Stathas, Lincoln, Nebraska, University of Nebraska Press, 1968 (1st edn 1718).

Certain Ancient Tracts Concerning the Management of Landed Property, London, C. Bathurst and J. Newbery, 1767.

Chabot, Isabelle, 'Widowhood and poverty in late medieval Florence', *C&C* 3:2 (1988), 291–311.

Chamberlain, John, *The Chamberlain Letters: A Selection of the Letters of John Chamberlain Concerning Life in England from 1597 to 1626*, ed. Elizabeth McClure Thomson, USA, Capricorn, 1966.

Chamberlayne, Edward, *Angliae Notitiae, or the Present State of England*, London, John Martyn, 1669.

Chambers, R., *Book of Days: A Miscellany of Popular Antiquities*, vol.1, London and Edinburgh, W. R. Chambers, 1863.

Chandos, John (ed.) *In God's Name: Examples of Preaching in England From the Act of Supremacy to the Act of Uniformity*, Indianapolis, Indiana, Bobbs-Merrill, 1971.

Chapman, A. Beatrice Wallis, and Chapman, Mary Wallis, *The Status of Women under the English Law*, London, George Routledge, 1909.

Chojnacki, Stanley, 'Patrician women in early renaissance Venice', *Studies in the Renaissance* 21 (1974), 174–203.

Chused, Richard H., 'Married women's property and inheritance by widows in Massachusetts: a study of wills probated between 1800 and 1850', *Berkeley Women's Law Journal* 2 (1986), 42–88.

Cioni, Maria L., 'Women and law in Elizabethan England, with particular reference to the Court of Chancery', unpublished PhD thesis, Cambridge University, 1974.

—— 'The Elizabethan Chancery and women's rights', in D. Guth and J. W. McKenna (eds) *Tudor Rule and Revolution*, Cambridge, Cambridge University Press, 1982.

Clark, Alice, *Working Life of Women in the Seventeenth Century*, with introduction by Miranda Chaytor and Jane Lewis, London, Routledge, 1982; with introduction by Amy Louise Erickson, London, Routledge, 1992 (1st edn 1919).

Clarkson, L. A., *The Pre-Industrial Economy in England 1500–1750*, London, Batsford, 1971.

Clay, Christopher, 'Marriage, inheritance and the rise of large estates in England 1660–1815', *EcHR* 21 (1968), 503–18.

—— 'The price of freehold land in the later seventeenth and eighteenth centuries', *EcHR* 27 (1974), 173–89.

—— 'Landlords and estate management in England', in Joan Thirsk (ed.) *The Agrarian History of England and Wales* V:ii, Cambridge, Cambridge University Press, 1985.

Clifford, Anne, *The Diary of the Lady Anne Clifford*, ed. Vita Sackville-West, London, William Heinemann, 1923.

Cockburn, J. S., *A History of English Assizes, 1558–1714*, Cambridge, Cambridge University Press, 1972.

Cockeram, Henry, *The English Dictionarie*, Menston, Yorkshire, Scolar Press, 1968 (1st edn 1623).

Cohn, Samuel Kline, Jr, *The Labouring Classes in Renaissance Florence*, New York, Academic Press, 1980.

Coke, Sir Edward, *The Institutes of the Laws of England*, London, E. R. Brooke, 1797 (1st edn 1628–44).

Coleman, D. C., *The Economy of England 1450–1750*, Oxford, Oxford University Press, 1977.

The Compleat Servant-Maid: Or, the Young Maiden's Tutor, 6th edn, London, Eben Tracy, 1700 (1st edn 1677).

Consett, Henry, *The Practice of the Spiritual or Ecclesiastical Courts*, London, T. Basset, 1685.

Considerations Touching the Dissolving . . . of the Court of Chancery, by F.L., London, Thomas Heath, 1653.

Cooper, J. P., 'Patterns of inheritance and settlement by great landowners from the fifteenth to the eighteenth centuries', in Jack Goody, Joan Thirsk and E. P. Thompson (eds) *Family and Inheritance: Rural Society in Western Europe 1200–1800*, Cambridge, Cambridge University Press, 1976.

Coppel, Stephen, 'Wills and the community: a case study of Tudor Grantham', in Philip Riden (ed.) *Probate Records and the Local Community*, Gloucester, Alan Sutton, 1985.

The Country-Man's Counsellor, by H. R., London, J. Clark, n.d., in MCC: Samuel Pepys's *Penny Merriments* II, 783–806.

Crawford, Barbara, 'Marriage and the status of women in Norse society', in R. B. Outhwaite (ed.) *Marriage and Society*, London, Europa, 1981; reprinted in Elizabeth Craik (ed.) *Marriage and Property*, Aberdeen, Aberdeen University Press, 1991 (1st edn 1984).

Crawford, Patricia, 'Katharine and Philip Henry and their children: a case study in family ideology', *Transactions of the Historic Society of Lancashire and Cheshire* 134 (1984), 39–73.

—— '"The only ornament in a woman": needlework in early modern England', in *All Her Labours* II: *Embroidering the Framework*, Sydney, Hale & Iremonger, 1984.

—— 'Women's published writings 1600–1700', in Mary Prior (ed.) *Women in English Society 1500–1800*, London, Methuen, 1985.

Cressy, David, *Education in Tudor and Stuart England*, London, Edward Arnold, 1975.

—— 'Describing the social order of Elizabethan and Stuart England', *Literature and History* 3 (1976), 29–44.

—— 'Kinship and kin interaction in early modern England', *P&P* 113 (1986), 38–69.

—— *Coming Over: Migration and Communication Between England and New England in the Seventeenth Century*, Cambridge, Cambridge University Press, 1987.

Cullum, Patricia, '"And hir name was charite": women and charity in medieval Yorkshire', in P. J. P Goldberg (ed.) *Woman is a Worthy Wight: Women in Medieval English Society 1200–1500*, Gloucester, Alan Sutton, 1992.

Curtis, M. H., 'Education and apprenticeship', *Shakespeare Survey* 17 (1964), 53–72.

Davidoff, Leonore, and Hall, Catherine, *Family Fortunes: Men and Women of the English Middle Class 1780–1850*, London, Hutchinson, 1987.

Day, John, 'On the status of women in medieval Sardinia', in Julius Kirshner and Suzanne F. Wemple (eds) *Women of the Medieval World*, Oxford, Blackwell, 1985.

Defoe, Daniel, *An Essay Upon Projects*, London, T. Cockerill, 1697.

—— *Roxana*, ed. David Blewett, Harmondsworth, Penguin, 1987 (1st edn 1724).

Depositions and Other Ecclesiastical Proceedings from the Church Courts of Durham, extending from 1311 to the reign of Elizabeth, Surtees Society Series 26 (1845).

Diefendorf, Barbara B., 'Widowhood and remarriage in sixteenth-century Paris', *JFH* 7:4 (1982), 379–95.

—— *Paris City Councillors in the Sixteenth Century: the Politics of Patrimony*, Princeton, New Jersey, Princeton University Press, 1983.

—— 'Women and property in *ancien régime* France: theory and practice in Dauphiné and Paris', in John Brewer and Susan Staves (eds) *Early Modern Conceptions of Property*, London and New York, Routledge, 1995.

Dobson, Austin, *Fielding*, London, Macmillan, 1883.

Dunlop, O. Jocelyn, *English Apprenticeship and Child Labour*, London, Unwin, 1912.

Dupaquier, J., Helin, E., Laslett, P., Livi-Bacci, M. and Sogner, S. (eds) *Marriage and Remarriage in Populations of the Past*, London, Academic Press, 1981.

Dyer, Christopher, 'Changes in the size of peasant holdings in some west midland villages 1400–1540', in R. M. Smith (ed.) *Land, Kinship and Life-Cycle*, Cambridge, Cambridge University Press, 1984.

Earle, Peter, *The Making of the English Middle Class: Business, Society and Family Life in London 1660–1730*, London, Methuen, 1989.

Eliot, George, *Adam Bede*, Edinburgh and London, William Blackwood, 1859.

—— *The Mill on the Floss*, Edinburgh and London, William Blackwood, 1860.

Emmison, F. G., *Elizabethan Life*, Chelmsford, Essex County Council, 1976.

English, Barbara, and Saville, John, 'Family settlement and the "rise of great estates"', *EcHR* 33:4 (1980), 556–8.

—— *Strict Settlement: A Guide for Historians*, University of Hull Occasional Papers in Economic and Social History 10 (1983).

Equal Opportunities Commission, *Women and Men in Britain: a Research Profile*, London, HMSO, 1988.

Erickson, Amy Louise, 'The property ownership and financial decisions of ordinary women in early modern England', unpublished PhD thesis, Cambridge University, 1990.

—— 'An introduction to probate accounts', in Geoffrey Martin and Peter Spufford (eds) *The Records of the Nation*, Woodbridge, Suffolk, Boydell Press, 1990.

—— 'Maternal management and the cost of raising children in early modern England', in Richard Wall and Osamu Saito (eds) *Social and Economic Aspects of the Family Life-Cycle*, Cambridge, Cambridge University Press, forthcoming.

Evans, Nesta, 'Inheritance, women, religion and education in early modern society as revealed by wills', in Philip Ride (ed.) *Probate Records and the Local Community*, Gloucester, Alan Sutton, 1985.

—— *The East Anglian Linen Industry: Rural Industry and Local Economy 1500–1800*, Aldershot, Hampshire, Gower for the Pasold Fund, 1985.

Everitt, Alan, 'Farm labourers', in Joan Thirsk (ed.) *The Agrarian History of England and Wales* IV, Cambridge, Cambridge University Press, 1967.

Ezell, Margaret J. M., *The Patriarch's Wife: Literary Evidence and the History of the Family*, Chapel Hill, North Carolina, University of North Carolina Press, 1987.

Faith, Rosamond Jane, 'Peasant families and inheritance customs in medieval England', *Agricultural History Review* 14 (1966), 77–95.

Fanshawe, Anne, *Memoirs of Lady Fanshawe, Wife of Sir Richard Fanshawe, Bt., Ambassador from Charles II to the Courts of Portugal and Madrid*, ed. Beatrice Marshall, London and New York, John Lane, 1905.

Farmer, David Hugh, *Oxford Dictionary of Saints*, Oxford, Oxford University Press, 1987.

Fell, Sarah, *The Household Account Book of Sarah Fell of Swarthmoor Hall*, ed. Norman Penny, Cambridge, Cambridge University Press, 1920.

Ferguson, Moira (ed.) *First Feminists: British Women Writers 1578–1799*, Bloomington, Indiana, Indiana University Press, 1985.

Fiennes, Celia, *The Journeys of Celia Fiennes*, ed. Christopher Morris, London, Cresset Press, 1949.

Finch, Sir Henry, *Law, or a Discourse Thereof*, London, Society of Stationers, 1627.

Finch, Mary E., *The Wealth of Five Northamptonshire Families 1540–1640*, Northamptonshire Record Society Series 19 (1956).

Fissell, Mary, 'Women and families: thoughts on life-cycle and poverty in eighteenth-century England', paper presented to the Cambridge Group for Population Studies, March 1991 (forthcoming).

Fitzherbert, John, *The Boke of Husbandry*, London, R. Kele, 1550.

Flandrin, Jean-Louis, *Families in Former Times: Kinship, Household and Sexuality*, transl. R. Southern, Cambridge, Cambridge University Press, 1979.

Fletcher, John, *The Woman's Prize or the Tamer Tamed*, ed. G. B. Ferguson, London, The Hague and Paris, Mouton, 1966 (written 1611).

Forte, A. D. M., 'Some aspects of the law of marriage in Scotland: 1500–1700', in Elizabeth Craik (ed.) *Marriage and Property*, Aberdeen, Aberdeen University Press, 1991 (1st edn 1984).

Franklin, Peter, 'Peasant widows' "liberation" and remarriage before the black death', *EcHR* 39:2 (1986), 186–204.

Fraser, Antonia, *The Weaker Vessel: Woman's Lot in Seventeenth-Century England*, London, Weidenfeld & Nicolson, 1984.

Gampel, Gwen, 'The planter's wife revisited: women, equity law and the Chancery Court in seventeenth-century Maryland', in Barbara J. Harris and JoAnn K. McNamara (eds) *Women and the Structure of Society*, Durham, North Carolina, Duke University Press, 1984.

Gardiner, Dorothy, *English Girlhood at School: A Study of Women's Education Through Twelve Centuries*, London, Oxford University Press, 1929.

Garrard, Rachel P., 'English probate inventories and their use in studying the significance of the domestic interior, 1570–1700', in A. van der Woude and Anton Schuurman (eds) *Probate Inventories*, Utrecht, HES Publishers, 1980.

Gay, John, *The Beggar's Opera*, 3rd edn, London, John Watts, 1728.

The Gentlewomans Companion; or, a Guide to the Female Sex, London, A. Maxwell for Edward Thomas, 1675.

George, Margaret, 'From "goodwife" to "mistress": the transformation of the female in bourgeois culture', *Science & Society* 37 (1973), 152–77.

Gibbon, Edward, *Memoirs of my Life*, Harmondsworth, Penguin, 1984 (written 1789).

Gillis, John R., 'Conjugal settlements: resort to clandestine and common law marriage in England and Wales 1650–1850', in John Bossy (ed.) *Disputes and Settlements*, Cambridge, Cambridge University Press, 1983.

—— *For Better, for Worse: British Marriages, 1600 to the Present*, New York, Oxford University Press, 1985.

Gittings, Clare, *Death, Burial and the Individual in Early Modern England*, London, Croom Helm, 1984.

Gottlieb, Beatrice, 'The problem of feminism in the fifteenth century', in Julius Kirshner and Suzanne F. Wemple (eds) *Women of the Medieval World*, Oxford, Blackwell, 1985.

Gough, Richard, *The History of Myddle*, ed. David Hey, Harmondsworth, Penguin, 1981.

Graham, Elspeth, 'Authority, resistance, and loss: gendered difference in the writings of John Bunyan and Hannah Allen', in Anne Laurence, W. R. Owens and Stuart Sim (eds) *The Pulpit Guarded: Confrontations Between Orthodox and Radicals in Revolutionary England*, London, Hambledon Press, 1990.

Graham, Elspeth, Hinds, Hilary, Hobby, Elaine, and Wilcox, Helen (eds) *Her Own Life: Autobiographical Writings by Seventeenth-Century English Women*, London, Routledge, 1989.

Graham, Rose, 'The civic position of women at common law before 1800', in Rose Graham, *English Ecclesiastical Studies*, London, Society for the Propagation of Christian Knowledge, 1929.

Gray, Charles Montgomery, *Copyhold, Equity and the Common Law*, Cambridge, Massachusetts, Harvard University Press, 1963.

Greenberg, Janelle, 'The legal status of the English woman in early eighteenth-century common law and equity', *Studies in Eighteenth-Century Culture* 4 (1975), 171–81.

Grey, Anchitell, *Debates of the House of Commons* I *1667–94*, London, T. Becket and P. A. De Hondt, 1769.

Griffiths, R. G., 'Joyce Jeffreys of Ham Castle: a 17th century business gentlewoman', *Transactions of the Worcestershire Archaeological Society* 10 (1933), 1–32.

Habakkuk, H. J., 'Marriage settlements in the eighteenth century', *TRHS* 4th ser. 32 (1950), 15–30.

——— 'The long-term rate of interest and the price of land in the seventeenth century', *EcHR* 5:1 (1952), 26–45.

Hanawalt, Barbara, 'Childrearing among the lower classes of late medieval England', *Journal of Interdisciplinary History* 8:1 (1977), 1–22.

The Hardships of the English Laws. In Relation to Wives. With an Explanation of the Original Curse of Subjection Passed Upon the Woman. In an Humble Address to the Legislature, London and Dublin, G. Faulkner, 1735.

Harland, John, and Wilkinson, T. T., *Lancashire Folk-Lore*, London, Frederick Warne, 1867.

Harley, Brilliana, *Letters of the Lady Brilliana Harley, Wife of Sir Robert Harley, of Brampton Bryan, Knight of the Bath*, ed. Thomas Taylor Lewis, Camden Society Series 58 (1854).

Harris, Barbara J., 'Marriage sixteenth-century style: Elizabeth Stafford and the third Duke of Norfolk', *Journal of Social History* 15:3 (1982), 371–82.

Haskell, Ann S., 'The Paston women on marriage in fifteenth-century England', *Viator* 4 (1973), 459–71.

Haskins, George L., 'The development of common law dower', *Harvard Law Review* 62:1 (1948), 42–55.

——— 'The estate by the marital right', *University of Pennsylvania Law Review* 97:3 (1949), 345–53.

Hays, Mary, *Appeal to the Men of Great Britain on Behalf of Women*, New York and London, Garland, 1974 (reprint of original 1798 edn).

Helmholz, R. H., *Marriage Litigation in Medieval England*, Cambridge, Cambridge University Press, 1974.

Henderson, Katherine Usher, and McManus, Barbara F., *Half Humankind: Contexts and Texts of the Controversy About Women in England, 1540–1640*, Urbana, Illinois, University of Illinois Press, 1985.

Henley, Nancy M., 'Power, sex, and nonverbal communication', in Barrie Thorne and Nancy Henley (eds) *Language and Sex: Difference and Dominance*, Rowley, Massachusetts, Newbury House, 1975.

Hey, David, 'Yorkshire and Lancashire', in Joan Thirsk (ed.) *The Agrarian History of England and Wales* V:i, Cambridge, Cambridge University Press, 1984.

Higgins, Patricia, 'The reaction of women, with special reference to women petitioners', in Brian Manning (ed.) *Politics, Religion and the English Civil War*, London, Edward Arnold, 1973.

Hill, Bridget (ed.) *Eighteenth-Century Women: An Anthology*, London, Allen & Unwin, 1984.

——— *Women, Work and Sexual Politics in Eighteenth-Century England*, Oxford, Blackwell, 1989.

Hindle, Steve, 'Aspects of the relationship of the state and local society in early modern England, with special reference to Cheshire, c.1590–1630', unpublished PhD thesis, Cambridge University, 1992 (forthcoming as *State and Society in Early Modern England*, London, Macmillan).

Hobby Elaine, *Virtue of Necessity: English Women's Writing 1649–88*, London, Virago, 1988.

Hoby, Margaret, *The Diary of Lady Margaret Hoby 1599–1605*, ed. Dorothy M. Meads, London, George Routledge, 1930.

Hogrefe, Pearl, 'The legal rights of Tudor women and their circumvention by men and women', *Sixteenth-Century Journal* 3 (1972), 97–105.

Holcombe, Lee, 'Victorian wives and property', in Martha Vicinus (ed.) *A Widening Sphere*, Bloomington, Indiana, Indiana University Press, 1977.

—— *Wives and Property: Reform of the Married Women's Property Law in Nineteenth-Century England*, Toronto and Buffalo, New York, University of Toronto Press, 1983.

Holderness, B. A., 'Elizabeth Parkin and her investments, 1733–66: aspects of the Sheffield money market in the eighteenth century', *Transactions of the Hunter Archaeological Society* 10:2 (1973), 81–7.

—— 'Credit in a rural community, 1660–1800: some neglected aspects of probate inventories', *Midland History* 3:2 (1975), 94–115.

—— 'Credit in a rural society before the nineteenth century, with special reference to the period 1650–1720', *Agricultural History Review* 24:2 (1976), 97–109.

—— 'Widows in pre-industrial society: an essay upon their economic functions', in R. M. Smith (ed.) *Land, Kinship and Life-Cycle*, Cambridge, Cambridge University Press, 1984.

Holdsworth, W. S., *A History of English Law* III, 3rd edn, London, Methuen, 1923, and V, 1st edn, London, Methuen, 1924.

Hopkins, Sheila V. and Phelps Brown, Henry, 'Seven centuries of building wages', in Henry Phelps Brown and Sheila Hopkins, *A Perspective of Wages and Prices*, London, Methuen, 1981.

Horsman, Gilbert, *Precedents in Conveyancing*, 3 vols, London, Henry Lintot for John and Paul Knapton, 1744.

Horwitz, Henry, 'Testamentary practice, family strategies, and the last phases of the custom of London, 1660–1725', *Law & History Review* 2:2 (1984), 223–39.

Houlbrooke, Ralph, *Church Courts and the People During the English Reformation 1520–70*, Oxford, Oxford University Press, 1979.

—— *The English Family 1450–1700*, London, Longmans, 1984.

—— 'Women's social life and common action in England from the fifteenth century to the eve of the civil war', *C&C* 1:2 (1986), 171–89.

Howell, Cicely, 'Peasant inheritance customs in the midlands, 1280–1700', in Jack Goody, Joan Thirsk and E. P. Thompson (eds) *Family and Inheritance: Rural Society in Western Europe 1200–1800*, Cambridge, Cambridge University Press, 1976.

—— *Land, Family and Inheritance in Transition: Kibworth Harcourt 1280–1700*, Cambridge, Cambridge University Press, 1983.

Howell, Martha C., *Women, Production, and Patriarchy in Late Medieval Cities*, Chicago, Illinois, University of Chicago Press, 1986.

Hufton, Olwen, 'Women in history: early modern Europe', *P&P* 101 (1983), 125–41.

—— 'Women without men: widows and spinsters in Britain and France in the eighteenth century', *JFH* 9:4 (1984), 355–76.

Hughes, Diane Owen, 'Domestic ideals and social behaviour: evidence from medieval Genoa', in Charles E. Rosenberg (ed.) *The Family in History*, Pittsburgh, Pennsylvania, University of Pennsylvania Press, 1975.

Hunt, Margaret, 'Wife-beating, domesticity and women's independence in eighteenth-century London', *Gender & History* 4:1 (1992).

Hunt, Richard, 'Quarter sessions order books', in Lionel M. Munby (ed.) *Short Guides to Records*, London, Historical Association, 1972.

Index of Chancery Proceedings, Bridges Division, 1613–1714, prepared by A. J. Gregory, 4 vols, Public Record Office Lists and Indexes Series 39, 42, 44, 45 (1913–17).

Ingram, Martin, *Church Courts, Sex and Marriage in England, 1570–1640*, Cambridge, Cambridge University Press, 1987.

Jefferies, Peggy, 'The medieval use as family law and custom: the Berkshire gentry in the fourteenth and fifteenth centuries', *Southern History* 1 (1979), 45–69.

Johnston, J. A., 'The probate inventories and wills of a Worcestershire parish 1676–1775', *Midland History* 1:1 (1971–2), 20–33.

Jones, John, *A Human Geography of Cambridgeshire*, London, Sidgwick & Jackson, 1924.

Jordan, W. K., *Philanthropy in England 1480–1660*, New York, Russell Sage Foundation, 1959.

Keeton, G. W., *Introduction to Equity*, 6th edn, London, Pitman, 1965.

Kenny, Courtney Stanhope, *The History of the Law of England as to the Effects of Marriage on Property and on the Wife's Legal Capacity*, London, Reeves & Turner, 1879.

Kerridge, Eric, *Agrarian Problems in the Sixteenth Century and After*, London, George Allen & Unwin, 1969.

Kettle, Ann J., '"My wife shall have it": marriage and property in the wills and testaments of later medieval England', in R. B. Outhwaite (ed.) *Marriage and Society*, London, Europa, 1981; reprinted in Elizabeth Craik (ed.) *Marriage and Property*, Aberdeen, Aberdeen University Press, 1991 (1st edn 1984).

King, Gregory, 'Observations . . . upon the state and condition of England, 1696', and 'Natural and political observations', in Peter Laslett (ed.) *The Earliest Classics: John Graunt and Gregory King*, Germany, Gregg International, 1973.

Kirshner, Julius, 'Pursuing honor while avoiding sin: the *Monte delle Doti* of Florence', *Studi Senesi* (1977), 177–258.

Kirshner, Julius, and Molho, Anthony, 'The dowry fund and the marriage market in early quattrocento Florence', *Journal of Modern History* 50:3 (1978), 403–38.

Kitching, Christopher, 'Probate during the civil war and interregnum', Parts I and 2, *Journal of the Society of Archivists* 5:5 and 5:6 (1976), 283–93, 346–56.

Klapisch-Zuber, Christiane, 'The Griselda complex: dowry and marriage gifts in the quattrocento', in her collected essays, *Women, Family and Ritual in Renaissance Italy*, transl. Lydia G. Cochraine, Chicago, Illinois, University of Chicago Press, 1985.

Knight, Marcus, 'Litigants and litigation in the seventeenth-century Palatinate of Durham', unpublished PhD thesis, Cambridge University, 1990.

Kussmaul, Ann, *Servants in Husbandry in Early Modern England*, Cambridge, Cambridge University Press, 1981.

Lacey, Kay E., 'Women and work in fourteenth- and fifteenth-century London', in Lindsey Charles and Lorna Duffin (eds) *Women and Work in Pre-Industrial England*, London, Croom Helm, 1985.

The Ladies' Dictionary, London, J. Dunton, 1694.

The Ladies' Library, 3 vols, London, Mr Steele, 1714.

Lambiri-Dimaki, Jane, 'Dowry in modern Greece', in Marion A. Kaplan (ed.) *The Marriage Bargain: Women and Dowries in European History*, New York, Harrington Park Press, 1985.

Lansberry, H. C. F., 'Free bench see-saw: Sevenoaks widows in the late seventeenth century', *Archaeologia Cantiana* 100 (1984), 281–93.

Lasansky, Jeannette, *A Good Start: The Aussteier or Dowry*, Lewisburg, Pennsylvania, Oral Traditions Project of the Union County Historical Society, 1990.

Laslett, Peter, 'Mean household size in England since the sixteenth century', in Peter Laslett and Richard Wall (eds) *Household and Family in Past Time*, Cambridge, Cambridge University Press, 1972.

—— *Family Life and Illicit Love in Earlier Generations*, Cambridge, Cambridge University Press, 1977.

Latt, David J., 'Praising virtuous ladies: the literary image and historical reality of women in seventeenth-century England', in Marlene Springer (ed.) *What Manner of*

Woman: Essays on English and American Life and Literature, New York, Blackwell, 1977.

Laughton, Jane, 'Aspects of the social and economic history of late medieval Chester, 1350–1500', unpublished PhD thesis, Cambridge University, 1994.

The Lawes Resolutions of Women's Rights: Or, the Lawes Provision for Woemen, London, John More, 1632.

Lawrence, Basil Edwin, *The History of the Laws Affecting the Property of Married Women in England*, London, Reeves & Turner, 1884.

Lebsock, Suzanne, *The Free Women of Petersburg: Status and Culture in a Southern Town, 1784–1860*, New York, Norton, 1984.

Levine, David, and Wrightson, Keith, *The Making of an Industrial Society: Whickham 1560–1765*, Oxford, Clarendon, 1991.

Loder, Robert, *Robert Loder's Farm Accounts 1610–20*, ed. G. E. Fussell, Camden Society 3rd Series 53 (1936).

Loengard, Janet Senderowitz, '"Of the gift of her husband": English dower and its consequences in the year 1200', in Julius Kirshner and Suzanne F. Wemple (eds) *Women of the Medieval World*, Oxford, Blackwell, 1985.

—— 'Legal history and the medieval Englishwoman: a fragmented view', *Law & History Review* 4:1 (1986), 161–78.

Lowe, Roger, *The Diary of Roger Lowe of Ashton-in-Makerfield, Lancs. 1663–74*, ed. William L. Sachse, London, Longmans, 1938.

Luther, Martin, *Luther's Works XXXIV*, transl. Lewis W. Spitz, gen. eds Jaroslav Pelikan and Helmut Lehmann, Philadelphia, Muhlenberg Press, 1960.

MacDonald, Michael, *Mystical Bedlam: Madness, Anxiety and Healing in Seventeenth-Century England*, Cambridge, Cambridge University Press, 1981.

Macfarlane, Alan, *The Family Life of Ralph Josselin, a Seventeenth-Century Clergyman*, Cambridge, Cambridge University Press, 1970.

—— 'The myth of the peasantry: family and economy in a northern parish', in R. M. Smith (ed.) *Land, Kinship and Life-Cycle*, Cambridge, Cambridge University Press, 1984.

—— *Marriage and Love in England 1300–1840*, Oxford, Blackwell, 1986.

MacLean, Iain, *The Renaissance Notion of Woman: A Study in the Fortunes of Scholasticism and Medical Science in European Intellectual Life*, Cambridge, Cambridge University Press, 1980.

Main, Gloria, 'Widows in rural Massachusetts on the eve of the revolution', in Ronald Hoffman and Peter J. Albert (eds) *Women in the Age of the American Revolution*, Charlottesville, Virginia, University Press of Virginia, 1989.

Makin, Bathsua, *An Essay to Revive the Antient Education of Gentlewomen* (1673), with introduction by Paula Barbour, Augustan Reprint Society Series 202 (1980).

Manley, Delarivier, *A Woman of No Character: An Autobiography of Mrs Manley*, ed. Fidelis Morgan, London, Faber & Faber, 1986.

Marchant, Ronald A., *The Church under the Law: Justice, Administration and Discipline in the Diocese of York 1560–1640*, Cambridge, Cambridge University Press, 1969.

Markham, Gervase, *The English Housewife*, 9th edn, London, Hannah Sawbridge, 1683.

Marshall, J. D., 'Agrarian wealth and social structure in pre-industrial Cumbria', *EcHR* 33:4 (1980), 503–21.

Martindale, Adam, *The Life of Adam Martindale, Written by Himself*, ed. Richard Parkinson, Chetham Society Old Series 4 (1845).

de Mause, Lloyd (ed.) *The History of Childhood*, New York, Psychohistory Press, 1974.

Mendelson, Sara Heller, *The Mental World of Stuart Women*, Brighton, Harvester, 1987.

Menefee, Samuel Pyeatt, *Wives for Sale: An Ethnographic Study of British Popular Divorce*, Oxford, Blackwell, 1981.

Meriton, George, *A Guide for Constables, Churchwardens, Overseers of the Poor*, London, A. Crook, W. Leak, A. Roper, F. Tyton, G. Sawbridge, J. Place, W. Place, J. Starkey, T. Basset, R. Pawley & S. Heyrick, 1669.

—— *The Touchstone of Wills, Testaments, and Administrations*, 3rd edn, London, W. Leak, 1674 (1st edn 1668).

The Merry Conceits and Passages of Simon and Cisley, London, n.d., in MCC: Samuel Pepys's *Penny Merriments* I, 1226–47.

Michel, Robert H., 'English attitudes towards women, 1640–1700', *Canadian Journal of History* 1 (1978), 35–60.

Middleton, Chris, 'Women's labour and the transition to pre-industrial capitalism', in Lindsey Charles and Lorna Duffin (eds) *Women and Work in Pre-Industrial England*, London, Croom Helm, 1985.

Miller, Barbara D., 'Female infanticide and child neglect in rural North India', in Nancy Scheper-Hughes (ed.) *Child Survival: Anthropological Perspectives on the Treatment and Maltreatment of Children*, Dordrecht, D. Reidel, 1987.

Mingay, G. E., *The Gentry: The Rise and Fall of a Ruling Class*, London, Longman, 1976.

—— 'The east midlands', in Joan Thirsk (ed.) *The Agrarian History of England and Wales* V:i, Cambridge, Cambridge University Press, 1984.

Mitterauer, Michael, and Sieder, Reinhard, *The European Family: Patriarchy to Partnership from the Middle Ages to the Present*, transl. Karla Oosterveen and Manfred Horzinger, Oxford, Blackwell, 1982.

Montagu, Mary Wortley, *Letters from the Right Honourable Lady Mary Wortley Montagu 1709 to 1762*, ed. R. Brimley Johnson, London, J. M. Dent, 1906.

Moore, Giles, *The Journal of Giles Moore*, ed. Ruth Bird, Sussex Record Society 68 (1970).

Morison, Fynes, *An Itinerary Written by Fynes Morison Gent*, London, J. Beale, 1617.

Mount, Ferdinand, *The Subversive Family: An Alternative History of Love and Marriage*, London, Cape, 1982.

Muldrew, James Craig, 'Credit, market relations and debt litigation in late seventeenth-century England, with specific reference to King's Lynn', unpublished PhD thesis, Cambridge University, 1990.

Munby, Lionel M. (ed.) *Life and Death in King's Langley: Wills and Inventories, 1498–1659*, King's Langley, King's Langley Local History & Museum Society in association with King's Langley Workers' Education Association, 1981.

Narrett, David E., 'Men's wills and women's property rights in colonial New York', in Ronald Hoffman and Peter J. Albert (eds) *Women in the Age of the American Revolution*, Charlottesville, Virginia, University Press of Virginia, 1989.

Nelson, William, *Lex Testamentaria*, London, J. Nutt, assignee of Edward Sayer, for T. Bever, 1714.

Notestein, Wallace, 'The English woman, 1580–1650', in J. H. Plumb (ed.) *Studies in Social History: A Tribute to G. M. Trevelyan*, London, Longmans, Green, 1955.

Nussbaum, Felicity A., introduction to *Satires on Women*, Augustan Reprint Society Series 180 (1976).

—— *The Brink of All We Hate: English Satires on Women 1660–1750*, Lexington, Kentucky, University Press of Kentucky, 1984.

O'Donovan, Katherine, 'The male appendage – legal definitions of women', in Sandra Burman (ed.) *Fit Work for Women*, London, Croom Helm for Oxford University Women's Studies Committee, 1979.

—— *Sexual Divisions in Law*, London, Hutchinson, 1985.

Okin, Susan Moller, *Women in Western Political Thought*, Princeton, New Jersey, Princeton University Press, 1979.

—— 'Patriarchy and married women's property in England: questions on some current views', *Eighteenth-Century Studies* 17:2 (1983–4), 121–38.

Oren, Laura, 'The welfare of women in labouring families: England, 1860–1950', *Feminist Studies* 1:3/4 (1973), 107–25.

Osborne, Dorothy, *The Letters of Dorothy Osborne to William Temple 1652–54*, ed. G. C. Moore Smith, Oxford, Clarendon Press, 1928.

Outhwaite, R. B., *Inflation in Tudor and Early Stuart England*, London, Macmillan, 1969.

—— 'Marriage as business: opinions on the rise in aristocratic bridal portions in early modern England', in Neil McKendrick and R. B. Outhwaite (eds) *Business Life and Public Policy*, Cambridge, Cambridge University Press, 1986.

Overton, Mark, 'Agricultural change in Norfolk and Suffolk, 1580–1740', unpublished PhD thesis, Cambridge University, 1980.

—— 'English probate inventories and the measurement of agricultural change', in A. van der Woude and Anton Schuurman (eds) *Probate Inventories*, Utrecht, HES Publishers, 1980.

Ozment, Steven, *When Fathers Ruled: Family Life in Reformation Europe*, Cambridge, Massachusetts, Harvard University Press, 1983.

Palazzi, Maura, 'Female solitude and patrilineage: unmarried women and widows during the eighteenth and nineteenth centuries', *JFH* 15:4 (1990), 443–59.

The Paston Letters, ed. Norman Davis, Oxford, Oxford University Press, 1983.

Pateman, Carole, *The Sexual Contract*, Cambridge, Polity, 1989.

Pearson, Lu Emily, 'Elizabethan widows', *Stanford Studies in Language and Literature* (1941), 124–42.

—— *Elizabethans at Home*, Stanford, California, Stanford University Press, 1957.

Perry, Ruth, *Women, Letters and the Novel*, New York, AMS Press, 1980.

—— 'Radical doubt and the liberation of women', *Eighteenth-Century Studies* 18:4 (1985), 472–93.

Pettit, Philip A. J., *The Royal Forests of Northamptonshire: A Study in their Economy 1558–1714*, Northamptonshire Record Society 23 (1962–3).

Phayer, Thomas, *A Newe Boke of Presidents*, New York, Da Capo Press, 1973 (reprint of original 1543 edn).

Phillimore Atlas and Index of Parish Registers, ed. Cecil Humphery-Smith, Chichester, Phillimore, 1984.

Phillipson, Laurel, 'Quakerism in Cambridge before the Act of Toleration (1653–1689)', *Proceedings of the Cambridge Antiquarian Society* 76 (1987), 1–25.

Pinchbeck, Ivy, *Women Workers and the Industrial Revolution 1750–1850*, London, Routledge, 1930.

Pinchbeck, Ivy, and Hewitt, Margaret, *Children in English Society* I, London, Routledge & Kegan Paul, 1969.

'A Pleasant Dialogue Betwixt Honest John and Loving Kate', London, 1685, in MCC: Samuel Pepys's *Penny Merriments* I, 209–32.

Pocock, J. G. A., *The Ancient Constitution and the Feudal Law: a Study of English Historical Thought in the Seventeenth Century*, Cambridge, Cambridge University Press, 1957.

Pollock, Sir Frederick, and Maitland, F. W., *A Concise History of the English Law Before the Time of Edward I*, 2 vols, Cambridge, Cambridge University Press, 1898.

Pollock, Linda, *Forgotten Children: Parent–Child Relations from 1500 to 1900*, Cambridge, Cambridge University Press, 1983.

—— '"Teach her to live under obedience": the making of women in the upper ranks of early modern England', *C&C* 4:2 (1989), 231–58.

Pomerleau, Cynthia S., 'The emergence of women's autobiography in England', in Estelle C. Jelinek (ed.) *Women's Autobiography: Essays in Criticism*, Bloomington, Indiana, Indiana University Press, 1980.

Poole, Eric, 'West's *Symboleography*: an Elizabethan formulary', in J. A. Guy and H.

G. Beale (eds) *Law and Social Change in British History*, London, Royal Historical Society, 1984.

Postan, M. M., *Medieval Economy and Society*, London, Weidenfeld & Nicolson, 1972.

Poster, Mark, *Critical Theory of the Family*, New York, Seabury Press, 1978.

Power, Eileen, 'The position of women', in C. G. Crump and E. F. Jacobs (eds) *The Legacy of the Middle Ages*, Oxford, Oxford University Press, 1926.

Prest, Wilfred, 'Law and women's rights in early modern England', *The Seventeenth Century* 6 (1991), 169–87.

Prior, Mary, *Fisher Row: Fishermen, Bargemen, and Canal Boatmen in Oxford, 1500–1900*, Oxford, Clarendon, 1982.

—— 'Women and the urban economy: Oxford 1500–1800', in Mary Prior (ed.) *Women in English Society 1500–1800*, London, Methuen, 1985 .

—— 'Wives and wills 1558–1700', in John Chartres and David Hey (eds) *English Rural Society, 1500–1800: Essays in Honour of Joan Thirsk*, Cambridge, Cambridge University Press, 1990.

Putnam, Bertha H., 'Northamptonshire wage assessments of 1560 and 1667', *EcHR* 1st ser. 1 (1927–8), 124–34.

Ray, John, *A Collection of English Proverbs*, 2nd edn, Cambridge, W. Morden, 1678 (1st edn 1670).

Redwood, B. C. (ed.) *Quarter Sessions Order Book 1642–9*, Sussex Record Society Series 54 (1954).

Reeves, Maud Pember, *Round About a Pound a Week*, 2nd edn, London, G. Bell, 1914.

Rice, Margery Spring, *Working Class Wives: Their Health and Conditions*, Harmondsworth, Penguin, 1939.

Roberts, Michael, '"Words they are women, and deeds they are men": images of work and gender in early modern England', in Lindsey Charles and Lorna Duffin (eds) *Women and Work in Pre-Industrial England*, London, Croom Helm, 1985.

Rogers, Alan, 'Three early maps of the Isle of Axholme', *Midland History* 1:2 (1971–2), 25–31.

Rosenthal, Joel T., 'Aristocratic widows in fifteenth-century England', in Barbara J. Harris and JoAnn K. McNamara (eds) *Women and the Structure of Society*, Durham, North Carolina, Duke University Press, 1984.

Russell, Conrad, *The Crisis of Parliaments 1509–1660*, Oxford, Oxford University Press, 1971.

Ryan, Mary P., *Womanhood in America: From Colonial Times to the Present*, New York, New Viewpoints, 1975.

St German, Christopher, *The Dialoges in Englishe, betwene a Docter of Divinitie, and a Student in the Lawes of Englande*, London, Richard Tottell, 1580 (1st edn 1528–31).

Salmon, Marylynn, 'Women and property in South Carolina: the evidence from marriage settlements, 1730–1830', *WMQ* 39 (1982), 655–85.

—— 'The legal status of women in early America: a reappraisal', *Law and History Review* 1 (1983), 129–51.

—— *Women and the Law of Property in Early America*, Chapel Hill, North Carolina, University of North Carolina Press, 1986.

Schofield, Roger, 'English marriage patterns revisited', *JFH* 10:1 (1985), 2–20.

—— 'Did the mothers really die? Three centuries of maternal mortality in "the world we have lost"', in Lloyd Bonfield, Richard M. Smith and Keith Wrightson (eds) *The World We Have Gained*, Oxford, Oxford University Press, 1986.

Schofield, Roger, and Wrigley, E. A., 'Infant and child mortality in England in the late Tudor and early Stuart period', in Charles Webster (ed.) *Health, Medicine and Mortality in the Sixteenth Century*, Cambridge, Cambridge University Press, 1979.

—— 'Remarriage intervals and the effect of marriage order on fertility', in J. Dupaquier, E. Helin, P. Laslett, M. Livi-Bacci and S. Sogner (eds) *Marriage and*

Remarriage in Populations of the Past, London, Academic Press, 1981.

Scott, Hilda, *Working Your Way to the Bottom: The Feminization of Poverty*, London, Pandora, 1984.

Searle, Eleanor, 'Freedom and marriage in medieval England: an alternative hypothesis', *EcHR* 29 (1976), 482–6.

Selby Wills, ed. F. Collins, Yorkshire Archaeological Society Record Series 47 (1911).

Sen, Amartya, 'More than 100 million women are missing', *New York Review of Books* 37:20 (20 December 1990), 61–6.

Shammas, Carole, 'Early American women and control over capital', in Ronald Hoffman and Peter J. Albert (eds) *Women in the Age of the American Revolution*, Charlottesville, Virginia, University Press of Virginia, 1989.

—— *The Pre-Industrial Consumer in England and America*, Oxford, Clarendon Press, 1990.

Shammas, Carole, Salmon, Marylynn, and Dahlin, Michel, *Inheritance in America From Colonial Times to the Present*, New Brunswick, New Jersey, Rutgers University Press, 1987.

Shanley, Mary Lyndon, *Feminism, Marriage, and the Law in Victorian England, 1850–1895*, London, I. B. Tauris, 1989.

Sharma, Ursula, *Women, Work and Property in North-West India*, London, Tavistock, 1980.

Sharpe, J. A., 'Such disagreement betwyx neighbours: litigation and human relations in early modern England', in John Bossy (ed.) *Disputes and Settlements: Law and Human Relations in the West*, Cambridge, Cambridge University Press, 1983.

—— 'Plebeian marriage in Stuart England', *TRHS* 5th ser. 35 (1985), 69–90.

Sharpe, Pamela, 'Marital separation in the eighteenth and early nineteenth centuries', *LPS* 45 (1990), 66–70.

—— 'Poor children as apprentices in Colyton, 1598–1830', *C&C* 6:2 (1991), 253–70.

Sheehan, Michael M., 'The influence of canon law on the property rights of married women in England', *Mediaeval Studies* 25 (1963), 109–24.

—— *The Will in Medieval England: From the Conversion of the Anglo-Saxons to the End of the Thirteenth Century*, Toronto, Pontifical Institute of Mediaeval Studies, 1963.

Shepherd, Simon (ed.) *The Women's Sharp Revenge: Five Women's Pamphlets from the Renaissance*, London, Fourth Estate, 1985.

Short, Brian M., 'The south-east', in Joan Thirsk (ed.) *The Agrarian History of England and Wales* V:i, Cambridge, Cambridge University Press, 1984.

Shorter, Edward, *The Making of the Modern Family*, New York, Basic Books, 1975.

Simpson, Alfred William Brian, *An Introduction to the History of the Land Law*, London, Oxford University Press, 1961.

Skipp, Victor, *Crisis and Development: An Ecological Case Study of the Forest of Arden 1570–1674*, Cambridge, Cambridge University Press, 1978.

Slater, Miriam, 'The weightiest business: marriage in an upper-gentry family in seventeenth-century England', *P&P* 72 (1976), 25–54.

—— *Family Life in the Seventeenth Century: The Verneys of Claydon House*, London, Routledge & Kegan Paul, 1984.

Smith, R. M., 'Women's property rights under customary law: some developments in the thirteenth and fourteenth centuries', *TRHS* 5th ser. 35 (1985), 165–94.

—— 'Some issues concerning families and their property in rural England 1250–1800', in R. M. Smith (ed.) *Land, Kinship and Life-Cycle*, Cambridge, Cambridge University Press, 1984.

Smith, Sir Thomas, *De Republica Anglorum*, Menston, Yorkshire, Scolar Press, 1970 (reprint of original 1583 edn).

Snell, Edmund Henry Turner, *The Principles of Equity*, London, Stevens & Haynes, 1868.

Snell, K. D. M., *Annals of the Labouring Poor: Social Change and Agrarian England*

1660–1900, Cambridge, Cambridge University Press, 1985.

Snell, K. D. M. and Millar, J., 'Lone-parent families and the welfare state: past and present', *C&C* 2:3 (1987), 387–422.

Somerville, James K., 'The Salem (Mass.) woman in the home, 1660–1770', *Eighteenth-Century Life* 1 (1974), 11–14.

'Sophia', *Woman Not Inferior to Man*, London, John Hawkins, 1739.

—— *Woman's Superior Excellence over Man: Or, a Reply to the Author of a Late Treatise, Entitled 'Man Superior to Woman'*, London, John Hawkins, 1740.

Spender, Dale, *Man Made Language*, London, Routledge & Kegan Paul, 1980.

—— *Invisible Women: The Schooling Scandal*, London, Writers & Readers, 1982.

Spring, Eileen, 'The family, strict settlement, and historians', *Canadian Journal of History* 18:3 (1983), 379–98; reprinted in G. R. Rubin and David Sugarman (eds) *Law, Economy and Society 1750–1914*, Abingdon, Oxfordshire, Professional Books, 1984.

—— 'Law and the theory of the affective family', *Albion* 16:1 (1984), 1–20.

—— 'The strict settlement: its role in family history', *EcHR* 41:3 (1988), 454–60.

—— 'The heiress-at-law: English real property law from a new point of view', *Law & History Review* 8:2 (1990), 273–96.

Spufford, Margaret, *Contrasting Communities: English Villagers in the Sixteenth and Seventeenth Centuries*, Cambridge, Cambridge University Press, 1974.

—— 'Peasant inheritance customs and land distribution in Cambridgeshire from the sixteenth to the eighteenth centuries', in Jack Goody, Joan Thirsk and E. P. Thompson (eds) *Family and Inheritance: Rural Society in Western Europe 1200–1800*, Cambridge, Cambridge University Press, 1976.

—— *Small Books and Pleasant Histories: Popular Fiction and its Readership in Seventeenth-Century England*, London, Methuen, 1981.

—— *The Great Reclothing of Rural England: Petty Chapmen and their Wares in the Seventeenth Century*, London, Hambledon Press, 1984.

—— 'The misleading nature of the probate inventory', in John Chartres and David Hey (eds) *English Rural Society 1500–1800: Essays in Honour of Joan Thirsk*, Cambridge, Cambridge University Press, 1990.

Spufford, Peter, 'A printed catalogue of the names of testators', in Geoffrey Martin and Peter Spufford (eds) *The Records of the Nation*, Woodbridge, Suffolk, Boydell Press, 1990.

Staves, Susan, *Married Women's Separate Property in England, 1660–1833*, Cambridge, Massachusetts, Harvard University Press, 1990.

Stenton, Doris Mary, *The English Woman in History*, London, George Allen & Unwin, 1957.

Stone, Lawrence, *The Crisis of the Aristocracy 1558–1641*, Oxford, Oxford University Press, 1967.

—— *The Family, Sex and Marriage in England 1500–1800*, London, Weidenfeld & Nicolson, 1977.

—— 'Only women', *New York Review of Books* 32:6 (11 April 1985), 21–7.

Stone, Lawrence, and Stone, Jeanne C. Fawtier, *An Open Elite? England 1540–1880*, Oxford, Clarendon, 1984.

Stout, William, *The Autobiography of William Stout of Lancaster, 1665–1752*, ed. J. D. Marshall, Manchester, Manchester University Press, 1967.

Stretton, Tim, 'Women and litigation in the Elizabethan Court of Requests', unpublished PhD thesis, Cambridge University, 1993 (forthcoming, Cambridge University Press).

—— 'Women, custom and equity in the Court of Requests', in Jenny Kermode and Garthine Walker (eds) *Women, Crime and the Courts in Early Modern England*, London, UCL Press, 1994.

Stuard, Susan Mosher, 'Dowry increase and increments in wealth in medieval Ragusa

(Dubrovnik)', *Journal of Economic History* 16:4 (1981), 795–811.

Swacker, Marjorie, 'The sex of the speaker as a sociolinguistic variable', in Barrie Thorne and Nancy Henley (eds) *Language and Sex: Difference and Dominance*, Rowley, Massachusetts, Newbury House, 1975.

Swinburne, Henry, *A Treatise of Testaments and Last Wills*, London, John Windet, 1590 (1635 edn, London, W. S. Tansby and T. Harper).

Symonds, E. M., 'The diary of John Green (1635–57)', *English Historical Review* 43 (1928), 385–94, 598–604, and 44 (1929), 106–17.

Tadmor, Naomi, '"Family" and "friend" in Pamela: a case study in the history of the family in eighteenth-century England', *Social History* 14:3 (1989), 290–306.

Takahashi, Motoyasu, 'The number of wills proved in the sixteenth and seventeenth centuries', in Geoffrey Martin and Peter Spufford (eds) *The Records of the Nation*, Woodbridge, Suffolk, Boydell Press, 1990.

Takas, Marianne, 'Divorce: who gets the blame in "no fault"?', *Ms Magazine* (February 1986), 48.

Tawney, R. H., *The Agrarian Problem in the Sixteenth Century*, New York, Harper & Row, 1967 (1st edn 1912).

Taylor, Jeremy, 'Married life', in John Chandos (ed.) *In God's Name: Examples of Preaching in England From the Act of Supremacy to the Act of Uniformity*, Indianapolis, Indiana, Bobbs-Merrill, 1971.

Taylor, Michael D., 'Gentile da Fabriano, St Nicholas, and an iconography of shame', *JFH* 4:7 (1982), 321–32.

Thirsk, Joan, *English Peasant Farming: The Agrarian History of Lincolnshire from Tudor to Recent Times*, London, Routledge & Kegan Paul, 1957.

—— 'Industries in the countryside', in F. J. Fisher (ed.) *Essays in the Economic and Social History of Tudor and Stuart England*, Cambridge, Cambridge University Press, 1961.

—— 'The common fields', *P&P* 29 (1974), 3–25.

—— 'The European debate on customs of inheritance, 1500–1700', in Jack Goody, Joan Thirsk and E. P. Thompson (eds) *Family and Inheritance: Rural Society in Western Europe 1200–1800*, Cambridge, Cambridge University Press, 1976.

Thomas, Keith, 'Numeracy in early modern England', *TRHS* 5th ser. 37 (1987), 103–32.

Thomas of Woodcock (1590s) Nottingham Drama Text, 1977.

Thompson, Roger (ed.) *Samuel Pepys' Penny Merriments*, London, Constable, 1976.

Thornton, Alice, *The Autobiography of Mrs Alice Thornton of East Newton, Co. York*, ed. C. Jackson, Surtees Society Series 62 (1873).

Thynne, Joan and Maria, *Two Elizabethan Women: The Correspondence of Joan and Maria Thynne 1575–1611*, ed. Alison D. Wall, Wiltshire Record Society Series 38 (1982).

Titow, J. Z., 'Some differences between manors and their effects on the condition of the peasant in the thirteenth century', *Agricultural History Review* 10 (1962), 1–13.

Todd, Barbara, 'Widowhood in a market town: Abingdon 1540–1720', unpublished PhD thesis, Oxford University, 1983.

—— 'The remarrying widow: a stereotype reconsidered', in Mary Prior (ed.) *Women in English Society 1500–1800*, London, Methuen, 1985.

—— 'Freebench and free enterprise: widows and their property in two Berkshire villages', in John Chartres and David Hey (eds) *English Rural Society 1500–1800: Essays in Honour of Joan Thirsk*, Cambridge, Cambridge University Press, 1990.

Todd, Janet (ed.) *Dictionary of British and American Women Writers 1660–1800*, London, Methuen, 1984.

A Treatise of Feme Coverts or, the Lady's Law, London, E. & R. Nutt and R. Gosling for B. Lintot, 1732 (reprinted New Jersey, 1974).

Trexler, Richard, 'In search of father: the experience of abandonment in the recollections of Giovanni di Pagolo Morelli', *History of Childhood Quarterly* 2 (1975), 225–51.

Trumbach, Randolph, *The Rise of the Egalitarian Family: Aristocratic Kinship and Domestic Relations in Eighteenth-Century England*, London, Academic Press, 1978.

Tryon, Thomas, *The Way to Health, Long Life and Happiness*, London, Andrew Sowle, 1683.

—— *The New Art of Brewing Beer*, London, Thomas Salusbury, 1691.

—— *Monthly Observations for the Preserving of Health*, 2nd edn, London, Andrew Sowle for Randal Taylor, 1691.

—— *The Good House-Wife Made a Doctor*, 2nd edn, London, H.N. and T.S., 1692.

Tusser, Thomas, *Five Hundred Pointes of Good Husbandrie . . . Over and Besides the Booke of Huswiferie*, London, Henry Denham, 1580.

Tysdale, William, *Tenours and Forme of Indentures*, London, 1546.

Ulrich, Laurel Thatcher, *Good Wives: Image and Reality in the Lives of Women in Northern New England 1650–1750*, New York, Knopf, 1982.

Underdown, D. E., 'The taming of the scold: the enforcement of patriarchal authority in early modern England', in Anthony Fletcher and John Stevenson (eds) *Order and Disorder in Early Modern England*, Cambridge, Cambridge University Press, 1985.

Unwin, R. W., 'Tradition and transition: market towns in the Vale of York, 1660–1830', *Northern History* 17 (1981), 72–116.

Vaisey, David, 'Probate inventories and provincial retailers in the seventeenth century', in Philip Riden (ed.) *Probate Records and the Local Community*, Gloucester, Alan Sutton, 1985.

Vanes, Jean, *Education and Apprenticeship in Sixteenth-Century Bristol*, Bristol History Association Local History Pamphlet 52 (1982).

—— *Apparelled in Red: The History of the Red Maids School*, Gloucester, Alan Sutton for the Governors of the Red Maids School, 1984.

Vann, Richard T., 'Wills and the family in an English town: Banbury, 1550–1800', *JFH* 4:3 (1979), 346–67.

Vaux, James, *Church Folk-Lore*, 2nd edn, London, Skeffington, 1902.

Veall, Donald, *The Popular Movement for Law Reform 1640–1660*, Oxford, Clarendon, 1970.

Verney, Frances Parthenope (ed.) *Memoirs of the Verney Family* I, London, Longmans, 1892.

Wales, Tim, 'Poverty, poor relief and the life-cycle: some evidence from seventeenth-century Norfolk', in R. M. Smith (ed.) *Land, Kinship and Life-Cycle*, Cambridge, Cambridge University Press, 1984.

Wall, Richard, 'Woman alone in English society', *Annales de Demographie Historique* (1981), 303–17.

—— 'Inferring differential neglect of females from mortality data', *Annales de Demographie Historique* (1981), 119–40.

—— 'The household: demographic and economic change in England, 1650–1970', in Richard Wall, Jean Robin and Peter Laslett (eds) *Family Forms in Historic Europe*, Cambridge, Cambridge University Press, 1983.

—— 'The will of Martin Luther', *LPS* 35 (1985), 53–4.

Wallas, Ada, *Before the Bluestockings*, London, George Allen & Unwin, 1929.

Waterman, Elizabeth L., 'Some new evidence on wage assessments in the eighteenth century', *English Historical Review* 43 (1928), 398–407.

Watt, Tessa, *Cheap Print and Popular Piety, 1550–1640*, Cambridge, Cambridge University Press, 1991.

Weatherill, Lorna, 'A possession of one's own: women and consumer behavior in England 1660–1740', *Journal of British Studies* 25:2 (1986), 131–56.

—— *Consumer Behaviour and Material Culture in Britain 1600–1760*, London Methuen, 1988.

Webb, John (ed.) *Poor Relief in Elzabethan Ipswich*, Suffolk Record Society 9 (1966)

Wedgwood, C. V., *The King's Peace 1637–1641*, London, Collins, 1955.

Weigall, Rachel, 'An Elizabethan gentlewoman: the journal of Lady Mildmay, circ 1570–1617', *Quarterly Review* 215:428 (July 1911), 119–38.

Weinstein, Helen (ed.) *A Catalogue of the Pepys Ballad Collection*, Woodbridge Suffolk, Boydell Press, 1992.

—— 'Religious preconceptions in the mind of the just-reading public in the seventeenth century' (forthcoming).

West, William, *Symbolaeography . . . or the Paterne of Praesidents, or the Notarie o Scrivener*, London, Charles Yetsweirt, 1594.

Whitelock, Dorothy (ed.) *Anglo-Saxon Wills*, Cambridge, Cambridge University Press, 1930.

Wiesner, Merry E., 'Guilds, male bonding and women's work in early modern Germany', *Gender & History* 1:2 (1989), 125–37.

Williams, Tamsyn Mary, 'Polemical prints of the English revolution, 1640–60' unpublished PhD thesis, University of London, 1986.

Wills at Chester, ed. J. P. Earwaker, Lancashire and Cheshire Record Society Series 15 (1887), 18 (1888), 20 (1889), 22 (1890).

Wilson, Stephen, 'The myth of motherhood a myth: the historical view of European child-rearing', *Social History* 9 (1984), 181–98.

Winter, Anne, 'Girl child', *Everywoman* (March 1991), 20–1.

Wood, Andy, 'Industrial development, social change and popular politics in the mining area of north-west Derbyshire c. 1600–1700', unpublished PhD thesis. Cambridge University, 1994 (forthcoming, Cambridge University Press).

Wright, Susan J., 'Family life and society in sixteenth and early seventeenth-century Salisbury', unpublished PhD thesis, University of Leicester, 1982.

—— '"Churmaids, huswyfes and hucksters": the employment of women in Tudor and Stuart Salisbury', in Lindsey Charles and Lorna Duffin (eds) *Women and Work in Pre-Industrial England*, London, Croom Helm, 1985.

Wrightson, Keith, 'Infanticide in the early seventeenth century', *LPS* 15 (1975), 10–22.

—— *English Society 1580–1680*, London, Hutchinson, 1982.

—— 'Kinship in an English village: Terling, Essex 1550–1700', in R. M. Smith (ed.) *Land, Kinship and Life-Cycle*, Cambridge, Cambridge University Press, 1984.

—— 'The social order of early modern England: three approaches', in Lloyd Bonfield, Richard M. Smith and Keith Wrightson (eds) *The World We Have Gained*, Oxford, Oxford University Press, 1986.

Wrightson, Keith, and Levine, David, *Poverty and Piety in an English Village: Terling 1525–1700*, New York, Academic Press, 1979.

Wrigley, E. A., 'Clandestine marriage in Tetbury in the late seventeenth century', *LPS* 10 (1973), 15–21.

Wrigley, E. A. and Schofield, Roger, *The Population History of England, 1541–1871: A Reconstruction*, London, Edward Arnold, 1981.

Wyman, A. L., 'The surgeoness: the female practitioner of surgery 1400–1800', *Medical History* 28 (1984), 22–41.

Zaretsky, Eli, *Capitalism, the Family and Personal Life*, London, Pluto Press, 1976.

Zimmerman, Don, and West, Candace, 'Sex roles, interruptions, and silences in conversation', in Barrie Thorne and Nancy Henley (eds) *Language and Sex: Difference and Dominance*, Rowley, Massachusetts, Newbury House, 1975.

Name index, 1550–1750

General index

Note: Towns and villages mentioned no more than twice appear under their county.